Readings in Management

A Course Supplement to
A D M N   6 0 1

University of Maryland University College
Graduate School of Management & Technology

SIMON & SCHUSTER
CUSTOM PUBLISHING

Excerpts taken from:
Management, Sixth Edition,
by James A. Stoner, R. Edward Freeman, and Daniel Gilbert
Copyright © 1995 by Prentice-Hall, Inc.
Simon & Schuster Company / A Viacom Company
Upper Saddle River, New Jersey 07458

American Business Values: with International Perspectives,
Fourth Edition, by Gerald F. Cavanaugh
Copyright © 1998, 1990, 1984, 1976 by Prentice-Hall, Inc.

Technology and American Society: A History,
by Gary Cross and Rick Szostak
Copyright © 1995 by Prentice-Hall, Inc.

Ethical Theory and Business, Fifth Edition,
edited by Tom L. Beauchamp and Norman E. Bowie
Copyright © 1997, 1993, 1988, 1983, 1979 by Prentice-Hall, Inc.

Managing Across Cultures,
by Susan C. Schneider and Jean-Louis Barsoux
Copyright © 1997 by Prentice-Hall Europe
Hertfordshire, England HP2 7EZ

This special edition published in cooperation with
Simon & Schuster Custom Publishing

Printed in the United States of America

10 9 8 7 6 5 4 3 2

Please visit our website at www.sscp.com

ISBN 0–536–01606-2

BA 98683

SIMON & SCHUSTER CUSTOM PUBLISHING
160 Gould Street/Needham Heights, MA 02494
Simon & Schuster Education Group

Copyright Acknowledgments

Contents

History of Management Thought

• The Evolution of Management Theory

CHAPTER 2

THE EVOLUTION
OF MANAGEMENT
THEORY

Upon completing this chapter, you should be able to:

1. Explain the setting in which management theory first developed.

2. Describe the ways in which a theory can be useful.

3. Distinguish the scientific management school, the classical organization theory school, the behavioral school, and the management science school of management theory.

4. Understand the historical context in which the systems approach, the contingency approach, and the dynamic engagement approach to management theory have developed.

THE APOSTLE OF MASS PRODUCTION[1]

enry Ford and the Model T have long been symbols of the modern industrial age. Even the subsequent growth and success of Ford's rival, General Motors, was due in large part to GM's need to find an innovative response to the Model T. In large measure, the managerial approach of Henry Ford, as well as his preferences in managerial theory, is a paradigm of much that was constructive and much that was imperfect—in early approaches to management.

The son of a poor Irish immigrant, Henry Ford was born in 1863 and grew up on a farm in rural Michigan. He was fascinated by machinery and was quite skilled in repairing and improving almost any machine. He started the Ford Motor Company in 1903, and by 1908, the Model T was built.

In the early part of the century when automobiles were introduced, they were a symbol of status and wealth, the near-exclusive province of the rich. Ford intended to change that: the Model T was to be for the masses—a car that virtually anyone could afford. He understood that the only way to make such a car was to produce it at high volume and low cost. Ford focused his factory efforts on efficiency, mechanizing wherever possible, and breaking down tasks into their smallest components. One worker would perform the same task over and over, producing not a finished part, but one of the operations necessary for the production of the whole; the incomplete part would then be passed on to another worker, who would contribute a successive operation. Ford was able to achieve remarkable efficiencies: Although the first Model T took over 12 ½ hours to produce, only 12 years later, in 1920,

Ford simply decided to double wages in order to get the best people...

Ford was producing one Model T every minute. By 1925, at the peak of the car's popularity, a Model T was rolling off Ford's assembly lines at the rate of one every 5 seconds.

However, mechanization of the plant had some adverse effects. The faster Ford pushed his workers, the more disgruntled they became. In 1913, turnover was 380 percent, and Ford had to hire ten times more workers than he needed just to keep the line moving. In an action that at the time was unprecedented, Ford simply decided to double wages in order to get the best people and motivate them to work even harder. In the days following the announcement that wages were being doubled, thousands and thousands of men came to the Ford plant in search of work. Police had to be called in to control the crowds.

When he died in 1945, Ford was worth over $600 million. He left an indelible mark on both American industry and society. His name is synonymous with mass production and the development of modern management theory. →

A REVOLUTION BEGINS. Henry Ford takes a spin in his first auto.

Most people associate Henry Ford with the Model T, the affordable mass-produced automobile that changed society. But Ford is also important as a management thinker because he developed ideas about how organizations function. Moreover, Ford hired theorists, such as Frederick Winslow Taylor, and gave them the chance to develop their management theories. In this chapter we will see how different management theories developed and continue to evolve. But first we will look at some early ideas about how to run organizations effectively.

EARLY THINKING ABOUT MANAGEMENT

People have been shaping and reshaping organizations for many centuries. Looking back through world history, we can trace the stories of people working together in formal organizations such as the Greek and Roman armies, the Roman Catholic Church, the East India Company, and the Hudson Bay Company. People have also long been writing about how to make organizations efficient and effective—since long before terms such as "management" came into common usage. Two prominent and instructive examples are the writings left for us by Niccolo Machiavelli and Sun Tzu.

MACHIAVELLI AND SUN TZU:
EARLY STRATEGISTS

Although the adjective "Machiavellian" is often used to describe cunning and manipulative opportunists, Machiavelli was a great believer in the virtues of a republic. This is evident in *Discourses*, a book Machiavelli wrote in 1531 while he lived in the early Italian republic of Florence. The principles he set forth can be adapted to apply to the management of organizations today:[2]

1. An organization is more stable if members have the right to express their differences and solve their conflicts within it.
2. While one person can begin an organization, "it is lasting when it is left in the care of many and when many desire to maintain it."
3. A weak manager can follow a strong one, but not another weak one, and maintain authority.
4. A manager seeking to change an established organization "should retain at least a shadow of the ancient customs."

Another classic work that offers insights to modern managers is *The Art of War* written by the Chinese philosopher Sun Tzu more than 2,000 years ago. It was modified and used by Mao Zedong, who founded the People's Republic of China in 1949. Among Sun Tzu's dictums are the following:[3]

1. When the enemy advances, we retreat!
2. When the enemy halts, we harass!
3. When the enemy seeks to avoid battle, we attack!
4. When the enemy retreats, we pursue!

AN ORGANIZATION WITH A LONG HISTORY. The Roman Catholic church is an organization with a formal structure and hierarchy that existed long before the term "management" came into common usage.

Although these rules were meant to guide military strategy, they have been used when planning a strategy to engage business competitors. Keep Sun Tzu in mind as you study the chapter about strategy and planning.

Although neither Machiavelli nor Sun Tzu was trying to develop a theory of management per se, their insights teach us an important lesson about history. Management is not something that originated in the United States in this century. We must be careful not to put on historical and cultural blinders when, from the perspective of this particular time and place, we think about the management of organizations. ▪▬

Before going on to our discussion of the major management theories, let's take a moment to look at the reasons studying management theory will help you understand management and today's complex organizations.

WHY STUDY MANAGEMENT THEORY?

theory:
Coherent group of assumptions put forth to explain the relationship between two or more observable facts and to provide a sound basis for predicting future events.

Theories are perspectives with which people make sense of their world experiences. Formally, a **theory** is a coherent group of assumptions put forth to explain the relationship between two or more observable facts. John Clancy calls such perspectives "invisible powers" to emphasize several crucial uses of theories, the "unseen" ways in which we approach our world.[4]

First, theories provide a *stable focus* for understanding what we experience. A theory provides criteria for determining what is relevant. To Henry Ford, a large and compliant work force was one relevant factor as he theorized about his business. In other words, his theory of management included, among other things, this assumption about the supply of labor.

Second, theories enable us to *communicate efficiently* and thus move into more and more complex relationships with other people. Imagine the frustration you would encounter if, in dealing with other people, you always had to define even the most basic assumptions you make about the world in which you live! Because Ford and his managers fully understood Ford's theory about manufacturing automobiles, they could interact easily as they faced day-to-day challenges.

Third, theories make it possible—indeed, challenge us—to *keep learning* about our world. By definition, theories have boundaries; there is only so much that can be covered by any one theory. Once we are aware of this, we are better able to ask ourselves if there are alternative ways of looking at the world (especially when our theories no longer seem to "fit" our experience) and to consider the consequences of adopting alternative beliefs. Two cases are instructive.

One example involves world politics. For years, what might be called a theory of the Cold War dominated diplomatic activity between the United States and the Soviet Union. During those years, most diplomats and military officials did not consider what the world would be like if the Cold War ended. Now, however, the  "Cold War" theory no longer fits our experience, and government and military officials, as well as managers of other organizations, are scrambling to develop new theories for dealing with former enemies on a more cooperative basis.[5] For example, the breakup of the Soviet Union and Russia's struggles toward financial stability have left some of the world's top scientists unemployed, struggling with poor equipment, and willing to work for little pay. In this breach U.S. firms such as Corning, American Telephone and Telegraph, and United Technologies have capitalized on the opportunity this presents by funding research facilities in Russia.[6]

The other case takes us back to Henry Ford. Ford has been criticized for not using his approach as a way to learn about better ways to run his company. While Ford was giving his customers no choice about anything other than price (which *was* attractive!) Alfred Sloan was transforming General Motors. Beginning in the 1920s, Sloan rejected part of Ford's theory about running a business in favor of alternative ways to design automobiles and organize manufacturing and distribution.[7] GM's marketing strategy had always been to market nationwide with cars of interest to different segments of the public. Sloan set up separate divisions, with central direction from headquarters, to market the Buick, Oldsmobile, Pontiac, Cadillac, and Chevrolet lines. In contrast to Ford, each type of car has its own distinction and price differential.[8]

In this chapter, we will focus on four well-established schools of management thought.[9] the *scientific management school*, the *classical organization theory school*, the *behavioral school*, and the *management science school*. Although these schools, or theoretical approaches, developed in historical sequence, later ideas have not *replaced* earlier ones. Instead, each new school has tended to complement or coexist with previous ones. At the same time, each school has continued to evolve, and some have even merged with others.[10] This takes us to three recent integrative approaches: the *systems approach*, the *contingency approach*, and what we call the *dynamic engagement approach* to management. Figure 2-1 shows the approximate date when each of these theoretical perspectives emerged, as well as key historical events that signaled the emergence of each way of thinking about organizations and management.

THE EVOLUTION OF MANAGEMENT THEORY

Management and organizations are products of their historical and social times and places. Thus, we can understand the evolution of management theory in terms of how people have wrestled with matters of *relationships* at particular *times* in history. One of the central lessons of this chapter, and of this book as a whole, is that we can learn from the trials and tribulations of those who have preceded us in steering the fortunes of formal organizations. As you study management theory you will learn that although the *particular* concerns of Henry Ford and Alfred Sloan are very different from those facing managers in the mid-1990s, we can still

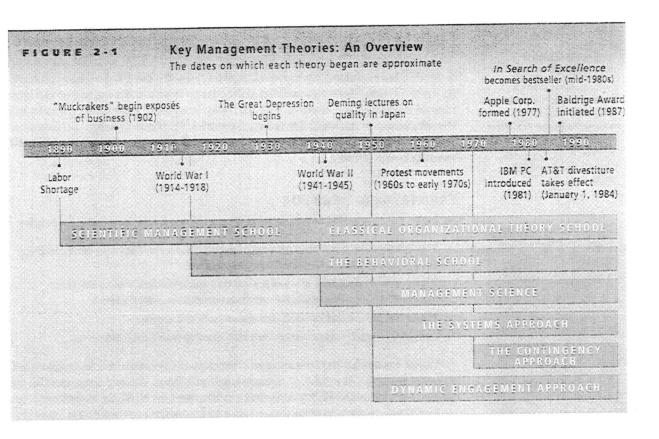

FIGURE 2-1   Key Management Theories: An Overview
The dates on which each theory began are approximate

In Search of Excellence becomes bestseller (mid-1980s)

"Muckrakers" begin exposés of business (1902)

The Great Depression begins

Deming lectures on quality in Japan

Apple Corp. formed (1977)

Baldrige Award initiated (1987)

1890 1900 1910 1920 1930 1940 1950 1960 1970 1980 1990

Labor Shortage

World War I (1914-1918)

World War II (1941-1945)

Protest movements (1960s to early 1970s)

IBM PC introduced (1981)

AT&T divestiture takes effect (January 1, 1984)

SCIENTIFIC MANAGEMENT SCHOOL

CLASSICAL ORGANIZATIONAL THEORY SCHOOL

THE BEHAVIORAL SCHOOL

MANAGEMENT SCIENCE

THE SYSTEMS APPROACH

THE CONTINGENCY APPROACH

DYNAMIC ENGAGEMENT APPROACH

see ourselves continuing the traditions that these individuals began long before our time. By keeping in mind a framework of relationships and time, we can put ourselves in their shoes as students of management.

Imagine that you are a manager at an American steel mill, textile factory, or one of Ford's plants in the early twentieth century. Your factory employs thousands of workers. This is a scale of enterprise unprecedented in Western history. Many of your employees were raised in agricultural communities. Industrial routines are new to them. Many of your employees, as well, are immigrants from other lands. They do not speak English well, if at all. As a manager under these

circumstances, you will probably be very curious about how you can develop working relationships with these people. Your managerial effectiveness depends on how well you understand what it is that is important to these people. Current-day challenges parallel some of those faced in the early twentieth century. In the 1980s 8.7 million foreign nationals entered the U.S. and joined the labor market. They often have distinct needs for skills and language proficiency, much as those before them at the advent of the industrial age.[11]

Early management theory consisted of numerous attempts at getting to know these newcomers to industrial life at the end of the nineteenth century and beginning of the twentieth century in Europe and the United States. In this section, we will survey a number of the better-known approaches to early management theory. These include scientific management, classical organization theory, the behavioral school, and management science. As you study these approaches, keep one important fact in mind: the managers and theorists who developed these assumptions about human relationships were doing so with little precedent. Large-scale industrial enterprise was very new. Some of the assumptions that they made might therefore seem simple or unimportant to you, but they were crucial to Ford and his contemporaries.

THE SCIENTIFIC MANAGEMENT SCHOOL

scientific management theory:

A management approach, formulated by Frederick W. Taylor and others between 1890 and 1930, that sought to determine scientifically the best methods for performing any task, and for selecting, training, and motivating workers.

Scientific Management theory arose in part from the need to increase productivity. In the United States especially, skilled labor was in short supply at the beginning of the twentieth century. The only way to expand productivity was to raise the efficiency of workers. Therefore, Frederick W. Taylor, Henry L. Gantt, and Frank and Lillian Gilbreth devised the body of principles known as **scientific management theory.**

FREDERICK W. TAYLOR

Frederick W. Taylor (1856-1915) rested his philosophy on four basic principles:[12]

1. *The development of a true science of management,* so that the best method for performing each task could be determined.
2. *The scientific selection of workers,* so that each worker would be given responsibility for the task for which he or she was best suited.
3. *The scientific education and development of the worker.*
4. *Intimate, friendly cooperation between management and labor.*

A SCIENTIFIC MANAGEMENT LEGACY. A General Electric engineer uses a teaching box to train an industrial robot to perform tasks that have been analyzed using motion studies.

differential rate system:

Frederick W. Taylor's compensation system involving the payment of higher wages to more efficient workers.

Taylor contended that the success of these principles required "a complete mental revolution" on the part of management and labor. Rather than quarrel over profits, both sides should try to increase production; by so doing, he believed, profits would rise to such an extent that labor and management would no longer have to fight over them. In short, Taylor believed that management and labor had a common interest in increasing productivity.

Taylor based his management system on production-line time studies. Instead of relying on traditional work methods, he analyzed and timed steel workers' movements on a series of jobs. Using time study as his base, he broke each job down into its components and designed the quickest and best methods of performing each component. In this way he established how much workers should be able to do with the equipment and materials at hand. He also encouraged employers to pay more productive workers at a higher rate than others, using a "scientifically correct" rate that would benefit both company and worker. Thus, workers were urged to surpass their previous performance standards to earn more pay. Taylor called his plan the **differential rate system.**

CONTRIBUTIONS OF SCIENTIFIC MANAGEMENT THEORY

The modern assembly line pours out finished products faster than Taylor could ever have imagined. This production "miracle" is just one legacy of scientific management. In addition, its efficiency techniques have been applied to many tasks in non-industrial organizations, ranging from fast-food service to the training of surgeons.[13]

LIMITATIONS OF SCIENTIFIC MANAGEMENT THEORY

Although Taylor's methods led to dramatic increases in productivity and to higher pay in a number of instances, workers and unions began to oppose his approach because they feared that working harder or faster would exhaust whatever work was available, causing layoffs.

Moreover, Taylor's system clearly meant that time was of the essence. His critics objected to the "speed up" conditions that placed undue pressures on employees to perform at faster and faster levels. The emphasis on *productivity*—and, by extension, *profitability*—led some managers to exploit both workers and cus-

8

tomers. As a result, more workers joined unions and thus reinforced a pattern of suspicion and mistrust that shaded labor-management relations for decades.

HENRY L. GANTT

Henry L. Gantt (1861-1919) worked with Taylor on several projects. But when he went out on his own as a consulting industrial engineer, Gantt began to reconsider Taylor's incentive system.

Abandoning the differential rate system as having too little motivational impact, Gantt came up with a new idea. Every worker who finished a day's assigned work load would win a 50-cent bonus. Then he added a second motivation. The *supervisor* would earn a bonus for each worker who reached the daily standard, plus an extra bonus if all the workers reached it. This, Gantt reasoned, would spur supervisors to train their workers to do a better job.

Every worker's progress was rated publicly and recorded on individual bar charts—in black on days the worker made the standard, in red when he or she fell below it. Going beyond this, Gantt originated a charting system for production  scheduling; the "Gantt chart" is still in use today. In fact, the Gantt Chart was translated into eight languages and used throughout the world. Starting in the 1920s, it was in use in Japan, Spain, and the Soviet Union. It also formed the basis for two charting devices which were developed to assist in planning, managing, and controlling complex organizations: the Critical Path Method (CPM), originated by Du Pont, and Program Evaluation and Review Technique (PERT), developed by the Navy. Lotus 1-2-3 is also a creative application of the Gantt Chart.[14]

THE GILBRETHS

Frank B. and Lillian M. Gilbreth (1868-1924 and 1878-1972) made their contribution to the scientific management movement as a husband-and-wife team. Lillian and Frank collaborated on fatigue and motion studies and focused on ways of promoting the individual worker's welfare. To them, the ultimate aim of scientific management was to help workers reach their full potential as human beings.

In their conception, motion and fatigue were intertwined—every motion that was eliminated reduced fatigue. Using motion picture cameras, they tried to find the most economical motions for each task in order to upgrade performance and reduce fatigue. The Gilbreths argued that motion study would raise worker morale because of its obvious physical benefits and because it demonstrated management's concern for the worker.

CLASSICAL ORGANIZATION THEORY SCHOOL

classical organization theory:
An early attempt, pioneered by Henri Fayol, to identify the principles and skills that underlie effective management.

Scientific management was concerned with increasing the productivity of the shop and the individual worker. **Classical organization theory** grew out of the need to find guidelines for managing such complex organizations as factories.

HENRI FAYOL

Henri Fayol (1841-1925) is generally hailed as the founder of the classical management school—not because he was the first to investigate managerial behavior, but because he was the first to systematize it. Fayol believed that sound manage-

EXHIBIT 2-1	Fayol's 14 Principles of Management

1. *Division of Labor.* The most people specialize, the more efficiently they can perform their work. This principle is epitomized by the modern assembly line.

2. *Authority.* Managers must give orders so that they can get things done. While their *formal* authority gives them the right to command, managers will not always compel obedience unless they have *personal* authority (such as relevant expertise) as well.

3. *Discipline.* Members in an organization need to respect the rules and agreements that govern the organization. To Fayol, discipline results from good leadership at all levels of the organization, fair agreements (such as provisions for rewarding superior performance), and judiciously enforced penalties for infractions.

4. *Unity of Command.* Each employee must receive instructions from only one person. Fayol believed that when an employee reported to more than one manager, conflicts in instructions and confusion of authority would result.

5. *Unity of Direction.* Those operations within the organization that have the same objective should be directed by only one manager using one plan. For example, the personnel department in a company should not have two directors, each with a different hiring policy.

6. *Subordination of Individual Interest to the Common Good.* In any undertaking, the interests of employees should not take precedence over the interests of the organization as a whole.

7. *Remuneration.* Compensation for work done should be fair to both employees and employers.

8. *Centralization.* Decreasing the role of subordinates in decision making is centralization; increasing their role is decentralization. Fayol believed that managers should retain final responsibility, but should at the same time give their subordinates enough authority to do their jobs properly. The problem is to find the proper degree of centralization in each case.

9. *The Hierarchy.* The line of authority in an organization—often represented today by the neat boxes and lines of the organization chart—runs in order of rank from top management to the lowest level of the enterprise.

10. *Order.* Materials and people should be in the right place at the right time. People, in particular, should be in the jobs or positions they are most suited to.

11. *Equity.* Managers should be both friendly and fair to their subordinates.

12. *Stability of Staff.* A high employee turnover rate undermines the efficient functioning of an organization.

13. *Initiative.* Subordinates should be given the freedom to conceive and carry out their plans, even though some mistakes may result.

14. *Esprit de Corps.* Promoting team spirit will give the organization a sense of unity. To Fayol, even small factors should help to develop the spirit. He suggested, for example, the use of verbal communication instead of formal, written communication whenever possible.

Source: Henri Fayol *Industrial and General Administration,* J.A. Coubrough, trans. (Geneva: International Management Institute, 1930).

ment practice falls into certain patterns that can be identified and analyzed. Fro this basic insight, he drew up a blueprint for a cohesive doctrine of managemer one that retains much of its force to this day.

With his faith in scientific methods, Fayol was like Taylor, his contempora While Taylor was basically concerned with *organizational functions,* howev

A SUCCESSFUL BUREAUCRACY. United Parcel Service (UPS) is a bureaucratic organization marked by a clear division of labor, a fixed hierachy of authority, and clearly defined regulations. Automation, computerization, and scientific management principles add to its efficiency.

Fayol was interested in the *total organization* and focused on management, which he felt had been the most neglected of business operations. Exhibit 2-1 lists the 14 principles of management Fayol "most frequently had to apply."[15] Before Fayol, it was generally believed that "managers are born, not made." Fayol insisted, however, that management was a skill like any other—one that could be taught once its underlying principles were understood.

MAX WEBER

bureaucracy:
Organization with a legalized formal and hierarchical structure; also refers to the formal structural process within an organization.

Reasoning that any goal-oriented organization consisting of thousands of individuals would require the carefully controlled regulation of its activities, the German sociologist Max Weber (1864-1920) developed a theory of bureaucratic management that stressed the need for a strictly defined hierarchy governed by clearly defined regulations and lines of authority.[16] He considered the ideal organization to be a **bureaucracy** whose activities and objectives were rationally thought out and whose divisions of labor were explicitly spelled out. Weber also believed that technical competence should be emphasized and that performance evaluations should be made entirely on the basis of merit.

Today we often think of bureaucracies as vast, impersonal organizations that put impersonal efficiency ahead of human needs. We should be careful, though, not to apply our negative connotations of the word *bureaucracy* to the term as Weber used it. Like the scientific management theorists, Weber sought to improve the performance of socially important organizations by making their operations predictable and productive. Although we now value innovation and flexibility as much as efficiency and predictability, Weber's model of bureaucratic management clearly advanced the formation of huge corporations such as Ford. Bureaucracy was a particular pattern of relationships for which Weber saw great promise.

Although bureaucracy has been successful for many companies, in the competitive global market of the 1990s organizations such as General Electric and Xerox

11

have become "bureaucracy busters," throwing away the organization chart and replacing it with ever-changing constellations of teams, projects, and alliances with the goal of unleashing employee creativity.[17]

MARY PARKER FOLLETT

Mary Parker Follett (1868-1933) was among those who built on   sic framework of the classical school. However, she introduced many new elements, especially in the area of human relations and organizational structure. In this, she initiated trends that would be further developed by the emerging behavioral and management science schools.

Follett was convinced that no one could become a whole person except as a member of a group; human beings grew through their relationships with others in organizations. In fact, she called management "the art of getting things done through people."[18] She took for granted Taylor's assertion that labor and management shared a common purpose as members of the same organization, but she believed that the artificial distinction between managers (order givers) and subordinates (order takers) obscured this natural partnership. She was a great believer in the power of the group, where individuals could combine their diverse talents into something bigger. Moreover, Follett's "holistic" model of control took into account not just individuals and groups, but the effects of such environmental factors as politics, economics, and biology.

Follett's model was an important forerunner of the idea that management meant more than just what was happening inside a particular organization. By explicitly adding the organizational environment to her theory, Follett paved the way for management theory to include a broader set of relationships, some inside the organization and some across the organization's borders. A diverse set of modern management theories pays homage to Follett on this point.

RELATIONSHIPS AND QUALITY AT HOME DEPOT

Home Depot, America's largest home-improvement retailer, practices much of what Follett had in mind. Before Home Depot opens a new store, all employees receive about four weeks of training. To maintain contact and to reinforce information about the company, the retailer holds quarterly Sunday morning meetings for its 23,000 employees using satellite TV hook-ups in each store. The sessions are know as "Breakfast with Bernie and Arthur" (the founders of Home Depot). The telecast is interactive, allowing for exchange of information and permitting employees to phone the company's top executives to ask questions. Home Depot also has an in-house TV station that produces programs designed to teach the Home Depot "service spirit" to new store employees.

Home Depot also educates customers. Stores offer clinics, taught by staff or by supplier representatives, on how to do a variety of home improvement projects. Home Depot also strives to make improvements based on customer experiences and suggestions. For instance, when contractors requested a special checkout area near the lumber racks, Home Depot complied, finding that the change speeded "front-of-store" check out. The team spirit, sharing of information, and quality customer service that define Home Depot has made it the dominant power in the $115 billion home improvement industry. In 1993, among 404 major corporations in the U.S., Home Depot was ranked as the second most admired company.[19]

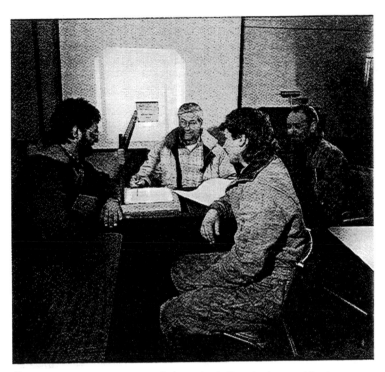

THE IMPORTANCE OF THE GROUP. Follett was ahead of her time in recognizing the power that comes from combining diverse talents in a group such as this team from Globe Metallurgical, a 1988 winner of the Baldrige award.

CHESTER I. BARNARD

Chester Barnard (1886-1961), like Follett, introduced elements to classical theory that would be further developed in later schools. Barnard, who became president of New Jersey Bell in 1927, used his work experience and his extensive readings in sociology and philosophy to formulate theories about organizations. According to Barnard, people come together in formal organizations to achieve ends they cannot accomplish working alone. But as they pursue the organization's goals, they must also satisfy their individual needs. And so Barnard arrived at his central thesis: An enterprise can operate efficiently and survive only when the organization's goals are kept in balance with the aims and needs of the individuals working for it. What Barnard was doing was specifying a principle by which people can work in stable and mutually beneficial relationships over time.

For example, to meet their personal goals within the confines of the formal organization, people come together in informal groups such as cliques. To ensure its survival, the firm must use these informal groups effectively, even if they sometimes work at purposes that run counter to management's objectives. Barnard's recognition of the importance and universality of this "informal organization" was a major contribution to management thought.

zone of indifference (area of acceptance):

According to Barnard and Simon, respectively, inclinations conditioning individuals to accept orders that fall within a familiar range of responsibility or activity.

Barnard believed that individual and organizational purposes could be kept in balance if managers understood an employee's **zone of indifference**—that is, what the employee would do without questioning the manager's authority. Obviously, the more activities that fell within an employee's zone of indifference (what the employee would accept), the smoother and more cooperative an organization would be. Barnard also believed that executives had a duty to instill a sense of moral purpose in their employees. To do this, they would have to learn to think beyond their narrow self-interest and make an ethical commitment to society. Although Barnard stressed the work of *executive* managers, he also focused considerable attention on the role of the individual worker as "the basic strategic factor in organization." When he went further to emphasize the organization as the cooperative enterprise of individuals working together as *groups,* he set the stage for the development of a great deal of current management thinking.[20]

EFFICIENCY AND
THE FACTORY

[Taking the advice of efficiency expert Walter Flanders in 1908,] Ford bought grounds in Highland Park, where he intended to employ the most modern ideas about production, particularly those of Frederick Winslow Taylor. Those would bring, as Taylor had prophe-

sied, an absolute rationality to the industrial process. The idea was to break each function down into much smaller units so that each could be mechanized and speeded up and eventually flow into a straight-line production of little pieces becoming steadily larger. The process began to change in the spring of 1913. The first piece on the modern assembly line was the magneto coil assembly. In the past, a worker—and he had to be a skilled worker—had made a flywheel magneto from start to finish. A good employee could make 34 or 40 a day. Now, however, there was an assembly line for magnetos, divided into 29 different operations performed by 29 different men. In the old system it took 20 minutes to make a magneto; now it took 13.

Ford and his men soon moved to bring the same rationality to the rest of the factory. Quickly, they imposed a comparable system for the assembly of motors and transmissions. Then, in the summer of 1913, they took on the final assembly, which, as the rest of the process had speeded up, had become the great bottleneck. The workers [now maneuvered] as quickly as they could around a stationary metal object, the car they were putting together. If the men could remain stationary as the semifinished car moved up the line through them, less of the workers' time—Ford's time—would be wasted.

Charles Sorensen, who had become one of Ford's top production people, [initiated the assembly line by pulling] a Model T chassis slowly by a windlass across 250 feet of factory floor, timing the process all the while. Behind him walked six workers, picking up parts from carefully spaced piles on the floor and fitting them to the chassis...[Soon,] the breakthroughs came even more rapidly...[By installing an automatic conveyor belt,] Ford could eventually assemble a car in [93 minutes].... Just a few years before, in the days of stationary chassis assembly, the best record for putting a car together had been 728 hours of one man's work. Ford's top executives celebrated their victory with a dinner at Detroit's Pontchartrain Hotel. Fittingly, they rigged a simple conveyor belt to a five-horsepower engine with a bicycle chain and used the conveyor to serve the food around the table. It typified the spirit, camaraderie, and confidence of the early days.

Nineteen years and more than fifteen million cars later, when Ford reluctantly came to the conclusion that he had to stop making the T, the company balance was $673 million. And this was not merely a company's success; it was the beginning of a social revolution. Ford himself [believed] he had achieved a breakthrough for the common man. "Mass production," he wrote later, "precedes mass consumption, and makes it possible by reducing costs and thus permitting both greater use-convenience and price-convenience."

[Not surprisingly,] the price of the Model T continued to come down, from $780 in the fiscal year 1910-11 to $690 the following year, then to $600, to $550, and, on the eve of World War I, to $360. At that price, Ford sold 730,041 cars, outproducing everyone else in the world....

Henry Ford, immigrant's son and one-time machinist's apprentice, had indeed become a very rich man. Obviously, he had become so by being a venturesome and successful theorist of industrial management. But both his practices and his personality drew fire from those who were critical of his implicit attitude toward those "masses" for whom he had originally perfected and prized the Model T. For example, his widely publicized doubling of wages for employees in 1914 was seen by some as a trailblazing maneuver in management-labor relations, by others as a scheme to solidify Ford's paternalistic power over those who depended upon him for a living. In addition, Ford stubbornly resisted the unionization of his employees long after his major competitors had made agreements with union organizations. Repression on the part of company police against union "agitators" was common on the company's grounds until, finally, having lost an election conducted by the National Labor Relations Board [a government agency established in 1935 to affirm labor's right to bargain collectively], Ford contracted with the United Auto Workers in 1941. →

INFORMAL GROUPS EXIST IN EVERY ORGANIZATION. In identifying the "informal organization," Barnard promoted the effectiveness of recognizing and using informal workplace groups such as this one.

For example, companies are increasingly using teams. In fact, some advocate using teams as the building blocks of the organization. Because teams are generally self-managing, supervisory roles are limited. Management provides direction by giving each team a common purpose and holds the teams accountable for measurable performance goals. Companies such as Motorola, DuPont, AT&T, and General Electric are moving in this direction.[21] We will discuss teams more fully in Chapter 18.

THE BEHAVIORAL SCHOOL: THE ORGANIZATION IS PEOPLE

behavioral school:
A group of management scholars trained in sociology, psychology, and related fields, who use their diverse knowledge to propose more effective ways to manage people in organizations.

The **behavioral school** emerged partly because the classical approach did not achieve sufficient production efficiency and workplace harmony. To managers' frustration, people did not always follow predicted or expected patterns of behavior. Thus there was increased interest in helping managers deal more effectively with the "people side" of their organizations. Several theorists tried to strengthen classical organization theory with the insights of sociology and psychology.

THE HUMAN RELATIONS MOVEMENT

human relations:
How managers interact with other employees or recruits.

Human relations is frequently used as a general term to describe the ways in which managers interact with their employees. When "employee management" stimulates more and better work, the organization has effective human relations; when morale and efficiency deteriorate, its human relations are said to be ineffective. The human relations movement arose from early attempts to systematically discover the social and psychological factors that would create effective human relations.

THE HAWTHORNE EXPERIMENTS. The human relations movement grew out of a famous series of studies conducted at the Western Electric Company from 1924 to 1933. These eventually became known as the "Hawthorne Studies" because many of them were performed at Western Electric's Hawthorne plant near Chicago. The Hawthorne Studies began as an attempt to investigate the relationship between the level of lighting in the workplace and worker productivity—the type of question Frederick Taylor and his colleagues might well have addressed.

In some of the early studies, the Western Electric researchers divided the employees into test groups, who were subjected to deliberate changes in lighting, and control groups, whose lighting remained constant throughout the experiments. The results of the experiments were ambiguous. When the test group's lighting was improved, productivity tended to increase, although erratically. But when lighting conditions were made worse, there was also a tendency for productivity to increase in the test group. To compound the mystery, the control group's output also rose over the course of the studies, even though it experienced no changes in illumination. Obviously, something besides lighting was influencing the workers' performance.

In a new set of experiments, a small group of workers was placed in a separate room and a number of variables were altered: Wages were increased; rest periods of varying length were introduced; the workday and work week were shortened. The researchers, who now acted as supervisors, also allowed the groups to choose their own rest periods and to have a say in other suggested changes. Again, the results were ambiguous. Performance tended to increase over time, but it also rose and fell erratically. Partway through this set of experiments, Elton Mayo (1880-1949) and some associates from Harvard, including Fritz J. Roethlisberger and William J. Dickson, became involved.

In these and subsequent experiments, Mayo and his associates decided that a complex chain of attitudes had touched off the productivity increases. Because they had been singled out for special attention, both the test and the control groups had developed a group pride that motivated them to improve their work performance. Sympathetic supervision had further reinforced their motivation. The researchers concluded that employees would work harder if they believed management was concerned about their welfare and supervisors paid special attention to them. This phenomenon was subsequently labeled the **Hawthorne effect**. Since the control group received no special supervisory treatment or enhancement of working conditions but still improved its performance, some people (including Mayo himself) speculated that the control group's productivity gains resulted from the special attention of the researchers themselves.

The researchers also concluded that informal work groups—the social environment of employees—have a positive influence on productivity. Many of Western Electric employees found their work dull and meaningless, but their associations and friendships with co-workers, sometimes influenced by a shared antagonism toward the "bosses," imparted some meaning to their working lives and provided some protection from management. For these reasons, group pressure was frequently a stronger influence on worker productivity than management demands.

To Mayo, then, the concept of "social man"—motivated by social needs, wanting rewarding on-the-job relationships, and responding more to work-group pressures than to management control—was necessary to complement the old concept of "rational man" motivated by personal economic needs.[22] All these findings might seem unremarkable today. But compare what Mayo and his associates considered relevant with what Ford and Weber found relevant, and you see what a change these ideas brought to management theory.

Hawthorne effect:
The possibility that workers who receive special attention will perform better simply because they received that attention: one interpretation of studies by Elton Mayo and his colleagues.

APPLYING QUALITY CONCEPTS TO HUMAN RELATIONS THEORIES

The application of these human relations theories can be seen in today's competitive environment. For example, with the restructuring of today's competitive global economy, many companies have made the decision to "downsize" or reduce the numbers of managers and workers. However, some companies, well aware of the dynamics pointed out by the Hawthorne studies, have approached employee reductions with great care. At Sky Chiefs, a $450 million airline in-flight services corporation, the problems experienced by the airlines industry such as price wars, brisk competition from foreign airlines, aging fleets, and the increasing cost of new planes, were directly affecting the company. Forced to reduce staff, management realized that if it managed the process poorly and didn't take into consideration the needs of employees, those who remained after the downsizing would be less loyal and cohesive as a group.

To minimize potential problems after the downsizing, the management adopted "total quality leadership" to provide the company with a framework for implementing the restructuring. It spent thousands of hours and dollars to fund training and improvement processes related to total quality leadership. The key to the success of the restructuring was that instead of management dictating what would happen and to whom, employees, seen as the backbone of the company, were empowered to facilitate the process. For example, prior to the restructuring process, employees participated in evaluating all headquarters functions. An employee-managed restructuring committee was selected by management to assemble, interpret, and evaluate the data. Then smaller action teams were created to address the downsizing. To help those who were to be let go, extensive counseling and outplacement services were provided, including group workshops on networking, interviewing techniques, and hiring, and employees were videotaped to help with future interviews.

Now, after the restructuring, productivity and operating profits are increasing. The remaining employees have accepted their new roles and responsibilities, and morale continues to improve.[23] ▬▬

FROM HUMAN RELATIONS TO THE BEHAVIORAL SCIENCE APPROACH

Mayo and his colleagues pioneered the use of the scientific method in their studies of people in the work environment. Later researchers, more rigorously trained in the social sciences (psychology, sociology, and anthropology), used more sophisticated research methods and became known as "behavioral scientists" rather than "human relations theorists."

The behavioral scientists brought two new dimensions to the study of management and organizations. First, they advanced an even more sophisticated view of human beings and their drives than did Mayo and his contemporaries. Abraham Maslow and Douglas McGregor, among others, wrote about "self-actualizing" people.[24] Their work spawned new thinking about how relationships can be beneficially arranged in organizations. They also determined that people wanted more than "instantaneous" pleasure or rewards. If people were this complex in the way they led their lives, then their organizational relationships needed to support that complexity.

Second, behavioral scientists applied the methods of scientific investigation to the study of how people behaved in organizations as whole entities. The classic example is the work of James March and Herbert Simon in the late 1950s.[25] March and Simon developed hundreds of propositions for scientific investigation, about patterns of behavior, particularly with regard to communication, in organizations. Their influence in the development of subsequent management theory has been significant and ongoing.

According to Maslow, the needs that people are motivated to satisfy fall into a hierarchy. Physical and safety needs are at the bottom of the hierarchy, and at the top are ego needs (the need for respect, for example) and self-actualizing needs (such as the need for meaning and personal growth). In general, Maslow said, lower-level needs must be satisfied before higher-level needs can be met. Since many lower-level needs are routinely satisfied in contemporary society, most people are motivated more by the higher-level ego and self-actualizing needs.

Some later behavioral scientists feel that even this model cannot explain all the factors that may motivate people in the workplace. They argue that not everyone goes predictably from one level of need to the next. For some people, work is only a means for meeting lower-level needs. Others are satisfied with nothing less than the fulfillment of their highest-level needs; they may even choose to work in jobs that threaten their safety if by doing so they can attain uniquely personal goals. The more realistic model of human motivation, these behavioral scientists argue, is "complex person." Using this model, the effective manager is aware that no two people are exactly alike and tailors motivational approaches according to individual needs.

As American corporations increasingly do business with other cultures, it is important to remember that theories can be culturally bounded. For example, Maslow's hierarchy of needs is not a description of a universal motivational process. In other nations the order of the hierarchy might be quite different, depending on the values of the country. In Sweden, quality of life is ranked most important, while in Japan and Germany, security is ranked highest.[20]

McGregor provided another angle on this "complex person" idea. He distinguished two alternative basic assumptions about people and their approach to work. These two assumptions, which he called **Theory X** and **Theory Y** take opposite views of people's commitment to work in organizations. Theory X managers, McGregor proposed, assume that people must be constantly coaxed into putting forth effort in their jobs. Theory Y managers, on the other hand, assume that people relish work and eagerly approach their work as an opportunity to develop their creative capacities. Theory Y was an example of a "complex person" perspective. Theory Y management, McGregor claimed, was stymied by the prevalence of Theory X practices in the organizations of the 1950s. As you are already able to see, the roots of Theory Y can be traced to the days of scientific management and the factories based on these principles. In accordance with McGregor's thinking, General Electric CEO Jack Welch argues that people must forget the old idea of "boss" and replace it with the idea that managers have the new duties of counseling groups, providing resources for them and helping people think for themselves. "We're going to win on our ideas," he says, "not by whip and chains."

A THEORY Y ATTITUDE. At Baldrige-Award-winning Westinghouse, employee Spencer Douglas says it best: "There's so much pride here and everybody here wants to do their very best.... They hate to work on a product and pass it on to the next person and find something that they've missed."

THE MANAGEMENT SCIENCE SCHOOL

At the beginning of World War II, Great Britain desperately needed to solve a number of new, complex problems in warfare. With their survival at stake, the British formed the first operational research (OR) teams. By pooling the expertise of mathematicians, physicists, and other scientists in OR teams, the British were able to achieve significant technological and tactical breakthroughs. When the

operations research:
Mathematical techniques for the modeling, analysis, and solution of management problems. Also called *management science.*

management science school:
Approaching management problems through the use of mathematical techniques for their modeling, analysis, and solution.

Americans entered the war, they formed what they called **operations research** teams, based on the successful British model, to solve similar problems. The teams used early computers to perform the thousands of calculations involved in mathematical modeling.

When the war was over, the applicability of operations research to problems in industry gradually became apparent. New industrial technologies were being put into use and transportation and communication were becoming more complicated. These developments brought with them a host of problems that could not be solved easily by conventional means. Increasingly, OR specialists were called on to help managers come up with answers to these new problems. Over the years, OR procedures were formalized into what is now more generally called the **management science school.**[27]

The management science school gained popularity through two postwar phenomena. First, the development of high-speed computers and of communications among computers provided the means for tackling complex and large-scale organizational problems. Second, Robert McNamara implemented a management science approach at Ford Motor Company in the 1950s and 1960s. (Later, he brought the same approach to his assignment as Secretary of Defense in the Johnson Administration.)[28] As McNamara's so-called "Whiz Kids" proteges moved to management positions at Ford and across American industry, the management science school flourished. If you find yourself working in an organization where "crunching the numbers" is the central way that management decisions are reached and justified, you can thank McNamara and his generation.

Today the management science approach to solving a problem begins when a mixed team of specialists from relevant disciplines is called in to analyze the problem and propose a course of action to management. The team constructs a mathematical model that shows, in symbolic terms, all relevant factors bearing on the problem and how they are interrelated. By changing the values of the variables in the model (such as increasing the cost of raw materials) and analyzing the different equations of the model with a computer, the team can determine the effects of each change. Eventually, the management science team presents management with an objective basis for making a decision.[29]

Management science offered a whole new way to think about time. With sophisticated mathematical models, and computers to crunch the numbers, forecasting the future based on the past and present became a popular activity. Managers can now play with the "what if the future looks like this?" questions that previous management theories could not handle. At the same time, the management science school pays less attention to relationships per se in organizations. Mathematical modeling tends to ignore relationships as data, emphasizing numerical data that can be relatively easily collected or estimated. The criticism is thus that management science promotes an emphasis on only the aspects of the organization that can be captured in numbers, missing the importance of people and relationships.

RECENT DEVELOPMENTS IN MANAGEMENT THEORY

Theories are powerful influences. The longer we use a given theory, the more comfortable we become with it and the more we tend to not seek out alternative theories unless events force us to change. This helps explain why "modern" management theory is really a rich mosaic of many theories that have endured over at least the past century. One benefit of understanding this concurrent popularity of many points of view about organizations is that it prepares you for your own organizational experiences. If this chapter has not already brought to mind different managerial styles to which you have been exposed, it will prepare you for the day when, for example, you work for a "management science" manager who in turn works for a manager who practices by one of the theories to follow in the next section! Or if you have already experienced such managers, it will help you understand their perspectives better.

While it is impossible to predict what future generations will be studying, at this point we can identify at least three additional perspectives on management theory that can grow in importance: the systems approach, the contingency approach, and what we call the dynamic engagement approach.

THE SYSTEMS APPROACH

systems approach:
View of the organization as a unified, directed system of interrelated parts.

Rather than dealing separately with the various segments of an organization, the **systems approach** to management views the organization as a unified, purposeful system composed of interrelated parts. This approach gives managers a way of looking at the organization as a whole and as a part of the larger, external environment (see Chapter 3). Systems theory tells us that the activity of any segment of an organization affects, in varying degrees, the activity of every other segment.[30]

Production managers in a manufacturing plant, for example, prefer long uninterrupted production runs of standardized products in order to maintain maximum efficiency and low costs. Marketing managers, on the other hand, who want to offer customers quick delivery of a wide range of products, would like a flexible manufacturing schedule that can fill special orders on short notice. *Systems-oriented* production managers make scheduling decisions only after they have identified the impact of these decisions on other departments and on the entire organization. The point of the systems approach is that managers cannot function wholly within the confines of the traditional organization chart. They must mesh their department with the whole enterprise. To do that, they have to communicate

SYNERGY AT CNN. Organizational synergy is possible at CNN through a global network of correspondents and camera crews who feed reports to the Atlanta anchor desk.

not only with other employees and departments, but frequently with representatives of other organizations as well.[31] Clearly, systems managers grasp the importance of webs of business relationships to their efforts.

SOME KEY CONCEPTS

Many of the concepts of general systems theory are finding their way into the language of management. Managers need to be familiar with the systems vocabulary so they can keep pace with current developments.

subsystems:
Those parts making up the whole system.

synergy:
The situation in which the whole is greater than its parts. In organizational terms, synergy means that departments that interact cooperatively are more productive than they would be if they operated in isolation.

open system:
A system that interacts with its environment.

closed system:
A system that does not interact with its environment.

system boundary:
The boundary that separates each system from its environment. It is rigid in a closed system, flexible in an open system

flows:
Components such as information, material, and energy that enter and leave a system.

feedback:
The part of system control in which the results of actions are returned to the individual, allowing work procedures to be analyzed and corrected.

SUBSYSTEMS. The parts that make up the whole of a system are called **subsystems**. And each system in turn may be a subsystem of a still larger whole. Thus a department is a subsystem of a plant, which may be a subsystem of a company, which may be a subsystem of a conglomerate or an industry, which is a subsystem of the national economy, which is a subsystem of the world system.

SYNERGY. Synergy means that the whole is greater than the sum of its parts. In organizational terms, **synergy** means that as separate departments within an organization cooperate and interact, they become more productive than if each were to act in isolation. For example, in a small firm, it is more efficient for each department to deal with one finance department than for each department to have a separate finance department of its own.

OPEN AND CLOSED SYSTEMS. A system is considered an **open system** if it interacts with its environment; it is considered a **closed system** if it does not. All organizations interact with their environment, but the extent to which they do so varies. An automobile plant, for example, is a far more open system than a monastery or a prison.

SYSTEM BOUNDARY. Each system has a boundary that separates it from its environment. In a closed system, the **system boundary** is rigid; in an open system, the boundary is more flexible. The system boundaries of many organizations have become increasingly flexible in recent years. For example, managers at oil companies wishing to engage in offshore drilling now must consider public concern for the environment. A trend is that American communities are demanding more and more environmental responsibility from companies. For example, Santa Rosa, California, a city of 125,000, treats environmental violations such as "off-gassing" a waste product, that is, allowing it to evaporate into the atmosphere, as a potential criminal offense.[32]

FLOW. A system has **flows** of information, materials, and energy (including human energy). These enter the system from the environment as *inputs* (raw materials, for example), undergo transformation processes within the system (operations that alter them), and exit the system as *outputs* (goods and services).

FEEDBACK. **Feedback** is the key to system controls. As operations of the system proceed, information is fed back to the appropriate people, and perhaps to a computer, so that the work can be assessed and, if necessary, corrected.[33] For example, when Aluminum Company of America began feeding production data back to the factory floor, workers in the Addy, Washington, magnesium plant quickly observed ways to improve operations, boosting productivity by 72 percent.[34] Figure 2-2 shows the flows of information, materials, energy, and feedback in an open system.

Systems theory calls attention to the dynamic and interrelated nature of organizations and the management task. Thus, it provides a framework within which

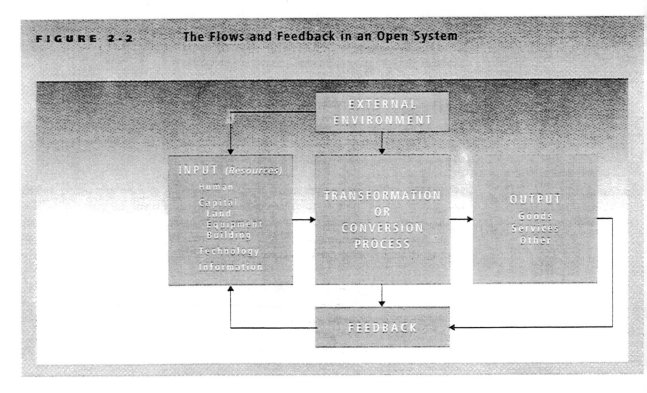

FIGURE 2-2   The Flows and Feedback in an Open System

we can plan actions and anticipate both immediate and far-reaching consequences while allowing us to understand unanticipated consequences as they develop. With a systems perspective, general managers can more easily maintain a balance between the needs of the various parts of the enterprise and the needs and goals of the whole firm.

THE CONTINGENCY APPROACH

The well-known international economist Charles Kindleberger was fond of telling his students at MIT that the answer to any really engrossing question in economics is: "It depends." The task of the economist, Kindleberger would continue, is to specify *upon what* it depends, and in what ways.

"It depends" is an appropriate response to the important questions in management as well. Management theory attempts to determine the predictable relationships between situations, actions, and outcomes. So it is not surprising that a recent approach seeks to integrate the various schools of management thought by focusing on the interdependence of the many factors involved in the managerial situation.

The **contingency approach** (sometimes called the *situational approach*) was developed by managers, consultants, and researchers who tried to apply the concepts of the major schools to real-life situations. When methods highly effective in one situation failed to work in other situations, they sought an explanation. Why, for example, did an organizational development program work brilliantly in one situation and fail miserably in another? Advocates of the contingency approach had a logical answer to all such questions: Results differ because situations differ; a technique that works in one case will not necessarily work in all cases.

According to the contingency approach, the manager's task is to identify which technique will, *in a particular situation, under particular circumstances, and at a particular time*, best contribute to the attainment of management goals. Where workers need to be encouraged to increase productivity, for example, the classical theorist may prescribe a new work-simplification scheme. The behavioral scientist

contingency approach:
The view that the management technique that best contributes to the attainment of organizational goals might vary in different types of situations or circumstances; also called the *situational approach*.

22

may instead seek to create a psychologically motivating climate and recommend some approach like *job enrichment*—the combination of tasks that are different in scope and responsibility and allow the worker greater autonomy in making decisions. But the manager trained in the contingency approach will ask, "Which method will *work best here?*" If the workers are unskilled and training opportunities and resources are limited, work simplification would be the best solution. However, with skilled workers driven by pride in their abilities, a job-enrichment program might be more effective. The contingency approach represents an important turn in modern management theory, because it portrays each set of organizational relationships in its unique circumstances.

For example, when managers at Taco Bell addressed the question of what would work best for its restaurants, they redefined business based on the simple premise that customers value food, service, and the physical appearance of the restaurant. To implement the new customer-focused goals, the company recruited new managers who were committed to creating or delivering goods that customers value and who could coach and support staff in the new direction. To concentrate on customers, Taco Bell outsourced much of the assembly-line food preparation, such as shredding lettuce, allowing employees to focus on customers. As a result, it has enjoyed a 60 percent growth in sales at company-owned stores.[35] Other fast food restaurants might base their business on different situational factors, by the contingency view.

ENTERING AN ERA OF DYNAMIC ENGAGEMENT

All of the preceding theories have come down to us in the late twentieth-century world of organizations and management. Here they are practiced against a backdrop of rapid change and profound rethinking about how management and organizations will evolve in the next century. At the heart of this rethinking, which is really occurring in numerous ways at the same time, are new ways of thinking about relationships and time.

As boundaries between cultures and nations are blurred and new communications technology makes it possible to think of the world as a "global village," the scope of international and intercultural relationships is rapidly expanding. The pace of organizational activity picks up dramatically. These trends indicate a heightened level of *intensity* in organizations and management today.

To emphasize the intensity of modern organizational relationships and the intensity of time pressures that govern these relationships, we call this flurry of new management theory the **dynamic engagement** approach. "Dynamic engagement" is our term. In times when theories are changing, it is often true that the last thing that happens is that someone assigns a name to the new theory. We use *dynamic engagement* to convey the mood of current thinking and debate about management and organizations. It is quite likely that twenty years from now, well into your organizational lives, you will look back and call this period of movement by some other name.

Dynamic—the opposite of static—implies continuous change, growth, and activity; engagement—the opposite of detachment—implies intense involvement with others. We therefore think the term *dynamic engagement* best expresses the vigorous way today's most successful managers focus on human relationships and quickly adjust to changing conditions over time.

Six different themes about management theory are emerging under the umbrella that we call dynamic engagement. To emphasize their importance to your

dynamic engagement:
The view that time and human relationships are forcing management to rethink traditional approaches in the face of constant, rapid change.

understanding of management in the 1990s and beyond, and to highlight the differences between them, we devote a chapter in Part Two to each of them.

NEW ORGANIZATIONAL ENVIRONMENTS (Chapter 3)

The dynamic engagement approach recognizes that an organization's environment is not some set of fixed, impersonal forces. Rather, it is a complex, dynamic web of people interacting with each other. As a result, managers must not only pay attention to their own concerns, but also understand what is important to other managers both within their organizations and at other organizations. They interact with these other managers to create jointly the conditions under which their organizations will prosper or struggle. The theory of competitive strategy, developed by Michael Porter, focuses on how managers can influence conditions in an industry when they interact as rivals, buyers, suppliers, and so on. Another variation on the dynamic engagement approach, most notably argued by Edward and Jean Gerner Stead in *Management for a Small Planet,* places ecological concerns at the center of management theory.

ETHICS AND SOCIAL RESPONSIBILITY (Chapter 4)

Managers using a dynamic engagement approach pay close attention to the values that guide people in their organizations, the corporate culture that embodies those values, and the values held by people outside the organization. This idea came into prominence with the publication in 1982 of *In Search of Excellence* by Thomas Peters and Robert Waterman. From their study of "excellent" companies, Peters and Waterman concluded that "the top performers create a broad, uplifting, shared culture, a coherent framework within which charged-up people search for appropriate adaptations."[36]

Robert Solomon has taken this idea a step further, arguing that managers must exercise moral courage by placing the value of *excellence* at the top of their agendas. In dynamic engagement, it is not enough for managers to do things the way they always have, or to be content with matching their competitors. Continually striving toward excellence has become an organizational theme of the 1990s. Because values, including excellence, are ethical concepts, the dynamic engagement approach moves ethics from the fringe of management theory to the heart of it.

CURRENT MANAGEMENT WRITING. The dynamic engagement approach is evident in much of the current literature in the field of management.

GLOBALIZATION AND MANAGEMENT (Chapter 5)

The dynamic engagement approach recognizes that the world is at the manager's doorstep in the 1990s. With world financial markets running 24 hours a day, and even the remotest corners of the planet only a telephone call away, managers facing the twenty-first century must think of themselves as global citizens. Kenichi Ohmae makes this point as he describes a "borderless" world where managers treat all customers as "equidistant" from their organizations.[37]

A simple comparison illustrates how things have changed. If you were to look through Alfred Sloan's autobiography about his long career as General Motors chairman through the 1940s, you would find very little about international factors—with good reason in that time and place. Today, however, if you tune into a CNN broadcast you will notice that the reporters do not use the word "foreign" at all. Or, consider the poster on the wall of Honda dealerships, which says the idea of an "American car" doesn't make any sense in an era when a single car contains parts made by people from all over the globe.

INVENTING AND REINVENTING ORGANIZATIONS (Chapter 6)

Managers who practice dynamic engagement continually search for ways to unleash the creative potential of their employees and themselves. A growing chorus of theorists are urging managers to rethink the standard organization structures to which they have become accustomed. Peters is once again at the forefront. His concept of "liberation management" challenges the kinds of rigid organization structures that inhibit people's creativity. Peters' heroes succeed in spite of those structures.[38] Michael Hammer and James Champy have made their concept of **"reengineering** the corporation" into a bestseller. Hammer and Champy urge managers to rethink the very processes by which organizations function and to be courageous about replacing processes that get in the way of organizational efficiency.

Reengineering

This occurs when an organization conducts a significant reassessment of what it is all about.

CULTURES AND MULTICULTURALISM (Chapter 7)

Managers who embrace the dynamic engagement approach recognize that the various perspectives and values that people of different cultural backgrounds bring to their organizations are not only a fact of life but a significant source of contributions.

Joanne Martin has pioneered the cultural analysis of organizations. She explains how differences create unprecedented challenges for modern managers. Charles Taylor is a prominent proponent of the so-called "communitarian" movement. Taylor claims that people can preserve their sense of uniqueness—their authenticity—only by valuing what they hold in common and seeking to extend what they hold in common in the organizations and communities in which they live. Cornel West grabs our attention to different cultures with the very title of his book, *Race Matters*. Martin, Taylor, and West all want us to see the benefits that come from welcoming and understanding differences among people. Still, none of them say that acceptance of different cultures will be easy. Multiculturalism is a moving target as more and more people become conscious of their particular cultural traditions and ties. Here is where both "dynamic" and "engagement" clearly come together as we envision the organizations of the twenty-first century.

QUALITY (Chapter 8)

By the dynamic engagement approach, Total Quality Management (TQM) should be in every manager's vocabulary. All managers should be thinking about how every organizational process can be conducted to provide products and services that are responsible to tougher and tougher customer and competitive standards. Strong and lasting relationships can be fruitful byproducts of a "quality" frame of mind and action, by this view. Total Quality Management adds one more dynamic dimension to management, because quality, too, is always a moving target.

Dynamic engagement is an example of the changing face of management theory. Not everyone we have mentioned in this overview of the dynamic engagement approach calls himself or herself a management theorist. Some are philosophers and some are political scientists. As we bring this chapter to a close, we want to point out an important lesson in this lineup of dynamic engagement theorists. The dynamic engagement approach challenges us to see organizations and management as integral parts of modern global society. This was not always a tenet of management theory. Once the door is opened between organizations and the larger world, however, many new influences can come to bear on questions about management theory and relationships.

REMEMBER TO CHANGE WITH THE TIMES

We have discovered two basic things in this chapter. First, theorists, whatever their fields of endeavor, tend to be people and products of their times. Second, management theories, like theories in all fields, tend to *evolve* to reflect everyday realities and changing circumstances. By the same token, managers must be sensitive to changing circumstances and equally willing to change. If they do not, they must be surpassed by more flexible competitors.

Both of these ideas apply to Henry Ford, the man who boldly embraced the ideas of scientific management, revolutionizing the auto industry and our society in the process.

Yet many of Ford's managerial practices were conservative or unresponsive to changing times, and his hold on the automotive market was eventually wrested from him by companies more farsighted in their managerial theories and practices. Hostile to the banking community, for example, Ford refused outside investments in his company throughout his lifetime, borrowing capital only when absolutely necessary and preferring to finance corporate activities solely through the company's own income. He was also inclined to ignore the dynamics of the industry that he had largely founded. Although he opened up branch factories to cater to a growing European market, he long failed to follow managerial advice to retool for both the hydraulic brake and six- or eight-cylinder engine; he also resisted management counsel regarding the advances in gearshift and transmission technology and even put off introducing color variety into his product line (Ford preferred his cars to be black). His disinterest in consumer demands for comfort and style ultimately cost him his industry's leadership, which passed to General Motors, a conglomerate assembled from over 20 diverse firms by founder William Durant and a second generation of American industrial organizers.

MANAGEMENT 2000 AND BEYOND

A COMPANY OF BUSINESSPEOPLE

For most of the twentieth century, the terms that have been used for relationships between people in the workplace have been supervisor/worker, manager/employee, the company/the union or us/them. It was expected that owners and managers would run the company, and workers would follow directions. Because of the dynamic marketplace changes of the past 20 years, many people are questioning whether this old thinking still works. Part of the story can be told in the recent history of failed American businesses and others that are struggling mightily.

Meanwhile, a number of pathbreaking managers in both large and small companies are ignoring old ideas—as well as the latest innovations such as TQM. Instead, these managers are creating a wholly different mind-set about business and a differ-

Organizational Ethics

- Ethical Norms for Business Decisions
- Business Values for the Future

ETHICAL NORMS FOR BUSINESS DECISIONS

Ethical norms and models have been the subject of much reflection over the centuries. The theory of rights and duties focuses on the entitlements of individual persons. Immanuel Kant[7] (personal rights) and John Locke[8] (property rights) were the first to fully develop the theory of rights and duties. The theory of justice has a longer tradition, going back to Plato and Aristotle in the fourth century B.C.[9]

Of all ethical norms, businesspeople feel most at home with utilitarianism. This is not surprising, as the norm traces its origins to Adam Smith, the father of modern economics. The main proponents of utilitarianism are Jeremy Bentham[10] and John Stuart Mill,[11] both of whom helped to formulate the theory

---

[7] Immanuel Kant, *The Metaphysical Elements of Justice*, trans. J. Ladd (New York: Library of Liberal Arts, 1965).

[8] John Locke, *The Second Treatise of Government* (New York: Liberal Arts Press, 1952).

[9] Aristotle, *Ethics*, trans. J. A. K. Thomson (London: Penguin, 1953).

[10] Jeremy Bentham, *An Introduction to the Principles of Morals and Legislation* (New York: Hafner, 1948).

[11] John Stuart Mill, *Utilitarianism* (Indianapolis: Bobbs-Merrill, 1957).

more precisely. Utilitarianism evaluates actions in terms of their consequences. In any given situation, the one action which would result in the greatest net gain for all concerned parties is considered to be the right, or morally obligatory, action.

The ethical norm of caring has developed more recently from feminist ethics.[12] Theoretical work in each of these ethical norms continues to the present.[13] For an overview of these four ethical norms—their history, strengths, weaknesses, and areas of application—see Table 3–1 on pp. 76–77.

The Norm of Individual Rights and Duties

A moral right is an important, normative, justifiable claim or entitlement to something.[14] Moral rights and duties flow from one's human dignity and ultimately from the Creator, and are sometimes supported by law, such as our constitutional rights of freedom of conscience or freedom of speech. Moral rights have these characteristics: (1) They enable individuals to pursue their own interests, and (2) they impose duties or correlative requirements or prohibitions on others.[15]

Legal rights are stated in rules, laws, or a constitutional system. The U.S. Bill of Rights and the United Nations Universal Declaration of Human Rights are examples of documents that spell out individual rights in detail. Most legal rights stem from moral rights; but not all moral rights are enacted into law, and some bad law can even abrogate human rights (for example, rights of blacks in pre-1960s United States and Jews in Nazi Germany).

Every right has a corresponding obligation or duty. My right to freedom of conscience is supported by the prohibition of other individuals from unnecessarily limiting that freedom of conscience. With regard to business, my right to be paid for my work corresponds to my duty to perform "a fair day's work for a fair day's pay." In the latter case, both the right and duty stem from the right to private property, which is a traditional pillar of American life and law. However, the right to private property is not absolute. A factory owner may be forced by law, as well as by morality, to spend money on pollution control or safety equipment. For a listing of selected rights and other ethical norms, see Figure 3–2.

People also have the right not to be lied to or deceived, especially on matters about which they have a right to know. Hence, a supervisor has the duty to be truthful in giving feedback on work performance even if it is difficult for the

---

[12] See Carol Gilligan, *In a Different Voice* (Cambridge: Harvard University Press, 1982), and Nel Noddings, *Caring* (Berkeley: University of California Press, 1984).

[13] For example, John Rawls, *A Theory of Justice* (Cambridge, Mass.: Harvard University Press, 1971). See two books of readings: Thomas Donaldson and Patricia Werhane, *Ethical Issues in Business: A Philosophical Approach*, 5th ed. (Englewood Cliffs, N.J.: Prentice-Hall, 1996); Tom Beauchamp and Norman Bowie, *Ethical Theory and Business*, 4th ed. (Englewood Cliffs, N.J.: Prentice-Hall, 1993).

[14] Richard T. De George, *Business Ethics* (Englewood Cliffs, N.J.: Prentice-Hall, 1995), pp. 101–4.

[15] Manuel Velasquez, *Business Ethics: Concepts and Cases* (Englewood Cliffs, N.J.: Prentice-Hall, 1992), p. 73; see also Thomas Donaldson, *Corporations and Morality* (Englewood Cliffs, N.J.: Prentice-Hall, 1982).

FIGURE 3–2 Selected Ethical Norms

RIGHTS AND DUTIES

1. *Life and safety*: The individual has the right not to have her or his life or safety unknowingly and unnecessarily endangered.

2. *Truthfulness*: The individual has the right not to be intentionally deceived by another, especially on matters about which the individual has the right to know.

3. *Privacy*: The individual has the right to do whatever he or she chooses to do outside working hours and to control information about his or her private life.

4. *Freedom of conscience*: The individual has the right to refrain from carrying out any order that violates those commonly accepted moral or religious norms to which the person adheres.

5. *Free speech*: The individual has the right to criticize conscientiously and truthfully the ethics or legality of corporate actions so long as the criticism does not violate the rights of other individuals within the organization.

6. *Private property*: The individual has the right to hold private property, especially insofar as this right enables the individual and his or her family to be sheltered and to have the basic necessities of life.

JUSTICE

1. *Fair treatment*: Persons who are similar to each other in the relevant respects should be treated similarly; persons who differ in some respect relevant to the job they perform should be treated differently in proportion to the difference between them.

2. *Fair administration of rules*: Rules should be administered consistently, fairly, and impartially.

3. *Fair compensation*: Individuals should be compensated for the cost of their injuries by the party that is responsible for those injuries.

4. *Fair blame*: Individuals should not be held responsible for matters over which they have no control.

5. *Due process*: The individual has a right to a fair and impartial hearing when he or she believes that personal rights are being violated.

UTILITARIANISM

1. *Organizational goals* should aim at *maximizing the satisfactions* of the organization's constituencies.

2. The members of an organization should attempt to attain its goals as *efficiently* as possible by consuming as few inputs as possible and by minimizing external costs which organizational activities impose to others.

3. The employee should use every *effective* means to achieve the goals of the organization and should neither jeopardize those goals nor enter situations in which personal interests conflict significantly with the goals.

CARING

1. Each person has responsibility for the well-being of those people with whom one has a relation.

2. The responsibility to care increases as the dependency of the other person increases.

3. One cannot be obligated to provide care that one is incapable of providing.

31

TABLE 3-1 Ethical Models for Business Decisions

Definition and Origin	Strengths	Weaknesses	When Used	
			Example	Summary
1. Norm of Rights and Duties Individual's freedom is not to be violated: Locke (1635–1701)—property Kant (1724–1804)—personal rights	1. Ensures respect for individual's personal freedom and property 2. Parallels political "Bill of Rights"	1. Emphasis on rights can encourage individualistic, selfish behavior	1. Unsafe workplace 2. Flammable children's toys 3. Lying to superior or subordinate	1. Where individual's personal rights or property are in question 2. Use with, for example, employee privacy, job tenure, work dangerous to person's health
2. Norm of Justice Equitable distribution of society's benefits and burdens: Aristotle (384–322 B.C.) Rawls (1921–)	1. The "democratic" principle 2. Does not allow a society to become status- or class-dominated 3. Ensures that minorities, handicapped poor, receive opportunities and a fair share of the output	1. Can result in less risk, incentive and innovation 2. Encourages sense of entitlement	1. Bribes, kickbacks, fraud 2. Delivery of shoddy goods 3. Low wages to Hispanic, African-American, or women workers	1. Fairness, equal opportunity, for poor and unemployed 2. Setting salaries for workers vs. executives 3. Public policy decisions: to maintain a floor of living standards for all 4. Use with, for example, performance appraisal, due process, distribution of rewards and punishment

(continued on next page)

TABLE 3–1 Ethical Models for Business Decisions *(continued)*

Definition and Origin	Strengths	Weaknesses	Example	Summary
				When Used
3. Utilitarianism "The greatest good for the greatest number": Bentham (1748–1832) Adam Smith (1723–1790) David Ricardo (1772–1823)	1. Concepts, terminology, methods are easiest for businesspeople to use 2. Promotes view of entire system of exchange beyond "this firm" 3. Encourages entrepreneurship, innovation, productivity	1. Impossible to measure or quantify all important elements 2. "Greatest good" can degenerate into self-interest 3. Can result in abridging another's rights 4. Can result in neglecting less powerful segments of society	1. Plant closing 2. Pollution 3. Condemnation of land or buildings for "development"	1. Use in all business decisions, and will be dominant criteria in most 2. Version of model is implicitly used already, although scope is generally limited to "this firm"
4. Caring Responsibility to a person because of relationship: Gilligan (1936–) Noddings (1929–)	1. Emphasizes care and responsibility for people 2. Builds trust, healthy communications and teamwork 3. Supports community and good for group	1. Poor at discriminating various responsibilities and equities 2. Without personal relationship there are no obligations	1. Mentoring colleagues and subordinates 2. Flexible hours and flexible leave policy for sake of family duties 3. At time of delivery of poor performance report or layoffs	1. Emphasizes interpersonal relationships 2. Care for employees and members of work group 3. Concern for those with personal or family needs

supervisor to do so. Each of us has the right not to be lied to by salespeople or advertisements. Perjury under oath is a serious crime; lying on matters where another has a right to accurate information is also seriously unethical. Truthfulness and honesty are basic ethical norms.

Rights and duties express the requirements of morality from the standpoint of the individual. Rights and duties protect the individual from the encroachment and demands of society or the state. Utilitarian standards promote the group's interests and are relatively insensitive regarding a single individual except insofar as the individual's welfare affects the good of the group.

A business contract establishes rights and duties that did not exist before: The right of the purchaser to receive what was agreed and the right of the seller to be paid what was agreed. Formal written contracts and informal verbal agreements are essential to business transactions.

Immanuel Kant recognized that an emphasis on rights can lead people to focus largely on what is due them. Kant sought to broaden this perspective, so he emphasized what he called the "categorical imperative." The first formulation is: *I ought never to act except in such a way that I can also will that my principle should become a universal law.* An equivalent statement is this: *An action is morally right for a person in a certain situation if and only if the person's reason for carrying out the action is a reason that he or she would be willing to have every person act on, in any similar situation.*[16]

Kant's second formulation of the categorical imperative cautions us against using other people as a means to our own ends: *Never treat humanity simply as a means, but always also as an end.* In effect, an action is morally right for a person if and only if in performing the action the person does not use others merely as a means for advancing his or her own interests, but also both respects and develops their capacity to choose for themselves. The Golden Rule, "Do unto others as you would have them do unto you," reflects the earlier words of Leviticus (19:18) and Jesus (Matthew 22:19), "Love your neighbor as yourself."

Capital, computers, and business firms are means, and are thus to be used to serve the purposes of people. A person, on the other hand, is not to be used merely as an instrument for achieving another's goals. This rules out deception, manipulation, and exploitation in dealing with people.

The Norm of Justice

Justice requires all persons, and thus managers too, to be guided by fairness, equity, and impartiality. Justice calls for evenhanded treatment of groups and individuals (1) in the distribution of the benefits and burdens of society, (2) in the administration of laws and regulations, and (3) in the imposition of sanctions

---

[16] Immanuel Kant, *Groundwork of the Metaphysics of Morals*, trans. H. J. Paton (New York: Harper & Row, 1964), pp. 62–90.

and the awarding of compensation for wrongs suffered. An action or policy is just if it is comparable to the treatment accorded to others.

Standards of justice are generally considered to be more important than the utilitarian consideration of consequences. If a society is unjust to a group (e.g., segregation, job discrimination), we generally consider that society to be unjust and we condemn it, even if the results of the injustices bring about greater economic productivity. On the other hand, we are willing to trade off some equality if the results will bring about greater benefits for all. For example, differences in income and wealth are justified *only* if they bring greater benefits for *all*.

Standards of justice are not as often in conflict with individual rights as are utilitarian norms.[17] This is not surprising, since justice is largely based on the moral rights of individuals. The moral right to be treated as a free and equal person, for example, undergirds the notion that benefits and burdens should be distributed equitably. Personal moral rights (e.g., right to life, freedom of conscience, the right to free consent) are so basic that they generally may not be taken away to bring about a better distribution of benefits within a society. On the other hand, property rights may be abridged for the sake of a fairer distribution of benefits and burdens (e.g., graduated income tax, limits on pollution).

Distributive justice becomes important when a society has sufficient goods but not everyone's basic needs are satisfied. The question then becomes, What is a just distribution? The fundamental principle is that equals should be treated equally and that unequals should be treated in accord with their inequality. For example, few would argue that a new person hired for a job should receive the same pay as a senior worker with 20 years experience. People who perform work of greater responsibility or who work longer hours should receive greater pay. Hence, pay differentials should be based on the work itself, not on some arbitrary bias of the employer.

Even knowing all of the above, we still wouldn't be able to determine what is a fair distribution of society's benefits and burdens. In fact, quite different notions of equity are proposed. For example, the capitalist model (benefits based on contribution) is radically different from the socialist (from each according to abilities, to each according to needs). An important contribution to the theory of justice has been made by John Rawls.[18] Rawls would have us construct a system of rules and laws for society as if we did not know what roles we were to play in that society. We do not know if we would be rich or poor, female or male, African or European, manager or slave, handicapped or physically and mentally fit. Rawls calls this the "veil of ignorance." Constructing a system of rules under the veil of ignorance is intended to allow us to rid ourselves of the biases we have as a result of our status. In such circumstances,

[17] Jerald Greenberg, "A Taxonomy of Organizational Justice Theories," *Academy of Management Review* 12 (January 1987): 9–22.

[18] John Rawls, *A Theory of Justice* (Cambridge, Mass.: Harvard University Press, 1971).

each of us would try to construct a system that would be of the greatest benefit to all and that would not undermine the position of any group. Rawls proposes that people under the veil of ignorance would agree to two principles:

1. Each person is to have an equal right to the most extensive liberty compatible with similar liberty for others.
2. Social and economic inequalities are to be arranged so that they are both reasonably expected to be to everyone's advantage and attached to positions and offices open to all.

The first principle is consonant with the American sense of liberty and thus is not controversial in the United States. The second principle is more egalitarian and also more controversial. However, Rawls maintains that if people honestly choose as if they were under the veil of ignorance, they would opt for a system of justice that is most fair to all members of society.[19] We now turn to a norm that observes the *consequences* of actions on the entire group.

The Norm of Utilitarianism

Utilitarianism examines the consequences of an act. It judges that an action is right if it produces the greatest utility, "the greatest good for the greatest number." The decision process is very much like a cost-benefit analysis applied to all parties who would be touched by the decision. That action is right which produces the greatest net benefit when all the costs and benefits to all the affected parties are taken into account. Although it would be convenient if these costs and benefits could be measured in some comparable unit, this is rarely possible. Many important values (e.g., human life and liberty) cannot be quantified. Thus, the best we can do is to list the effects and estimate the magnitude of their costs and benefits as accurately as possible.

The utilitarian principle says that the right action is that which produces the greatest net benefit over any other possible action. This does not mean that the right action produces the greatest good for the person performing the action. Rather, it is the action that produces the greatest net good for all those who are affected by the action. The utilitarian norm is best for cases that are complex and affect many parties. Although the model and the methodology are clear in theory, carrying out the calculations is often difficult. Taking into account so many affected parties, along with the extent to which the action effects them, can be a tallying nightmare.

Hence several shortcuts have been proposed that can reduce the complexity of utilitarian calculations. Each shortcut involves a sacrifice of accuracy for ease of calculation. Among these shortcuts are (1) calculation of costs and bene-

[19] An organization that treats its employees justly reaps many rewards; see Blair H. Shepart, Roy J. Lewicki, and John W. Minton, *Organizational Justice: The Search for Fairness in the Workplace* (New York: Lexington, 1992).

fits in dollar terms for ease of comparison; (2) restriction of consideration to those directly affected by the action, putting aside indirect effects. In using these shortcuts, an individual should be aware that they result in simplification and that some interests may not be sufficiently taken into consideration.

In the popular mind, the term *utilitarianism* sometimes suggests selfishness and exploitation. For our purposes, the term should be considered not to have these connotations. However, a noteworthy weakness of utilitarianism as an ethical norm is that it can advocate, for example, abridging an individual's right to a job or even life for the sake of the greater good of a larger number of people. This and other difficulties are discussed elsewhere.[20] One additional caution in using utilitarian rules is in order: It is considered unethical to opt for narrower benefits (e.g., personal goals, career, or money) at the expense of the good of a larger number, such as a firm, neighborhood, or a nation. Utilitarian norms emphasize the good of the *group*; it is a large-scale ethical model. As a result, an individual and what is due that individual may be overlooked. Hence the norm of utilitarianism must be balanced by the use of the norms of justice, rights and duties, and the norm we will discuss next, caring.

The Norm of Caring

Over the centuries, ethicists, who were almost all male, developed the norms of rights and duties, justice and utilitarianism. These norms emphasize impartiality and abstract principles. A new norm of *caring* has been presented by scholars in the last few decades.[21] Caring is built upon relations between people and is an extension of family life. Rather than autonomous individuals making objective, impartial ethical judgments, in reality we experience numerous relationships, and each of these relationships influences our ethical obligations. We care for each other, and we have responsibilities to each other.

Ethicists who use caring as their norm demonstrate how womens' moral experience up to this time has been neglected. Carol Gilligan was among the first to point out that, when faced with moral dilemmas, women tend to focus on the relationships of people rather than on impartial, theoretical principles.[22] As we saw in Chapter 2, Gilligan amended the existing descriptions of the levels of moral development in the light of the experience of women. The male matures by developing autonomy and sees himself in opposition to the other, thus the insistence on personal rights. In the limiting case, a businessperson's values, if they are unduly influenced by rights, economics, and the market-

---

[20] Gerald F. Cavanagh, Dennis J. Moberg, and Manuel Velasquez, "The Ethics of Organizational Politics," *Academy of Management Review* 6 (July 1981): 363–74. For a more complete treatment, see Manuel Velasquez, *Business Ethics: Concepts and Cases* 3rd. ed. (Englewood Cliffs, N.J.: Prentice-Hall, 1992), pp. 58–72.

[21] See Rosemarie Tong, *Feminine and Feminist Ethics* (Belmont, Calif.: Wadsworth, 1993), esp. Chapters 3 and 4.

[22] Carol Gilligan, *In a Different Voice* (Cambridge, Mass.: Harvard University Press, 1982).

place, can result in paranoid tendencies which can cause him either not to relate to others or to relate to others only by contract.

The female matures by developing relationship-based morality. Although feminist ethicists are reluctant to analyze caring too exactly, we can note some qualifications of the norm of caring. First, the obligation to care is proportional to one's relationship. In extended relationships, caring does not require action if that action is very costly. Second, one's roles and obligations influence the responsibility to care. Caring for one's child has greater priority than caring for someone in one's work group. Third, one cannot be obligated to provide care that one is incapable of providing.[23] From the viewpoint of the organization and the manager, caring is a very relevant norm for many current business challenges. Trust, teamwork, good personal relationships, and communications build upon caring, and must be achieved, if the firm is to be competitive.[24]

Caring clearly engages our emotions, but in order to do *any* ethical reasoning, our emotions must be involved. While ethics is not to be equated with feeling, it is a sterile intellectual exercise if one's feelings are not engaged in the process. In making ethical judgments it is essential to consider the interests of others. In order to incorporate the interests of others into one's decision-making processes, one must be able to feel and to empathize with those that are affected by one's decisions. In Kohlberg's terms, one must at least have achieved Level 2 moral development (see Chapter 2). Ethical decision-makers must learn how to regularly and habitually put themselves in the position of other persons. They must learn how others perceive a situation and sense what others feel and suffer. Without this ability to care for others on a sensible level, it is impossible to examine the moral dimensions of life in any significant way.[25]

Ethical Norms for Global Business

Some business ethics scholars have examined the varying business customs and practices in various countries throughout the world, and they have concluded that new norms are needed in international business ethics. They have proposed a variety of different models, based upon rights, social contract, and negative and modified utilitarianism.[26] Other scholars, however, have found similar fundamental ethical values in business in different cultures.[27]

---

[23] Gerald F. Cavanagh, Dennis J. Moberg, and Manuel Velasquez, "Making Business Ethics Practical," *Business Ethics Quarterly* 5 (July 1995): 399–418.

[24] Jeanne M. Liedtka, "Feminist Morality and Competitive Reality: A Role for the Ethic of Care?," *Business Ethics Quarterly* 6 (April 1996): 179–200.

[25] On the importance of empathy in ethical decision making, I thank Manuel Velasquez.

[26] Thomas Donaldson, *The Ethics of International Business* (New York: Oxford University Press, 1989); Richard T. DeGeorge, *Competing with Integrity in International Business* (New York: Oxford University Press, 1993); Thomas Donaldson and Thomas Dunfee, "Toward a Unified Conception of Business Ethics: Integrative Social Contract Theory," *Academy of Management Review* 19 (April 1994): 252–84.

[27] For example, Japanese businesspeople have roughly the same values as do American, even though business ethics is not as institutionalized in Japan. See Chaiki Nakano, "A Survey on Japanese Managers' Views of Business ethics," *op. cit.*

FUTURE BUSINESS VALUES

American business and its values have shifted over the last decade; earlier chapters of this book charted these shifts. Because changes continue at a rapid rate, it is imperative that we understand the direction and the substance of current changes.

In this final section we will review the changes that are taking place and try to assess their potential impact on American business. We will identify emerging values that will significantly affect people, firms, and American business ideology. Note that these emerging values are extensions of traditional American values; there are few sharp breaks (see Table 9–1). We will attempt to make projections by using data and expert opinion.

Central Role of the Person

The importance of the individual person pervades American life, literature, and thought. Individualism is increasingly important also in China, Singapore, South Korea, Japan, and other Asian countries.[32] Individualism, democracy, human rights, the free market, and the courts build on the centrality of the dignity

---

[32] For a comparison of and demonstration of the similarity of basic Asian and American values, see John Naisbitt, *Megatrends Asia, op. cit.,* pp. 53–55.

40

TABLE 9–1 Traditional American Values Lead to Future Business Values	
Traditional American Values . . . Lead to . . .	*Future Business Values*
Dignity of the individual	Central role of the person
Entrepreneurship and democratic spirit	Participation in management decisions
Self-reliance	Sustainable development
Planning ahead	Long-range perspective
Business as a provider of goods and services	Business as a servant of society
Growth and progress	Technology and innovation
Democratic nation	A nation among nations
Respect for the land	Harmony with the environment
Frontier and self-sufficiency	Local control: small is beautiful
Influence of religion and churches on American life	Spiritual roots of the new business mission
Helping neighbors (building barns, labor unions, charitable organizations)	Concern for others
Centrality of the individual, the family, and the local community	New measures of success
Optimism and openness	Vision and hope

of the individual person. Demands for greater productivity, coupled with the central role of the person, will bring more upgrading of skills and management development, along with flexibility in peoples' workday, workweek, and career. Most recognize that teams and loyalty bring success and satisfaction. The family will again be emphasized as the bedrock of America's social structure.

A firm in which the talents of each employee are challenged, in which coworkers communicate and supervisors provide feedback on work, is one in which each individual will grow in skills, satisfaction, and as a person. For a business firm to succeed, its workers must be committed to a quality product or service. The firm must enlist the efforts of all workers in pursuing its goals by communicating its mission statement, creating a cooperative climate, allowing time in the work week for group sessions on better quality, and rewarding groups and individuals that contribute to reaching the goals.

Firms recognize that the best way to succeed is to draw on the full talents of all workers. Workers feel that they are part of the team when they are asked their opinions of products and processes. Workers then develop a sense of ownership with respect to the job and the firm, and they work better, experience less fatigue, and enjoy greater satisfaction as a result.[33]

---

[33] See Gerald F. Cavanagh, "Evolution of Corporate Social Responsibility: Educating Stakeholders and Virtuous Entrepreneurs," in John W. Houck and Oliver F. Williams, eds., *Is the Good Corporation Dead?— Social Responsibility in a Global Economy* (Lanham, Md.: Rowman & Littlefield, 1996), pp. 169–99.

Participation in Management Decisions

Managers now also encourage participation in decisions. Various schemes have been developed in the United States, Sweden, Japan, and elsewhere to obtain worker input and to share the responsibility for decision making with workers. Decision making through consensus at the grass roots level among workers, as opposed to decision making only at the top, is now common. The American Catholic bishops devoted an entire section in their letter on the U.S. economy to participation.[34] However, Sar Levitan, veteran observer of work, cautions,

> In most cases . . . management preaches worker cooperation but ignores workers' priorities if they conflict with immediate profit-maximization efforts. Employees are encouraged to participate in corporate decision making only if it does not infringe on management prerogatives.[35]

Most people find that liking their coworkers is essential to job satisfaction. If coworkers are friendly, cooperative, and interested in each other, work can be something to look forward to. Firms that previously would transfer talented, high-potential managers every few years now recognize the needs people have for family, friendships, and some stability. Life on the job and in the suburbs can be impersonal, and friendships there can be superficial. If one might be transferred and thus forced to go through the pain of leaving friends, it can be too great a risk to get to know people well. It is easier and less painful not to get involved. Recognition of the need for stability for the sake of spouse and children has caused some firms not to demand that their achievement-oriented executives move as often. Thus, managers can become more involved with their family, neighborhood, and local community, and thereby increase their own confidence and self-esteem.

Most American firms now have programs designed to increase employee involvement and satisfaction. For example, Ford reduced the number of defects in its vehicles by 48 percent in a 2-year period by enlisting the efforts of workers. Where labor relations are not adversarial, management is able to ask employees to help improve quality by monitoring the product as it is made and by suggesting better manufacturing processes. Ford engineers took a prototype of a pickup truck to line workers and asked for their suggestions. Larry Graham, an assembly-line worker who had worked on a previous model pickup, suggested that the design be altered to allow assemblers to bolt the pickup cargo box from above rather than from below. When bolting from below, an assembler had to lift a heavy pneumatic wrench over his or her head from a pit beneath the truck.

---

[34] United States Catholic Bishops, *Catholic Teaching and the United States Economy* (Washington, D.C.: United States Catholic Conference, 1986), part 4, nos. 295–325. For a discussion of the development of the document, see Manuel Velasquez and Gerald F. Cavanagh, S.J., "Religion and Business: The Catholic Church and the American Economy," *California Management Review* 30 (Summer 1988): 124–41.

[35] Sar A. Levitan, "Beyond 'Trendy' Forecasts," *The Futurist* (November–December 1987): 30.

Bolts were not firmly tightened, and customer complaints came in. The engineers used Graham's suggestions to redesign the assembly process, resulting in easier assembly and far fewer consumer complaints.[36]

Sustainable Development

The last 2 decades have been sobering, not only to Americans but to all peoples. Citizens in Europe, Japan, and the United States now realize that they will never again attain the supremacy in world markets or the growth rate that they had in the 1950s and 1960s.[37] Rainforests are being destroyed in Latin America, Africa, Indonesia, and India.[38] No substantial housing for millions plagues Mexico City, Jakarta, Bombay, and hundreds of other cities. Moreover, we anticipate one billion people in China and India owning autos that use petroleum and add to pollution. Hence, we realize that development and growth must be such that the generation following us may enjoy both a decent standard of living and a liveable world.[39]

In the United States, data shows that 15 percent of citizens have family incomes below the poverty level. In the last chapter we cited the huge compensation of top executives. This gap between the rich and the poor is widening each year. During the last 25 years, while the gross domestic product has doubled, an index of social health has declined to about one-half its former level. Developed at Fordham University, this index includes 16 items such as infant mortality, drug abuse, high school dropouts, elderly poverty, child abuse, teen suicides, child poverty, health insurance coverage, unemployment, real wages, homicides and the gap between the incomes of the rich and the poor.[40]

The gap between the rich and the poor is larger and more apparent in many Asian, Latin, and African countries, also. It will be extremely difficult for business to prosper in the long term, given such problems, both because potential markets are thus limited, and also because of the danger of social instability.[41] Moreover, many of the new service and some high-tech jobs are not challenging. They do not provide the opportunity for expanding one's skills or for advancement, as we note at Burger King, McDonald's, and retailing.

---

[36] "A Better Idea: American Car Firms Stress Quality to Fend off Imports," *Wall Street Journal*, August 26, 1982, pp. 1, 14.

[37] Katherine S. Newman, *Declining Fortunes: The Withering of the American Dream* (New York: Basic Books, 1993).

[38] Anjali Acharya, "Tropical Rainforests Vanishing," in Lester R. Brown, Nicholas Lenssen, and Hal Kane, eds., *Vital Signs, 1995—The Trends That Are Shaping Our Future* (New York: W. W. Norton, 1994), pp. 116–17.

[39] Hal Kane, "Shifting to Sustainable Industries," and Lester R. Brown, "An Acceleration of History," in Lester R. Brown, et. al., *State of the World—1996* (New York: W. W. Norton, 1996); see also the special issue of *Academy of Management Review*, 20 (October 1995): 873–1089, which is dedicated to seven studies of ecologically sustainable organizations.

[40] "A Warning Sign," *U.S. News & World Report*, October 21, 1996, p. 30.

[41] Paul Krugman, *The Age of Diminished Expectations* (Cambridge: MIT Press and Washington Post, 1994).

In addition to the above, resources are now more expensive. Most manufacturing and services add to pollution, and the cost to clean it up increases our cost of living. Finally, all peoples must compete for markets with every other country. This was discussed in Chapters 1 and 8.

In contrast to the "cowboy economy" of the 1980s, in which gross production and consumption measured success, the newer "spaceship economy" of the twenty-first century recognizes that all men and women live together on a fragile planet. This planet has only finite resources and a limited ability to cleanse itself of pollution. Thus, if human needs and desires could be met with less use of resources, less production, and less consumption, that economy would be superior. To say this is economic heresy. However, if we can meet human needs with less resources, waste, and pollution, are we not better off? Consumption and production without limit harm all people and the environment, and they should hardly be considered as goals in themselves.

There is resistance to this reformulation of goals and to the new criteria of success that this demands. The reformulation requires that we make judgments on the type of growth and the products we want and on the tradeoffs and costs we are willing to accept. Such judgments require discussion, common understandings, and building consensus—an immense task in a fractured democracy. It is easier to allow the "free market" to decide all issues. However, giving such power to the market wastes resources, arable land, and human lives, and thus is not a responsible policy.

As for work and home life, many already opt for simplification. For example, note transportation. Much of the time that was saved in shortening the workday is lost in driving to and from work, schools, church, and stores. In older neighborhoods one could walk to each; many suburbs do not even have sidewalks upon which one could walk. This total reliance on the automobile wastes not only time but also petroleum and other natural resources. It constitutes not progress, but a loss of freedom. Similarly, time is lost in filling out income tax returns, insurance forms, and questionnaires and in listening to advertisements. Some urge: wherever there is a choice between making more money and simplifying life, the latter road should be taken.

From another point of view, a new series of cultural "thou shalt nots" may be required in the future. Humankind will not be able to survive if individual humans do not set limits to their appetites, do not develop an habitual willingness to conserve and preserve, and do not maintain a conscientious concern for others. Although these attitudes are difficult to achieve, they are essential if we are to prevent mass starvation, war, and chaos.[42] The development of spiritual, human values that are integrated into everyday life and institutional decision making is a priority. Developing countries, especially Asian nations, are also experiencing many of these dilemmas. Fortunately, most of these nations still have

---

[42] Daniel Callahan, *The Tyranny of Survival* (New York: Macmillan, 1974).

their traditional religions and respect for family to support concern for future generations. On this shrinking planet, economic and political planning must consider the larger issues.

Fortunately, many of the above attitudes are now taking hold in our society. They will have a significant impact on the firm and its activities. The successful leader is alert to changes in attitudes and will gear actions and policies to the new situation. Future sources of jobs, government policy, and personal values will all be heavily influenced by the coming era of entrepreneurship and sustainable development.[43]

Long-Range Perspective

Every business executive agrees that future business thinking must include planning that includes a long-range perspective. In a survey of CEOs, 89 percent said that they thought that American companies were too oriented toward the short term.[44] New business and new products depend on R & D, but cost-cutting and short-term thinking often results in too little time and money being devoted to it. In their study of effective business leaders, James Kouzes and Barry Posner summarize their findings:

> Traditional management teaching focuses our attention on the short term, the Wall Street analysts, the quarterly statements, and the annual report. Yet all the effective leaders we've seen have had a long-term, future orientation. They've looked beyond the horizon of the present.[45]

The survival and growth of American business demands an increased attention to long-term concerns. Pressure resulting from short-term financial interests makes long-term planning difficult but does not alter its importance for the future. This issue was also discussed in Chapters 1 and 8.

Business as a Servant of Society

The free market model views the business firm as independent, isolated, and competing with other firms to survive and grow. As long as a firm shows a profit, financial analysts and *Forbes* call it a success. The firm is thus judged successful whether it makes high-quality, energy-efficient necessities with less pollution (for example, Hewlett-Packard: computers; Merck: medications) or dangerous, trivial products (RJR Nabisco: cigarettes). The firm's "success"

---

[43] See Paul Hawken, *The Ecology of Commerce: A Declaration of Sustainability* (New York: Harper Collins, 1993). Excellent data for planning and for sustainable development are in Lester R. Brown, Christopher Flavin, and Hal Kane, *Vital Signs—1996: Trends that are Shaping Our Future* (New York: W. W. Norton, 1996), also Lester R. Brown, et al., *State of the World—1996* (New York: W. W. Norton, 1996).

[44] Ben J. Wattenberg, "Their Deepest Concerns," *Business Monthly* (January 1988): 27–36.

[45] James M. Kouzes and Barry Z. Posner, *The Leadership Challenge* (San Francisco: Jossey-Bass, 1995), p. 15.

might even be at the cost of unsafe working conditions (sweatshops in the United States and overseas) and the pollution of neighborhoods. The models and ideology of old-school economists and businesspeople urged profit making, production, and consumption. To many people even today, any increase in gross national product (GNP) indicates success. However, note that the manufacture of cigarettes and the hospital expenses for those with lung cancer or heart disease due to smoking add to GNP. A serious injury auto accident and the generation of pollution also leads to an increase in GNP—the cost of the work required to repair the damage to humans and the physical environment. What does it mean to consider unnecessary hospital bills, accidents, or pollution as success?

It is therefore apparent that these criteria of success are not complete. businesspeople and business firms are servants of society. Their purpose is to provide for the needs of citizens, to provide family incomes, and to make lives safer, healthier, and happier.[46]

An innovative and related perspective on leadership has been developed by the servant-leadership movement. The movement shows how a leader is most effective when the leader is able to elicit the best efforts from each member of the group. The leader empowers each worker to do their best and thus be a "servant of the group." This viewpoint is now popular and is aided by the writings of Robert Greenleaf, who had been an executive and management researcher at AT&T, and later at the Greenleaf Center.[47] The Center holds seminars and publishes books and a newsletter. Community volunteer work develops leadership skills and attitudes of service, and builds upon servant-leadership theory. Volunteer programs are now common among secondary and university students.

Conscientious corporate executives have long acted on the notion that the firm should serve society. CEOs have redirected their firms to ensure that social objectives are met.[48] Many new and developing industries that have high growth potential are geared to genuine human needs, such as robotics, solar power, office technology, energy conservation, cable TV, and genetic engineering.

A major criteria of the worth of any skill or work up to the time of the Industrial Revolution was the relative value of the good or service to society. As we have seen in earlier chapters, with the growth of industry and the division of

---

[46] For a plan to achieve a just economic order, see John Paul II, *Centesimus Annus* (*On the Hundreth Anniversary of Rerum Novarum*) (St. Paul: Media Books, 1991). For an assessment of the influence of the letter on business ethics, see S. Prakash Sethi and Paul Steidlmeier, "Religion's Moral Compass and a Just Economic Order: Reflections on Pope John Paul II's Encyclical *Centesimus Annus*," *Journal of Business Ethics* 12 (1993): 901–17.

[47] Robert K. Greenleaf, *The Servant as Leader* (Newton Center, Mass.: Greenleaf Center, 1970). Greenleaf also wrote *The Institution as Servant*, and several other essays. The newsletter is *The Servant Leader* and is published by the Greenleaf Center, now located at 1100 W. 42nd St., Suite 321, Indianapolis, Ind. 46208.

[48] See Business Roundtable, *Statement on Corporate Responsibility* (New York: Business Roundtable, 1981), pp. 1, 8, 12–14. The Business Roundtable is an organization composed of the CEOs of 170 large firms in the United States.

labor, an ideology developed that bestowed value on any work regardless of its outcome. The amount of financial return received became more important than what was accomplished. However, a growing number of men and women now question the value of some work no matter how well paid it may be. Some people will not work for a strip-mining firm, a hard-sell advertiser, a manufacturer of automatic weapons, or a junk bond firm with a shady reputation. On the other hand, individual transportation vehicles are important for society, and thus an auto worker's efforts take on value beyond the paycheck and benefits. Thus we reintroduce criteria that had been pushed aside. The value of a job or position is judged both by the contribution of the worker to a product or service *and* by the contribution the product or service makes to society.

Does it make any difference whether one is helping to produce electricity, tractors, cigarettes, throw-away bottles, nutritious foods, or Coca-Cola? All goods are not of equal value to society, and judgments can be made on the relative merits of these goods. In a small, primitive economy, these questions do not arise, since there are only enough resources and energy available to provide the necessities. Our society has many goods along with diminishing and more expensive resources, so questions about relative values are forced on us. It is necessary to determine which goods are more valuable to society. A principle might help in developing these criteria: Goods and services might be judged to be worthy insofar as they support life, families, neighborhoods, give freedom, and provide joy and happiness.

Technology and Innovation

Reliance on technology has been the principal means of increased business efficiency and productivity over the decades. In the future, technology will continue to be a generator of business "progress." However, what is seldom realized is that the sort of technology chosen reflects the values of the chooser, and, perhaps more importantly, that same technology has a profound influence on the values and life-styles of all who use it. The choice of electrical power generation grids and large manufacturing plants influence the hours that we work and the way we live, even outside of work. Asbestos insulation and chlorofluorocarbon aerosol propellants are examples of choices whose costs we later learned were greater than their benefits. The promotion of the automobile with a tax supported freeway system over rapid public transportation is a choice that reflects a "triumph of individualistic over communal values."[49]

In the future telecommuting, that is, doing work from a computer work station at home or at a substation, will increase flexibility and freedom, but will

---

[49] John M. Staudenmaier, S.J., "Technology," *A Companion to American Thought*, ed. Richard W. Fox and James T. Kloppenberg (Oxford: Blackwell, 1995). See also Staudenmaier's "Computerization" and "Technology" in *A New Dictionary of Catholic Thought*, ed. Judith A. Dwyer and Elizabeth L. Montgomery (Collegeville, Minn.: Michael Glazer, 1994).

decrease teamwork and the sense of community that is found at a central work site. Computers, and their ability to store data, also pose ethical questions of how this data is used. TRW holds credit records on each of us that can be obtained for a fee. Some of this record is personal and some of it is in error, yet people use this information to make decisions on hiring, making loans, and for many other purposes. The Internet with its extraordinary advantages for swift, global communications, also allows adolescent or less innocent hackers into the most sensitive and personal data that is available.

Emerging technologies will give firms and their employees access to data about individuals that many would prefer remain private. Are there any limits to using this information to sell products? It is essential that we use our moral and ethical skills in deciding how this information can be used.

The technology that one adopts and how one uses it depends upon the values of the one who chooses. The technological systems themselves are generally selected by elites—that is, leaders of business and government. Hence it is even more essential for justice and the stability of society to keep in mind the needs of *all people*, including those without a voice: the poor and disadvantaged.

A Nation Among Nations

In this world of increasing population, faster transportation and communication, and more choices in life-styles, people are becoming more interdependent. On the individual level, each of us depends on each other and requires interaction to develop as a person. For example, when people flee the problems of the city, their affluent children, without parks, libraries, and corner stores within walking distance, find little to do and become bored. Bus service is not readily available in most of these communities, leading to isolation for anyone who does not drive. Many children then use alcohol, drugs, drop out of school, and run away from home. On the international scene, a war or a revolution in the Middle East, Latin America, or Asia is brought to us by TV within hours. Starvation among refugees in Africa also comes into our living rooms, along with the fact that our use of dog food, lawn fertilizer, and red meat may play a role in depriving those Africans of life-giving grain. No nation can any longer assume that what is good for them is therefore good for all peoples.

Many problems that face the world cannot be solved by any single nation acting alone. Take, for example, acid rain, the greenhouse effect, malnutrition, toxic waste, dwindling finite resources, the threat of terrorism, and even a balance of trade deficit. Too often U.S. officials are insensitive to worldwide reaction to U.S. policies. This country's lone vote against the World Health Organization's code for marketing infant formula and its repudiation of the Law of the Sea Treaty lost the United States much international respect. Business managers know that nationalistic attitudes that might have served well a generation ago are no longer sufficient. They now operate in world markets and must be responsible citizens of more than one country. As the world gets smaller, all people depend more on each other. Yet, paradoxically, a new nationalism is afoot. Many nations are unwilling to limit their sovereignty or their self-interest. Hence we see individualism clash with the reality of interdependence.

Sociologist Robert Bellah thinks America's failure lies in its emphasis on the atomistic self and on rational self-interest and in its break with the basic understandings of the Founding Fathers. In early America, there was a strong social, collective emphasis: Citizens were together responsible for the state. Bellah demonstrates how this emphasis derived from the biblical covenant between God and God's people and from the gospel notion of a loving community based on membership in the common body of Christ. Bellah is convinced that the economic system of contemporary industrial America no longer is based on the early American view that economic interdependence is the foundation of the political order.[50] Perhaps our early ideals can be recaptured. The urgency and importance of the problems that face the peoples of the world demand that leaders work together for solutions.

Harmony with the Environment

In the course of meeting people's needs, business firms will operate with greater respect for the natural environment. Scarcity of resources, pollution, and undesirable by-products place constraints on the direction and pace of economic and business growth. These physical constraints will become more pressing, and citizens' expectations that firms will respect those constraints will become more pronounced. Hazardous industrial waste looms as an ever-increasing problem during the coming decade. The cost of its transportation and disposal, as well as the effort to determine liability, will increase; this, in turn, poses costly problems for business in the future.

Is it then surprising that West Africa is becoming the dumping ground for American and European toxic waste? As the costs of disposing of this waste go up, it becomes cheaper to pay Morocco, Congo, or Niger to bury it on their land. For example, in early 1988 American and European private waste disposal firms offered Guinea-Bissau $120 million annually to bury 15 million tons of toxic waste from tanneries and pharmaceutical companies. This is slightly less than the African country's gross national product of $150 million.[51] This practice has created a furor in West Africa, with many people in these nations demanding that the contracts be repudiated.

Local Control: Small Is Beautiful

The entrepreneur and the small firm has been respected, encouraged, and often preferred to the large firm in the United States. In a time when there are many

---

[50] Robert N. Bellah, *The Broken Covenant: American Civil Religion in Time of Trial* (New York: Seabury, 1975).

[51] "West Africa Attracts Toxic Waste Dumpers," *Cleveland Plain Dealer*, July 17, 1988, p. 19.

new and changing needs, the flexible entrepreneur has a very important role.[52] Small businesses are encouraged in the United States by lower tax rates. Large size is necessary, when economies of scale are required for the purpose of competing in large international markets, for example autos and computers. Nevertheless, encouraging entrepreneurs and keeping the government's role limited are traditional American values. Even in providing human services, such as education, health, and retirement, the independent sector can generally deliver better services at a lower cost than can the government. As long as these services are provided to the poor and disadvantaged, local control in both the public and private sectors has several advantages: (1) It gives people more control over their work and lives and thus provides increased personal involvement; (2) it more clearly locates responsibility; (3) it eliminates layers of organizational bureaucracy; (4) it is less costly; and (5) it is in the American tradition of self-reliance.

Spiritual Roots of the New Business Mission

Personal and national goals in the United States have been heavily influenced by religion, especially Christianity. We live on a foundation provided by the Judeo-Christian culture. Although our values and attitudes are currently not well anchored, the older roots continue to provide sustenance and life. As our society became more pluralistic (each person's values are deemed as good as any other person's) and atheistic (the existence of God is denied), our values became more free-floating. Although it soon became secular, the Protestant ethic stemmed from Christianity. Religious values have had a profound influence on business and economic life in the past, so it is appropriate to ask: will spiritual and religious ideals have an impact in the future?

There has always been a strong streak of moralism in American culture. Witness our condemnation of buying votes in government, the sexual infidelities of political leaders, and the selfish activities of corporate raiders like Ivan Boesky, Charles Hurwitz, and Sir James Goldsmith. This sort of reaction is not new; our history is replete with morally rooted reaction to issues. In the nineteenth century, the powerful antislavery (abolition) and antitrust (muckraking) movements were morally motivated and received their inspiration from the Gospels.

The civil rights movement in the United States was led by Martin Luther King, Jr., a Baptist minister. He preached "love for the oppressor" and espoused nonviolent techniques to gain social justice for blacks. The record shows how effective the movement and his leadership were. The role of the churches in political life is increasing, and polls indicate that most people want that. Many of the most committed social activists are inspired by the Gospels. Ralph Nader comes from a religious family with high ideals, and Common Cause appeals to

---

[52] Rosabeth Moss Kanter, *World Class: Thriving Locally in the Global Economy* (New York: Simon & Schuster, 1995), p. 26.

the generosity and moral qualities of Americans. Mahatma Gandhi was an inspiration to many of these people, and he was inspired by the life of Christ. Moreover, his nonviolent approach to gaining India's independence from England was successful.

In Poland and other Eastern European countries, religious convictions moved people to overthrow dictatorships. Many Catholic priests and sisters have defended the interests of the poor, and as a result have been murdered in Guatemala, El Salvador, Brazil, Bolivia, Chile, and other Latin American countries.[53] Their inspiration comes from Jesus, his love for the poor, and his commitment to bring justice to those at the bottom of the socioeconomic ladder (Matt. 5:3; Luke 6:20). The goal of these Gospel-inspired leaders is freedom. They want the poor, ordinary citizen to have the freedom to own land, to vote, and to be a self-respecting citizen, as well as the freedom to work and earn a fair day's pay. They want self-determination for peoples around the world. Thus they often find themselves in opposition to a global business firm or a military government. Hindu and Muslim fundamentalist groups are having a profound influence in Asia, Africa, and the Middle East. They reject the Western values of violence and free sex that they see on our films and exported TV. Westerners, who have been influenced by the Enlightenment, have difficulty in understanding the appeal of the fundamentalists.

It is no accident that 11 of the *100 Best Companies to Work for in America*[54] are located in two areas of the United States that are heavily influenced by religious values. The 100 firms are rated on: pay and benefits, opportunities, pride in work, job security, openness and fairness, and camaraderie and friendliness. Minneapolis-St. Paul is home to 3M, Dayton Hudson, General Mills, H.B. Fuller, and many other firms with outstanding records in social responsibility. The area is strongly Lutheran and Catholic and has long been a leader in the United States with regard to firms having a strong sense of social responsibility. Western Michigan is home to Donnelly, Herman Miller, Kellogg, Steelcase, and others and is much influenced by the Calvinist Dutch Reformed Church.

Religion views the manager or owner as a steward. Thus wealth and power constitute a trust that is held for others. Based on the understanding that the world and all its goods come from and ultimately belong to God, the individual businessperson holds all this in stewardship—in trust for others.[55] Numerous organizations and prayer groups now meet to enable businesspeople

---

[53] "Roman Catholic Priest Has Struggle Changing Lives in Rural Brazil: Father Ricardo Resende Faces Violence, Makes Enemies in Fight to Aid Landless," *Wall Street Journal*, August 28, 1986, pp. 1, 16. For additional examples, see Penny Lernoux, *Cry of the People* (New York: Penguin, 1980); Martin Lange and Reinhold Iblacker, *Witness of Hope: The Persecution of Christians in Latin America* (Maryknoll, N.Y.: Orbis, 1981).

[54] Robert Levering and Milton Moskowitz (New York: Penguin, 1994).

[55] See Oliver F. Williams, C.S.C., "Religion: The Spirit or Enemy of Capitalism," *Business Horizons* (November–December, 1983): 6–13; also Williams's, "Who Cast the First Stone?" *Harvard Business Review* (September–October 1984): 151–60.

to better understand: faith, family, and firm. Paradoxically, it is "old-fashioned" religion that has traditionally urged concern for others, especially poor people in other nations and future generations.

Concern for Others

People who are loved develop into more mature persons, are less turned in on themselves, and more concerned about others. Self-centeredness and insularity are vices of the immature, as we saw in Chapter 2. Love for others is a basic human virtue. Expressing such love is a matter of giving—often without hope of return. Altruistic love is possible for anyone, although it is more readily achieved by those who have been loved. It is essential for the development of persons, families, and society, yet it is sometimes difficult. Speaking of this sort of love, economist Kenneth Boulding says,

> It always builds up, it never tears down, and it does not merely establish islands of order in a society at the cost of disorder elsewhere. It is hard for us, however, to learn to love, and the teaching of love is something at which we are still very inept.[56]

Much of the energy of the poor is spent on obtaining the necessities of life. Once a person's basic needs are reasonably satisfied, that person is more inclined to consider the needs of others in society. Thus, material security is often a foundation for loving and giving. Having food and shelter enables people to reach beyond themselves and their own problems to other human beings and to realize the interdependence of people and institutions.

Concern for others is an important part of the organizational climate at Hewlett-Packard and IBM. The Ford worker-involvement program encourages all Ford employees to focus on quality. The Parts and Services Division has called itself "the loving and caring division of Ford." Aetna, L.L. Bean, Dow, Steelcase, and Johnson & Johnson have all established model programs to better the health of their employees. With less illness and injury, it also saves money for the firm.[57]

New Measures of Success

A goal of most people is to obtain happiness. If, however, happiness is measured by more compensation or more wealth, one can never achieve happiness. "People are prosperous as long as they can say, 'We have enough.' "[58] In a parallel fashion, to be successful a business firm must be efficient and profitable. However, corporate leaders no longer claim that profit maximization is the only goal of

---

[56] Kenneth E. Boulding, *The Meaning of the Twentieth Century* (New York: Harper & Row, 1964), p. 146. The importance of the manager's love and caring was reinforced in the 1995 study by Kouzes and Posner, *The Leadership Challenge, op. cit.*

[57] Shawn Tully, "America's Healthiest Companies," *Fortune*, June 12, 1995, pp. 98–106.

[58] Richard C. Haas, *We All Have a Share* (Chicago: ACTA Publications, 1995), p. 32.

business or that such a goal automatically benefits society. Chapter 8 described many situations where what was good for a firm was not good for society.

New measures of success for business firms arise when we realize that such firms operate to benefit people.[59] They are essentially instruments of service to people—all kinds of people. Those who benefit include customers and shareholders but also employees, suppliers, and members of the local community. Benefits to one constituency are generally not at the expense of another group; business is not a zero-sum game. When J&J acts out its statement that its first obligation is to customers and its last to shareholders, the shareholders do better than they would otherwise.

Just as a financial audit sketches a firm's financial performance, a social audit outlines the impact of the firm's operations on its other constituents. Criteria for judging social performance are crucial if we are adequately to decide the degree of success achieved by a firm.[60]

Business firms are aware of the need for corporate social performance measures. The Business Roundtable, composed of the CEOs of the largest U.S. firms, described the importance of social goals and how to structure a firm so that these social goals are achieved.[61] These CEOs also sponsored a handbook that aids firms in the achievement of their social goals.[62] Government policy, too, both national and international, must be assessed using the same criteria: what is better for all people?

The new measures of success focus on the benefits that accrue to people—all the stakeholders of the firm. This focus constitutes a fundamental change in perspective for corporate managers. Because achievement of social goals is increasingly among the criteria for measuring the success of business managers, social goals have an impact on the values and perspective of managers.

Vision and Hope

The problems that we face—trade and budget deficits, pollution, refugees, unjust governments, lack of jobs, broken families—are so immense that many find it easier to deny them. These problems are often the result of trying to achieve other goods or, in some cases, of callously disregarding the welfare of people. We then must ask: are we motivated to seek a solution when the solution has a cost to me? And are we able to alter our actions to make more ethical tradeoffs? Can we build the values and institutions necessary for justice and peace throughout the world?

---

[59] See the alternate definition of productivity in Haas, *We all Have a Share, op cit.,* p. 12.

[60] Cetron, Rocha, and Luckins, "Into the 21st Century," p. 40.

[61] Business Roundtable, *Statement on Corporate Responsibility*; see also the earlier Roundtable statement, *The Role and Composition of the Board of Directors of the Large Publicly Held Corporation* (New York: Business Roundtable, 1978).

[62] Francis W. Steckmest, ed., *Corporate Performance: The Key to Public Trust* (New York: McGraw-Hill, 1982).

Vision and hope have always been American virtues. Ever since the days of the frontier, we have never been defeatists or fatalists. Nevertheless, it would be foolish to underestimate the enormous problems before us. Many people today are concerned mainly with their own personal lives and careers and care little about what they can do to help solve others' problems. Yet, as we have seen, a single individual or a small group of talented, generous people can have a profound impact on the lives of others and on the world as a whole.

Summary and Conclusions

The challenge of the future is to provide products, services, jobs, and a reasonable standard of living for all people, and yet not needlessly exploit finite natural resources or leave the world more polluted than we found it. Business firms have achieved unprecedented efficiency, productivity, and growth. Nevertheless, it is clear that the free market is not able to provide such goods as clean air and water, safe products, or even fair competition. A firm that provides jobs and goods sometimes also destroys natural beauty and harms people's health. Its operations may be demeaning or dangerous, use nonrenewable resources, or cause pollution.

Generating cooperation and providing benefits to people are appropriate goals for business and government. Pressure from special interest groups, coupled with apathy and lack of clear goals, has pushed American society into many unfruitful, expensive, and frustrating traps. Note, for example, defective and dangerous products, collapsing railroads and urban public transportation systems, disappearing farmlands, defective nuclear power plants, and expensive and wasteful defense systems. Exacerbating the problem is the fact that traditional business ideology justifies and rewards selfishness. More humane personal values and an acknowledgment of public goals helps to avoid these costly blunders. Most firms forecast future values so that they can initiate product planning, employee participation, and advertising to meet new needs.

Future business values require business efficiency and innovativeness. Moreover, citizens now demand that business decisions contribute to the overall goals of society. A business firm is not merely a *private* enterprise; its role is to serve the needs of society. If business firms do not choose to act responsibly, legislation or tax incentives will be required to encourage such behavior.

Americans want greater independence, even in the face of the dehumanizing factors of modern life. In spite of large corporations and big government, individuals still prefer autonomy, personal responsibility, and the ability to share decisions. Businesses will be structured to encourage such self-reliance and responsibility.

Religion has in the past, and will in the future, provide a foundation for business values. Religious values run counter to self-interest and what has come to be known as the consumer ethic. The Protestant ethic demanded moderation, planning, and self-sacrifice. Budget deficits, pollution, anxiety, crime, and substance abuse demonstrate the failure of current values. Americans now may be

Impact of Technology

- Modern Americans in a Technological World

- Into the Future? Government Policy and Technological Innovation: Lessons from the Past

_____ *chapter* **20** _____

Modern Americans in a Technological World

_____

Since World War II, technological change has had a complex and ambiguous impact on American society. The atomic bomb's use in August 1945 suggested an epochal leap in humanity's ability to harness the hitherto secret power of the atom. Moreover, hundreds of mundane developments from the pesticide DDT and numerical control (or automated) machine tools to tape recorders and ballpoint pens seemed to promise an endless transformation of work and leisure. In addition to new technologies (some of which were in the works long before 1945), the postwar generation experienced unprecedented prosperity made possible by the conversion of the engineering might of the American war machine into the creation of a new world of consumer goods. Technology was hardly the only cause of this affluence: Temporary American dominance of the global marketplace, higher wages won by unions, and government investments in infrastructure were other factors. Even so, Americans became accustomed to thinking of technology as the key agent of change. General Motors' "Futurama" exhibit at the New York World's Fair of 1939 encouraged Americans to look forward to 1960 when they would drive radio-controlled cars on super highways that provided "safety with increased speed." During World War II, popular magazines offered images of technological wonders awaiting Americans after the "boys came home." Americans willingly invested billions in taxes for science and technology

309

to find medical cures and to explore outer space (as well as to engage in a nuclear arms race).

The postwar years also greeted Americans with the threat of losing jobs to automation, of cities polluted by smog, and of invisible but deadly radioactivity from nuclear testing. More subtly, there was an abiding discomfort at the prospect of technology that could run endless quantities of refrigerators and cars off the production lines but did not seem to make people happy or to create social harmony.

Immediately after the war, many industrial workers worried that the unemployment of the depression years would return now that the munitions factories were no longer needed and new technology would take away jobs. In 1943, the glamorous boom town of Los Angeles experienced its first bout with smog resulting from dust mixed with industrial and automobile emissions. New by-products of affluence were pollution from DDT (first used as a pesticide in 1939), detergents (which began replacing soap in 1946), and plastics. Beginning in 1945, the *Bulletin of Atomic Scientists* warned of the imminent danger of nuclear warfare and John Hersey's description of that devastation in his *Hiroshima* (1946) graphically illustrated this threat. In 1953, this fear was brought home when fallout from nuclear tests in Nevada was detected in radioactive rain that fell over Troy, New York. Most Americans supported the cold war and the linkages between big science and the arms race. But the use of advanced physics in the 1960s to bomb Vietnam and of chemistry to defoliate jungle changed some Americans' perception of science. Much earlier, British authors Aldous Huxley, in *Brave New World*, and George Orwell, in *1984*, haunted many thoughtful Americans with their images of a technological future. Dominating these visions were the passive artificial pleasures of "feelies" and the thought control of "Big Brother." Today, these fantasies may remind us of the promise of "virtual reality" toys and sound much like the intrusive power of the modern computer.

In the years between 1945 and the present, technology has frequently been understood as both a panacea and an enemy. Technology continues to inspire those fascinated with science's ingenuity in mastering nature, reducing routine and arduous labor, and diversifying life through mass consumption. To others, the increased pace of technological change only seems to propel humanity into a world where gadgetry replaces social life and new problems of pollution and affluence replace the old concerns of toil, insecurity, and scarcity. While some technological "pessimists" seem to look back nostalgically on a "lost" past and fearfully toward the future, others advocate a technology that is "appropriate" to the dignity of work, a clean environment, and a less materialist culture.

AN ABIDING AMBIVALENCE: MODERN TECHNOLOGICAL OPTIMISTS AND PESSIMISTS

The debate over technology turned on how opposing sides envisioned the future. In chapter 9, we noted the contrasting technological futures offered by Edward

Bellamy and Ignatius Donnelly in the 1880s. Again in the 1920s and 1930s, technological optimists looked to planned cities where broad tree-lined avenues would
lead to sleek skyscrapers surrounded by neat plazas. In 1927, the young Buckmin-
ster Fuller dreamed of a "Dymaxion House" that would offer mass-produced ul-
tramodern convenience: Small bedrooms would have pneumatic beds without
blankets (unnecessary in this climate-controlled house); a "get-on-with-life room"
was to be equipped with a television, phonograph, and a mimeograph machine all
in one unit; beneath was space for an amphibious auto-airplane. Presumably Dymaxion Houses could be stacked on top of one another and could be easily moved
(perhaps by zeppelin) at will. This was a "machine for modern living." More modest futurologists such as Lewis Mumford stressed that electricity would free cities
from air-fouling industry and instantaneous communications would allow for decentralized communities and choice in where people lived and worked.

Yet, as we noted in chapter 15, many other Americans in the 1930s were
deeply suspicious that technology was responsible for the depression and blamed
machines for displacing workers. MIT professor L.M. Passano wrote that the chief
purpose of scientific research was "to enable those who already receive an undue
share of the wealth produced by industry and research, to appropriate a share still
larger."[1] Charlie Chaplin's film *Modern Times* portrays a nearly worker-less factory where the boss supervised assembly line workers by television from a comfortable office and even experimented with a mechanical lunch feeder to keep
workers constantly on the job.

These divergent views of the technological future persisted after 1945. Most
engineers and scientists willingly abandoned questions about the wider impact of
their work, preferring to concentrate on their area of competence. For some, this
attitude was merely an expression of the modern scientist's intellectual modesty
and commitment to being value free; for others it betrayed the effects of overspe-
cialization or the "seductiveness of technological detail."[2] Perhaps an even more
important reason for this common indifference to the apparent side effects of innovation was the widespread American confidence in the "technological fix"—
faith in technology to solve all problems with less effort and cost than required to
change social behavior or political realities. Nuclear power was far more effective
in overcoming problems of air pollution and depleted fossil fuels than was trying
to persuade people to conserve.

This technological optimism pervaded the thinking of futurists such as Herman Kahn and Alvin Toffler. In the 1950s, Kahn became famous when he advocated that Americans "think [optimistically] about the unthinkable" effect of
thermonuclear war that humanity would survive. From the late 1960s, he argued
that energy and other resources were in no danger of exhaustion. For example, the
damming of the Amazon River would create a valuable inland "Mediterranean"
sea as well as cheap electricity. Those who insisted that industrialism had to be restrained ignored the fact that the earth was "resourceful." Sufficient food could be
produced if the pesticides and new hybrids of the "green revolution" were used to
greatly increase agricultural output. New technologies, Kahn argued, such as
communications satellites, would replace dependence on scarce resources (e.g.,

copper wiring). Continued industrial growth assured that by the end of the century the work year could drop in half to about 1,000 hours. In his *The Year 2000* (1967), Kahn predicted the coming of a "postindustrial society" that would be dominated by "services" rather than production. In this society, scientists rather than politicians and businesspeople would make the major decisions and lifelong education, guaranteed personal income, and greater leisure would become realities. Kahn worried that these changes could undermine the work ethic and create a hedonistic society without motivation or ethical standards, but he had faith that a minority of educated technicians could monitor and support the rest of the population.

Toffler's *The Third Wave* (1980) reminds us of the optimism of the utopian thought of Bellamy and the youthful Mumford: The next technological wave would eliminate dependence on fossil fuels and shift to limitless energy sources (i.e., biomass, alcohol fuel from grain, as well as nuclear and solar power). In any case, new products and forms of communications would become less energy dependent, Toffler argued. The old centralized mass media would give way to interactive and individually chosen media. Thanks to microelectronics, consumers would be able to design their own products (as "prosumers"). And goods would be manufactured by robots regulated by a skilled human workforce. Labor would no longer be arduous and confined to centralized authoritarian factories or offices; instead the home-based computer terminal would allow for a return of work to the home, transformed into an "electronic cottage," where one could adapt working hours to personal needs. Thus, technology would allow us to avoid the fate of the centralized "Brave New World": Choice and privacy would prevail over the mass culture of the industrial era. Toffler, like his predecessors, found in the technological future the solution to today's problems of pollution, resource depletion, and alienating work and social life. Toffler insisted that technology, not political or moral reform, would usher in a world of greater health, cleanliness, and choice. Somehow the technology of the information age would make corporations less obsessed with profits and more interested in ecology and personal needs.

Challenging these views was a vocal group of technological pessimists. These writers shared with many nineteenth-century romantics the belief that technology had become essentially autonomous or separate from social needs and operated according to mechanistic rules. These ideas were often expressed by Europeans (such as Jacques Ellul and Herbert Marcuse), even if these pessimists often lived in the United States. But American writers such as Theodore Roszak, Barry Commoner, and others shared similar perspectives. An international group of natural and social scientists, often identified as the "Club of Rome," offered a concrete expression of this pessimism in *The Limits to Growth* (1972). The authors concluded that output per person would decline sharply in the twenty-first century, claiming that technology could delay, but not prevent, collapse. The problem, they argued, was a culture that was dedicated to exponential growth but ignored the natural limits of the physical world. Even the technological fixes of the green revolution, wherein new rice varieties dramatically increased agricultural output in poor countries, these pessimists argued, had only increased the division between rich and poor regions of the world: Disadvantaged peoples could not afford the new technologies or were victims of lost agricultural employment. Even in the advanced West, this group noted, the suburbanization of cities had solved nothing. It led only to traffic jams, additional pollution, and the confinement, but not eradication, of drug- and crime-infested hopelessness in the urban core. Economists have forcefully challenged the assumptions of the "limits to growth" model. But the technological pessimism behind this model remained.

The debate about the future declined in the 1980s. This was caused partly by growing skepticism in global economic projections, but even more by a new conservative political climate that embraced the optimistic scenarios of Kahn and Toffler. Ronald Reagan's space-based missile defense program met with a great deal of criticism from scientists; but this dream of a "space shield" from nuclear attack had obvious popular appeal in a country still looking for technological fixes. And growing concern that Americans were losing their advantage in manufacturing and product innovation led to a renewed interest in technological solutions. Still the pessimistic perspective survived in new concerns about "global warming" in the late 1980s. Despite the ideological triumph of market economics in the late 1980s with the collapse of European communism, concerns remained that a "third wave" of growth (following the first and second industrializations analyzed in this book) would lead to greater global economic inequality and irrationalities of consumerism. Others, of course, continued to predict a closing of the income gap between the rich and poor nations: This more rosy scenario was based on the ongoing transfer of technology and the lower population growth in less developed nations.

These are powerful and contradictory visions of the future. Without taking sides (leaving that to the reader), let us try to sort out these disparate ideas about the impact of recent technology by considering in turn the themes of (1) jobs and automation, (2) the environment, and (3) consumerism.

TECHNOLOGY, JOBS, AND THE POSTWAR ECONOMY

During the Great Depression, many argued that mechanization permanently displaced wage earners. The only solution was to reduce the workday. In 1932, a 30-hour workweek bill was introduced in Congress in an attempt to increase the number of employed workers. But work sharing seemed to many in business and government to be unnecessary. This view was encouraged by economists such as the American Wesley Mitchell and Britain-based Colin Clark who argued that mechanization did not eliminate jobs in the long run, at least; rather it created new employment. Occupational migration from the mining, agricultural, and industrial sectors of the economy to the service sector was an inevitable consequence of increased productivity, they argued. Not only did this mean new jobs, but efficiency would create new forms of consumption in education, recreation, and health.

This optimistic assessment of the impact of new technology on employment

61

dominated much thinking by economists about the relationship between industrial technology and employment for a decade after World War II (even if trade unions were less optimistic). According to W.W. Rostow's famous *Stages of Economic Growth* (1961), industrial society culminated in "the age of high mass-consumption." The goal of a technological society was clearly not the four-day workweek advocated by those that Rostow labeled as "utopians" nor was it endemic unemployment.[3] It was a society of continuously increasing jobs and consumption. At the same time, optimists predicted that new technology would eliminate boring repetitive assembly work and provide employees with more varied and interesting opportunities in problem solving.

This optimistic appraisal of the impact of mechanization on employment and work quality was the conventional wisdom of the 1950s. It largely coincided with the reality of that decade: It was an era of exceptional job stability and income growth of factory and service workers. But by the end of that decade, the specter of automation began haunting wage earners. Since 1945, engineers at MIT, supported with contracts from the Defense Department, developed the precursors to the modern computerized factory in numerical control machine tools. By the early 1960s, these devices entered civilian manufacturing to the distress of skilled machinists. At the same time, unionized longshoremen faced containerization (reducing dock work by shipping goods in large, often railcar-size containers) and printers confronted teletypesetting and computers. The shift in mining from labor-intensive deep ore mining to the continuous miner (a machine that cut and hauled coal) and strip mining had a similar impact on workers. Few unions directly opposed the new machinery or suggested alternatives (even though automation did spark strikes and informal efforts to slow down production in the 1960s). But fears that numerical control machine tools and later robots would displace skilled machinists led unions to demand retraining programs for displaced workers and higher job classifications for those who remained. The boom years of the Vietnam War era after 1964 reduced these pressures from organized labor, and union power declined with the recessions and deteriorating industrial base of the 1970s and 1980s.

By the 1980s, integrated computer technology further reduced the role of the machinist; increasingly the designer set up machinery directly from a terminal. The ability of computers to track and coordinate the flow of materials through the production process centralized control and eliminated jobs. As we have already seen, the new flexibility not only lowered start-up and modification costs and facilitated "just-in-time" and batch production, it also eliminated skilled labor. In Europe these trends contributed to persistent jobless rates at 10 percent or more in the 1980s. It is true that the percentage of Americans in the workforce increased from 59.56 percent to 63 percent in the 1980s. But this did not mean that the new service jobs were as well paying or as secure as the old industrial jobs. Rather much of this job growth came in low-paying clerical and service employment, especially for women. The role of the highly paid, mostly male factory and construction worker, upon which American "Fordism" was built, declined sharply: This worker constituted a quarter of the labor force in 1950 but comprised only an eighth by the 1980s.

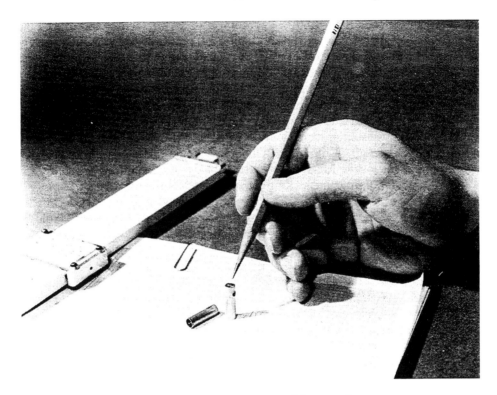

Bell Labs publicity photo of the transistor, 1949. In addition to the transistor's small size, the company emphasized the fact it needed neither a vacuum nor a long warmup period. (Library of Congress)

Pessimists not only feared that new technology destroyed high-paying factory jobs but that it undermined the skill and dignity of work. Although the computerized office may have enhanced the competence of some typists and file clerks, "user friendly" programs have deskilled other jobs. Constant labor at the computer has had its price in muscle and eye strain. Work in the electronic cottage may have reduced employee costs for commuting, clothing, and perhaps child care; and it has provided flexible hours and supplemental income for home-bound workers. But feminist critics have associated home computer work with the nineteenth-century domestic sweatshop. In both situations workers were isolated from others doing the same job; thus, they were less able to exert collective pressure on employers to improve conditions or pay. Critics have argued that these employees have become part of a flexible and often temporary workforce that has little job security and few benefits.

The economic advantage of automation to stockholders, managers, and perhaps consumers was clear. But observers such as historian David Noble and labor activists argue that a major advantage of computer-controlled machinery and factories has been the displacement of the traditional power of the skilled machinist

63

on the shop floor. In this way, computer-driven factory and office machinery is a new form of Taylorism (see chapter 14) that expands management's control over the pace and method of work by almost completely eliminating the human factor in the worker. Electronic monitoring of performance might be more subtle than Taylor's "functional foremen," but the new methods may be more effective. The result, critics charge, has been more stressful and intimidating work.

Since the 1970s, unorthodox economists, including the Nobel prize winner Wassily Leontief have resurrected the old theme of technological unemployment by challenging Colin Clark's theory of occupational migration: They argued that it was illusory to hope that new technology would simply be followed by a further transfer of full-time jobs from the industrial to the service sector as had happened earlier in the century. Instead, computers would reduce white-collar jobs as well. Some doubted that the new technology (such as computers) could generate the consumer demand that the automobile and electric goods industries had created early in this century.

Many Americans feared that the rapid transference of technology abroad took away the advantages that blue-collar American workers enjoyed in the 1950s and 1960s. Japanese and other Pacific rim Asians became innovators in robotics, for example. Low-cost electronic communications allowed American insurance companies to employ low-wage data-entry clerks from Ireland. And reduced transport costs and global markets allowed manufacturers to export factories and their jobs to low-wage regions such as Mexico and Indonesia. The traditional advantage of experienced industrial workers in the United States also declined. Other peoples had learned to adapt to the discipline of industrial work and were more willing than Americans to work for less money. Americans grew more concerned about whether the U.S. standard of living remained the world's highest, especially as the Japanese seemed to be catching up and (by some estimates) West Germans were surging ahead.

In the 1980s, the impact of these trends was clear to authorities such as the political economist Robert Reich: The new technology created opportunity for a class of Americans engaged in design, marketing, and finance; but their loyalties were to an international economic system rather than to the city or even country that they happened to live in. And this left out the less trained Americans with no stake in the global technological network. The social and moral bonds between these groups upon which a national community was based appeared to be eroding.

Most economists remained convinced that expanding trade links increased average American incomes. They could also point to the benefits achieved by importing Japanese and European technology. Still, numerous jobs were threatened by foreign competition, and government retraining efforts seemed insufficient to alleviate the distress of the workers affected.

Many solutions were offered in the 1980s. Most agreed that the traditional palliative of public works jobs was inadequate to a problem generated by a technological shift (some, though, remained convinced that New Deal policies still had their place). The politically dominant doctrine was to encourage investment and innovation by lowering taxes (especially for the investor classes) and to reduce government regulation of the market. Others, such as Lester Thurow and Robert Reich, argued for greater incentives for investment in new technology, hoping that this would overcome the loss of jobs from traditional industrial employment. "Unproductive" employment in the bloated military, legal, and administrative sectors could be supplanted by jobs that would create wealth and increase the American share of world trade, thus assuring higher American living standards. According to more radical reformers, however, this approach did not address the wider problem of income inequality or unemployment related to technological change. Many authorities advocated retraining. But others argued that this would be only a stop-gap measure: CAD/CAM (computer-assisted design/computer-assisted manufacturing) would greatly increase industrial job loss. Pro-labor writers called for the revitalization of the trade union movement as a vehicle that could assure a more equal distribution of the fruits of new technology. But could the new workplace, where employees have become more dispersed and less permanent, produce a stronger labor movement? The call for global and coordinated economic stimulation was a logical, but problematic, solution as was the demand for job protection through more regulated trade.

Another remedy, of course, was the resurrection of the old demand that technological unemployment be averted by work sharing. By reducing the average work year, not only would jobs be created but demand for goods and services would be raised. From the beginning of the automation scare in the late 1950s, members of the American auto workers' union returned to the old demand for the 30-hour week; even the AFL-CIO endorsed the 35-five hour week in 1961. Especially in Western Europe, the nagging threat of unemployment sparked numerous demands for a 35-hour workweek, longer vacations, and earlier retirement. But after the French reduced working hours slightly in the early 1980s, few jobs were created. American intellectuals and labor leaders have called for similar measures but without success. Instead the trend has been in the opposite direction toward longer workweeks. Economist Juliet Schor claimed that employed Americans worked an average of a month more per year in 1987 than they did in 1969.

The relationship between work and technological change has always been complex. Many economists remain convinced that new technologies will create new jobs just as they have in the past. Any solution to the problem of adapting skills and job needs to technological change is as difficult as it has ever been.

ENVIRONMENTALISM AND GROWTH

Accelerated technological change after 1945 raised anew old questions about the quality and security of American jobs in a competitive global economy. That change also forced Americans to reevaluate the impact of modern industrialism on the natural environment. From about 1900, Americans took an interest in the conservation of wilderness and in the creation of sustainable agriculture and forestry. The new environmentalism had a wider focus: It looked to the impact of farming, mining, and manufacturing on the "biosphere." In *Silent Spring* (1962),

Rachel Carson showed the impact of chemical pesticides (DDT especially) and fertilizers on water quality and the food chain. Carson's ecological approach was adopted by scientists who studied the wide-ranging and unanticipated environmental costs of refineries, automobiles, mines, and factories. But the older reverence for the "rights" of the natural world remained at the heart of the environmental movement. In *The Closing Circle* (1970), Barry Commoner proclaimed "four laws of ecology" that neatly summarized this perspective:

Everything is connected to everything else.

Everything must go somewhere.

Nature knows best.

There is no such thing as a free lunch.[4]

The environmentalists' concerns mounted with evidence of the ecological costs of technology and growth. The increased pace of the depletion of resources had become worrisome. The Ogallala Aquifer, which lies under six states in the southern Midwest and is essential for irrigation, was being rapidly drained. The drainage rate increased threefold from 1950 to 1980, and investigators reported that the Aquifer would be useless for irrigating farm land by the year 2000. Power outages in New York in November 1965 affected 30 million people and brought home how dependent Americans had become on a complex and imperfect energy/power system. In 1972, 95 percent of U.S. energy was supplied by burning fossil fuels. Americans, representing 6 percent of the world's population, used 35 percent of global energy in 1973. In that year U.S. dependence on foreign oil was starkly revealed by the OPEC price increase and temporary Arab ban on sales of oil to the United States. Groundwater contamination from storage tanks, hazardous water sites, and landfills was becoming a major problem by the 1960s. Love Canal, an industrial dump that had become a housing development in the 1950s in Niagara Falls, New York, had begun sinking in the mid-1970s. In 1980, after residents complained of diseases of mysterious causes, Love Canal was declared a disaster area and 719 families were evacuated. When oil spills fouled California beaches in 1967 and 250 million gallons of crude oil polluted the beautiful coastline along the Santa Barbara Channel in 1969, a cry rose against off-shore petroleum development. In 1969, the Cuyahoga River that flowed through Cleveland burst into flame because of an unidentified oil spill. By the early 1970s ecologists attacked the practice of strip mining for defacing the landscape.

The environmental movement was more successful than was the response to automation: Between 1965, with the passing of the Water Quality Act, and the early 1970s, a number of environmental bills became law. The first Earth Day on April 22, 1970, gave national media attention to the problem. The Air Quality Act (1967) required states to submit plans to Washington to control air pollution. The National Environmental Policy Act of 1970 demanded environmental impact studies from developers of potentially dangerous industrial sites. The Environmental Protection Agency was established at the same time. In 1972, the pesticide

DDT was finally banned. Local efforts to clean up decades of industrial and sewage pollution in Lake Erie, Lake Washington (in Seattle), and the Cuyahoga River were relatively successful. Local action reduced air pollution in Los Angeles, Pittsburgh, and New York. In 1966, Californians were required to have a catalytic converter on all new cars. In response to the threat of dependence on foreign oil and domestic petroleum depletion, there was a flurry of interest in solar, geothermal, wind, and other new technologies in the late 1970s.

A related topic was the strain of population growth. Paul Ehrlich in his *The Population Bomb* (1968) warned of impending mass starvation because of failure to control global birthrates. This prediction was in error and Ehrlich's stress on birth control was criticized by both liberals and conservatives. Still, movements for family planning were fairly successful in both advanced and less developed countries. Birthrates began dropping sharply in the 1970s in poorer regions. Choosing to have small families and using contraception pills in the 1960s became virtues, not the signs of selfishness or impotence they had often been in many cultures. Still, the U.S. population alone increased by 26 percent from 1960 to 1980.

In the conservative 1980s, environmentalism suffered the same decline as did other movements critical of unfettered technological growth. In any case, the price of environmental cleanup seemed increasingly beyond reach, as government deficits mounted. But American trust in technology also seemed to decline

Los Angeles skyline, 1954: Smog had already reared its ugly head on the West Coast. (Library of Congress)

in the 1980s. The explosion of the Challenger spacecraft in 1986 led people to question the competence of those who since the mid-1950s had been lionized as the champions of advanced science. The scare of the partial meltdown of the reactor core at Three Mile Island in Pennsylvania in 1979 was followed by the catastrophe at Chernobyl in 1986. Expenses for meeting safety standards made nuclear power, which in the 1950s had been touted as "too cheap to meter," too costly to build in the 1980s. In 1988, scientists widely discussed global warming, caused by gases such as carbon dioxide from burned fuels that trapped solar heat. Pessimists predicted that higher temperatures would melt polar caps, flood coastal cities, and create deserts out of pastures and wheat fields. This prognosis remains controversial. Still, community groups increasingly rejected government and industry plans to place waste or potentially hazardous facilities in their neighborhoods—despite promises of jobs and safeguards.

Of course, technological optimists continued to deny the severity of the problem. In 1978, J. Peter Vajk argued that "with virtually unlimited solar power available in space, we eventually could build countless new settlements" in outer space.[5] Most opponents emphasized that environmentalism was a threat to economic growth and jobs. Lumbermen and their families were pitted against "sentimentalists" who were portrayed as more concerned with the spotted owl than American jobs. Businesses resisted making investment in technology that reduced pollution; these expenditures, after all, did not contribute to immediate profits and had contributed to the decline in the productivity of mining and manufacturing in the 1970s. Still, in the Reagan years, support for research into alternative energy and environmental protection waned as market forces and developmentalist ideas were dominant. Reports of the possibility of inexhaustible energy (for example, from bioengineering or from hydrogen-based fusion that could be drawn from the sea) assuaged some people's fears of global economic collapse.

But underlying these shifts in the political winds remained a fundamental division: On one side stood those who believed that technology could fix the problems that it has created. On the other side were those who thought that a changed social ethic was also required. This might mean fewer goods and reduced mobility, but it would also secure an inhabitable planet for the future.

TECHNOLOGY AND PERSONAL LIFE

The intellectual battles over the impact of technology on jobs and the environment often led to a still broader concern about the effect of innovation on personal life. From the beginnings of industrialization, visionaries predicted that mechanization would lead to a progressive and universal reduction of work—as well as mass affluence. As we saw in chapter 13, optimists assumed that the mechanization of the home would free women for wider participation in public and economic life. The famous economist J.M. Keynes wrote in 1931 that in the near future "man will be faced with his real, his permanent problem—how to use his freedom from pressing economic cares, how to occupy the leisure, which science and compound interest will have won for him, to live wisely and agreeably, and well."[6] Further mechanization could only free all for longer and richer hours of leisure.

But increased free time also disturbed many: Early in this century, cultural conservatives anguished over what wage earners would do with their free time; businesspeople feared that reduced work would mean the end of economic growth upon which their wealth depended. Most important, the expectation that increased productivity meant greater leisure was based on a false assumption: that the demand for goods would decline with affluence. If anything, the opposite has occurred. As demand for consumer goods has grown, so has the commitment of most Americans to steady or even longer periods of wage work in order to purchase this growing array of goods. Thus leisure did not increase as predicted.

It is not difficult to explain why consumer demand should increase, especially after 1945, despite the satisfaction of many needs: After all technology promised not only leisure but greater material goods and comfort. A constant theme of this book has been the virtual identity of the "American way of life" with the material benefits of technology. This was a common viewpoint in the nineteenth century despite the American ideals of the pastoral and the work ethic. Early twentieth-century intellectuals such as Simon Patten and Bertrand Russell argued that technology would create a mass-consumer culture wherein old class divisions would disappear. Mass-produced clothing would reduce social distinctions, especially after work. The radio, the phonograph, and the movies could bridge gaps between peoples of different ethnic groups and regions.

These expectations seemed to become a reality to the generation living in the affluence that followed World War II. Popular magazines gloried in the apparent fact that old luxuries were becoming mass-consumer goods and all Americans were joining the middle class to the envy of the world. In the 1950s and early 1960s, academic sociologists predicted the convergence of social classes as an inevitable consequence of postindustrial consumer society. Work, even if boring and repetitive, was an inevitable and ultimately satisfactory price to pay for the freedoms and comforts of consumption and leisure.

But intellectuals regularly challenged the tendency to equate manufactured goods and mass entertainment with "the good life." This critique had roots deep in the romantic movements of the early nineteenth century and survived in the early twentieth century in the rising chorus of disenchantment with technology's impact on culture. While technocrats praised a productivity that brought high wages and consumer choice, humanistic intellectuals, such as Erich Fromm, argued that mass-assembly jobs disabled workers. Such labor prevented wage earners from marshalling the initiative and imagination required for anything more than passive leisure and manipulated consumption. Mass-production work, these critics argued, diminished the capacity for spontaneity and community.

Postwar affluence also brought forth similar criticism. The popular American sociologists Vance Packard and William Whyte found that mass consumption produced not happy families but status-seeking consumers. In 1970 the economist Staffan Linder argued that affluence had not brought additional leisure. Rather,

69

with rising real wages, the "cost" of free time rose, obliging practical wage earners to work additional overtime and to moonlight; economic maximizing induced them also to intensify their consumption of leisure time by purchasing time-saving devices (such as stereos with remote controls as opposed to time-consuming books). Ironically this meant that leisure hours were rushed with the "work" of consumption. People might long for community and self-expression, but goods got in the way of their enjoyment of time and each other. Another economist, Fred Hirsch, noted in 1974 that while many had predicted that affluence would create social harmony and personal security, this had not occurred. Instead members of the great middle class crowded each other on the beach; they found that the more they had, the more they competed with others who had still more. Finally, economist Tibor Scitovsky in *The Joyless Economy* argued that technological and economic success did not enable Americans to enjoy the fruits of technology in leisure and sophisticated consumption, for they valued these goals less than invention and business. Thus much of the time saved in work was spent watching television, driving cars, or shopping instead of cultivating the arts, reading, conversation, or even good cuisine. Thus, technology became not a means to an end but an end in itself.

These critical views were shared by opponents of centralized technology. Lewis Mumford, who in the 1930s wrote hopefully about a new more humane society based on electric power, by 1970 had radically changed his perspective. In the *Pentagon of Power*, he argued that technology had been captured by the militarists, elitist system builders, and profit-mad corporations. In 1973, Ivan Illich called for "tools of conviviality" where technologies would help people to relate to each other rather than serve authoritarian managers. Machines and techniques should maximize personal competence, argued Illich, rather than increase the individual's dependence on "experts," be they physicians, bureaucrats, engineers, or educators. This perspective had much in common with E.F. Schumacher's idea that decentralized power and manufacturing would benefit poor peoples of the less developed world where capital is scarce but labor plentiful. Schumaker's "small is beautiful" ethic also appealed to Americans tired of overcrowded cities and dependence on distant and presumably manipulative authorities for everyday needs.

Inspired by Illich, Schumacher, and others, Americans have sought practical alternative technologies. *The Whole Earth Catalog* (first appearing in 1968) offered an array of small machines and utensils that promised not to pollute or require large amounts of energy and capital. The same motives inspired advocates of decentralized energy in solar, wind, and biomass. In the 1970s some joined communes in California and many more added solar heating to backyard swimming pools.

However, this movement had a short-lived and ambiguous impact. For most Americans these ideas seemed impractical and too negative toward the variety and comfort in life brought by technology. To many, doomsday scenarios of ecological collapse were simply alarmist. And the appeal of convivial tools seemed to be merely romantic nostalgia for good old days that never were. In any case, as historian Thomas Hughes notes, these proposals for alternative technology ignored the "inertia, or conservative momentum of technological systems."[7] The centralized system of control over innovation has faced few effective challenges since it emerged in the last quarter of the nineteenth century with the birth of AT&T and GE. Despite dire warnings of impending ecological and psychological disaster, few Americans have been willing to think about this future. Even the advocates of convivial tools and restrained growth have not been able to imagine how society might embrace a new technology without the shock of some economic or ecological crisis.

TECHNOLOGY AND SOCIAL CHANGE

This book has been about the complex linkages between technological and social change. A persistent American doctrine has been the expectation that invention could solve all social problems. Another pervasive notion is that the United States was blessed with particular advantages because of its Yankee ingenuity. Recent trends suggest that these orthodoxies are, at least, incomplete: American superiority has vanished with the coming of a global technological network of satellite communications and the portability of the computer chip. The desire of other peoples to share in the bounty of innovation has challenged our educational system and culture to find new ways of competing. Technology has perhaps created almost as many problems as it has solved—even if we may dispute which set of problems is worse. Whatever you may think of the critiques of modern industrialism, they do suggest that technology has not, and probably cannot, make our choices for us. To a great extent, what sort of society we wish to become depends on how we evaluate those choices between growth and environment, between goods and free time, and between change and continuity. Technology helps inform and direct those choices. But they remain ours to make.

SUGGESTED READINGS

Bailes, Kendall, ed., *Environmental History, Critical Issues in Comparative Perspective* (Lanham, MD, 1985).

Bluestone, Barry, and B. Harrison, *The Deindustrialization of America* (New York, 1982).

Corn, Joseph, ed., *Imagining Tomorrow: History, Technology and the American Future* (Cambridge, MA, 1986).

Cross, Gary, *Time and Money: The Making of Consumer Culture* (New York, 1993).

Dickson, David, *The New Politics of Science* (New York, 1984).

Illich, Ivan, *Tools of Conviviality* (New York, 1973).

Mumford, Lewis, *Technics and Civilization* (New York, 1934).

National Research Council, *Computer Chips and Paper Clips: Technology and Women's Employment* (Washington, DC, 1986).

Petulla, J.M., *American Environmentalism: Values, Tactics and Priorities* (New York, 1980).

Scheffer, Victor, *The Shaping of Environmentalism in America* (Seattle, 1991).

Schor, Juliet, *The Overworked American* (New York, 1992).

Schumacher, E.P., *Small Is Beautiful* (London, 1973).

Shaiken, Harley, *Work Transformed: Automation and Labor in the Computer Age* (New York, 1984).

Winner, Langdon, *The Whale and the Reactor: A Search for Limits in an Age of High Tech* (New York, 1986).

NOTES

1. L.M. Passano, *Science* (1935), cited in Peter Kuznick, *Beyond the Laboratory: Scientists as Political Activists in 1930s America* (Chicago, 1987), p. 58. See also Robert Proctor, *Value Free Science?* (Cambridge, MA, 1992), p. 238.

2. Robert Morison, "A Future Note on Visions," *Daedalus* 109 (1): 55–64 Winter 1980.

3. W.W. Rostow, *The Stages of Economic Growth* (New York, 1961), p. 81.

4. Barry Commoner, *The Closing Circle* (New York, 1971), pp. 33, 39, 41, and 45.

5. J. Peter Vajk, *Doomsday Has Been Cancelled* (Culver City, CA, 1978), p. xiv, cited in V. Scheffer, *The Shaping of Environmentalism in America* (Seattle, 1991), p. 12.

6. John M. Keynes, *Essays in Persuasion* (London, 1931), p. 370.

7. Thomas Hughes, *American Genesis: A Century of Invention and Technological Enthusiasm* (New York, 1989), pp. 470–71.

Into the Future?
Government Policy
and Technological Innovation:
Lessons from the Past

The historical record of technological innovation is rich and varied, and thus one must be careful in drawing implications for government policy. Innovations have many effects on society, and not all of these are beneficial. In the previous chapter, we discussed a number of grave problems facing humankind because of our abuse of the potential of modern technology. Still, while our present technological situation raises legitimate concerns about the environment and our future, most of us would admit that we are better off now than were our grandparents. Certainly, we cannot deny that innovation has been the primary driving force behind economic growth over the past centuries and thus has made our per capita incomes much higher than those of our forebears (and we buy goods and services they could scarcely imagine). Moreover, we saw in chapter 15 that a lengthy temporal gap in product innovation can contribute significantly to economic decline.

Before World War II, much of the advance in workplace productivity resulted in a shorter workweek, but this has not continued since. In the home as well, we have not seized the full potential for greater leisure that has resulted from mechanization. Still, the further advance of technology must enhance the possibility that humankind can devote less of its time to earning a living and more to discovering its inner potential.

If we accept, then, that we would in general wish to see the continuation of rapid technological progress in the future (we might, of course, wish to affect the

325

direction of that progress), what can we say about the role of government policy? Most of the innovations we have discussed in this volume have emerged in the private sector, either from the hands of independent innovators or from industrial research laboratories. The clearest role for government in such cases was the maintenance of a patent system that would reward innovators while not unduly preventing others from adapting and building on their innovations. There may still be areas for improvement—some have claimed that industrial research labs abuse the patent system with a series of minor improvements designed primarily to keep competitors out of their industry—but little justification at first glance for government expenditure.

Some of our innovations have had government support. The government has always taken an interest in military technology. There is a long-standing debate on the extent of the civilian spillovers from military research. We would certainly expect that civilians would have gained much more if the money spent on the military had been devoted to nonmilitary research. Yet, for various reasons, this was not politically feasible. We cannot deny, however, that there have been substantial spillovers. In the early days, there was little difference between military guns and civilian guns, or between military ships and civilian ships. Thus, most advances in one were quickly adopted by the other (and government armories played a significant role in the development of the American system of manufacture). In this century, many would argue that military and civilian technologies have increasingly diverged. Military aircraft stress high speed and maneuverability, and relatively little attention is paid to cost. Commercial airlines trying to reduce cost per ton mile of passenger travel may find little of use to them (although supersonic air transport has some commercial future).

One should not take this argument too far. Many would say that the commercial airplane is the single most important spinoff from military research. Not only was aircraft production given a boost by World War I, but the navy continued to finance research during the interwar period. Airplanes were complex and thus well suited to the efforts of industrial research labs: With commercialization well in the future, these labs relied heavily on government funding through the interwar years. Then, in World War II, the development of jet engines was among the areas that saw rapid advance due to military research spending.

Not all government research support has been oriented toward the military. The space program is one example (although military motives were not totally absent). This program has given us Teflon, communications satellites, and the promise of widespread future benefits from experiments in space and space exploration itself. The Atomic Energy Commission has done much to harness the atom to peaceful power production (although many might wish it had never done so). Many government departments financed the early development of the computer. Medical and agricultural research are two other areas in which government has long played an active role.

Moreover, the American government has a long tradition of backing scientific research. Many technological innovations such as X rays, lasers, and biotechnology, which might appear to have emerged unaided from the private sector, were in fact based on publicly supported scientific discoveries. (Many foreign innovations have likewise depended on scientific breakthroughs at U.S. universities and research facilities.) As technological innovation increasingly occurs near the frontier of scientific knowledge, the importance of a productive scientific establishment has steadily increased. American scientists have used this fact to lobby for increased government support since the 1920s.

Was this government support necessary? In the case of airplanes, it would seem that commercial aviation would have been delayed at least for decades without it. Many examples—the transistor leaps to mind—of the science/technology link could be cited. Even with the most generous of patent systems, private innovators cannot be recompensed for all of the benefits that their breakthroughs bestow on society. This provides an economic rationale for government support: In the absence of public subsidy the private sector will not pursue many innovations that are socially beneficial. This is especially so the more basic the research: Scientists have had little opportunity to profit from their discoveries (although some have recently done so in electronics and biotechnology). Scientific advances over the last century would have been much slower if they had depended on profit-oriented private support (not only are the benefits diffuse, but the cost and degree of uncertainty are generally greater). Without public support of basic technology, the ability of independent innovators or research labs to develop new technology would have been severely hampered.

Over the last decades, the countries with the best records of innovation have also experienced higher rates of economic growth and lower levels of unemployment. One answer to the competitive threat faced by the United States in many industries is to increase research efforts. Scholars disagree about the role played by the Japanese government in that country's impressive postwar economic growth, but it does appear that the Japanese government perceived a role for itself in long-term support of innovation long before other governments did; and it has pursued a range of policies to that end: education, improvements in transportation and communication systems, and direct support of science and basic research.

History points to the type of government research strategy that will work best. Over and over, we have seen the cooperative nature of innovation: the necessity for scientists, engineers, production people, and marketing people to work together (think especially of the transistor or nylon). The government cannot expect to create basic innovations and have these quickly adopted by industry. To maximize the benefit from government research efforts, it should look for long-term cooperation with the private sector. Given the different roles played by large and small firms in the innovative process, governments should try to work with both (the success of agricultural research shows that governments can successfully work with small firms).

In the early chapters of this book we described how the United States borrowed and adapted advanced European technology. For much of the twentieth century, the United States has been the world leader in most technological fields and has not had to borrow foreign technology. This is increasingly not the case now, for competitors in both Europe and Asia are challenging America's leadership. This must enhance the overall rate of advance (think of the improvements in just automobile performance and consumer electronics that have emanated from Japan in the last decades). To maintain the competitive position of American industry internationally, however, American innovators must do as they did in the beginning and be prepared to import and improve foreign technology.

As we will see in the next section, it is very difficult to predict the future course of technological change. We should be wary, then, of public policy that explicitly tries to pick winners. Although the Japanese government may have had some success at this, it has also recorded important failures: Government planners were initially hostile to the idea of Japanese firms' entering the automobile industry. Still, government research efforts could legitimately be biased toward certain goals. Improving the environment is the most obvious of these. We discussed in the previous chapter the pressing need to take better care of our environment. Even with existing technology, we can have both economic growth and a better environment. The technology of the future should make it even easier to pursue both of these goals.[1]

TECHNOLOGICAL FORECASTS PAST AND PRESENT

Forecasters in 1941 correctly predicted the growth potential of pharmaceuticals, nuclear power, and television. They also, however, foresaw great advances in long-term weather forecasting, photosynthesis, and prefabricated housing. Their success rate is fairly typical of those who have had the audacity to predict the future. Even when one thinks one sees the early stages of the emergence of a new technology, it is difficult to foresee how successful it may be. Decades after the first "horseless carriage" hit the roads, urban planners and others still could not imagine the dominant role that the automobile was destined to play in American society. In recent years, producers have been disappointed by the failure of picturephones, and pleasantly surprised by the success of cellular phones and fax machines.

Guessing at new areas of technological discovery is even more dangerous. Writers of science fiction, at least, had imagined space travel centuries before it became possible, although they could not be very precise about the particular form this travel would take. On the other hand, nobody imagined radio before scientists discovered the existence of electromagnetic waves. Perhaps the only thing we can say with certainty about the future is that there are sure to be surprises.

Some might even question that conclusion. Perhaps we have already exhausted most of the technological potential in this world, and thus rates of innovation must fall in the future. Because the rate of innovation has been rising, in general, for centuries, we might expect that it will continue to rise into the future. (Of course, the rate of growth of the world's population also rose over the previous couple of centuries before tapering off in the last decades.) Some have argued that industry has much greater technological potential than the service sector, and thus as the latter grows in importance the rate of innovation must fall. However, the service sector has been expanding in importance for at least a century without having this effect. Moreover, the information revolution within the service sector could prove to be the most far-reaching set of innovations of the late twentieth century. Certainly, entertainment, education, and medicine seem susceptible to a considerable degree of innovation in the future.

It is only natural in times of poor economic performance to wonder if the rate of innovation is falling. As we saw in chapter 15, this is a reasonable conjecture. The general manager of the National Machine Tool Business Association worried in the mid-1920s that the age of invention was drawing to a close. With the advantage of hindsight we now know that although few new products reached the market in the interwar period, research was well under way that would unleash a host of new products on the postwar market. With no compelling reason to think otherwise, we are well advised to expect that the future course of innovation will be at least as impressive as the past.[2]

It is not as if we cannot point to areas in which we have good reason to expect substantial innovation. We have already touched on the information revolution. The mating of the computer with advances in telecommunications creates enormous potential: Retailing, for example, may be transformed by shopping from home. In the factory, computerized design and production are changing both what and how we produce. As computer chips become smaller and more sophisticated, they will find applications in almost all aspects of our existence. Superconductivity—the transmission of electricity with virtually no resistance as occurs at temperatures approaching absolute zero—is now practicable in laboratories with materials, temperatures, and pressures inexpensive enough for commercial use; this too is likely to yield a revolution in electronic devices before the end of the twentieth century, with almost costless long-distance power transmission. Lasers, industrial ceramics (a term used to apply to processed materials with no metallic content), and biotechnology are other areas in which we can be confident of major breakthroughs over the next decades. This list could be extended: We stop lest some historian in 2050 laugh at us for our errors in judgment.

This analysis applies to the United States. As many developed countries increase their expenditures on research, and as many less developed countries grow and begin to make their own contributions to worldwide innovation (think of the Japanese contribution in recent decades), there is even better reason to expect innovation to continue to expand at the global level. Care must be taken that future technology is harnessed in a way that protects the dignity of our world and ourselves, but we should not turn our backs on the potential good that can come from innovation. Any country that does not share in this expansion risks falling behind.

SUGGESTED READING

Mowery, David C., and Nathan Rosenberg, *Technology and the Pursuit of Economic Growth* (Cambridge, UK, 1989).

77

———— NOTES

1. Just as the urban manure problem caused by horse transport was solved by the car, the pollution problem caused by the modern car may be alleviated by not only innovations in transport, but also innovations that facilitate working and shopping from home.
2. If it is correct to view the 1950s and 1960s as an unusual period in which a backlog of technology from the depression and World War II was developed, then we might not see such a period again.

Global Issues

- Managing Cultural Differences
- Ethical Issues in International Business:
  International Norms

CHAPTER FOUR

Culture and organization

> Intuitively, people have always assumed that bu-
> reaucratic structures and patterns of action differ in
> the different countries of the Western world and even
> more markedly between East and West. Practitioners
> know it and never fail to take it into account. But
> contemporary social scientists . . . have not been
> concerned with such comparisons.
>
> Michel Crozier[1]

Just how does culture influence organization structure and process? To what extent do organizational structures and processes have an inherent logic which overrides cultural considerations? Given the nature of today's business demands, do we find convergence in the ways of organizing? To what extent will popular techniques such as team management and empowerment be adopted across cultures? With what speed and with what possible (re)interpretation? What cultural dimensions need to be recognized which may facilitate or hinder organizational change efforts?

In order to demonstrate the impact of culture on organizational structure, systems, and processes, we present the evidence for national differences and consider the cultural reasons for these differences. Examining the degree to which organizations have centralized power, specialized jobs and roles, and formalized rules and procedures, we find distinct patterns of organizing which prevail despite pressures for convergence. This raises concerns regarding the transferability of organizational forms across borders and questions the logic of universal "best practices".

Different schools, different cultures

While many managers are ready to accept that national culture may influence the way people relate to each other, or the "soft stuff", they are less convinced that it can really affect the nuts and bolts of organization: structure, systems, and processes. The culture-free (or *emic*) argument is that structure is determined by *organizational* features such as size and technology. For example, the famous Aston studies,[2] conducted in the late 1960s in the United Kingdom and widely replicated, point to size as the most important factor influencing structure: larger firms tend to have greater division of labor (specialized) and more formal policies and procedures (formalized) but are not necessarily more centralized. Furthermore, the nature of technology, such as mass production, is considered to favor a more centralized and formal (mechanistic) rather than decentralized and informal (organic) approach.[3]

Other management scholars argue that the *societal* context creates differences in structure in different countries (*etic*).[4] In effect, the "structuralists" argue that structure creates culture, while the "culturalists" argue that culture creates structure. The debate continues, with each side arming up with more sophisticated weapons: measurements and methodologies.

Taking an historical perspective, theories about how best to organize – Max Weber's (German) bureaucracy, Henri Fayol's (French) administrative model, and Frederick Taylor's (American) scientific management – all reflect societal concerns of the times as well as the cultural backgrounds of the individuals.[5] Today, their legacies can be seen in the German emphasis on structure and competence, the French emphasis on social systems, roles and relationships (unity of command), and the American emphasis on the task system or machine model of organization, now popularized in the form of re-engineering.

Indeed, many of the techniques of modern management – performance management, participative management, team approach, and job enrichment all have their roots firmly embedded in a particular historical and societal context: *scientific management* in the United States at the turn of the century; *human relations*, brought about by Hawthorne studies (1930s) in the United States; *socio-technical* brought by the Tavistock studies of the coal mines in the United Kingdom (1930s); and *human resources* brought about in Sweden (1970s) with Saab Scania's and Volvo's redesign of auto assembly into autonomous teams.

These approaches reflect different cultural assumptions regarding, for example, human nature and the importance of task and relationships. While the scientific management approach focused on how best to accomplish the task, the human relations approach focused on how best to establish relationships with employees. The human resources approach assumed that workers were self-motivated, while earlier schools assumed that workers needed to be motivated by more or less benevolent management.

These models of management have diffused across countries at different rates and in different ways. For example, mass-production techniques promoted by scientific management were quickly adopted in Germany, while practices associated with the human relations school transferred more readily to Spain.[6] For this reason the historical and societal context needs to be considered to understand the adoption and diffusion of different forms of organization across countries. While some theorists focus on the *institutional arrangements*,[7] such as the nature of markets, the educational system, or the relationships between business and government, to explain these differences, we focus here, more specifically, on the cultural reasons.

This does not mean that institutional factors are irrelevant. In effect, it is quite difficult to separate out the influence of institutions from culture as they have both evolved together over time and are thus intricately linked. For example, the strong role of the state and the cultural emphasis on power and hierarchy often go hand in hand, as in the case of France. Or in the words of the French *roi soleil* Louis XIV, *L'état, c'est moi* ("The state is me"). Our argument (the culturalist perspective) is that different forms of organization emerge which reflect underlying cultural dimensions.

Culture and structure

Hofstede's findings

One of the most important studies which attempted to establish the impact of culture differences on management was conducted by Geert Hofstede, first in the late 1960s, and continuing through the next three decades.[8] The original study, now considered a classic, was based on an employee opinion survey involving 116,000 IBM employees in 40 different countries. From the results of this survey, which asked people for their preferences in terms of management style and work environment, Hofstede identified four "value" dimensions on which countries differed: power distance, uncertainty avoidance, individualism/collectivism, and masculinity/femininity.

Power distance indicates the extent to which a society accepts the unequal distribution of power in institutions and organizations. **Uncertainty avoidance** refers to a society's discomfort with uncertainty, preferring predictability and stability. **Individualism/collectivism** reflects the extent to which people prefer to take care of themselves and their immediate families, remaining emotionally independent from groups, organizations, and other collectivities. And the **masculinity/femininity** dimension reveals the bias towards either "masculine" values of assertiveness, competitiveness, and materialism, or towards "feminine" values of nurturing, and the quality of life and relationships. Country rankings on each dimension are provided in Table 4.1.

Given the differences in value orientations, Hofstede questioned whether American theories could be applied abroad and discussed the consequences of cultural differences in terms of motivation, leadership, and organization.[9] He argued, for example, that organizations in countries with high power distance would tend to have more levels of hierarchy (vertical differentiation), a higher proportion of supervisory personnel (narrow span of control), and more centralized decision-making. Status and power would serve as motivators, and leaders would be revered or obeyed as authorities.

In countries with high uncertainty avoidance, organizations would tend to have more formalization evident in greater amount of written rules and procedures. Also there would be greater specialization evident in the importance attached to technical competence in the role of staff and in defining jobs and functions. Managers would avoid taking risks and would be motivated by stability and security. The role of leadership would be more one of planning, organizing, coordinating, and controlling.

In countries with a high collectivist orientation, there would be a preference for group as opposed to individual decision-making. Consensus and cooperation would be more valued than individual initiative and effort. Motivation derives from a sense of belonging, and rewards are based on being part of the group (loyalty and tenure). The role of leadership in such cultures is to facilitate team effort and integration, to foster a supportive atmosphere, and to create the necessary context or group culture.

Table 4.1   Hofstede's rankings

Country	Power distance		Individualism		Masculinity		Uncertainty avoidance	
	Index	Rank	Index	Rank	Index	Rank	Index	Rank
Argentina	49	35–6	46	22–3	56	20–1	86	10–15
Australia	36	41	90	2	61	16	51	37
Austria	11	53	55	18	79	2	70	24–5
Belgium	65	20	75	8	54	22	94	5–6
Brazil	69	14	38	26–7	49	27	76	21–2
Canada	39	39	80	4–5	52	24	48	41–2
Chile	63	24–5	23	38	28	46	86	10–15
Colombia	67	17	13	49	64	11–12	80	20
Costa Rica	35	42–4	15	46	21	48–9	86	10–15
Denmark	18	51	74	9	16	50	23	51
Equador	78	8–9	8	52	63	13–14	67	28
Finland	33	46	63	17	26	47	59	31–2
France	68	15–16	71	10–11	43	35–6	86	10–15
Germany (F.R.)	35	42–4	67	15	66	9–10	65	29
Great Britain	35	42–4	89	3	66	9–10	35	47–8
Greece	60	27–8	35	30	57	18–19	112	1
Guatemala	95	2–3	6	53	37	43	101	3
Hong Kong	68	15–16	25	37	57	18–19	29	49–50
Indonesia	78	8–9	14	47–8	46	30–1	48	41–2
India	77	10–11	48	21	56	20–1	40	45
Iran	58	19–20	41	24	43	35–6	59	31–2
Ireland	28	49	70	12	68	7–8	35	47–8
Israel	13	52	54	19	47	29	81	19
Italy	50	34	76	7	70	4–5	75	23
Jamaica	45	37	39	25	68	7–8	13	52
Japan	54	33	46	22–3	95	1	92	7
Korea (S)	60	27–8	187	43	39	41	85	16–17
Malaysia	104	1	26	36	50	25–6	36	46
Mexico	81	5–6	30	32	69	6	82	18
Netherlands	38	40	80	4–5	14	51	53	35
Norway	31	47–8	69	13	8	52	50	38
New Zealand	22	50	79	6	58	17	49	39–40
Pakistan	55	32	14	47–8	50	25–6	70	24–5
Panama	95	2–3	11	51	44	34	86	10–15
Peru	64	21–3	16	45	42	37–8	87	9
Philippines	94	4	32	31	64	11–12	44	44
Portugal	63	24–5	27	33–5	31	45	104	2
South Africa	49	36–7	65	16	63	13–14	49	39–40
Salvador	66	18–19	19	42	40	40	94	5–6
Singapore	74	13	20	39–41	48	28	8	53
Spain	57	31	51	20	42	37–8	86	10–15
Sweden	31	47–8	71	10–11	5	52	29	49–50
Switzerland	34	45	68	14	70	4–5	58	33
Taiwan	58	29–30	17	44	45	32–3	69	26
Thailand	64	21–3	20	39–41	34	44	64	30
Turkey	66	18–19	37	28	45	31–3	85	16–17
Uruguay	61	26	36	29	38	42	100	4
United States	40	38	91	1	62	15	46	43
Venezuela	81	5–6	12	50	73	3	76	21–2
Yugoslavia	76	12	27	33–5	21	48–9	88	8
Regions:								
East Africa	64	21–3	27	33–5	41	39	52	36
West Africa	77	10–11	20	39–41	46	30–1	54	34
Arab countries	80	7	38	26–7	53	23	68	27

Rank numbers: 1 – Highest; 53 – Lowest.
Source: G. Hofstede (1991) *Cultures and Organizations: Software of the Mind*, McGraw-Hill, Maidenhead.

84

In countries ranked high on masculinity, the management style is likely to be more concerned with task accomplishment than nurturing social relationships. Motivation will be based on the acquisition of money and things rather than quality of life. In such cultures, the role of leadership is to ensure bottom-line profits in order to satisfy shareholders, and to set demanding targets. In more feminine cultures, the role of the leader would be to safeguard employee well-being, and to demonstrate concern for social responsibility.

Having ranked countries on each dimension, Hofstede then positioned them along two dimensions at a time, creating a series of cultural maps. He too found country clusters – Anglo, Nordic, Latin, and Asian – similar to those reported in the previous chapter.[10] While some concern has been voiced that the country differences found in Hofstede's research are not representative due to the single company sample, further research by him and others supports these dimensions and the preferences for different profiles of organization.

One such cultural map, as shown in Figure 4.1 (see also Table 4.2), is particularly relevant to structure in that it simultaneously considers power distance (acceptance of hierarchy) and uncertainty avoidance (the desire for formalized rules and procedures).

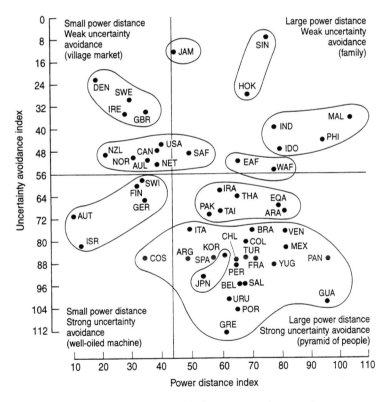

Figure 4.1 Hofstede's maps. (*Source*: G. Hofstede (1991) *Cultures and Organizations*, McGraw-Hill, Maidenhead.)

85

Table 4.2   Abbreviations for the countries and regions studied

Abbreviation	Country or region	Abbreviation	Country or region
ARA	Arab-speaking countries (Egypt, Iraq, Kuwait, Lebanon, Libya, Saudi Arabia, United Arab Emirates)	ITA	Italy
		JAM	Jamaica
		JPN	Japan
		KOR	South Korea
ARG	Argentina	MAL	Malaysia
AUL	Australia	MEX	Mexico
AUT	Austria	NET	Netherlands
BEL	Belgium	NOR	Norway
BRA	Brazil	NZL	New Zealand
CAN	Canada	PAK	Pakistan
CHL	Chile	PAN	Panama
COL	Colombia	PER	Peru
COS	Costa Rica	PHI	Philippines
DEN	Denmark	POR	Portugal
EAF	East Africa (Ethiopia, Kenya, Tanzania, Zambia)	SAF	South Africa
		SAL	Salvador
EQA	Equador	SIN	Singapore
FIN	Finland	SPA	Spain
FRA	France	SWE	Sweden
GBR	Great Britain	SWI	Switzerland
GER	Germany F.R.	TAI	Taiwan
GRE	Greece	THA	Thailand
GUA	Guatemala	TUR	Turkey
HOK	Hong Kong	URU	Uruguay
IDO	Indonesia	USA	United States
IND	India	VEN	Venezuela
IRA	Iran	WAF	West Africa (Ghana, Nigeria, Sierra Leone)
IRE	Ireland (Republic of)		
ISR	Israel	YUG	Yugoslavia

Source: G. Hofstede (1991) *Cultures and Organizations*, McGraw-Hill, Maidenhead.

Countries which ranked high both on power distance and uncertainty avoidance would be expected to be more "mechanistic"[11] or what is commonly known as bureaucratic. In this corner we find the Latin countries.

In the opposite quadrant, countries which rank low both on power distance and uncertainty avoidance are expected to be more "organic"[12] – less hierarchic, more decentralized, having less formalized rules and procedures. Here we find the Nordic countries clustered and to a lesser extent, the Anglo countries.

In societies where power distance is low but uncertainty avoidance is high, we expect to find organizations where hierarchy is downplayed, decisions are decentralized, but where rules and regulations are more formal, and task roles and responsibilities are more clearly defined. Thus there is no need for a boss, as the organization runs by routines. This is characteristic of the Germanic cluster.

In societies where power distance is high but uncertainty avoidance is low, organizations resemble families or tribes. Here, "the boss is the boss", and the organization may be described as paternalistic. Subordinates do not have clearly defined task roles and responsibilities (formalization), but instead social roles. Here we find the Asian countries where business enterprise is often characterized by centralized power and personalized relationships.

Emerging cultural profiles: converging evidence

These differences in structural preferences also emerged in a study conducted by Stevens[13] at INSEAD. When presented with an organizational problem, a conflict between two department heads within a company, MBA students from Britain, France, and Germany proposed markedly different solutions. The majority of French students referred the problem to the next level up, the president. The Germans argued that the major problem was a lack of structure; the expertise, roles, and responsibilities of the two conflicting department heads had never been clearly defined. Their suggested solution involved establishing procedures for better coordination. The British saw it as an interpersonal communication problem between the two department heads which could be solved by sending them for interpersonal skills training, preferably together.

On the basis of these findings, Stevens described the "implicit model" of the organization held by each culture. For the French, the organization represents a "pyramid of people" (formalized and centralized). For the Germans, the organization is like a "well-oiled machine" (formalized but not centralized), in which management intervention is limited to exceptional cases because the rules resolve problems. And for the British, it was more like a "village market" (neither formalized nor centralized) in which neither the hierarchy nor the rules, but rather the demands of the situation determine structure.

Going beyond questionnaires by observing the actual behavior of managers and company practices, further research reveals such cultural profiles as shown in Figure 4.2. Indeed, in studies comparing firms in France, Germany, and the United Kingdom,[14] French firms were found to be more centralized and formalized with less delegation when compared with either German or British firms. The role of the PDG (French CEO) was to provide coordination at the top and to make key decisions, which demands a high level of analytical and conceptual ability that need not be industry- or company-specific. The staff function plays an important role in providing analytic expertise. These capabilities are developed in the elite *grandes écoles* of engineering and administration.

The research findings confirmed the image of German firms as "well-oiled machines" as they were more likely to be decentralized, specialized, and formalized. In fact, German managers were more likely to cite structure as a key success factor, having a logic of its own, apart from people. German firms were more likely to be organized by function (sometimes to the extent that they are referred to as "chimney" organizations) with coordination achieved through routines and procedures.

Although German organizations tended to be flatter and to have a broader span of control when compared with the French, middle managers had less discretion than their British counterparts as they were limited to their specific technical competence. The

87

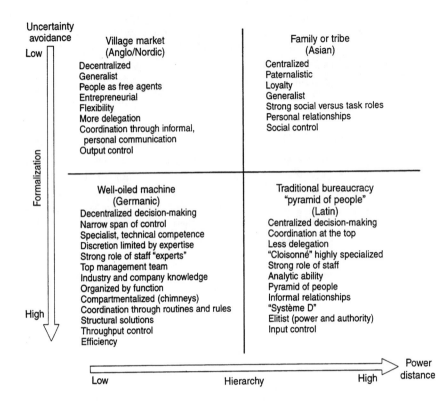

Figure 4.2 Emerging cultural profiles.

premium placed on competence was expressed in the concern to find competent people to perform specialized tasks, the strong role of staff to provide technical expertise, and expectations that top management not only has specific technical competence, but also in-depth company knowledge. Furthermore, top management typically consists of a managing board, *Vorstand*, which integrates the specialized knowledge of the various top managers (rather than in the head of a lone individual as in the case of France, Britain, or the United States).

In contrast to the well-oiled machine model with its greater concern for efficiency, the "village market" model reflects a greater concern for flexibility. Indeed, structure in British firms was found to be far more flexible, more decentralized and less formalized, when compared with the French and German firms. Organized by divisions, there is greater decentralization and delegation in the company and the role of central staff is far less important. Here, the burden of coordinating functions was placed on individual managers requiring a constant need for persuasion and negotiation to achieve cooperation.[15]

British managers, compared with Germans, were more ready to adapt the structure to the people working in it. Changes in personnel were often used as opportunities to reshuffle the jobs and responsibilities in order to accommodate available talent, and to create opportunities for personal development (free agents). Top management's role was to identify market opportunities and convince others to pursue them, underlining the importance of taking a more strategic view and of being able to communicate it persuasively.[16]

Studies in Asia have also found companies to fit the "family model", being more hierarchic and less formalized, with the exception of Japan. When compared with the Japanese, Hong Kong Chinese firms were less likely to have written manuals and Hong Kong Chinese bosses were also found to be more autocratic and paternalistic.[17] Another study of thirty-nine multinational commercial banks from fourteen different countries operating in Hong Kong found the Hong Kong banks to have the greatest number of hierarchical levels (eleven); the banks from Singapore, the Philippines, and India were also among those most centralized.[18]

A recent study of Chinese entrepreneurs found the Confucian tradition of patriarchal authority to be remarkably persistent. Being part of the family is seen as a way of achieving security. Social roles are clearly spelled out in line with Confucian precepts, which designate the responsibilities for the roles of father–son, brothers, and so on. Control is exerted through authority, which is not questioned. In 70 percent of the entrepreneurial firms studied, even large ones, the structure of Chinese organizations was found to resemble a hub with spokes around a powerful founder, or a management structure with only two layers.[19]

What begins to emerge from these various research studies is a converging and coherent picture of different management structures when comparing countries within Europe, as well as when comparing countries in Europe, the United States, and Asia. The primary cultural determinants appear to be those related to relationships between people in terms of power and status and relationship with nature, for example how uncertainty is managed and how control is exercised.

These underlying cultural assumptions are expressed in beliefs (and their subsequent importance, or value) regarding the need for hierarchy, for formal rules and procedures, specialized jobs and functions. These beliefs and values, in turn, are observable in behavior and artifacts, such as deference to the boss, the presence of executive parking and dining facilities ("perks"), and the existence of written policies and procedures, specific job descriptions, or manuals outlining standard operating procedures.

The research findings in the above-mentioned studies were based on observations as well as questionnaires and interviews of managers and companies in different countries. The same, of course, can be done comparing companies in different industries or within the same industry, and managers in different functions providing corresponding models of industry, corporate and/or functional cultures. From these findings, management scholars interpret underlying meaning.

The meaning of organizations: task versus social systems

André Laurent argues that the country differences in structure described above reflect different conceptions (or understandings) of what is an organization.[20] These different

Table 4.3   Management questionnaire

A = Strongly agree
B = Tend to agree
C = Neither agree, nor disagree
D = Tend to disagree
E = Strongly disagree

1. When the respective roles of the members of a department become complex, detailed job descriptions are a useful way of clarifying.	A B C D E
2. In order to have efficient work relationships, it is often necessary to bypass the hierarchical line.	A B C D E
8. An organizational structure in which certain subordinates have two direct bosses should be avoided at all costs.	A B C D E
13. The more complex a department's activities, the more important it is for each individual's functions to be well-defined.	A B C D E
14. The main reason for having a hierarchical structure is so that everyone knows who has authority over whom.	A B C D E
19. Most organizations would be better off if conflict could be eliminated forever.	A B C D E
24. It is important for a manager to have at hand precise answers to most of the questions that his/her subordinates may raise about their work.	A B C D E
33. Most managers have a clear notion of what we call an organizational structure.	A B C D E
38. Most managers would achieve better results if their roles were less precisely defined.	A B C D E
40. Through their professional activity, managers play an important role in society.	A B C D E
43. The manager of tomorrow will be, primarily, a negotiator.	A B C D E
49. Most managers seem to be more motivated by obtaining power than by achieving objectives.	A B C D E
52. Today there seems to be an authority crisis in organizations.	A B C D E

Source: A. Laurent. Reproduced by permission.

conceptions were discovered in surveys which asked managers to agree or disagree with statements regarding beliefs about organization and management. A sample of the questions are shown in Table 4.3.

The results of this survey are very much in line with the discussion above in that they show similar cultural differences regarding power and uncertainty in views of organizations as systems of hierarchy, authority, politics, and role formalization. What would these different views of organization actually look like, were we to observe managers at work and even to question them? What arguments would managers from different countries put forth to support their responses?

Having a view of organizations as **hierarchical systems** would make it difficult, for example, to tolerate having to report to two bosses, as required in a matrix organization, and it would make it difficult to accept bypassing or going over or around the boss. The boss would also be expected to have precise answers to most of the questions that subordinates have about their work. Asian and Latin managers argue that in order for bosses to be respected, or to have power and authority, they must demonstrate expert knowledge. And if the most efficient way to get things done is to bypass the hierarchical line they would consider that there was something wrong with the hierarchy.

Scandinavian and Anglo managers, on the other hand, argue that it is perfectly normal to go directly to anyone in the organization in order to accomplish the task. It would seem intolerable, for example, to have to go through one's own boss, who would contact his or her counterpart in a neighboring department before making contact with someone in that other department.

Furthermore, they argue that it is impossible to have precise answers, since the world is far too complex and ambiguous, and even if you could provide precise answers, this would not develop the capability of your subordinates to solve problems. Thus a Swedish boss with a French subordinate can anticipate some problems: the French subordinate is likely to think that the boss, not knowing the answers, is incompetent, while the Swedish boss may think that the French subordinate does not know what to do and is therefore incompetent.

Those who view the organization as a **political system** consider managers to play an important political role in society, and to negotiate within the organization. Thus obtaining power is seen as more important than achieving specific objectives. Here again, Latin European managers are more likely to adhere to this view than their Nordic and Anglo counterparts.

In France, for example, executives have often played important roles in the French administration before assuming top positions in companies. Furthermore, Latin managers are acutely aware that it is necessary to have power in order to get things done in the organization. Nordic and Anglo managers, however, tend to downplay the importance of power and therefore reject the need for political maneuvering.

When organizations are viewed as systems of **role formalization**, managers prefer detailed job descriptions, and well-defined roles and functions. These serve to clarify complex situations and tasks. Otherwise it is difficult to know who is responsible for what and to hold people accountable. In addition they argue that lack of clear job descriptions or role definitions creates overlap and inefficiency. Nordic and Anglo managers, on the other hand, argue that the world is too complex to be able to clearly define roles and functions. Furthermore they say that detailed descriptions interfere with maintaining flexibility and achieving coordination.

From his research, Laurent concluded that underlying these arguments managers had different conceptions of organization: one which focused on the task, called **instrumental**, and one which focused on relationships, called **social**. For Latin European managers, organizations are considered as **social systems**, or systems of relationships, where

91

personal networks and social positioning are important. The organization achieves its goals through relationships and how they are managed (as prescribed by Fayol). Roles and relationships are defined formally (by the hierarchy) and informally, based on authority, power, and status which are seen as attributes of the person, not the task or function. Personal loyalty and deference to the boss are expected.

However, getting things done means working around the system – using informal, personal networks to circumvent the hierarchy as well as the rules and regulations – what the French call *Système D*. According to sociologist Michel Crozier, it is this informal system that gives the French "bureaucratic model" its flexibility.[21] Organizations are thus considered to be necessarily political in nature. When asked to diagnose organizational problems, French social scientists and consultants typically start by analyzing the power relationships and power games (*les enjeux*).[22]

In contrast, for Anglo–Saxon, and northern European managers, the organization is a system of tasks where it is important to know what has to be done, rather than who has power and authority to do so (as in the socio/political view). This instrumental or functionalist view of organizations (very much in keeping with Taylor's scientific management) focuses on what is to be achieved and whether objectives are met (achievement orientation). Structure is defined by activities – what has to be done – and the hierarchy exists only to assign responsibility. It follows that authority is defined by function and is limited, specific to the job not the person.

Here, coordination and control are impersonal, decentralized, and reside in the structure and systems. Rules and regulations are applied universally. If the rules and regulations are dysfunctional, then they are changed rather than circumvented or broken. Management consultants are called in to figure out the best way to devise strategy, design structure, classify jobs and set salary scales, and develop concrete programs such as "total quality" or "performance management".

These different conceptions of organization were confirmed recently when Trompenaars[23] asked 15,000 managers to choose between the following statements:

> A company is a system designed to perform functions and tasks in an efficient way. People are hired to fulfill these functions with the help of machines and other equipment. They are paid for the tasks they perform.

> A company is a group of people working together. The people have social relations with other people and with the organization. The functioning is dependent upon these relations.

He too found large differences between Anglo and Nordic managers compared with Latin and Asian managers, as shown in Figure 4.3. These different beliefs reveal the underlying cultural meaning of organizations as task versus social systems.

As we see us . . . (revisited)

These findings can be further corroborated by asking managers to describe the approach to management in their countries, or "how we see us", as discussed in Chapter 1. For example, many of the research results discussed above place Scandinavian managers at

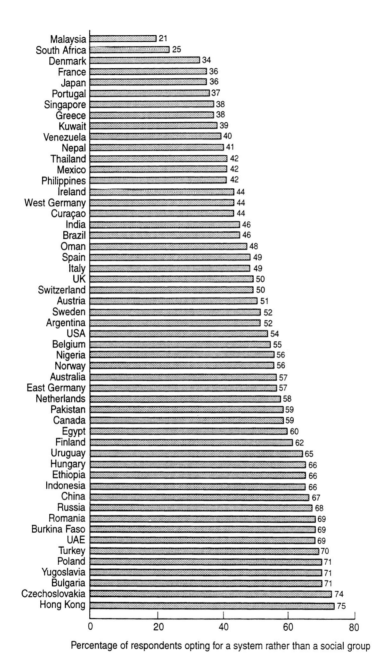

Figure 4.3   Organizations as task versus social systems. (*Source*: F. Trompenaars (1993) *Riding the Waves of Culture: Understanding cultural diversity in business*, Nicholas Brealey, London.)

93

one end of a continuum, with Latin and Asian managers at the other. Jan Selmer,[24] a Swedish management professor, proposed the following profile of "Viking Management". Compare this with the self-descriptions of Brazilian[25] and Indonesian managers in Table 4.4.

According to self-reports, clear differences and similarities emerge in terms of the nature of relationships (hierarchy) and the relationship with nature (uncertainty and control). For example, in keeping with the findings discussed above, Viking Management is characterized as decentralized (less hierarchy) when compared with the Brazilian and Indonesian views, which emphasize status and power or respect for elders.

On the other hand, in each case there is a strong emphasis on the importance of relationships: family (mother–daughter) and friends, avoiding conflict, being tolerant,

Table 4.4   As we see us . . . .

Viking management
Decentralized decision-making
Organization structure is often ambiguous
Perceived by others to be indecisive
Goal formulation, long-range objectives, and performance evaluation criteria are vague and implicit
Informal channels of communication
Coordinate by values not rules (normative versus coercive)
Case by case approach versus standard procedures
Consensus-oriented
Avoid conflict
Informal relationships between foreign subsidiaries and headquarters (mother–daughter
   relationships)

Brazilian management
Hierarchy and authority; status and power are important
Centralized decision-making
Personal relationships are more important than the task
Rules and regulations are for enemies
Flexible and adaptable (too much?) *Jeitiñho*
Anything is possible
Short-term oriented – immediatism
Avoid conflict – seen as win/lose
Rely on magic – low control over environment
Decisions based on intuition and feeling

Indonesian management
Respect for hierarchy and elders
Family-oriented
Group- versus individual-oriented
Friendly and helpful, hospitable
Tolerant
Decisions based on compromise – "keep everyone happy"
Importance of religion – (Islam)
Five principles
Bhinneka Tunggal Ika (unity through diversity)

seeking consensus, and "keeping everyone happy". For the Swedes, this corresponds to their keen concern for social well-being and quality of relationships, reflected in their number one ranking on Hofstede's femininity dimension.

In all three self-descriptions there is less emphasis placed on formalization. For the Swedes, organization goals and structures are experienced as vague and ambiguous. Uncertainty is managed with a "case by case" (and *not* a universal) approach, through informal communication channels, and "through values not rules". For the Indonesians, it is the "Five principles" established by President Suharto that provide the rules, rather than organizational ones. In comparison with the Swedes, however, the Indonesians perceive little control over their environment, *Insh'allah* (if God wills . . .)". Thus the Swedish approach to getting things done may be frustrated by the Indonesian sense of letting things happen.

Brazilian managers, faced with great uncertainty in the day-to-day business environment over which they feel they have little control, say that they have developed a finely tuned sense of intuition, having learned to trust their "gut" feel, as previously mentioned. For the Brazilians, the notion of *Jeitiñho* is similar to that of the French *Système D*, going around the system in order to get things done. This assures flexibility and adaptability such that anything is possible (although perhaps too much so as Brazilian managers themselves acknowledge).

Now imagine a Brazil–Sweden–Indonesia joint venture. This raises the possibility that three firms would have to resolve their differences on several fronts while using their similarities to create a shared sense of purpose. In particular, there would probably be a clash between the cultural assumptions underlying Swedish management – little concern with power and status and high perceived control over the environment – with those of Brazilian and Indonesian management – more emphasis on power and authority and less perceived control.

This would probably cause the biggest headaches for the Swedes when it came to efforts to delegate decision-making and to encourage individual responsibility and accountability. For the Indonesian and Brazilian managers, the frustration would come from confusion as to "who is the boss?" and "why isn't he/she making decisions?", and "how can I be held responsible when I have no control over what happens?". In decision-making, the Brazilians would find the Indonesians and Swedes interminably slow, seeking consensus or democratic compromise, while they in turn would see the Brazilians as impetuous, and too individualistic. On the other hand, the similarity in importance placed on relationships, on informal communication, and on avoiding conflict can help to work through these difficulties together, on a personal basis.

Although there are variations within countries, due to industry and corporate culture, as well as individual styles of key managers, the above research findings and self-descriptions point to different cultural profiles of organization. The underlying assumptions can be interpreted to reveal the nature of relationships, as seen in the importance of hierarchy, and control over nature, as seen in the need for formal or social rules and procedures. The underlying cultural meaning of the organization can then be interpreted as systems of tasks versus systems of relationships. These cultural profiles provide a starting point to explore different structural preferences and to begin to anticipate potential problems when transferring practices from one country to another or in forming joint ventures and strategic alliances.

On a less serious note, these differences have been caricatured in the organizational charts shown in Figure 4.4. Using these caricatures can provoke discussion of structural differences across countries in a humorous mode while allowing us to discover the grain of truth within and to imagine how our own organization chart might seem to others.

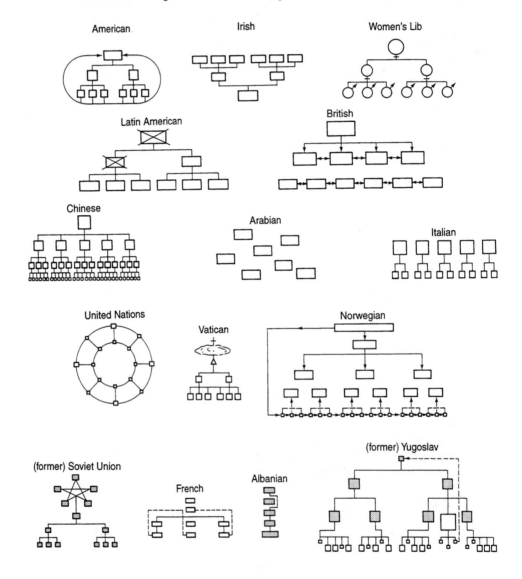

Figure 4.4   The organization chart. (*Source*: *International Management*. Copyright © Reed Business Publishing.)

Constructing cultural profiles enables us to appreciate the impact of culture on management as multidimensional. It would therefore be a mistake to base a prediction regarding structure or process on a single cultural dimension.

In addition, managers need to recognize that the relationships between cultural dimensions and structure (or processes) are not simple cause–effect links, but instead, are multidetermined. Similar approaches may exist for different cultural reasons, and different approaches may exist for the same reason. Thus formalized rules and procedures or participative management approaches may have a different *raison d'être* on different sides of the national border.

Having considered cultural differences in organization and structure, we can now turn our attention to organizational processes. In addition to cultural preferences regarding hierarchy and formalization, other cultural dimensions are considered to explain the reasons for some of the country differences that may seem contradictory. And to show why similar business practices may have different underlying cultural roots, or meaning.

Culture and processes

The characterization of organizations as pyramids, well-oiled machines, village markets, and family tribes, and the structural correlates are further reflected in the organizational processes. In effect, structures are similar to fossils, as they bear the traces of organizational processes over time. Thus the influence of culture can also be seen in organizational processes such as the nature of policies and procedures, planning and control, information processing and communication, and decision-making.

Policies and procedures

The formalization and standardization of policies and procedures may reflect low tolerance for uncertainty, as they can be clearly spelled out, leaving little room for doubt. Other cultural dimensions may also have a hand in explaining differences found between cultures. For instance, although the United States ranks low on uncertainty avoidance, European managers working for US multinationals often complain about the formal reporting systems, and volume of written policies and procedures that come down from headquarters.

This is perhaps more understandable given the contractual view of employment in the United States, an instrumental view of the firm, and low-context communication. All of these dimensions encourage a high level of explicitness which is evident in the ubiquitous standard operating procedures. Policies and job descriptions are thus written down and standardized so that anyone can perform them. Information is embedded in the system not in the person, as the organization is thought to exist independently from its members. This might seem contrary to the primacy of the individual, but in fact it is this standardization which allows individuals to move easily in and out of jobs/organizations and guarantees their career mobility in the village market. Also, given US commitment to universalism, rules and procedures are necessary to assure that all people are treated equally.[26]

A comparison of British and German firms[27] showed that all the British firms had detailed job descriptions while only one of the German firms did. This seems contrary to expectations, given the respective attitudes to uncertainty avoidance in the two countries (Germany high, Britain low). However, as German managers are specialists and tend to stay longer in one job, job descriptions are well-internalized, and there is less of a need to formalize them.

On the other hand, British managers are generalists, and tend to rotate jobs more often. One study found that in matched companies twenty-five out of thirty British managers had changed jobs within four years, compared with ten out of thirty German managers.[28] Therefore job descriptions are formalized to provide general guidelines to new incumbents.

Furthermore, British managers had a higher tolerance for mismatch between written expectations and actual responsibilities and thus did not feel constrained to follow the job descriptions. German resistance to written descriptions stemmed from the desire to preserve flexibility. Unlike the British managers, the German managers would have felt uncomfortable with any divergence between written procedures and practice (uncertainty).

Procedures or job descriptions are less likely to be made explicit where communication is more embedded in relationships and in situations (high context). Japanese managers tend to have broader general knowledge of the company, which is often tacit, having been gained through observation and on-the-job experience, like a craft.[29] In addition, tasks are assigned to groups not individuals, and individual accountability remains vague. This creates a stronger link between people, the group, and the organization, making knowledge company-specific, thereby reducing career mobility outside the organization, keeping it all in the family.

Systems and controls

Control systems also reflect different cultural assumptions regarding relationships with people (in terms of power and human nature) and relationship with nature (uncertainty and control). For example, French managers indicate that the most important function for a manager is to control, while British managers say it is to coordinate.[30] This reflects different attitudes towards power. For the French, control derives from the hierarchy; for the British, coordination is achieved through persuasion and negotiation, since the boss is not seen as all-powerful.

Furthermore, the nature of control depends on assumptions regarding human nature. When employees are seen as capable and self-directed (Theory Y),[31] there is more reliance on communication, rather than direct supervision. When managers assume that workers are basically lazy and need to be directed by others (Theory X), they are more likely to set up tight control processes.

Different types of control – input, throughout, and output – are also evident across cultures. The French are particularly careful about recruiting future senior managers from the top schools. This reflects input control – choosing the best and the brightest – and then assuming that they will manage and produce results. German companies are less concerned with hiring elites than with developing managers through rigorous apprenticeships and in-depth job-specific experience. The focus on detailed plans and operational controls also reflects the importance of throughput controls. In the United States and Britain, the emphasis is on budgets, financial controls, and reporting procedures, which reflects more output control.

This can be seen in different ideas regarding the purpose of budgets. One comparative study[32] of managers in US and French subsidiaries of the same firm found that for the American managers, budgets were treated as useful tools which provided concrete objectives against which performance could be measured. French managers, on the other hand, were more concerned with the overall logic and perfection of the budgeting system. These differences reflect American managers' confidence in their ability to control events by being pragmatic (instrumental) and results (achievement)-oriented, while French managers rely more on their analytic (Cartesian) capability, or the quality of thinking.

Planning practices also reflect underlying cultural assumptions. A study by Horovitz[33] comparing planning practices in the United Kingdom, Germany and France found that planning practices in the United Kingdom were more strategic in focus, more long term (six year horizon), with more participation in the process. In Germany, planning was more operational (including stringent, detailed one year plans), more short term (three year horizon), with little participation from the ranks. In France, planning was also more short term (less than half of the firms had long-range planning), more administrative (three year financial forecasts), and also less participative. The shorter term and the more operational/administrative orientation reflects the need to limit uncertainty to more manageable time frames and with more concrete outcomes. Thus the need to reduce uncertainty and to impose controls will result in planning that is more operational than strategic, more short term, and less participative.

Information and communication

Organizations must process information in order to make decisions, to communicate policies and procedures, and to coordinate across units. Yet what kind of information is sought or heeded, how information circulates, and what information is shared with whom, are likely to reflect cultural preferences for hierarchy, formalization, and participation.

For example, French companies are often characterized by French managers as *cloisonné* (compartmentalized), very clearly structured vertically as well as horizontally. This makes very clear the personal roles and responsibility, privileges and obligations, and hence the degree of discretion in performing one's job.[34] Thus the flow of information between groups is limited.

Furthermore, given the view of organization as a social system based on relationships, information may not be readily shared as it is viewed as personal, not public. Information is passed through personal connections. According to one French manager, "Information which is widely distributed is obviously useless".[35] In addition, the political nature of French organizations encourages information to be seen as a source of power, and therefore not easily given away.

For these reasons, it is not surprising that informal communication assumes considerable importance in French companies. A survey in the *Nouvel Economiste*[36] found that information was more likely obtained from rumours than from one's immediate boss.

Informal channels compensate for the centralized, formalized, and limited participative nature of information flows.

In contrast, managers in Sweden, which is more egalitarian and more tolerant of uncertainty, pay very little attention to formal structure or hierarchy. Communication patterns are much more open and informal. This is supported in the research findings of André Laurent that Swedish managers were far less inhibited than their French counter-parts about bypassing the hierarchical line.[37] Given the Swedish view of organizations as instrumental rather than socio-political, there is a greater willingness to share information with anyone who has an interest in it. Information can be put to use; its value is instrumental, not social.

The Swedish insistence on transparency, or the open sharing of information, created initial difficulties for Electrolux when they acquired Italian company, Zanussi.[38] The Italian managers and labor unions, although first surprised by this transparency, came to respect and trust the "Viking" acquirers because of it. Nevertheless, Zanussi managers had trouble unlearning the previous habit of keeping information to themselves as a way of preserving power.[39]

In Japanese companies, intensive and extensive discussion is encouraged at all levels both within (among employees) and outside (with suppliers and customers) the organization. The adaptability of Japanese companies is often attributed to this cross-boundary, open flow of information. By maximizing the informal exchange of information, Japanese firms are able to generate and leverage knowledge, to create a "learning company".[40]

Consider the special case of Kao, the Japanese competitor of Proctor & Gamble and Unilever.[41] CEO Dr. Maruta strongly believes that,

> If everyone discusses on an equal footing, there is nothing that cannot be resolved . . . [As such,] the organization was designed to "run as a flowing system" which would stimulate interaction and the spread of ideas in every direction and at every level . . . [Thus] organizational boundaries and titles were abolished.

Kao's head office is indeed designed in such a way as to encourage the cross-fertilization of ideas.

> On the 10th floor, known as the top management floor, sat the Chairman, the President, four executive vice presidents, and a pool of secretaries. A large part of the floor was open space, with one large conference table and two smaller ones, and chairs, blackboards and overhead projectors strewn around; this was known as the Decision Space, where all discussions with and among the top management took place. Anyone passing, including the President, could sit down and join in any discussion on any topic . . . This layout was duplicated on the other floors . . . Workplaces looked like large rooms; there were no partitions, but again tables and chairs for spontaneous or planned discussions at which everyone contributed as equals. Access was free to all, and any manager could thus find himself sitting round the table next to the President, who was often seen waiting in line in Kao's Tokyo cafateria.

Furthermore, any employee can retrieve data on sales or product development, the latest findings from R&D, details of yesterday's production and inventory at every plant, and can even check up on the President's expense account.

100

Thus office design, building layout, and information technology can encourage managers to share information or to keep it to themselves, and can facilitate whether communication channels are open and multiple, or limited to a one-to-one basis, serial, and secretive. The Japanese scientists from Toshiba, assigned to a joint venture with IBM and Siemens, found it unproductive to be in separate little rooms. So they spent most of their time standing in the halls discussing ideas.[42] The German scientists preferred privacy.

This use of physical space and the consequent patterns of interaction are cultural artifacts which reveal different beliefs regarding the optimal degree of hierarchy, formalization, and level of participation. These beliefs influence the flow of information and communication within companies in different countries. Digging deeper, we find differences in the assumptions regarding the use of information under conditions of uncertainty, whether people are seen as trustworthy and capable, and whether information is used to preserve power or to be shared. In addition we find the underlying cultural meaning of information as serving instrumental versus political purposes.

Decision-making

The nature of decision-making is also culturally rooted. Who makes the decision, who is involved in the process, and where decisions are made (in formal committees or more informally in the hallways and corridors, or on the golf course) reflect different cultural assumptions. In turn, the very nature of the decision-making processes as well as different time horizons influences the speed with which decisions are taken.

It is perhaps not surprising that in countries such as Sweden and Germany, where power and hierarchy are played down, there is the greatest evidence of participation in decision-making. In Sweden, perhaps furthest along on the road of industrial democracy, union leaders often sit on the management board and are involved in making major strategic decisions, including decisions to relocate factories abroad. Everyone has the right to contribute to a decision. Decision-making means seeking consensus.

In The Netherlands and Germany, the works council, or labor representation, also plays an important role in deciding business affairs. The strong commitment to consensus, social equality, and human welfare reveals assumptions regarding collectivism and the importance of the quality of working life.[43]

In contrast, companies in cultures which emphasize power and hierarchy are more likely to centralize decision-making. In France, for example, the government plays an important role in determining company strategy and policy, often choosing top management. This has earned France the reputation of being "the father of industrial policy".[44] The PDG (CEO) may well have more experience in government than in business. Furthermore, he (in rare cases she) is expected to make decisions and is respected for it. Power is jealously guarded by each actor, such that management and unions often end up in violent confrontation, neither willing to concede to the other party. While industry is currently being privatized, and employees have become more involved through participation and through quality circles, French management is criticized for remaining centralized and elitist.[45]

The difference in decision-making between Nordic and Latin European firms was sharply illustrated when Sweden's Electrolux acquired Italy's Zanussi. The Swedish top

101

management was often frustrated in its efforts to get Italian managers to arrive at a consensus among themselves in solving problems. The Italian managers, in turn, expected the senior management to settle problems such as transfer pricing between Italian product lines and the UK sales offices. According to one senior Italian manager, ". . . the key in this complex international organization is to have active mechanisms in place to create – and force – the necessary integration". However, the Swedish CEO preferred to let them solve their own problems; "Force is a word that is rarely heard in the Electrolux culture".[46]

Japanese firms, with their collectivist orientation, take yet another approach to decision-making. In the Japanese *Ringi* system, petitions (decision proposals) are circulated requiring individuals to "sign on". Signing, however, does not necessarily mean approval, but means that if the decision is taken, the person agrees to support it. While the opinions of superiors are sought, these opinions tend to be more implicit than explicit. Therefore, Japanese managers devote extra time in trying to "read their boss" to find out what is actually desired. In this way, Japanese firms reconcile the importance placed on both collectivism and the hierarchy.

Northern European and American managers often complain about the "slowness" with which Japanese companies *make* decisions. Japanese managers, on the other hand, often complain about the time it takes American and European companies to *implement* decisions. Although in Japan more time is taken to reach decisions, once the decision is taken it can be implemented more quickly as everyone has been involved and understands why the decision has been taken, what has been decided, and what needs to be done. Americans may pride themselves on being "decisive", making decisions quickly on their own. However, they then have to spend more time back at the office selling these decisions, explaining why, what, and how, and gathering support. Inevitably, implementation takes longer.

These different approaches to decision-making therefore have repercussions on the time taken to reach decisions, even in countries that appear to share cultural assumptions. For example, one study comparing strategic decision-making in Sweden and Britain demonstrated that it took twice as long in Sweden, not just to identify strategic issues (37 months versus 17 months), but also to decide what to do about those issues (23 months versus 13 months).[47]

These differences in the amount of time for reaching decisions was explained by the degree of involvement of others in the process and desire for consensus. In Sweden, more participants are involved in contributing information and more time is taken to collect information and compare alternatives. Also, strategic decisions were more often taken by the management board (a collective) in Sweden rather than, as in Britain, by the Managing Director (CEO), an individual. The Swedish consensus-driven approach (which includes government and union officials) results in the tendency to appoint commissions or special working groups which are often time-consuming.

The speed of decision-making reflects not just the process, but also the prevailing attitude towards time. Many Western managers complain that their sense of urgency is not shared in other parts of the world where the attitude seems to be "what's the big hurry?". Yet in Asia and the Middle East, a decision made quickly may indicate that it has little importance. Otherwise, more time for consideration, reflection, and discussion would be warranted. Thus taking quick decisions is not universally admired as a sign of determination and strong leadership but can be regarded as a sign of immaturity and irresponsibility, or even stupidity.

Furthermore, in cultures where the past plays an important role, traditions cannot be dismissed so quickly. Therefore, decisions need to be taken and implemented more slowly. While this may be more obvious in Asian cultures, important differences exist between countries with otherwise similar cultural profiles. American managers, who are less tradition-bound, may perceive European managers as rather slow in making decisions.

British society, for example, has been described as conservative and tradition-bound, with a marked reluctance to change.[48] The slower speed of decision-making in British firms is also attributed to its being more decentralized (assigned to standing committees) and more informal (guided by unwritten rules and procedures which are maintained through personal connections).[49]

A study comparing strategic decision-making in British and Brazilian firms found that Brazilian executives tend to take decisions more quickly.[50] This was attributed to their centralized power which enables them to take decisions individually. Also according to Brazilian managers, the greater perceived uncertainty and lack of control over the environment contributes to a strong sense of urgency (or as referred to in Table 4.3 "immediatism") and need for change.

Thus differences in approaches to decision-making can be attributed to multiple, interacting cultural dimensions. In addition to cultural preferences for hierarchy, and formalization, assumptions regarding time and change are important considerations in *how* and *how quickly* decisions will be made. In addition, the level of participation in decision-making may be similar but for different reasons. In some countries, such as the United States, participation may be seen as a way of integrating different individual perspectives and preserving everyone's right to decide. In other cultures, such as Japan, it is a way to preserve group harmony and relationships, while in The Netherlands and Sweden it serves to promote social welfare. This results in different underlying cultural reasons for empowerment.

In Sweden where interested parties have the "right to negotiate" (*forhandlingsratt*), and in Germany where they have the "right to decide" (*Mitbestimmung*),[51] "empowerment" signifies power sharing in order to arrive at a consensus regarding collective well-being. In countries, such as the United States, where you are supposed to be self-sufficient and take care of yourself (high degree of individualism), labor and management relationships are more characterized by distributive bargaining. Each actor insists on safeguarding their own interests at the expense of the others and having the resources, support, and authority to pursue individual well-being independently.[52]

Transferability of best practice? Alternative approaches

By pulling together the various experiences of managers and more systematic research studies, we have demonstrated how culture affects organization structure and process.

103

We have proposed different profiles or models of organizing which evolve from different underlying cultural assumptions. This raises questions about what is considered to be "universal wisdom" and the transferability of "best practice". For the most part, arguments for transferability are in line with convergence notions which claim universality; "Management is management and best practice can be transferred anywhere". This was the rationale behind the 1980s rush to copy Japanese management practice and current rash of American-style restructuring and re-engineering.

Those that question transferability point to differences in the cultural or national (institutional) context. The culturalists question the effectiveness with which Japanese quality circles, say, can be transferred to individualist countries, such as the United States and France. The institutionalists stress the nature of ownership, and the role of government, and of labour unions in promoting such practices. Whether the success of Japanese management practices is due to cultural or institutional factors remains a matter of ongoing debate.[53]

The transfer of best practice nevertheless assumes, to some extent, universality. For example, matrix structures were heralded in the 1970s as a means of combining the benefits of product, geographic, and functional structures. In theory, decentralized decision-making, overlapping roles and responsibilities, and multiple information channels were all supposed to enable the organization to capture and analyze external complexity, to overcome internal parochialism, and to enhance response time and flexibility.[54]

While matrix management may have promised more than it could deliver, Laurent found deep resistance to matrix structures among both French and German managers, but for different reasons.[55] For the French, matrix structures violated the principle of "unity of command" and clear hierarchical reporting relationships. The idea of having two bosses was undesirable, as it created divided loyalties and caused unwelcome conflict. On the other hand, German managers resisted matrix structures, as they frustrated the need for clear-cut structure, information channels, roles and responsibilities. Again, the principles underlying matrix management ran counter to the German need to reduce uncertainty.

Thus cultural differences often undermine the best intentions and the assumed rationality of best practices. Different logics of organization exist in different countries, which can be equally effective, if not more so, given different societal contexts. In fact, there seems to be little doubt that some contexts are more favorable to the success of certain management practices, and it need not always be the country where that practice originated. Japanese quality-control methods originally came from the American gurus, Demming and Juran. Quality circles were the Japanese value-added.

Effectively transferring management structures and processes relies on the ability to recognize their inherent assumptions and to compare them with the cultural assumptions of the potential host country recipient. Countries also differ in their readiness to adopt or adapt foreign models, or to manifest a NIH (not invented here) syndrome. Throughout their history, the Japanese have borrowed models from China and then Europe. Other countries, such as Germany, may be more resistant to importing alien management practices. In eastern European countries, such as Poland, and in the developing Asian

104

countries, such as Thailand, the eagerness to adopt foreign models is tempered by the desire to develop their own models which are more culturally appropriate.

For example, managers in eastern Europe may reject "team" approaches looking for strong leadership and a sense of clear direction in an effort to break with the more collective approach of the past.[56] Despite the prevailing wisdom that organizations need to be less hierarchical and more flexible, some managers argue that faced with competitive threats and conditions of economic decline or instability, greater centralization and stronger controls are needed.

Indeed, companies in Hong Kong, Japan, and Singapore, where the hierarchy remains firmly in place, have performed well in industries, such as banking, which are facing turbulent environments. Here, other value orientations, not readily apparent in Western business, may be at work. For example, when trying to replicate Hofstede's original study in China, another dimension was discovered – "Confucian dynamism", thrift, persistence and a long-term perspective. This added dimension was considered to account for the competitiveness of the "Five Asian Dragons": China, Hong Kong, Taiwan, Japan, and South Korea.[57]

Consider this testimony regarding the entrepreneurial, family model characteristic of the overseas Chinese business community which has been quite successful whether transplanted to Malaysia or Canada.

> . . . The Confucian tradition of hard work, thrift and respect for one's social network may provide continuity with the right twist for today's fast-changing markets. And the central strategic question for all current multinationals – be they Chinese, Japanese or Western – is how to gather and integrate power through many small units. The evolution of a worldwide web of relatively small Chinese businesses, bound by undeniable strong cultural links, offers a working model for the future.[58]

Whatever the model of the future, be it team management or network organizations, we need to consider how culture may facilitate or hinder their diffusion. Will the more collective culture of Russia facilitate the team approach, while the greater relationship orientation of Chinese culture facilitates creating networks? Could it be that the greater emphasis on the task and the individual, which prevails in the performance management approach, will actually hinder American firms in their attempts to become more team- and network-oriented?

Given recent trends in the United States and Europe towards participative management and empowerment, the role of the leadership is changing. Rather than the more authoritarian notion of being the "boss", the role model is that of the "coach". Rather than directing and controlling, the new role calls for facilitating and developing. Notions of empowerment and the leader as coach, however, may not readily transfer.

Take, for example, two items from the Management Questionnaire designed by Laurent regarding the role of the boss (hierarchy) and of power as shown in Figure 4.5. Comparing the responses of managers attending training seminars from 1990 to 1994 with the results reported in 1980, we find some signs of convergence. According to self-reports, managers are becoming less authoritarian and more concerned with achieving objectives than obtaining power. Nevertheless, while country differences may have eroded, the different country rankings remain in place.

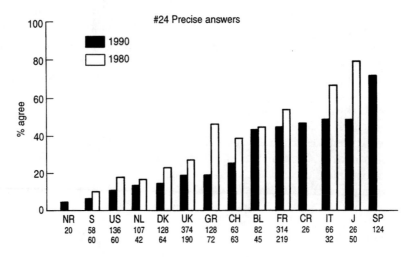

It is important for a manager to have at hand precise answers to most of the questions his/her subordinates may raise about their work.

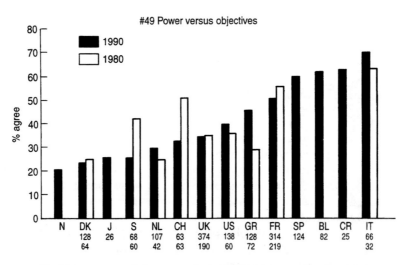

Most managers seem to be more motivated by obtaining power than by achieving objectives.

Figure 4.5 Convergence? (Reproduced by permission of A. Laurent.)

Even in countries which supposedly do not put much stock in hierarchy, such as The Netherlands and the United Kingdom, this new leadership behavior may be difficult to achieve. Therefore, what will that mean for countries in Asia where the hierarchy is still revered? What would the Asian version of empowerment look like? Perhaps there are different means of achieving this end. In the case of Japanese firms, the hierarchy is clearly, albeit implicitly, present. Nevertheless, there are apparently high levels of participation.

And as hierarchies collapse and as cooperation between units becomes more of a necessity, there is a greater need for negotiation and persuasion. Managers will increasingly have to elicit the cooperation of people over whom they have no formal authority. In fact this may demand a more political view of organizations to which Latin firms may be more attuned.

These are the challenges facing many companies as they remodel their corporate structures. They must not lose sight of the impact of national culture in their search for a model of organization that can respond best to the demands of the rapidly changing business context, and the pressures for internationalization. They must also recognize that the "best models" are not necessarily "home grown", but that other ways of organizing may be equally, if not more, effective.

Notes

1. Crozier, M. (1964) *The Bureaucratic Phenomenon*, Chicago: University of Chicago Press, p. 210.
2. Pugh, D.S., Hickson, D.J., Hinings, C.R., and Turner, C. (1969) "The context of organization structure", *Administrative Science Quarterly*, 14, 91–114; Miller, G.A. (1987) "Meta-analysis and the culture-free hypothesis", *Organization Studies*, 8(4), 309–25; Hickson, D.J. and McMillan, I. (eds) (1981) *Organization and Nation: The Aston Programme IV*, Farnborough: Gower.
3. Burns, T. and Stalker, G.M. (1961) *The Management of Innovation*, London: Tavistock.
4. Child, J. (1981) "Culture, contingency and capitalism in the cross-national study of organizations" in L.L. Cummings and B.M. Staw (eds) *Research in Organizational Behavior*, Vol. 3, 303–356, Greenwich, CT: JAI Press; Scott, W.R. (1987) "The adolescence of institutional theory", *Administrative Science Quarterly*, 32, 493–511; Lincoln, J.R., Hanada, M. and McBride, K. (1986) "Organizational structures in Japanese and US manufacturing", *Administrative Science Quarterly*, 31, 338–64.
5. Weber, M. (1947) *The Theory of Social and Economic Organization*, New York: Free Press; Fayol, H. (1949) *General Industrial Management*, London: Pitman; Taylor, F. (1947, first published 1912) *Scientific Management*, New York: Harper & Row.
6. Kogut, B. (1991) "Country capabilities and the permeability of borders", *Strategic Management Journal*, 12, 33–47; Kogut, B. and Parkinson, D. (1993) "The diffusion of American organizing principles to Europe" in B. Kogut (ed.) *Country Competitiveness: Technology and the Organizing of Work*, Ch. 10, New York: Oxford University Press, 179–202; Guillen, M. (1994) "The age of eclecticism: Current organizational trends and the evolution of managerial models", *Sloan Management Review*, Fall, 75–86.
7. Westney, D.E. (1987) *Imitation and Innovation*, Cambridge, MA: Harvard University Press.
8. Hofstede, G. (1980) *Cultures Consequences*, Beverly Hills, CA: Sage; Hofstede, G. (1991) *Cultures and Organizations: Software of the Mind*, London: McGraw-Hill.

9. Hofstede, G. (1980) "Motivation, leadership, and organization: Do American theories apply abroad?", *Organizational Dynamics*, Summer, 42–63.

10. Ronen, S. and Shenekar, O. (1985) "Clustering countries on attitudinal dimensions: A review and synthesis", *Academy of Management Review*, 10(3), 435–54.

11. Burns and Stalker, *Op. cit.*

12. *Ibid.*

12. Stevens, O.J., cited in Hofstede, G. (1991) *Cultures and Organizations*, London: McGraw-Hill, 140–2.

14. Brossard, A. and Maurice, M. (1976) "Is there a universal model of organization structure?", *International Studies of Management and Organization*, 6, 11–45; Horovitz, J. (1980) *Top Management Control in Europe*, London: Macmillan; Stewart, R., Barsoux, J.-L., Kieser, A., Ganter, D. and Walgenbach, P. (1994) *Managing in Britain and Germany*, London: Macmillan.

15. Stewart *et al.*, *Op. cit.*

16. *Ibid.*

17. Redding, S.G. and Pugh, D.S. (1986) "The formal and the informal: Japanese and Chinese organization structures" in S. Clegg, D. Dunphy, and S.G. Redding (eds) *The Enterprise and Management in East Asia*, Hong Kong: Center of Asian Studies, University of Hong Kong, 153–168; Vertinsky, I., Tse, D.K., Wehrung, D.A. and Lee, K. (1990) "Organization design and management norms: A comparative study of managers' perceptions in the People's Republic of China, Hong Kong and Canada", *Journal of Management*, 16(4), 853–67.

18. Wong, G.Y.Y. and Birnbaum-More, P.H. (1994) "Culture, context and structure: A test on Hong Kong banks", *Organization Studies*, 15(1), 99–123.

19. Kao, J. (1993) "The worldwide web of Chinese business", *Harvard Business Review*, March–April, 24–35.

20. Laurent, A. (1983) "The cultural diversity of western conception of management", *International Studies of Management and Organization*, 13(1–2), 75–96.

21. Crozier, M. (1964) *The Bureaucratic Phenomenon*, Chicago: University of Chicago Press.

22. Crozier, M. and Friedberg, E. (1977) *L'Acteur et le système: Les contraintes de l'action collective*, Paris: Seuil.

23. Trompenaars, F. (1993) *Riding the Waves of Culture*, London: Nicholas Brealey.

24. Selmer, J. (1988) Presentation, International Conference on Personnel and Human Resource Management Conference, Singapore.

25. Amado, G. and Brasil, H.V. (1991) "Organizational behaviors and cultural context: The Brazilian 'Jeitiñho' ", *International Studies of Management and Organization*, 21(3), 38–61.

26. Hampden-Turner, C. and Trompenaars, F. (1994) *Seven Cultures of Capitalism*, London: Piatkus.

27. Stewart *et al.*, *Op. cit.*

28. *Ibid.*

29. Nonaka, I. (1991) "The knowledge-creating company", *Harvard Business Review*, November–December, 96–104.

30. Laurent, A. (1986) "The cross-cultural puzzle of global human resource management", *Human Resource Management*, 25(1), 91—102.

31. McGregor, D. (1960) *The Nature of Human Enterprise*, New York: McGraw-Hill.

32. Perret, M.S. (1988) "The impact of cultural differences in budgeting", unpublished Ph.D. dissertation, University of Western Ontario.

33. Horovitz, *Op. cit.*

34. D'Iribarne, P. (1989) *La logique de l'honneur*, Paris: Seuil.

35. Orleman, P.A. (1992) The global corporation: Managing across cultures, Masters thesis, University of Pennsylvania.

36. "La communication dans l'entreprise", *Nouvel Economiste*, May 12, 1980, 42–7.

108

37. Laurent, *Op. cit.*
38. Haspeslagh, P. and Ghoshal, S. (1992) *Electrolux Zanussi*, INSEAD case.
39. Lorenz, C. (1989) "The Italian connection – a stark contrast in corporate manners", *Financial Times*, June 23, 20.
40. Nonaka, *Op. cit.*; Schütte, H. (1993) "Competing and cooperating with Japanese firms", Euro–Asia Center, INSEAD.
41. Ghoshal, S. and Butler, C. (1991) KAO Corporation, INSEAD case.
42. Browning, E.S. (1994) "Computer chip project brings rivals together, but the cultures clash", *Wall Street Journal*, May 3, A7.
43. Fry, J.A. (ed.) (1979) *Limits of the Welfare State: Critical Views on Post-war Sweden*, Farnborough: Saxon House.
44. Aubert, N., Ramantsoa, B. and Reitter, R. (1984) "Nationalizations, managerial power, and societal change", Working paper Harvard Business School.
45. Schmidt, V.A. (1993) "An end to French economic exceptionalism: The transformation of business under Mitterand", *California Management Review*, Fall, 75–98.
46. Lorenz, *Op. cit.*
47. Axelsson, R., Cray, D., Mallory, G.R. and Wilson, D.C. (1991) "Decision style in British and Swedish organizations: A comparative examination of strategic decision making", *British Journal of Management*, 2, 67–79.
48. Tayeb, M.H. (1988) *Organizations and National Culture: A Comparative Analysis*, London: Sage.
49. Mallory, G.R., Butler, R.J., Cray, D., Hickson, D.J. and Wilson, D.C. (1983) "Implanted decision making: American owned firms in Britain", *Journal of Management Studies*, 20, 191–211; Fry, *Op. cit.*
50. Oliveira, B. and Hickson, D.J. (1991) "Cultural bases of strategic decision making: A Brazilian and English comparison", presented at EGOS conference, Vienna.
51. Lawrence, P. and Spybey, T. (1986) *Management and Society in Sweden*, London: Routledge and Kegan Paul.
52. Irene Rodgers, Cross-cultural consultant, personal communication.
53. See Whitley, R.D. (ed.) (1992) *Business Systems in East Asia: Firms, Markets and Societies*, London: Sage.
54. Davis, S. and Lawrence, P.R. (1977) *Matrix*, Reading, MA: Addison-Wesley.
55. Laurent, A. (1981) "Matrix organization and Latin cultures", *International Studies of Management and Organization*, 10(4), 101–14.
56. Cyr, D.J. and Schneider, S.C. (1996) "Implications for learning: human resources management in east–west joint ventures", *Organization Studies*, 17(2), 207–226.
57. Hofstede, G. and Bond, M.H. (1988) "The Confucius connection: From cultural roots to economic growth", *Organizational Dynamics*, 16, 4–21; see also Hofstede, G. (1991) *Cultures and Organizations: Software of the Mind*, London: McGraw-Hill.
58. Kao, *Op. cit.*, p. 36.

CHAPTER FIVE

Culture and strategy

It is as if there were a common set of issues in organizations that some of us choose to call culture and others choose to call strategy.

Karl Weick[1]

The close link between culture and strategy, as noted above, was recognized by Karl Weick, a renowned organizational scholar, when he provided a set of statements to readers and asked them to decide whether the first word in each should be "strategy" or "culture". He demonstrated that by substituting the word culture in each statement (which were in fact traditional definitions of strategy), the meaning of the text remained unchanged.

Indeed, as stated earlier the definition of **culture** (provided in this book) as solutions to problems of external adaptation and internal integration could be taken as a fitting definition of **strategy**. In devising and implementing strategies, organizations need to assess their external environments as well as their internal capabilities. Strategic decisions are, in effect, intended to achieve external adaptation. Implementing these decisions requires configuring internal resources, including people, to achieve the necessary internal integration.

This chapter addresses the questions: How does national culture affect strategy? To what extent do different approaches to strategy, different ways of thinking about strategy, reflect different underlying cultural assumptions? Faced with similar business environments, how do managers from different cultures perceive and respond to that environment? In what ways does culture affect not only what decisions are taken (content), but also the way that these decisions are made (process)? And, in what ways does culture impact the interaction between strategic content and process? Having addressed these questions we then consider the implications for competitive analysis, for anticipating the strategic moves of different national competitors, and for the roles of headquarters and subsidiaries in both formulating and implementing strategy.

The cultural roots of strategy

Interest in strategy dates far back in history, often discussed in the context of war and the military. From the Greek *strategos* (commander of the army), to military maneuvers described in *The Art of War*,[2] and the personal maneuvers of Machiavelli's *Prince*,[3] strategies have been devised to achieve national or personal gain. For organizations too, strategy is considered to be the means for achieving corporate objectives.

In business, the notion of strategy became popularized in the 1960s when companies faced increased competition and limited resources. Strategic planning armies were mobilized to centralize and formalize the process. For companies like GE and Shell, strategic planning was sacrosanct, becoming something of a religious ritual. According to one former Shell executive, "Managers concerned with such [planning] systems fight a continuous battle to prevent them degenerating into a 'corporate rain dance' ".[4]

Corporate soldiers were trained to analyze organizational *strengths* and *weaknesses* and environmental *opportunities* and *threats* (SWOT) in order to create the appropriate strategic alignment, or "fit".[5] Strategic management weapons/tools, such as the Boston Consulting Group (BCG) matrices, were called upon to analyze the market (in terms of growth and position) and to assist in making strategic decisions as to where to attack (invest or divest). The language of SWOT analyses, cash cows, dogs, and stars became part of the shared corporate jargon.

Later on, models based on Industrial Organization economics, such as that of Michael Porter,[6] became the rage, and managers were off analyzing barriers to entry and exit, substitutability, desperately seeking other sources of competitive advantage. More recently, the search has been for "core competencies" and "strategic intent" with abundant examples taken from the Japanese management practices of Canon, NEC, and Matsushita.[7]

These strategic planning departments, rituals, tools, models, and jargon, in effect, represent cultural artifacts. The waves of fads and fashions which have carried strategic (as well as other) management practices promote certain sets of beliefs and values, such as "analytic rationality". However, it is important to understand the assumptions underlying these practices, beliefs, and values in order to question whether they have, in fact, the same meaning in different cultures. We need to consider alternative models of strategy formulation and implementation that may be equally viable. This has implications for developing strategies at the local and global levels, for communicating head office as well as local strategies, and for anticipating the strategic moves of local and global competitors and partners.

The rational/economic view

Many of the strategic management frameworks mentioned above, including the prescribed tools and techniques, affirm the belief and value of a "rational analytic" approach. This approach takes for granted certain assumptions. It assumes, for example, that the environment and the organization are objective realities that are similarly perceived and analyzed by intelligent managers.

111

Yet those managers making strategic decisions often find themselves confronted with environmental uncertainty, ill-structured problems, and socio-political processes.[8] In fact, rather than taking them as objective realities, it can be argued that both environments and organizations are *subjective* realities that are perceived and enacted in different ways.[9] This means that managers see different things, create different realities, and then act accordingly. Thus multiple interpretations of and responses to supposedly similar situations are likely. As such, national culture can play an important role in determining different types of strategic behavior.[10]

The rational analytic approach also assumes that managers making strategic decisions follow a similar route, gathering all relevant information, generating all possible alternatives, evaluating the costs and benefits of each alternative, choosing the optimal solution, and then acting upon it. While widely acknowledged that managers and organizations are limited in their capacity to digest all this information, thus subject to "bounded rationality",[11] the precise ways in which rationality in decision-making is limited, or more specifically culture-bound, have remained unexplored. In other words, how does culture influence the way managers gather and interpret information, choose between decision alternatives, and establish criteria for action?[12]

Clearly, much of the discussion to date regarding strategic management has been based on beliefs that environments and organizations are objective realities and that strategic decision-making is a rational and analytic process. Digging deeper, we discover underlying assumptions that environments are intelligible and predictable, and that by taking action, or doing, strategic objectives can be achieved. This functionalist, instrumental view of the world, however, may be challenged in other cultures.

Another view of strategy

Consider the speech given by the CEO of a major international bank, managed in accordance with Islamic principles.

> Strategy is a dynamic process, not a static perception, which is energized through feelings. It is not a bundle of facts, figures, and ideas assembled in order by the logical mind. Planning is the reflection of the flow of collective psyche synthesized with Purpose.

Underlying this notion of strategy we find dramatically different cultural assumptions. It highlights the role of feelings, or emotions, not just analytic rationality. It questions the nature of truth as determined by facts and figures, and logic, rather than by spiritual purpose. Furthermore, it views strategy as a collective process, and as dynamic – what is needed is to go with the flow.

Different cultural assumptions are also clearly evident in the approach of Matsushita. In 1932, the CEO announced a **250 year** corporate plan, divided into 10 segments of 25 years. He then codified the company creed, known as the "Seven Spirits of Matsushita", to explicitly articulate the following beliefs: harmony between man and nature, the need for co-prosperity and coexistence, the unlimited potential of people to grow and change, that the goal to improve life is never attainable, and that profit as an objective is a *means*

112

not an *end*.[13] Here, underlying assumptions regarding the relationship with nature (harmony), human nature (unlimited potential), and the nature of human relationships (collective prosperity and existence) are easily surfaced.

According to Pascale,[14] coauthor of *The Art of Japanese Management*, Japanese companies adopt a broader notion of strategy. They challenge the Western view of strategic management, considering these rational analytic approaches to be "myopic" and "an oversimplification of reality".

> The Japanese are somewhat distrustful of a single "strategy", for in their view any idea that focuses attention does so at the expense of peripheral vision. They strongly believe that *peripheral vision* is essential to discerning changes in the customer, the technology or competition, and is the key to corporate survival over the long haul. They regard any propensity to be driven by a single-minded strategy as a weakness. (pp. 47–48)
>
> The Japanese have a particular discomfort with strategic concepts. While they do not reject ideas such as the experience curve or portfolio theory outright they regard them as a stimulus to perception.
>
> Western consultants, academics, and executives express a preference for oversimplifications of reality and cognitively linear explanations of events . . . We tend to impute coherence and purposive rationality to events when the opposite may be closer to the truth. (p. 57)

Here too, assumptions regarding the nature of truth and reality are different: that reality cannot be boxed into two-by-two matrices; and that truth cannot be determined by simplistic theories of cause and effect.

But other Western management scholars have also challenged the rational analytic approach. Consider these comments by Henry Mintzberg, who has been a rather outspoken opponent to the "strategic planning" approach. "Strategy formation is a process of learning only partially under the control of conscious thought . . . Strategies emerge informally, sometimes gradually, sometimes spontaneously, usually in a collective process."[15] Rather than planned, strategy is considered as *emergent*, or as *evolutionary*.[16] This view assumes that managers have less control over their environments which are difficult to know, and that taking action does not necessarily make things happen. Strategy unfolds in response to current events, within the historical as well as organizational context (structures and procedures). Thus the "intended" strategy and the "emergent" one may not necessarily coincide. Strategies designed at the top and those that emerge through more autonomous activities further down the organization may be more or less loosely coupled. Strategies as such are thought to emerge and to evolve over time, as "a pattern in a stream of decisions".

More recently in the field of strategic management, there has been a growing interest in developing organizational resources and capabilities.[17] These resource-based and core competencies views suggest that building "corporate" character (or developing resource bases) provides the capability and flexibility to respond to environmental events. These approaches reflect different underlying assumptions by placing the emphasis on what the company *is* versus what the company *does* (*being* versus *doing* at the corporate level). The focus is on having the "right stuff", or strategic traits, rather than necessarily making the "right moves", or strategic actions.

The success of Japanese companies such as Canon and NEC is attributed to developing such competencies which enables them to capitalize on unexpected opportunities and to create, or re-create markets. In fact, many Japanese companies have managed to resurrect markets previously written off as mature by Western firms. For example, while Honda entered the mature US motorcycle market intending to sell big bikes to the "tough guy" market, they ended up selling mini-bikes to the "nicest people" (their advertising slogan). "History has it that Honda 'redefined' the U.S. motorcycle industry. In the view of American Honda's start-up team, this was an innovation they backed into – and reluctantly."[18]

Indeed, many American and European companies, such as Xerox and Philips, became concerned when they realized that not only were their markets being invaded, but also that the technologies that they had developed were appearing as Japanese products. The apparent Japanese competitive edge forced companies to reconsider their own way of thinking about strategy. It provided dramatic evidence that strategy could be viewed through different lenses, shaped by different cultural assumptions.

The extensive body of research comparing Japanese and Western companies points to distinctive national patterns in strategic management.[19] Yet the underlying cultural reasons for these differences have not been sufficiently examined. While the emphasis in this chapter is on national culture, industry and corporate cultures also play an important role in determining strategy, which will be discussed further on.

Cultural models of strategy

Cultural assumptions regarding external adaptation are particularly relevant to strategy, as its very purpose is to align the organization with its environment. Assumptions regarding internal integration are relevant to questions such as who is involved and who takes the decision. For example, managers from different countries have different assumptions regarding uncertainty and control, as established in the previous chapter. Consider the potential consequences of these assumptions in the following hypothetical scenarios.

Managers from Nordic and Anglo countries are less likely to see environments as uncertain. They believe that environments can be analyzed and known. They therefore are attracted to analytic tools and techniques such as strategic forecasting or scenario planning. They call for industry reports and market research, and call upon industry experts to provide objective information to assist in making strategic decisions. Armed with this information and decision tools, they have faith in their ability to analyze and to predict their environments which provides a sense of control over the course of events. Thus strategic actions are taken to make things happen.

Managers from countries within Latin Europe or Asia are likely to perceive greater uncertainty when faced with similar environments, and perceive less control over what will happen. Thus they are more inclined to go with the flow, to adapt. Information is gathered through informal channels and personal relationships, and is thus more subjective. They prefer to interpret this information through intense, face-to-face discussion and debate, believing that multiple perspectives, broader involvement, and more extensive information sharing are necessary to comprehend the external uncertainty and ambiguity.[20] More time is required to analyze and to decide how to respond.

Thus assumptions having to do with the relationship with nature (control), human beings (as capable), the nature of truth and reality (facts and figures, logic), and the nature of relationships (the role of the hierarchy and the collective) influence the sources and type of information sought, and the methods of interpreting that information.[21] These assumptions also influence who is involved in the process, experts or colleagues, and the nature of strategic response. Different assumptions lead to different models of strategic management which can be categorized as "controlling" versus "adapting".[22]

In Table 5.1, we present these two models in more detail, albeit oversimplified, as they are intended to represent endpoints on a continuum along which different countries, or

Table 5.1 Cultural models of strategy

CONTROLLING		ADAPTING
Scanning is:		
Active search	├───┼───┼───┼───┤	Monitor
Focused and systematic	├───┼───┼───┤	Broad and sporadic
Centralized (scanning department)	├───┼───┼───┤	Decentralized
Planning is:		
Formalized (systems)	├───┼───┼───┼───┤	Informal (discussion)
Centralized (strategic planning department)	├───┼───┼───┤	Decentralized
Types and sources of information:		
Quantitative	├───┼───┼───┼───┼───┤	Qualitative
Objective	├───┼───┼───┼───┼───┤	Subjective
Impersonal	├───┼───┼───┼───┼───┤	Personal
Interpreting information relies on:		
Formal models and methods (e.g. strategic forecasting)	├───┼───┤	Informal methods ("home grown" models)
Scenario planning	├───┼───┼───┼───┤	Discussion and debate
People involved are:		
Mostly at the top	├───┼───┼───┼───┤	Across the ranks
Experts	├───┼───┼───┼───┤	Employees
Decisions are made:		
Primarily at the top	├───┼───┼───┼───┤	On the front lines
Tend to be political	├───┼───┼───┼───┤	Consensual
Strategic goals and action plans are:		
Clearly defined and articulated	├───┼───┤	Broad and implicit
Explicitly measured and rewarded	├───┼───┤	Vaguely monitored
Time horizons are:		
Short term	├───┼───┼───┼───┤	Long term
Action plans are:		
Sequential	├───┼───┼───┼───┼───┤	Simultaneous

indeed industries and companies, can be positioned accordingly. They are presented as "caricatures" to help surface and decipher the underlying cultural assumptions. These models are intended to help generate hypotheses, and to assist managers to know what questions to ask.

Controlling model

The "controlling" model can be characterized as centralized and formalized. Top management may call in expert consultants to assist in devising strategies. Formal strategic planning units may be established to devise plans to be submitted to top management or the board for deliberation. Formal scanning units may also exist that are responsible for tracking environmental events. Scanning is focused and in-depth in order to obtain the necessary information.

Information is often obtained from industry reports, or consultants, and tends to be quantitative and objective. Forecasting, econometric models, and structured scenarios are used to analyze the information. Based on this information and analysis, top management makes the decisions and then hands them down to be implemented. Implementation entails thorough planning, setting clear and specific targets (milestones), explicit communication of what is to be done and how, persistent follow through, and then linking performance goals with rewards.

What cultural assumptions are embedded in this model? First there is the assumption that the environment can be known (is intelligible and predictable). Specific information can be obtained (by active and focused scanning) and analyzed (interpreted) to reduce environmental uncertainty. Truth is determined by facts and figures manipulated by mathematical models. Strategic vision can be expressed as concrete targets ("$15 billion by the next year 2000"), explicit and tangible (low context). Even the vision of British Airways as "the world's favorite airline" is subject to be measured.

Decisions are taken by those presumed to have the most power or knowledge, namely top management. As the top managers are considered to be rational economic actors, or agents, they are assumed to make the best decisions in line with individual interests. Therefore they need to be held accountable, and controlled by systems (reporting) or supervisory boards. Given different individual interests, the decision-making process is seen as more political.

The monochronic view of time as linear and segmented means that strategic decisions are seen as discrete events, and action steps can be planned within a given timetable. Thus implementation is highly task- and achievement-oriented: concrete actions can be planned and the results measured. According to this perspective, the purpose of strategic management is to achieve control of what happens both outside as well as inside the organization, hence "controlling".

Adapting model

In contrast, the "adapting" model is more decentralized and informal. Responsibility for strategy is diffused throughout the organization. Scanning is broader based and less

116

sytematic. Information is gathered from personal sources, friends and colleagues, and through observation (field visits) and thus tends to be more qualitative and subjective. Information is interpreted through "home grown" or intuitive models. Intense discussion is encouraged involving many people from all levels within the organization. Strategic decisions are expected to be reached through consensus (socially constructed).

Rather than a discrete strategic decision *per se*, a strategic direction tends to emerge. Implementation is then locally determined, keeping within this general strategic frame. Adjustments can then be made to unforeseen events and strategy can be refined on an ongoing basis. Responsibility and accountability are assigned to the collective.

The underlying assumptions in this model are that the environment cannot be readily known or controlled. Therefore the organization must be flexible and prepared to react to unforeseeable environmental events. A broad scan – peripheral vision again – is needed to detect subtle changes in the environment. Personal relationships and interactions are considered key to developing shared understanding, thus information sources are more personal and subjective. Truth and reality, or knowledge, are more likely to be arrived at through a "sixth sense", feelings or intuition. Strategic vision is often vague and philosophical. Strategy implementation is considered to hinge on the development of internal capabilities – knowledge, competencies, and learning – in order to be able to continuously improve, hence "adapting".

Returning to Japan . . .

In order to contrast the adapting and controlling models, let us return to Japan. Pascale explains the initial failure and subsequent success of Honda, as well as other Japanese companies, as follows.

> Their success did not result from a bold insight by a few big brains at the top. On the contrary, success was achieved by senior managers humble enough not to take their initial strategic positions too seriously. What saved Japan's near-failures was the cumulative impact of "little brains" in the form of salesmen and dealers and production workers, all contributing incrementally to the quality and market position these companies enjoy today. Middle and upper management saw their primary task as guiding and orchestrating this input from below rather than steering the organization from above along a predetermined strategic course.
>
> The Japanese don't use the term "strategy" to describe a crisp business definition or competitive master plan. They think more in terms of "strategic accommodation" or "adaptive persistence", underscoring their belief that corporate direction evolves from an incremental adjustment to unfolding events. Rarely, in their view, does one leader (or a strategic planning group) produce a bold strategy that guides a firm unerringly. Far more frequently, the input is from below. It is this ability of an organization to move information and ideas from the bottom to the top and back again in continuous *dialogdialogue that the Japanese value above all things.*[23]

Thus the strategy that emerges tends to be adaptive rather than being constrained by industry definitions, and fixed strategic plans. The success of Japanese firms is attributed to the absence of rigid planning systems, their willingness to adapt and shift to changing

117

environments, and their use of intuition and feel as guides. Their success is also attributed to their taking a long-term perspective, being willing to invest time and effort without immediate results.

More recently, management scholars, both East and West, support Pascale's assertions. For example, Burgelman[24] describes Japanese strategy as "evolutionary", wherein top management sets an open-ended vision and "vaguely delineated fields of strategic action". He argues that innovation evolves from the tension created by ". . . setting ambiguous directions together with very challenging parameters which serve as criteria for supporting emerging projects".[25] In this way, peripheral activities are encouraged which provide opportunities for learning new capabilities.

Japanese management scholar Nonaka also supports this Japanese version of strategy. He argues that the role of middle management is to simultaneously translate the abstract philosophies of top management and the concrete practical experience of the front lines. Strategies evolve and knowledge is created through this "middle-up-down" management.[26] Furthermore, he argues that

> The centerpiece of the Japanese approach is the recognition that creating new knowledge is not simply a matter of "processing" objective information. Rather it depends on tapping the tacit and often highly subjective insights, intuitions, and hunches of individual employees and making those insights available to testing and use by the company as a whole.[27]

These examples from Japan provide evidence for a model of strategy that is adapting rather than controlling. The different cultural behaviors, beliefs and values, and underlying assumptions that support the two models can be surfaced and deciphered, as shown in Table 5.2.

In the West, current interest in developing core competencies and in creating learning organizations represents a shift towards the adapting model. The rapidly, and sometimes radically, changing business environments represent serious challenges to assumptions of environmental certainty and organizational control.

These challenges are strongly felt in traditionally stable industries such as banking, notably in Europe, where the creation of the European Union has dramatically changed the rules of doing business. For this reason, it is worth examining the strategic approaches of two large European banks, one in Spain and one in Denmark, faced with the arrival of 1992, the date set for the opening of a single European market when these new rules were to be put in place. As this research was conducted in the summer of 1989, the story will be told in the perspective of what was about to happen rather than what actually occurred.[28]

The tale of two banks (circa 1989)

The date was set. As of January 1, 1992, capital, goods, and labor would be allowed to circulate freely among the (then twelve) member states. For the banking industry this meant the possibility of setting up branches in other countries, of playing on a "level

Table 5.2 Cultural determinants of strategy

External adaptation	Strategy

Relationship with nature
  Uncertainty
  Control
	Controlling/adapting

Human activity
  Doing versus being
  Achievement versus ascription
	Right moves versus right stuff
	Actions versus competences

Truth and reality	Facts and figures Intuition and philosophy

Internal integration	
Human nature	Who is capable of making decision

Nature of relationships
  Power and status
  Individual/collective
  Task/social
	Who has the right, legitimacy
	Who is responsible/accountable

Language High context/low context	Goals are explicit Strategy clearly articulated

Time
  Monochronic/polychronic
 	
  Long term/short term
	Decisions discrete
	Step-by-step action plans
	Speed of decisions
	Time frames for implementing

field" (harmonization of standards and practices), and of being able to sell their own products and services abroad (mutual recognition and home country supervision). The establishment of a central European bank and a common currency was also envisioned. By the year 1989 there was "much ado" in the press, in national government debates, and among business consultants preparing for what became known simply as "1992".

In this context, senior executives were interviewed in two banks, one in Denmark and one in Spain, to explore how information was gathered and interpreted, and how strategic decisions would be taken with regard to "1992". Both banks were among the top three in their respective countries and were similar in the nature of their activities' retail (primarily) and commercial banking. Both banks had also gone through crises in the mid-1980s and subsequent organizational changes, including a new CEO. Neither bank had significant international experience, except for currency trading and taking care of private and corporate (national) clients abroad.

119

Both countries were "overbanked", meaning that the market was saturated but fragmented (although more concentrated in the hands of fewer players in Denmark, where the top four banks had 47 percent as compared with 21 percent market share in Spain). Competition was, nevertheless, greater in Denmark; Spanish bankers sat more comfortably with higher margins. The level of government regulation and involvement was somewhat greater in Spain.

While the banks were comparable in many respects, the economic and political contexts in which they were situated differed.[29] Denmark had just emerged from a recession with less than 1 percent growth predicted while the growth rate of the Spanish economy was over 5 percent. Politically, Denmark had been more ambivalent about joining the EEC (as was later to be evident in their initial NO vote to the Maastricht Treaty). This ambivalence was linked to their superior standard of living (despite accompanying higher taxes) and their strong Scandinavian identity. In Spain, there had been great excitement about joining the EEC, as it was symbolically linked with democracy, Spain having been denied entry under the Franco regime, and laying to rest an old fifteenth century saying that "Europe ends at the Pyrenees"!

The Danish approach to "1992"

Executives within the Danish bank, described "1992" as "business as usual". It was essentially seen as a political event external to the bank. The planning department was seen as primarily responsible for "1992". The interpretation and response to "1992" would be managed within the formal decision-making process: the planning department would provide input to the board and CEO, who would then take the final decision. Little information regarding "1992" was disseminated to the rest of the bank.

The primary sources of information were considered to be external, particularly from contacts within the government or in Brussels. Internal sources were given less attention. One executive had written a book about the Single Market in his "own time" and was permitted to give talks (outside the bank) on the subject of "1992" as long as it "didn't interfere with his job". Formal information about "1992" was not very actively sought. It was estimated that only 10 percent came from written documentation, and industry reports were not relied upon. Analyses of costs and budgets provided the framework for interpreting information. However, the CEO considered that having a vision was more useful than economic scenarios, as it was more open and adaptive to changing events.

According to senior managers, discussions regarding "1992" were expected to be political, open to "wild debate", but "like the Communist party, they would be loyal to the outcome". Although some expressed concern that the far-reaching consequences were ill-understood by top management, one senior executive stated, "We're pretty cocksure we can manage it".

The Spanish approach to "1992"

In the Spanish bank, "1992" generated much excitement and enthusiasm. It was viewed as stimulating, as an impetus for change. A task force, called "Project Europe 1992", was created to develop a strategy for the bank. This task force consisted of 15 middle managers drawn from throughout the bank, assigned on a full-time basis. Members of the task force then interviewed the top 100 managers regarding their views on what the strategy should be. Information was also gathered by talking to people at meetings and at other banks, visiting best practice companies, and attending seminars. Information was interpreted by meeting and talking and using home grown models emphasizing market share and customer profitability.

The CEO gave "1992" top priority by placing it as the first item on the agenda for each meeting. The debate around "1992" was seen as consensus-seeking. To discourage political behavior, the CEO encouraged open sharing of information with an explicit rule of "no secrets". Any member of the task force thought to be protecting "home turf" interests was asked to leave. The primary challenge was "the task of getting 15,000 people ready to accept the challenge of 1992".

Different approaches, different assumptions

While not fitting neatly into the two models of a strategy previously discussed, the Danish bank's strategy can be considered more in line with the controlling approach, while the Spanish bank took a more adapting approach. This raises several questions: Why these differences? To what extent can they be attributed to national culture? To what extent does the national context, beyond culture, play a role? What other spheres of influence may be involved?

The Danish bank's approach reveals cultural assumptions of environmental certainty ("business as usual") and of organizational control ("We're pretty cocksure we can manage it."). There were no committees specially created to address the issue, nor extra resources devoted to intelligence gathering. Responsibility was clearly assigned to the strategic planning unit, with limited involvement of others. Top management was expected to make the decisions, and individual interests were expected to result in political debate. Thus the Danish bank approach corresponds to the controlling model, in that it was formalized, centralized, and political.

The Spanish bank's approach to "1992" reveals assumptions of environmental uncertainty and little organizational control. Here we find broader based environmental scanning, a special task force was created to access input from employees at all levels, greater reliance on home grown models, and more intense discussion and interaction to socially construct the meaning of "1992". This approach corresponds to the adapting model, described as decentralized, informal, and consensual.

Thus different assumptions regarding environmental uncertainty and organizational control, and the role of the individual versus the collective may contribute to explaining the different approaches in the cases described above. The different assumptions are also in line with the cultural differences reported in the previous chapter.[30] Indeed, Spain and Denmark represent opposite ends of the spectrum on many cultural dimensions. The Danish are more tolerant of uncertainty and have greater perceived control over their environment compared with the Spanish. The Danes are also more individualistic. Furthermore, for Danish managers organizations are task systems, while for Spanish managers they are social systems.

The Spanish bank's approach appears closer to that of the Japanese described earlier in the chapter. In fact, Japan and Spain are quite similar on dimensions of uncertainty avoidance, hierarchy, and collectivism. They also share the view of organizations as social systems. The role of the boss is to orchestrate decisions, based on the input and interest of the collective.

The Danish bank's approach, on the other hand, appears to have more in common with the approach associated with US companies. They indeed share similar cultural assumptions about control over nature, and tolerance of uncertainty, individualism, and the view of organizations as task systems. The role of the boss is to make decisions based on expert, individual input and interests.

Although we have focused primarily on the role of national culture, the different assumptions underlying the controlling versus adapting models may derive from interaction with other spheres of cultural influence. The behavior, beliefs and values, and assumptions embedded in national as well as other cultural spheres are determined, in part, by the national context, as discussed in Chapter 3.

Interaction effects

The national context, or *institutional environment*, includes the role of government and unions (the degree and nature of regulation), the market conditions (protected versus free), economic and political systems, educational systems, and history.[31] These factors play an important role in determining strategy. Compare, for example, the 1980s strategies of cost-cutting and rationalizing in US firms with Japanese firms' strategies of R&D investment, market growth, and expansion.

The contrast was often attributed to cultural differences regarding short- versus long-term time horizons. However, differences in government policies (such as protectionism), ownership structures, strength of currency, and sources of financing (from banks versus equity market) were also considered to be some of the institutional reasons for differences in short-term versus long-term orientation.[32]

These institutional arrangements were also considered to be the cause of differences in the strategies of US and European firms. In Germany, for example, banks have an important influence on corporate strategy, and in France, it is the government which plays a key role. Longer term views, greater concern for social welfare, and larger investment in developing internal capabilities are more feasible when investors are committed to the company (as the shareholders are in fact the banks or the government) and are not demanding quarterly reports and short-term return on investment. Compare that with institutional investors in the United States and United Kingdom who, on average, hold on to stocks for less than two years.[33]

These institutional arrangements interact with national culture to encourage different strategies. In addition to the national context, the increasing cross-border economic and political integration, as in the cases of the European Union and North American Free Trade Area (NAFTA), creates institutional pressures that go beyond national borders, contributing to a supraregional culture. Thus the institutional environment determines

122

the rules of doing business, both at the national or international level, and thereby shapes the different cultural spheres.

Let us examine how the national context interacts with national culture and other spheres of cultural influence which may help to explain the different strategic approaches in the cases of the Spanish and Danish banks. In Denmark, the economic recession, the previous ambivalence expressed towards joining the EEC, and the impending "shakeout" of the domestic market created an environment that was hostile and threatening. Indeed, research has shown that under conditions of threat, information flows are restricted, decision-making is centralized, and behavior reverts to well-known routines.[34]

In Spain, the economic and political context was different, marked by strong economic growth and a political climate that was pro-business and pro-integration. These conditions encouraged the Spanish bank to be more market-driven, to actively seek opportunities within the domestic market, and to develop internal capability. This is similar to the opportunity-driven, market-oriented, international strategies of Japanese companies in the 1980s.

Being faced with a hostile environment may have led the Danish bank to focus on costs and profitability, the bottom line. This corresponds to a strategic profile of *defender*, wherein efficiency and control are considered necessary to protect product/market niches and core businesses.[35] In the Spanish bank, the search for new product and market opportunities and the emphasis on flexibility and adaptability characterize organizations that are *prospectors*.[36] It can therefore be argued that these differences in the national context created conditions that encouraged the Danish bank to be defenders and the Spanish bank to be prospectors.

Organizations that are defenders tend to be more centralized and formalized, which would also explain the controlling approach. Prospector organizations tend to have structures that are more decentralized and informal, which reinforce an adaptive approach. Research has also demonstrated that organizations described as defenders are more likely to interpret strategic issues as threats, whereas entrepreneurial organizations, or prospectors, are more likely to interpret the same issues as opportunities.[37] This, in turn, reinforces the strategic actions noted above; seeking control and efficiency or seeking new products and markets. Thus the strategic process, content and profile interact in mutually reinforcing ways, as in Figure 5.1.

National context also helps to explain the different approaches to strategy through its effect on other spheres of cultural influence, such as corporate and industry cultures. *Corporate culture*, for example, is shaped in part by government regulation and resulting market conditions. Deregulation in the United States in the 1980s and in Europe in the 1990s, has forced companies on both sides of the Atlantic to become more competitive. This may mean becoming more cost-conscious and efficient on one hand, or more customer-driven and market-oriented on the other, or both.

The organization structures are adapted to meet these efforts by becoming either more centralized and formalized (in the name of efficiency), or more decentralized and informal (to be market-oriented), or by creating structures combining loose–tight properties in order to do both. The extent to which organization strategy drives structure or vice versa

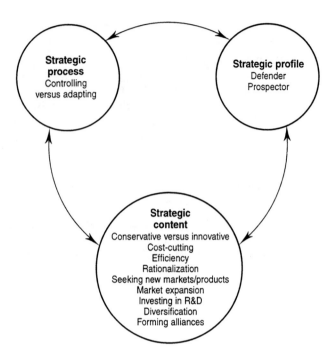

Figure 5.1   Interaction between strategic process, content and profile.

is open to debate.[38] Nevertheless, this interaction influences which strategies are pursued (content) and how they are chosen (process).

Industry culture is also driven by national context, or the institutional environment. For example, the degree to which technologies or markets are protected determines the level of competitiveness required as previously discussed. This can be seen in industries such as telecommunication, transportation, and banking. As a result of deregulation, many of these industries have had to become more customer-oriented and more efficient.

Industry culture is also being driven by broader, supraregional institutional pressures, such as EU regulations in the case of "1992". These pressures encourage the emergence of certain practices of strategic management either by coercion (through regulation or professionalization) or by copying best practices promoted by business consultants, professors, and the media to gain legitimacy.[39] For example, similar scanning practices found in Korean firms were attributed to their hiring the same US consulting firm.[40]

Industry recipes are passed on providing the key ingredients and the right procedures.[41] Evidence of this can be found in banking. In Norway, banks imitated each others' strategies, leading to greater decentralization and subsequent lessening of control, resulting in financial disaster.[42] In the 1980s, many US banks faced with intensifying competition, engaged in greater risk-taking, resulting in dramatic write-offs later on. Nor did following the fashion of financial supermarkets produce the anticipated synergies.

Further evidence may be found in the increasing number of domestic, or home-court, mergers in banking, in the United States, Europe, and Japan. These mergers continue, despite ongoing debates about whether the supposed benefits (such as economies of scale) outweigh the costs of integration, whether greater international competitiveness is derived by promoting greater competition at home, and whether developing assets and competencies within national borders neglects developing cross-border competencies.[43] Nevertheless, the uncertainties and anxieties that surround strategic issues, particularly in the current environment of economic recession and massive industry restructuring, provide fertile ground for the creation of business or industry myths that are often difficult to evaluate.

Thus corporate and industry cultures are influenced by both the national and supraregional contexts in ways that can influence which strategies are taken, as well as how those strategies are determined.[44] The prospectors of the 1980s became the defenders of the 1990s, with different emphases on expansion versus cost controls, risk-taking versus risk-minimizing, and innovative versus conservative actions. The controlling and adapting models of strategy may in fact represent alternative approaches that must be managed simultaneously in order to face the competitive challenge of being both market-oriented and cost-efficient.

Strategic implications of culture

In this chapter we have argued that assumptions regarding *external adaptation*, such as control and uncertainty, and those related to *internal integration*, such as hierarchy and individualism/collectivism, lead to different models of how organizations make sense of and respond to their environment. This can be observed in the way they gather, interpret and act on information about strategic issues: what is attended to and what is not, what kinds of information are considered useful, what models and methods are used to analyze this information, who is involved in the process, and what strategic decisions are taken.

These two models, called controlling and adapting, were illustrated by the example of how two banks in different countries, Denmark and Spain, went about making sense of a strategic issue – "1992". We further argued that this strategic process interacts with strategic profiles, such as defenders and prospectors, and strategic content, for example, cost-cutting or market expansion, in mutually reinforcing ways.

In addition, we discussed the way other cultural spheres may interact with strategy. We showed how the national context or institutional environment favors different approaches to strategy. We argued that the institutional environment, both at the national and supraregional levels, shapes corporate and industry culture, which in turn influences which strategies are chosen and how. We now need to consider the implications of these arguments in the roles of headquarters and subsidiaries in developing global strategies and in anticipating the moves of international competitors and partners.

The relationship between headquarters and subsidiaries

Different cultural assumptions drive different models of strategic process. In multinational corporations (MNCs), those at headquarters need to understand and appreciate

125

how at the local level strategy is formulated and implemented in order to best integrate it with corporate-level strategic management. For example, if the predominant model at headquarters is controlling, the strategic planning staff are likely to be frustrated in their discussions with managers in subsidiaries that opt for the adapting model.

For one, requests for objective information, e.g. market research or industry data, may be ignored. Headquarters may also have difficulty in getting managers in these subsidiaries to use the same models or methods of analysis, such as strategic forecasting and scenario planning. Matrices depicting market growth and position, along with its cash cows and dogs, may be dismissed as having little credibility. The insistence on facts and figures may be met with insistence on gut feel and philosophical debate. Furthermore, it will be difficult to know whom to address, as responsibility for strategic planning may be more diffused. For these reasons strategies pursued by headquarters and those pursued by subsidiaries may be very loosely coupled.

On the other hand, headquarters, in cultures that prefer the adapting approach, may be equally frustrated by managers in subsidiaries where the controlling approach is preferred. Requests from these subsidiaries for greater precision regarding corporate goals and intended strategies, for concrete action steps, for implementation timetables, for clear-cut assignment of responsibility and accountability, and for ways of measuring follow-up may seem unnecessary, and even irritating.

The problems caused by this mismatch are illustrated by the case of a Japanese bank headquarters with an American subsidiary where managers on both sides were frustrated since nothing was happening. It turned out that the Americans were waiting for clear direction from the Japanese headquarters, while the Japanese were waiting for initiatives from the American subsidiary.[45] Therefore, it is important to know what information is considered relevant, what models and methods of interpretation are considered useful, and who expects to be involved or to take the decision.

Different assumptions will also drive different strategic content. Thus it is essential to recognize that strategies which are considered by HQ to be crucial to survival may not be similarly appreciated by the subsidiaries. For example, strategies to improve efficiency and control costs by reducing R&D budgets and head counts, may be seen as short-sighted, and considered "penny-wise and pound-foolish", if these actions are seen to undermine the development of competencies needed for long-term adaptability.

Nor will HQ strategies designed to develop organizational competencies, to enhance flexibility, and stimulate entrepreneurship necessarily be readily embraced at the local level. For example, heavily investing in management training and development, or allowing scientists to "tinker about in laboratories removed from the real world", in other words, to conduct basic research with no clearly defined product applications or market need, may be seen as a wasteful, inefficient use of resources. Engaging in peripheral activities which have little apparent value for the existing business might frustrate those looking for a clear-cut strategic direction, and for more resources to be devoted to core businesses.

Cultural assumptions will also influence the strategic profile, such as defender or prospector. Headquarters and subsidiaries may not share assumptions regarding the ability to impose control. Headquarters located in cultures that promote prospectors looking to develop new product market opportunities may feel blocked by subsidiaries located in cultures that encourage defenders, trying to protect market niches and core technologies. A defender head office may refuse to invest in, and thereby miss opportunities discovered by its prospector subsidiary.

The pursuit of greater efficiency through rationalization and restructuring may overlook the importance of market and customer knowledge. For example, when Xerox reorganized its US operations by product lines, it expected its European subsidiary, Rank Xerox, to follow suit. This caused problems in Europe, with the managing director reluctant to lose the specific market (customer) knowledge of the geographically organized units. In the end, Rank Xerox proposed a matrix structure which allowed it to retain its market focus.

The above discussion of the mismatch between headquarters and subsidiaries highlights the potential frustrations and misunderstandings that can occur in formulating and implementing strategies, especially when the strategic decisions are assumed to come primarily from the top; HQ decides what to do, and the subsidiaries are supposed to implement these decisions. This depiction is, or course, somewhat exaggerated. However, what it highlights is the need to question the roles of HQ and subsidiaries in formulating as well as implementing strategies. Research has shown that the more subsidiaries are involved in formulating the strategies, the more readily they are implemented.[46]

Furthermore, the mismatch, rather than provoking frustration and irritation can be used to set up creative tensions, so that alternative models can coexist and codetermine which strategies are pursued and how. Different pieces of the strategic puzzle may be best suited to one approach over the other. Having access to both approaches may help to solve the competitive dilemma of having to improve efficiency in the short term, while at the same time having to develop core competencies for the long run.

The existence of different approaches to strategy is also in tune with the view of multinationals as differentiated organizational networks.[47] This view encourages us to consider that strategies can be developed at the local level for local and global implementation. This means that global strategies do not necessarily have to come from the top, HQ. This notion seems to surprise some HQ managers, and some local managers who protest "not invented here!".

Anticipating competitive and cooperative relationships

As the same environmental event may be interpreted and responded to in different ways in different countries, understanding these differences can provide a competitive advantage in facing international competitors. Recognizing key cultural dimensions can help anticipate the way in which a competitor may interpret and respond to strategic issues such as new regulations or new market opportunities.

For example, interpretations of threat versus opportunity may have more to do with the degree of perceived environmental uncertainty and organizational control than with objective reality. Strategic issues are likely to be interpreted as a threat given perceptions of low control.[48] Furthermore, interpreting a strategic issue as a threat has consequences for strategic response, leading to more risk-taking behavior, more investment of time and money, and a greater internal orientation.[49]

127

Research has shown that Latin European managers were more likely to interpret issues as threats or even crises, when compared with northern Europeans. They were also more willing to invest resources in training and information technology, in other words, in developing internal capabilities.[50] In another study, Japanese managers were found to be more likely to identify a strategic issue as a threat than were American managers.[51] Thus interpretations of and reactions to threat are more likely among Japanese and Latin European managers as they are more likely to perceive greater uncertainty and less control over their environments than their US or northern European counterparts.

Again, this is supported in the case of the Danish bank, discussed earlier, where despite a hostile and threatening environment, "1992" was seen as "business as usual". Assumptions of control meant that "1992" was not interpreted as a threat, even if conditions may have warranted it. Furthermore, given this assumption, investing extra resources in gathering intelligence or developing additional capabilities was considered unnecessary. As a result, they were quite surprised when they merged with (some say "taken over" by) their arch-rivals (who lived literally next door in the same building), only three months later.

In the case of a joint venture, these different interpretations of strategic issues may cause problems. Latin European managers may be seen as overreacting by their colleagues from the north, while the Latin Europeans themselves may be frustrated because the northerners cannot be convinced that a situation is really a crisis. In addition, the shared interpretation of strategic issues across cultures is vital to the mobilization of resources and efforts in these alliances.

Thus by deciphering the underlying assumptions of uncertainty and control that influence the interpretation of strategic issues as threats or opportunities, the strategic actions, or non-actions, of competitors or partners might be better anticipated.

Other cultural dimensions have also been found to explain the strategic actions, such as the mode of entry into foreign markets. For example, Japanese companies, in their desire to reduce uncertainty, tend to prefer greenfield operations and joint ventures rather than acquisitions, especially when there is greater cultural distance.[52]

When entering the US market, companies from countries that are quite culturally different from the United States and more power-oriented tend to prefer foreign direct investment over licensing agreements.[53] In this way they are able to maintain control through hierarchies rather than bargaining.

Given cultural distance, they also tend to rely more on rules rather than value-based controls. When cultures are similar, companies can rely on shared values to create high degrees of trust, as in the case of Japan, where norms of obligation and reciprocity tend to reduce opportunistic behavior.[54] However, the high level of trust among insiders may not necessarily be extended to outsiders. In fact, the reverse may be true. Thus while licensing arrangements and networks (keiretsu) may be preferred within cultural borders, there is a preference for direct ownership, such as greenfield sites, outside cultural borders.

The impact of national culture on strategy needs to be further explored. It is only recently that the relationship of strategy and national culture has been demonstrated empirically. More research is needed to test the hypotheses presented above. The sudden interest in corporate culture was largely the result of failed strategic change initiatives and the realization that organization cultures could constrain the choice or implementation of strategy. The same could be said for national culture.

In fact, the growing interest in managing across cultures may be driven by difficulties encountered when trying to implement global strategies, or to initiate strategic change across borders. The recognition of national cultural differences enables us to question our own assumptions and ways of thinking about strategy, to recognize potential "competitive blinders",[55] as well as to anticipate the strategic moves of competitors and the strategic concerns of partners in other cultures.

Notes

1. Weick, K.E. (1985) "The significance of corporate culture" in P. Frost, L.F. Moore, M.R. Louis, C.C. Lundberg and J. Martin (eds) *Organizational Culture*, Beverly Hills: Sage, 381–90, 382.
2. Sun-Tzu (1988) *The Art of War*, Boston: Shambhala (translated by T. Clearly).
3. Machiavelli, N. (1958) *The Prince*, London: J.M. Dent and Sons (translated by W.K. Marriot).
4. Galer, G. (1994) "The elements of scenario planning", Presented at the Organizational Learning Kolleg, Ladenburg, Germany, April 5.
5. Hofer, C.W. and Schendel, D. (1978) *Strategy Formulation: Analytic Concepts*, St. Paul: West Publishing.
6. Porter, M. (1980) *Competitive Strategy*, New York: Free Press.
7. Hamel, G. and Prahalad, C.K. (1989) "Strategic intent", *Harvard Business Review*, 67(3), 63–76; Prahalad, C.K. and Hamel, G. (1990) "The core competence of the corporation", *Harvard Business Review*, 68(3), 79–91.
8. Lyles, M.A. and Mitroff, I. (1985) "The impact of sociopolitical influences on strategic problem formulation" in R. Lamb and P. Shrivastava (eds) *Advances in Strategic Management*, Vol. 3, Greenwich, CT: JAI Press, 69–82; Mintzberg, H., Raisinghani, D. and Theoret, A. (1976) "The structure of unstructured decision processes", *Administrative Science Quarterly*, 21, 246–75; Bower, J.L. and Doz, Y. (1979) *Strategy Formulation: A Social and Political Process*, Boston: Little, Brown & Co; Allison, G. (1971) *The Essence of Decision: Explaining the Cuban Missile Crisis*, Boston, MA: Little, Brown & Co.
9. Smircich, L. and Stubbart, C. (1985) "Strategic management in an enacted world", *Academy of Management Review*, 10(4), 724–36; Weick, K.E. (1979) *The Social Psychology of Organizing*, Reading, MA: Addison-Wesley.
10. See Schneider, S.C. and DeMeyer, A. (1991) "Interpreting and responding to strategic issues: The impact of national culture", *Strategic Management Journal*, 12, 307–20.
11. March, J.G. and Simon, H. (1958) *Organizations*, New York: John Wiley.
12. Schneider, S.C. (1989) "Strategy formulation: The impact of national culture", *Organization Studies*, 10(2), 149–68; Schneider, S.C. (1994) "Interpreting strategic issues: Making sense of 1992" in C. Stubbart, J.R. Meindl and J.F. Porac (eds) *Advances in Managerial Cognition and Organizational Information Processing*, Vol. 5, Greenwich, CT: JAI Press, pp. 243–74.
13. Lightfoot, R.W. (1992) "Philips and Matsushita: A Portrait of two evolving companies", Harvard Business School.
14. Pascale, R.T. (1984) "Perspectives on strategy: The real story behind Honda's success", *California Management Review*, 26(3), 47–72.
15. Mintzberg, H. (1995) *The Rise and Fall of Strategic Planning*, Englewood Cliffs, NJ: Prentice Hall.
16. Mintzberg, H. (1978) "Patterns in strategy formation", *Management Science*, 24(9), 934–48; Mintzberg, H. and Waters, J. (1985) "Of strategies deliberate and emergent",

Strategic Management Journal, 6, 257–72; Burgelman, R.A. (1983) "A process model of internal corporate venturing in the diversified major firm", *Administrative Science Quarterly*, 28, 223–44; Nelson, R. and Winter, S. (1982) *An Evolutionary Theory of Economic Change*, Cambridge, MA: Harvard University Press.

17. Prahalad, C.K. and Hamel, G. (1990), *Op. cit.*; Wernerfelt, B. (1984) "A resource based view of the firm", *Strategic Management Journal*, 5, 171–80; Bower, J.L. (1970) *Managing the Resource Allocation Process*, Boston, MA: Harvard Business School Press.

18. Pascale, *Op. cit.*, p. 56.

19. Pascale, R.T. and Athos, A.G. (1981) *The Art of Japanese Management*, New York: Warner Books; Pascale, *Op. cit.*; Kagono, T., Nonaka, I., Sakakibara, K. and Okumura, A. (1985) *Strategic vs. Evolutionary Management: A U.S.–Japan Comparison of Strategy and Organization*, Amsterdam: North Holland Elsevier Science Publishers, B.V.; Nonaka, I. and Johansson, J.K. (1985) "Japanese management: What about 'hard' skills?", *Academy of Management Review*, 10(2), 181–91.

20. (Law of requisite variety) Ashby, W.R. (1956) *Introduction to Cybernetics*, London: Chapman & Hall; Daft, R.L. and Lengel, R.H. (1986) "Organizational information requirements, media richness and structural design", *Management Science*, 32(5), 554–71.

21. See also Daft, R.L. and Weick, K.E. (1984) "Toward a model of organizations as interpretation systems", *Academy of Management Review*, 9(2), 284–95.

22. See Schneider, S.C. (1989), *Op. cit.*

23. Pascale, *Op. cit.*, pp. 63–64.

24. Burgelman, R.A. (1988) "A comparative evolutionary perspective on strategy-making: Advantages and limitations of the Japanese approach" in K. Urabe, J. Child and T. Kagono (eds) *Innovation and Management: International Comparisons*, Berlin: Walter de Gruyter, 63–80.

25. *Ibid.*, p. 73.

26. Nonaka, I. (1988) "Toward middle-up-down management: Accelerating information creation", *Sloan Management Review*, 29(3), 9–18.

27. Nonaka, I. (1991) "The knowledge-creating company", *Harvard Business Review*, November–December, 96–104.

28. Schneider, S.C. (1994), *Op. cit.*

29. Evaris, R.M. (1990) "Spain in the grip of Eurofever", *International Management*, February, 38–42; Caminal, R., Gual, J. and Vives, X. (1989) "Competition in Spanish banking" in J. Dermine (ed.) *European Banking in the 1990's*, Oxford: Basil Blackwell, pp. 261–305; Laurie, S. (1989) "Shoot-out in Danish city", *The Banker*, May, 38–43; Fairlamb, D. (1989) "The Nordic countries play-it-safe strategy for 1992", *Institutional Investor*, August, 99–106.

30. Hofstede, G. (1980) *Cultures Consequences*, Beverly Hills: Sage; Laurent, A. (1983) "The cultural diversity of western conceptions of management", *International Studies of Management and Organizations*, 13(1–2), 75–96.

31. Child, J. (1981) "Culture, contingency and capitalism in the cross-national study of organizations" in L.L. Cummings and B.M. Staw (eds) *Research in Organizational Behavior*, Vol. 3, Greenwich, CT: JAI Press, pp. 303–56; Scott, W.R. (1987) "The adolescence of institutional theory", *Administrative Science Quarterly*, 32, 493–511.

32. Westney, D.E. (1987) *Imitation and Innovation*, Cambridge, MA: Harvard University Press.

33. "A conversation with Michael Porter", *European Management Journal*, 9(4), 1991, 355–59.

34. Staw, B.M., Sandelands, L. and Dutton, J.E. (1981) "Threat rigidity cycles in organizational behavior", *Administrative Science Quarterly*, 26, 501–24; Billings, T., Milburn, S.W. and Shaalman, M.L. (1980) "Crisis perception: A theoretical and empirical analysis", *Administrative Science Quarterly*, 25, 300–15.

35. Miles, R.H. and Snow, C.C. (1978) *Organizational Strategy, Structure and Process*, New York: McGraw-Hill.
36. *Ibid.*
37. Meyer, A.D. (1982) "Adapting to environmental jolts", *Administrative Science Quarterly*, 27, 515–37.
38. Chandler, A.D. (1962) *Strategy and Structure*, Cambridge, MA: MIT Press.
39. Meyer, J.W. and Rowan, B. (1977) "Institutionalized organizations: Formal structure as myth and ceremony", *American Journal of Scoiology*, 83(2), 340–63.
40. Ghoshal, S. (1985) "Environmental scanning: An individual and organizational level analysis", Unpublished doctoral dissertation, Cambridge, MA, MIT Sloan School of Management.
41. Spender, J.C. (1989) *Industry Recipes*, Oxford: Basil Blackwell.
42. Reve, T. (1990) "Mimetic strategic behavior in banking", Presented at the 10th annual Strategic Management Society meeting, Stockholm.
43. Ballarin, E. (1988) "The process of concentration in Spanish banks: Theory and practice", Working paper, IESE; Porter, M. (1990) "The competitive advantage of nations", *Harvard Business Review*, March/April, 73–93; Dunning, J.H. (1993) "Internationalizing Porter's diamond", *Management International Review*, 33(2), 7–15.
44. Huff, A.S. (1982) "Industry influences on strategy reformulation", *Strategic Management Journal*, 3, 119–31.
45. Ouchi, W.G. and Jaeger, A.M. (1978) "Theory Z organization: Stability in the midst of mobility", *Academy of Management Review*, 3(20), 305–14.
46. Kim, W.C. and Mauborgne, R.A. (1993) "Making global strategies work", *Sloan Management Review*, Spring, 11–27.
47. Ghoshal, S. and Nohria, N. (1989) "Internal differentiation within multinational corporations", *Strategic Management Journal*, 10(4), 323–37.
48. Dutton, J.E. and Jackson, S.E. (1987) "The categorization of strategic issues by decision makers and its links to organizational action", *Academy of Management Review*, 12, 76–90.
49. Tversky, A. and Kahnemann, D. (1974) "Judgement under uncertainty: Heuristics and biases", *Science*, 185, 1124–31; Dutton, J.E., Walton, E. and Abrahamson, E. (1989) "Important dimensions of strategic issues: Separating the wheat from the chaff", *Journal of Management Studies*, 26, 379–96; Dutton, J.E., Stumpf, S.A. and Wagner, D. (1990) "Diagnosing strategic issues and the investment of resources" in R. Lamb and P. Shrivastava (eds) *Advances in Strategic Management*, Vol. 6, Greenwich, CT: JAI Press, 143–67; Milliken, F.J. and Dukerich, J.M. (1987) "Insights into issue interpretation: The effect of issue characteristics on judgements of importance and information search", Academy of Management Meeting, New Orleans.
50. Schneider, S.C. and DeMeyer, A., *Op. cit.*
51. Sallivan, J. and Nonaka, I. (1988) "Culture and strategic issue categorization theory", *Management International Review*, 28(3), 6–10.
52. Kogut, B. and Singh, H. (1988) "The effect of national culture on the choice of entry model", *Journal of International Business Studies*, 19, 411–32.
53. Shane, S.A. (1994) "The effect of national culture on the choice between licensing and direct foreign investment", *Strategic Management Journal*, 15(8), 627–42.
54. Black, J.S. and Mendenhall, M. (1993) "Resolving conflicts with the Japanese: Mission impossible", *Sloan Management Review*, Spring, 49–59.
55. Zajac, E.J. and Bazerman, M.H. (1991) "Blind spots in industry and competitor analysis", *Academy of Management Review*, 16, 37–56.

131

CHAPTER TEN

Citizens of the world: business ethics and social responsibility

L'éthique, c'est le désir d'une vie accomplie, avec et pour les autres, dans le cadre d'institutions justes.

Paul Ricoeur[1]

(Ethics is the desire for a life accomplished, with and for others, within the framework of fair institutions.)

We now come to the end of our journey. In navigating the seas of international business, we have come to recognize culture as a powerful force which can either undermine our best intentions and efforts or push forward our business activities. We have used as our guide a map which indicates the cultural terrain, or key dimensions, and suggests methods for discovery through observation, questioning, and interpretation. This map can also serve to reveal different spheres of cultural influence – regional, industry, and corporate – and to consider the consequences of their interaction. We then examined the evidence of how and why culture influences management practice: in designing organization structure and processes, strategies, and human resource management practices. And finally, we brought to light the issues and concerns of how to manage these cultural differences as international managers, as multicultural teams, and as global organizations.

Throughout this journey we have demonstrated the impact of culture on management practices around the world. In this concluding chapter, we question to what extent notions of business ethics and social responsibility are also culture-bound, and whether we can ever hope to arrive at a culturally shared understanding of and response to ethical dilemmas and social responsibility. What, indeed, is the role of managers and companies as **global citizens** and what is the best path to follow in conducting international business?

We start by recognizing a long tradition of different cultural assumptions regarding business and profit, which are also revealed in theories of economic growth and of the firm ("why firms exist"). These different assumptions provide the fuel for the debate over "ethics versus profit"; do they go hand in hand or are there inherent, irreconcilable trade-offs? Despite this debate, ethical and socially responsible behavior can be considered to be an imperative for conducting business on a global scale. Indeed, attempts to establish a "level playing field" have already created cultural shock waves around the world.

Nevertheless attitudes and behavior towards ethics among managers and companies differ across cultures. Here we consider the *evidence* and explore *reasons* for similarities as well as differences. We question whether it is best to adopt a policy of "When in Rome do as the Romans do", or to impose home country or company ethical standards and risk being accused of "cultural imperialism". In addressing these questions, managers and companies can better define their role as citizens of the world, and develop guidelines to keep them on track in their continuing journey towards a global civilization.

Taking care of business

According to David Vogel, Professor of Business at the University of California at Berkeley, the current interest in business ethics represents "an ongoing moral dialogue with deep secular and religious roots" regarding the nature of market economy and human nature.[2]

> [As] medieval Catholic thought held that money-making was morally suspect . . . a moral businessman was thus a contradiction in terms . . .
> It was by morally sanctifying the pursuit of profit that Protestantism made business ethics possible . . . Not only could one serve God by working, but the correct use of wealth was precisely to improve it for the glory of God. Consequently, the pursuit of profit and the pursuit of heaven become not only compatible, but mutually reinforcing . . . In short, the Reformation made it possible for the first time to be both a good person and a successful businessman.[3]

In the Catholic church, profit was sanctioned for the benefit of the community, not for individual enhancement. The role of the hierarchy was to intervene on behalf of the people to ensure collective well-being and to mediate in upholding the word of God. For Protestants, access to God was more direct (no intermediary was necessary). Work, rather than a necessary evil, was considered to be the means to redemption. "The profile of the PWE [Protestant work ethic] believer then is of an independently minded, competitive, hard-working individual who is prepared to persevere at a task to achieve desirable ends."[4] This Protestant work ethic encouraged a strong need for individual achievement, perceived control over the environment, an instrumental approach, and the belief of a just world (equity).[5] It was this work ethic which, according to Max Weber, promoted capitalism.[6] Vogel argues that the doctrine of corporate social responsibility can be understood in part as the ongoing effort to reconcile the intentions and results of capitalism.

In France, for example, making money has long been viewed with some suspicion. Status and prestige came from family lineage and relationships – better to be an indebted aristocrat (*ancien pauvre*) than *nouveau riche*. Your personal value is derived from what you *are* rather than what you *do* or earn (ascription versus achievement).

In Russia, the power of the ruling elites and the concern for the collective in both traditional Russian culture, as well as under Communist ideology, also led to suspicion and mistrust of business. Engaging in business and making profit are still held as evidence

133

of selfishness and unethical motives. Parents are ashamed of children who go into private business to make money.[7]

Economic development is also thought to be rooted in culture. Hofstede found that country GNP strongly correlated (0.82) with rankings on individualism.[8] He then went on to explain the more recent impressive economic growth of southeast Asian "tigers" as related to "Confucian dynamism" which includes values of persistence, thrift, well-defined social roles, and a long-term, future orientation.[9]

Why firms exist

The very reason for "why firms exist", or the theory of the firm, is also strongly influenced by culture. Many Western business schools preach profit maximization as the ultimate goal to be *achieved*. They promote the idea that firms exist in order to provide benefits to shareholders, or to reduce transaction costs. These notions reflect underlying assumptions of organizations as instrumental, and of managers as "rational economic" actors, driven by self-interest (individualism).

In contrast, the idea that firms exist in order to promote the well-being of society (social responsibility) reflects assumptions of organizations as "systems of relationships", and of managers as "paternalistic", driven by concern for the "collective" (multiple stakeholders). These notions can be found in a growing number of company mission statements. Consider the following excerpts from Matsushita's creed and philosophy.

> Through our industrial activities, we strive to foster progress, to promote the general welfare of society, and to devote ourselves to furthering the development of world culture.

> The purpose of an enterprise is to contribute to society by supplying goods of high quality and low prices in ample quantity.

> Profit comes in compensation for contribution to society . . . [it] is a result rather than a goal.[10]

This vision clashes with assumptions underlying free market ideology; the *raison d'être* is not necessarily to provide shareholder benefits, nor to improve efficiency in market-driven economies. Responding to the question, "Is the only real goal of a company to make a profit or should the well-being of the various stakeholders be taken into account?", 47 percent of US managers chose the profit motive; this was true for a mere 4 percent of the Japanese.[11] The very meaning of profit may also be subject to cultural differences in interpretation. A study conducted with US and Japanese business students found such differences.

> For the Japanese, only one factor emerged. Profit is the reward to businessmen for taking risks to produce innovations society needs to develop the future. The American students had multiple concepts of profit, some emphasizing personal gain, some social value. To the Japanese, however, only one concept of profit exists and in it social and self interest are the same.[12]

134

In Portugal, one may find a more or less explicit theory of the firm including the belief that it exists to take care of workers. This theory reflects values of paternalism (hierarchy) and collectivism which makes the idea of layoffs in economic downturn particularly difficult to accept or implement. Moreover, this is reinforced by law.[13] For many Europeans (both west and east) and Asians, Americans are seen as behaving unethically when closing factories, laying off workers, and neglecting their social obligations. This lack of social conscience is what is perceived as "harsh capitalism". It comes as a shock to many to see the huge gap between the rich and poor in the United States, or the ratio of CEO to employee salary (Japan 17:1, Europe 21:1, US 155:1),[14] taken as evidence of unethical exploitation.

When Reader's Digest decided to withdraw from the Japanese market after 24 years, having been profitable for only 11 of those years, they were accused of a "crime akin to child abandonment". The affected labor union placed advertisements in the *New York Times* saying that the company's behavior was "unfair, unscrupulous, and irresponsible".[15]

Also, although it is common for Americans to change jobs often, and to trade up (change company for an increase in pay), company-hopping is seen as immoral in Japan; even if changing companies is now becoming more acceptable, frequent moves remain suspect. Faced with economic recession and increased competition, many European and even Japanese companies are restructuring (downsizing), creating moral *angst* over the breakdown of the psychological contract: employee loyalty in return for lifetime employment and company commitment to employee welfare.

Nevertheless, many American companies also make it their business to be socially responsible. These companies take seriously their role in improving society and providing benefit to multiple *stakeholders*, not just shareholders. Johnson & Johnson's credo makes it clear that providing benefits to shareholders is not first on the list of priorities, as shown in Figure 10.1. The strength of this credo, or corporate philosophy was credited with the socially responsible behavior of recalling Tylenol from market shelves. Thus different theories of the firm can be found in different cultures, both national and corporate.

These different underlying assumptions regarding the purpose of the firm – economic or social – drive the debate regarding the relationship between profit and social responsibility. Does profit represent an end in itself or does it provide the means for creating a better society? Does social responsibility make economic sense or is it a moral imperative? While some managers may remain cynical faced with such discussions, the social role and responsibility, particularly of global organizations, can no longer be side-stepped.

Making economic versus moral sense

The motivation for ethical behavior and for social responsibility has recently become a hot topic in the business press and within academic circles. What *really* drives such behavior: corporate philanthropy or corporate profit? For example, the furniture company, Herman Miller, banned the use of certain species of wood in order to prevent the destruction of rainforests (no more rosewood). While the corporate concern for ethics

135

Our Credo

We believe our first responsibility is to the doctors, nurses and patients,
to mothers and all others who use our products and services.
In meeting their needs everything we do must be of high quality.
We must constantly strive to reduce our costs
in order to maintain reasonable prices.
Customers' orders must be serviced promptly and accurately.
Our suppliers and distributors must have an opportunity
to make a fair profit.

We are responsible to our employees,
the men and women who work with us throughout the world.
Everyone must be considered as an individual.
We must respect their dignity and recognize their merit.
They must have a sense of security in their jobs.
Compensation must be fair and adequate,
and working conditions clean, orderly and safe.
Employees must feel free to make suggestions and complaints.
There must be equal opportunity for employment, development
and advancement for those qualified.
We must provide competent management,
and their actions must be just and ethical.

We are responsible to the communities in which we live and work
and to the world community as well.
We must be good citizens — support good works and charities
and bear our fair share of taxes.
We must encourage civic improvements and better health and education.
We must maintain in good order
the property we are privileged to use,
protecting the environment and natural resources.

Our final responsibility is to our stockholders.
Business must make a sound profit.
We must experiment with new ideas.
Research must be carried on, innovative programs developed
and mistakes paid for.
New equipment must be purchased, new facilities provided
and new products launched.
Reserves must be created to provide for adverse times.
When we operate according to these principles,
the stockholders should realize a fair return.

Johnson & Johnson

Figure 10.1 Johnson & Johnson credo. (Reproduced by permission of Johnson & Johnson, New York.)

dates back to 1923, thanks to the founder, D.J. DePree, a devout Baptist, top management also argues that these initiatives, such as recycling, make economic sense.[16]

In the United Kingdom, Anita Roddick's Body Shop, a soaps and cosmetics company, has made a fortune selling "natural" products. Company practices appeal to the consumer's conscience by recycling bottles, sourcing natural materials from the rainforest and other exotic locations, and setting up operations in developing countries under the slogan "Trade not Aid".[17] Their policy of "no animal testing" in developing products (and the highly visible campaign to stop such industry practices) came under attack, when they were accused of not upholding their own policy and of playing on political correctness. Despite such criticism, since the stock went public in 1984, the stock price (by 1992) had increased by over 10,000 percent.[18]

Interest in investing in "ethical" companies or "ethical" funds has grown. These funds (the first ethical fund, Pax World, was set up in the United States in the early 1970s) are restricted from investing in companies, for example, that produce alcohol and tobacco, or defense contractors. Supporters of these funds argue that paying attention to stakeholders as well as shareholders will, in the long term, boost profits by motivating the workforce, developing community goodwill, and avoiding fines. US and UK charities constrained to invest in ethical funds did, in fact, marginally outperform others not so constrained.[19]

Economists, however, protest that "ethical fund investing is a clever marketing tool that dupes people into thinking they are doing something moral".[20] They argue that the stock market carries no moral value, merely a price. German investment firms argue that "we couldn't offer an ethical investment because if we offered a moral alternative that would mean that other investments were not moral".[21]

Many managers believe that there is an inherent trade-off between being profitable and socially responsible. For this reason, John Shad, former SEC chairman, gave Harvard Business School $30 million in order to convince students that "Ethics pays: It's smart to be ethical".[22] A survey of business school deans and congressmen found 63 percent agreement with that notion. However, David Vogel, professor at Berkeley, argues that the statement "ethics pays" undermines its very intention. He insists that "it is unethical to base the case for ethics on economic self interest". Sometimes ethics costs, making decisions to engage in ethical behavior far from trivial, nor devoid of moral choice.[23]

Acts of corporate social responsibility may in fact be the consequence of profitability rather than the cause. It is easy to be magnanimous when things are going well. The real test is when there is a choice between acting ethically and making a profit, as in the case of the decision of US jeans company, Levi-Strauss, to pull their $40 million business out of the lucrative Chinese market in protest against human rights violations. While being a family-held business means that there is less need to worry about shareholders, Levi-Strauss has a long tradition of upholding core values (called aspirations) that have been promoted by family members over several generations.[24]

The relationship between profit and ethics (or morality) may be doomed to an eternal debate between the "economists" and the "humanists", or on the front lines, between the finance and human resource departments. The question remains whether morality and personal (or corporate) self-interest are necessarily mutually exclusive. Does ethics make good business sense, or does it represent a personal (or organizational) "way of being", or integrity?[25] (What you are versus what you do.) Or should ethics be considered a fundamental necessity, an unassailable assumption, in conducting international business?

137

No free society or free economy can long survive without an ethical base . . . a shared moral foundation, a set of binding rules for fair conduct . . . Far from being a luxury, a sound business ethic is essential to the preservation of free enterprise.[26]

Some may argue that this statement can be taken as evidence of cultural imperialism. According to a report in the *Financial Times*, many Asian leaders are rejecting such Western liberal democratic ideas, insisting on economic growth "the Asian way".

. . . Neoconfucianists argue that authoritarian governments such as China's are acceptable, even essential, because discipline is necessary to bring prosperity to developing countries. Full democracy as understood in the west would lead to chaos. Freedom of expression is undesirable . . . because it encourages instability and could provoke conflict between ethnic groups. The rights of individuals must be respected only insofar as they do not impinge on the greater rights of the community as a whole . . .

The west should stop arrogantly trying to impose inappropriate western standards of human rights, democracy and environmental protection on Asia, especially since Asia is on the rise and the west is declining as the "Pacific century" approaches.[27]

Others contend that ethical behavior provides the moral underpinnings of a free society and a free economy and can thereby be justified as an **imperative of globalization**. Yet notions of what is moral and ethical do not necessarily translate across national borders. For example, does the notion of "human rights" in China have a different meaning than in the West? Still, the push towards globalization is causing culture shocks in the way business is conducted around the world, as shown in Figure 10.2.

"It's either a shift away from Reaganomics, a shift in moral values, or an earthquake!"

Figure 10.2 Culture shocks. (*Source: Harvard Business Review*, May–June 1989. Adapted and reprinted by permission of *Harvard Business Review*. Copyright © 1989 by the President and Fellows of Harvard College, all rights reserved.)

The globalization imperative

The globalization of business activities calls for a "level playing field" where the rules of the game are clearly spelled out and apply to everyone. Clearly embedded in this imperative are assumptions of *universalism* and *fairness*. "Being fair" means providing equal opportunities and access to markets, not playing favorites, nor protecting home interests. It also implies distributive justice, such that everyone should get their "fair share". However these assumptions may not be shared in cultures that are relationship-driven and rely on personal networks, where belonging is more important than performing, and where *les droits du seigneur* (the rights of the lord) apply. After all, what does "equal access" or "fair share" mean in the context of a family and, more specifically, in the relationship between parent and child?

Nevertheless, as business continues to globalize, the role of multinationals and their missionaries in establishing and adhering to a shared set of business practices needs to be addressed. This is the case whether the primary motivation is to create a better world or simply to reduce the personal and company liabilities or perils of operating abroad, and now even at home.

Titans tumble

In many countries, chief executives and senior managers are waking up to some harsh realities of doing business across borders, as when the CEO of a French conglomerate found himself locked up in a Belgian jail. Indeed many senior executives are faced with some surprising consequences of becoming international players, finding themselves in jail in their own countries.[28] The "clean hands" (*mani pulite*) campaign launched in Italy in February 1992, for example, caused the resignation of top company and country officials, including ex-prime ministers, as well as the suicides of several prominent businessmen.[29] Many practices formerly considered "business as usual" are coming into public scrutiny, in Europe and in Asia, creating economic and political havoc.

The impact of the globalization imperative, that the rules of the game need to be the same for all players, is particularly evident in the financial industry. It started with scandals in the United States: E.F. Hutton gets nailed for check kiting schemes, Bank of Boston for laundering money, Citibank for parking funds off shore in the Caribbean, and Wall Street millionaire heroes (Mike Milliken, Dennis Levine, Ivan Boesky) are convicted of trading insider information. Questionable practices caused the sudden death of Drexel Burnham and the near death of Solomon Brothers (caught in treasury bond fiasco).

It may be that the nature of the industry plays an important role here. In investment banking, the "gray areas" are often where the money is to be made (no risk, no gain). Walking the thin line of legality provides the thrill as vividly portrayed by Michael Douglas as Gordon Gecko in the movie, *Wall Street*. Or, the corporate culture may be the culprit. The "profit above all" culture of GE was considered to be partly responsible for the Kidder Peabody scandal, as was the highly competitive "score at all costs" culture at Salomon Brothers.[30] But different countries also have different assumptions about what is considered "business as usual".

139

At first, many Europeans did not understand what all the noise was about in the United States. Insider trading, for example, was considered the normal state of affairs in the "City" (London). Then, in 1987 British courts convicted Ernest Saunders, then CEO of Guinness, of stock fraud. In Germany, insider trading was not considered illegal; "It's part of the culture here, and traders accept it as their due".[31] Nevertheless, Deutsche Bank has had to face up to its share of problems. The recent scandals of questionable financial trading practices at Metallgesellschaft and of Jurgen Schneider, who ended up owing the bank $3 billion, have challenged fundamental assumptions regarding the role of banks and business in Germany.[32]

In France, cultural aftershocks have been felt ever since the 1989 Pechiney insider trading fiasco and continue in more recent scandals involving shareholder- or taxpayer-financed home improvements, kickbacks, and political party contributions. These scandals have shaken up the "Gallic old boy network", and challenged the previously tight relationship between the judicial system and the government. This has resulted in a more open and accountable power structure where "the boss is no longer a sacred image".[33]

Continuing east, the banking scandals in Japan in 1991, and the bribery and corruption scandals in India and South Korea have seriously shaken economic and political stability in these countries. Thus the globalization imperative has challenged fundamental business, as well as cultural, assumptions in many countries: the long-cherished relationships between companies, or with customers in Japan, between banks and companies in Germany, or between companies and government in France.

Throughout the world, the resulting public outcry has challenged the long-entrenched social power structures, resulting in the growing demand for greater transparency and accountability to the public interest. In Japan this greater concern is attributed to the increasing vote (and louder voice) of women in society. Such cultural and political upheaval is due in part to globalization. Indeed, the very hope of arriving at "global civilization" depends upon being able to establish a shared meaning of what is considered to be ethical and socially responsible behavior. But to what extent is this really possible? The key question "what is ethical?" is itself a cultural minefield.

Are ethics culture-free?

St Thomas Aquinas, the thirteenth century philosopher, argued that there exists a "natural law" that transcends national boundaries and which "encompasses the preservation of human life, the promotion of family life, an orderly social life, and the quest for knowledge".[34] And throughout history, philosophers have been arguing over the proper criteria for determining ethical behavior: utilitarianism (Bentham and Mill), rights (Kant and Locke), justice (Aristotle), or filial piety (Confucius).

These criteria clearly reflect underlying cultural assumptions. For example, utilitarianism (the greatest good for the greatest number) implies an instrumental, functionalist approach. And rights, by what right: by hierarchy, or, as D'Iribarne argued,[35] by role as in France, by contract as in the United States, or by consensus as in The Netherlands? Does ethics take on different shades of truth on different sides of the Pyrenees (as stated by the sixteenth century French philosopher, Michel de Montaigne), or different sides of the Atlantic and Pacific oceans for that matter?

To address this issue we need to consider what is shared (*etic*) and what is culture-specific (*emic*), and perhaps more fundamentally, *why* we find similarities and differences. Only then can we consider the possibility of arriving at a shared understanding of the issues (such as corruption) and a shared way of responding to those issues, or an agreed upon code of conduct. Again, rather than imposing our own standards, the hope is to find ways of utilizing different cultural assumptions in order to become truly global citizens. With this aim in mind, we first consider the research evidence for cultural differences and similarities in attitudes and responses to issues of ethics and social responsibility. We then search for the underlying reasons. Let us consider the case of corruption.

What is corruption?

Corruption can be defined as

> . . . the misuse of authority as a result of considerations of personal gain which need not be monetary and includes bribery, nepotism, extortion, embezzlement, and utilization of resources and facilities which do not belong to the individual for his own private purposes.[36]

More recently sexual harassment has been added to the list.

In 1977, following scandals which implicated ITT in the effort to overthrow then President Allende in Chile and bribery at Lockheed, the United States passed the Foreign Corrupt Practices Act which made "unethical" behavior abroad subject to the same penalties as at home.

As certain practices, such as bribery, were sometimes considered the only way of doing business in certain environments, American companies had to find other ways or had to leave. IBM managers, for example, sign ethics pledges, swearing to uphold the Foreign Corrupt Practices Act and the company's ethics policies. ITT managers, having signed similar documents, are regularly audited (unannounced). Other companies hire local "watchdogs" to monitor their employee's lifestyles.[37]

Yet differences in local business practices continue to challenge international managers when confronted with what at home would be considered corrupt practices. And managers from different countries report different attitudes when faced with these situations.

For example, in a comparative study of US and European managers,[38] bribery was more often considered the price of doing business or necessary given the competitor's behavior by French (55 percent) and German (38 percent) managers than by US (17 percent). Forty-seven percent of American managers said that the action called for in the scenario presented was a bribe and therefore unethical, illegal, or against company policy (as compared with 15 percent French or 9 percent German). While bribery is illegal at home in France (French Penal Code, 1960) and in Germany, there is no such legislation that applies abroad.

In the same study it was found that all managers indicated similar concern in cases involving personal injury or protecting society. However, different reactions to such scenarios were evident. French and US managers were found more likely to blow the whistle (report on organizational activities to outside authorities) than were German managers. In addition, managers in France and Germany were more willing to let slide a minor infraction concerning pollution (despite having major environmental laws since early 1970s), than were American managers. The greater likelihood of enforcement in the United States was considered a key factor in explaining the differences found in this study.

Another study found both similarities and differences when comparing attitudes of managers in the United States and Hong Kong.[39] While differences were evident with regard to attitudes towards patent protection and price-fixing, almost all managers agreed on reporting defective or unsafe products to superiors even if their job was potentially jeopardized (94 percent HK versus 99 percent US). Although Hong Kong managers indicated that they were less inclined towards whistle blowing (50 percent HK versus 77 percent US), they reported often having to compromise personal principles to conform (92 percent HK versus 41 percent US).

Differences were also found in the way of resolving ethical dilemmas: US managers were more likely to consult with their boss (42 percent US versus 26 percent HK), while Hong Kong managers were more likely to discuss the issue with a friend (20 percent HK versus 6 percent US). These differences can be taken as evidence of greater collectivism when compared to the United States: sharing of information and consensual agreements, loyalty, and pressures for conformity.

The study also asked managers to rank the factors which they considered to contribute to unethical behavior. Neither group considered the society's moral climate or personal financial needs as important determinants. For both groups, the most important factor was the behavior of superiors. US managers placed more importance on the behavior of peers as a determining factor, while for managers in Hong Kong company policy and industry norms were given more importance.

According to the authors of this study, laws and regulations were considered unnecessary in Hong Kong due to the strong social controls created by intense interpersonal relationships. For example, insider trading is not considered a criminal offense; public exposure, loss of face, is considered to be sufficient punishment. Nonetheless, 82 percent of Hong Kong citizens indicated a need for regulation to improve ethical conduct in business. Apparently, more formal guidelines would be welcomed.

Codes of conduct

Codes of conduct provide such formal guidelines. One study conducted by the Conference Board found that by 1986, 92 percent of US companies had codes of conduct, 36 percent had ethics training, 16 percent indicated board level discussion of ethics, and 11 percent had assigned an ombudsman.[40] Another study compared codes of conduct in the top 200 firms in the United Kingdom, France, and (West) Germany and compared the results with that of a US survey of "Fortune 500" firms. Differences in the existence and content of codes of conduct were found not only between US and European firms, but among European firms as well.[41]

Codes of conduct were defined as "A statement setting down corporate principles, ethics, rules of conduct, codes of practice or company philosophy concerning responsibility to employees, shareholders, consumers, the environment or any other aspects of society external to the company". While 75 percent of the US "Fortune 500" firms surveyed has such codes, 59 percent of the 189 European companies responding did not. Most of the European companies had introduced codes in 1986 and only 56 percent intended to introduce them by 1990. These findings were taken as evidence of an "ethics gap" between the United States and Europe.

Differences within Europe were also found: only 30 percent of the French firms surveyed had codes of conduct, compared with 51 percent of the firms in Germany, and 41 percent in the United Kingdom. Controlling for local companies which were US affiliates, the "ethics gap" was found to be even greater: only 33 percent of European firms had codes – in France 18 percent, Germany 47 percent, and in the United Kingdom 31 percent. Of the US affiliates, only 2 percent did *not* have such codes.

The content of these codes of conduct was also found to be different. While all of the European company codes addressed the question of employee conduct (as compared with 55 percent of US firms), differences were found in what that meant. For US firms, it meant treating employees with "fairness and equity", for example, ensuring equal opportunity. The French and British codes stressed the importance of employees to the organization, reinforcing a sense of belonging and collective goals. In Germany, the rights of codetermination and shared responsibility were emphasized, as were specific expectations that the company had of its employees: reliability and loyalty. Thus the European codes focused on employee attitude and behavior towards the company (the collective), while in the United States the focus was placed on company policy towards employees (the individual).

Other differences in the content of codes were also reported: 60 percent of German companies stressed the importance of technology and innovation, and in France 93 percent addressed customer relations. This may indicate efforts to compensate for what is perceived as country-level competitive weaknesses discussed earlier: the reputation of German firms as not being terribly innovative and French firms not being particularly customer- or service-oriented. Given the French interest in high technology, it may not be surprising that one French construction company, Bouygues, included the use of advanced computerized information systems as its 11th commandment.

Other differences found to be culture-specific related to concern for political issues. For US managers this referred to the legal environment and was taken to mean being law-abiding. For the German publisher, Bertelsmann (Germany), this was expressed more generally as support for "a free, democratic and socially responsible society". Despite these differences, the study found that most ethical issues transcended national barriers: fairness and honesty; and concern for customers, suppliers, and community.

In the studies discussed above, it appears that there are concerns which cut across cultural boundaries, concern for society and for employee and customer safety, for example. However, differences were found in how they would respond to these issues. This difference was related to the legal context (regulation and enforcement) as well as the cultural context (hierarchy and collectivism).

143

Yet the questions remain: Why has this issue attracted so much attention in the United States? Is there indeed an "ethics gap"? Are US companies and managers more moral than their European and Asian counterparts? Or do they manage this issue in ways that are just more explicit, and public? Is insisting on ethical behavior, for example with regard to human rights, an excuse for meddling in internal national affairs, as China's Prime Minister has asserted? To what extent can a shared approach to business ethics be hoped for?

Reasons for differences

David Vogel, Professor at Berkeley, believes that there are persistent fundamental national differences in terms of how business ethics is defined, debated, and judged which are due to distinctive institutional, legal, social, and cultural contexts.[42]

Notions of ethics in the United States, for example, are more legalistic and universalist, based on rules and regulations that apply to everyone. These are often made explicit (low context), in written codes of conduct or lists of principles displayed proudly throughout the company, or distributed on wallet-sized cards. This approach annoyed one French manager of a firm acquired by Americans,

> I resent having notions of right and wrong boiled down to a checklist. I come from a nation whose ethical traditions date back hundreds of years. Its values have been transmitted to me by my church and through my family. I don't need to be told by some American lawyers how I should conduct myself in my business activities.[43]

In contrast with the United States where ethical decisions are considered personal, moral judgements, requiring individual responsibility and accountability, in Europe and Asia moral standards are considered to be more "consensual". "Legitimate moral expectations for a company are shaped by the norms of the community not the personal values or reflections of the individual."[44] Ethics is thus *particularist*, applied according to specific circumstances, and strongly affected by the nature of one's social ties and obligations.[45] As such, greater emphasis is placed on informal, social control.

The importance of this more collective, consensual approach is that outsiders, very often entrepreneurs, are the first to take the fall (Bernard Tapie in France, Resaat El-Sayed in Sweden. Even Saunders and Maxwell in the United Kingdom, and Milliken and Boesky in the United States are outsiders in these predominantly Anglo–Saxon Protestant cultures). The economic power of the entrepreneurial overseas Chinese makes them a target for local economic or political problems, as in Malaysia and Indonesia.

For the Japanese, the insider/outsider (*uchi/soto*) ethic is extremely powerful, making it difficult to do business without the proper connections. According to an old Japanese saying, "When you see a stranger, regard him as a thief".[46] Thus outsiders are viewed suspiciously, as they may not share the same values, nor be concerned for the welfare of the group.

In many Asian countries, the teachings of Confucius, which serve as moral guidelines, promote the importance of authority and the collective expressed as clearly structured role relationships. This means that morality is more likely to be defined in terms of

144

others, in terms of interdependence rather than independence.[47] Japanese mothers, for example, coax their children to eat their vegetables by having them consider the feelings of the farmer who produced them.

Notions of reciprocity result in common practices of gift giving and exchanging favors, of saving face and giving face. Shame serves as the most powerful form of social control. Not living up to obligations results in being seen as unreliable, and may lead to ostracism. In Japan, taking individual responsibility has even more serious implications; mitigating circumstances are no excuse. This led to the suicide of the CEO of Japan Airlines following a plane crash.

In contrast, America's Protestant heritage encourages *individual* moral scrutiny and self-criticism (if not self-righteousness). "Ethics [is] considered as a question of personal scruples, a confidential matter between individuals and their consciences."[48] Feelings of guilt rather than shame rest upon living up to internalized ideals rather than external expectations. Morality is based on having to live with yourself rather than with others.

The insistence on individualism thus requires universalism, that the same set of morals or rules and regulations apply to everyone. This results in the US legalistic approach to ethics. The emphasis on individualism results in attributing ethical behavior to the CEO, as in the case of Tylenol, and downplaying the possibility that this behavior may not have happened without the supporting organizational culture. The legalistic approach may also result in an emphasis on compliance (*doing*) rather than on encouraging integrity (*being*).[49]

While the above discussion points to different cultural determinants of ethical behavior, institutional factors need to be considered as well. Some of the institutional reasons may have to do with the roles of government and legislation, of the media, and of the stakeholders, shareholders as well as consumers. For example, the more vocal concern for ethics in the United States may be due to stricter government disclosure laws and more active enforcement, more aggressive journalism (or less fear of libel suits, as in Britain) and "best company" rankings in the business press, and greater risk of shareholder activism and consumer boycotts.

Role of government

Vogel argues that the prevalence of private rather than state ownership in the United States makes corporate social responsibility and philanthropy "primarily an American phenomenon".[50] In Europe, until very recently, business has been largely state rather than privately owned, and populated by small rather than large organizations. Thus the responsibility of business was more narrowly defined. The government was considered primarily responsible for economic development and social welfare.

In the United States private ownership and "big" business put more of the onus and spotlight on company behavior. According to Vogel, "Because the public's expectations of business conduct are so high, the invariable result is a consistently high level of public dissatisfaction with the actual ethical performance of business".[51] It seems more likely, however, that the experience with big business has been such that there is a greater perceived need to be vigilant. Given a history of questionable business practices, some of

145

the richest Americans, the Rockefellers, Carnegies, and Kennedys, were held morally (and legally) suspect in how they made their fortunes.

In fact, in the last ten years, two-thirds of American business has been found to be involved in illegal behavior.[52] And public perceptions of business ethics are indeed quite negative: 59 percent of Americans surveyed believed corporate executives to be dishonest, 58 percent thought ethical standards of business fair or poor, and 49 percent thought business crime was *very* common (41 percent *somewhat* common).[53]

Rather than the "values of 'business civilization' [being] so deeply engrained", as Vogel argues, it is more likely that the perceived excesses of capitalism have to be carefully checked. For example, the oil shortages in the 1970s were viewed by the public as having been manipulated by the oil companies for profit at their expense. This created an outcry that turned some of them into corporate philanthropists, demonstrating concern for social responsibility by creating foundations and by providing highly visible endowments to the arts.

Regulation: the legal context

Differences in legal context, the nature of regulation and the likelihood of enforcement, also play an important role. In Germany, strict environmental laws make these issues more salient. Still, there are few laws against bribery, kickbacks and pay-offs in the corporate sector.[54] In France, the "commission des operations de la bourse" has become a more powerful watchdog. However, in Britain, enforcement remains infrequent, despite the conviction of Ernest Saunders in the Guinness affair. Many were surprised at the lenient ruling on the Maxwell brothers, accused of misappropriating pension funds.

In the United States, between 1988 and 1990, financial penalties have increased by a factor of eight. This cost Exxon $100 million in fines for the Valdez disaster (oil spill), Salomon $200 million, and Drexel Burnham $650 million (which put it into bankruptcy). US managers have learned that crime does not pay.[55] In response to federal guidelines that went into effect on November 1, **1991**, many US companies have adopted codes of conduct and training programs to reduce liabilities and potential fines: $1–2 million fines could be knocked down to $50,000 if they had comprehensive programs such as codes of conduct, ombudsmen, employee hotlines, and mandatory training programs.[56]

At Citibank, for example, ethics training tools were designed such as "Work Ethic" which poses ethical dilemmas for managers to solve, such as that shown in Figure 10.3.[57] Implementing such programs may be viewed cynically as a way to avoid fines rather than as the right way of doing business. Indeed, no amount of ethical programs can make a company immune. The existence of a business conduct committee since 1976, did not stop Dow Corning from continuing to manufacture potentially dangerous breast implants.[58] Compliance with these guidelines does not address the fundamental ways of doing business which may put company integrity at risk.

The role of the media

Public scrutiny of ethical behavior in companies has been made possible by the increased attention to these issues by the media. Ethical breaches have become front page news:

146

Ethics: part of the game at Citicorp

■ Citicorp managers, ever circumspect, do not like to call their newly designed training tool, the Work Ethic, a game. But it is.

Players move markers around a game board by correctly answering multiple-choice questions presented on cards. Each card poses an ethical dilemma a bank employee might encounter in the office or with customers. As the game progresses, players are "promoted" from entry-level employee to supervisor, and eventually to senior manager. As the rank in the company rises, the score for a correct answer drops.

Should you talk to a credit applicant about his loan in public at a cocktail party? If you know not to and you're a supervisor, you gain 30 points; if you're an executive, add only 10. What if the manager of a competing bank calls to suggest colluding on interest rates? If you pick "ask to meet him and discuss it further", you're "fired for cause", and out of the game.

Citicorp thinks the game, which is still under development, could become part of its comprehensive corporate-ethics training program. Says Citicorp assistant secretary Christopher York: "We wanted to increase people's involvement by adding a little bit of competition to the training exercise."

After successfully completing a complex deal for a Japanese client, he presents you with a vase to express his appreciation. It's an expensive item and accepting a gift of such value is clearly against Citicorp policy. Yet, returning it would insult your client.

You:
a) return the vase to the client and explain diplomatically that it's against Citicorp policy to accept gifts from clients.
b) accept the gift because you can't risk insulting an importamt client.
c) accept the gift on behalf of Citicorp, log it with premises management as a furnishing, and display it in a public area of the office.
d) accept the gift and use it as an award for an employee who displays service excellence.

Citicorp likes answer c.

Figure 10.3 Citibank's ethics game. (*Source*: *FORTUNE*, 26 October 1987. Reprinted by permission.)

Exxon's Valdez oil spill, Union Carbide's Bhopal disaster, the BCCI débâcle, and the Barings fiasco. Journalists are increasingly becoming the "moral watchdogs" of corporate behavior. This has led to the dictum for managers: "Don't do anything that you wouldn't want to read in the newspaper".

The CNN coverage of the Anita Hill/Clarence Day affair made sexual harassment a global concern, highlighting the role of the media in the debate and definition of ethics. While Europeans tend to view the American public as excessively moralistic, puritanical, and hypocritical, some were nevertheless impressed with the openness and the transparency with which such ethical concerns were addressed, or publicly aired.

Media attention can also promote "good behavior". Companies have come to realize that well-publicized ethical actions can provide a competitive edge in the "caring nineties" (public backlash to the 1980s as the decade of corporate greed). Company image is enhanced not only with consumers but also with the internal workforce. Company pride can serve as a powerful motivator. Best company rankings provided by business journals such as *Fortune* or *Business Week* (which take into account ethical behavior) not only attract investment and customers but also top talent. Anita Roddick of the Body Shop recognizes the value of media attention in promoting public relations; the company does not advertise.

The role of stakeholders

Company stakeholders – the local community, customers, employees as well as shareholders – play an increasingly important role in monitoring ethical behavior. Striking employees protest over the closing of factories. Employees may also "blow the whistle" on unethical activities, such as employee safety practices in the famous case of Karen Silkwood. A Japanese engineer at Honda recently testified against the company's safety practices, sending shock waves in Japan where whistle-blowing is unheard of, akin to high treason.[59]

Customers boycott companies engaged in questionable practices, for example refusing to buy grapes picked by migrant workers in California. Local communities have become much more active in insisting on environmental protection, as in the case of Swiss pharmaceutical company Sandoz, which was burned in effigy, accused of polluting the Rhine. US government agencies are prohibited from doing business with suppliers or distributors that do not uphold affirmative action guidelines.

There is also growing pressure to hold company boards of directors more accountable. In the United States, members of the board are subject to increased personal liability for company actions and risk landing in jail or receiving heavy fines. Shareholders have become more vigilant and vocal in questioning the behavior of top management. In France this has led to the resignation of CEOs accused of using company resources for private purposes.

Despite the reasons, both cultural and institutional, for similarities and differences in ethical behavior, as discussed above, the question remains: to what extent should personal values, parent company, or home-country values and rules apply? Head-office efforts to insist on ethical practices or to install ethics programs in foreign subsidiaries may be taken as another sign of cultural imperialism. These efforts may even be disparaged as moral hypocrisy. Americans are often accused of excessive self-righteousness, and worse yet, of missionary zeal. Should we play by the local rules? Or is it possible to find a better way?

Strategies for managing ethical dilemmas

While the globalization imperative has challenged fundamental cultural and business assumptions throughout the world, many practices which may seem objectionable, remain firmly embedded in the host-country environment. The decision has to be made whether to impose parent company or home-country rules in host countries or to play by the local rules of the game. Journalist Roger Williams argues that,

> Corporations are not formed to effect change but to sell goods. It can be pressured into treating employees more equitably. But it cannot be expected to challenge the laws of a society. Those who insist otherwise are trying to get a businessman to do the job of a diplomat or a soldier.

However, during investigations of Italy's bribery scandals, the activities of foreign multinationals operating in Italy (such as ABB, Siemens, and Ericsson) came under scrutiny. Although kickbacks had been considered necessary to win public contracts, as openly acknowledged by top Italian industrialist, Carlo Di Benedetti, many major multinationals and their executives, both foreign and domestic, found themselves under arrest.

148

In fact, succession planning at some of the major Italian multinationals has been held up pending outcomes of such investigations. This experience provided a literal warning that the advice "when in Rome . . ." had serious limitations.[60]

Apparently, few American companies were implicated. This was attributed to taking seriously US anticorruption legislation and corporate ethics policies. At Honeywell Europe, the Italian Vice-President responsible for southern Europe acknowledged that while upholding company principles regarding ethical behavior sometimes meant walking away from certain markets, most managers felt pride in being able to do this.[61] But to what extent does imposing home country or company rules reflect cultural imperialism? In the words of Citibank,

> We must never lose sight of the fact that we are guests in foreign countries. We must conduct ourselves accordingly. Local governments can pass any kind of legislation, and whether we like it or not, we must conform to it. Under these circumstances, Citibank can survive only if we are successful in demonstrating to the local authorities that our presence is useful to them.[62]

Consider the case of South Africa, under apartheid, where different decisions were taken for different reasons. Some companies such as Polaroid or General Motors chose the path of "civil disobedience", operating in ways to bring about social change by breaking the rules of apartheid. Insisting on the corporate ethic of racial equality and opportunity, for example, these companies integrated factory washrooms and community neighborhoods.[63] Over one hundred (125) of the US "Fortune 500" companies (accounting for $2.5 billion in US FDI in Africa) signed up promising to adhere to the Sullivan Principles, a code of conduct for operating in South Africa.[64] These principles are shown in Figure 10.4.

The Sullivan Principles

• Non-segregation of the races in all eating, comfort, locker room, and work facilities
• Equal and fair employment practices for all employees
• Equal pay for all employees doing equal or comparable work for the same period of time
► Initiation and development of training programs that will prepare blacks, coloreds, and Asians in substantial numbers for supervisory, administrative, clerical, and technical jobs
► Increasing the number of blacks, coloreds, and Asians in management and supervisory positions
► Improving the quality of employees' lives outside the work environment in such areas as housing, transportation, schooling, recreation, and health facilities

Figure 10.4 The Sullivan principles. (*Source*: "The case for doing business in South Africa", *Fortune*, 19 June 1978. Reprinted by permission.)

Other companies chose to play by the host-country (apartheid) rules for reasons such as those expressed by Citibank. Eventually, economic sanctions imposed by the US Comprehensive Anti-Apartheid Act in November 1986 forced forty-nine US firms (including IBM, GM, and P&G) to withdraw from South Africa, and another forty the year after.

Several European companies, however, were reluctant to pull out, given the substantial amounts of investment, notably by British and West German firms less subject to the same kind of sanctions and shareholder pressures as in the United States. "The big difference between American and European business is the lesser moral tone".[65] However, British bank Barclays did pull out in 1986 after pressure from local special interest groups.[66] Dutch interests also succumbed to external pressures. Other foreign investors, particularly Asian companies, went in, buying up companies at fire-sale prices. The same has since happened in Burma.

Thus, as the case of South Africa demonstrates, different countries and different companies adopt different decisions when faced with these ethical dilemmas. Powerful multinational companies, such as Shell or IBM, may be able to convince local governments to play by the company rules or not to play at all. Thus the relationship of the home company or country to the host country, being considered an insider, powerful, and important, is critical.[67] Nevertheless, despite instances of countries agreeing to impose economic sanctions or boycotts for political reasons (Bosnia, Iran, Israel), arriving at a common approach to operating in other countries for economic reasons remains elusive. French President Chirac's recent promotion of business activities in China, to the chagrin of US President Clinton, may be a case in point.

In choosing to play by the local rules or to impose home-court rules, the following questions need to be open for discussion: Is following the dictum "when in Rome . . ." an easy way out, the path of least resistance? Does this mean that there is no difference between cultural relativism and ethical relativism, that there is no absolute good versus bad, right versus wrong? By accepting that different cultures have different notions of what is considered moral behavior, are we respecting cultural differences or are we contributing to social problems?

As Alan Christie, Director of Community Affairs, Levi-Strauss Europe, puts it, "The private sector may not be able to answer the social problems of the world – but it can stop being part of those problems". But does this mean that it is better to pull out or to stay and insist on doing it your way? Is it better to refuse to play (withdraw) or to fight the system from within? Which was more effective in the case of South Africa: economic sanctions or civil disobedience?

While it may not always be clear what is right and wrong (acute dilemmas), it may also be the case that one knows what is right or wrong but fails to do it (acute rationalization).[68] What are the appropriate criteria for judging ethical behavior: "How would it look in the press" (the "best disinfectant is sunlight"); or "How it would look in the mirror"? Is it enough to consult your personal sense of right and wrong?[69] Or is this an individual or collective (company, community, or national) process? These issues need to be addressed by both managers and their companies, in order to define their role as global citizens.

150

Global citizens: the role of managers and companies

Individual managers need to take stock not only of their own cultural and moral baggage, but also that of their company, industry, or host country. It is important to assess how these different spheres of cultural influence contribute to ethical behavior. While one's own moral position needs to be well defined ("To thine own self be true"), one must recognize how these external pressures, however subtle, may influence our judgement. In this way, morality is both an individual and collective affair.

In a study of recent Harvard MBA graduates, most reported using the "sleep test" to resolve ethical dilemmas and that the family was the primary source of ethical wisdom. They also reported company pressure to act unethically in the following messages: performance is what counts – meet your numbers, be loyal, be a team player, do not break the law, and do not overinvest in ethical behavior.[70]

In today's competitive environment, performance pressures are ever-increasing, making it more and more necessary to establish realistic performance goals. Pressure to achieve objectives above all else has led to a "means justify the ends attitude". Indeed, one study reports 20–30 percent of middle managers wrote deceptive internal reports, and 12–24 percent of job applicants deceptive resumés.[71]

Four rationalizations are found to be common in explaining unethical behavior: it is not really illegal or immoral; it serves the best interest of the individual or corporation; it is safe because it will never be found out or publicized; the activity helps the company and therefore will be condoned and protected.[72] These arguments reflect psychologically primitive systems of defense (denial). According to psychoanalyst, Abraham Zaleznik, this type of thinking derives from a narcissistic sense of entitlement that weakens conscience. Also, more than greed, there is the thrill of flirting with danger and a similar high to that of being on a winning streak, which may represent meglomania or a cover for depression.[73]

These rationalizations also reflect stages of moral development. An individual's sense of morality is developed quite early on. Kohlberg identified a sequence of six stages of moral development in children (ranging from obedience and fear of punishment if caught through adhering to universal principles of justice and welfare) which he considered to be invariant and universal.[74]

A study of Hong Kong managers found that although what managers said they would do corresponded to specific stages of development as described by Kohlberg, what they actually did when faced with different scenarios demonstrated reasoning at several stages simultaneously.[75] While some cultural differences were found when compared with American managers, the key issue was being able to capture what managers of whatever nationality would actually do or have done, rather than what they say they would do.

Using Kohlberg's model, different stages of moral development can also be found among companies, as shown in Figure 10.5.[76] **Amoral** organizations are driven by "winning at all costs", by greed, and short-term orientation. Their approach to ethics is "we won't get caught". **Legalistic** organizations are driven by concerns for economic performance. Their approach is reactive: "Don't do any harm", and obey the law to the letter. They avoid writing codes of ethics, as this can create legal problems later on. In

A summary of the moral development of corporations

Stage in moral development	Management attitude and approach	Ethical aspects of corporate culture	Corporate ethics artifacts	Defining corporate behavior
Stage I – the amoral organization	Get away with all you can; it's ethical as long as we're not caught; ethical violations, when caught, are a cost of doing business	Outlaw culture; live hard and fast; damn the risks; get what you can and get out	No meaningful code of ethics or other documentation; no set of values other than greed	Film Recovery System Numerous penny stock companies
Stage II – the legalistic organization	Play within the legal rules; fight changes that affect your economic outcome; use damage control through public relations when social problems occur; a reactive concern for damage to organizations from social problems	If it's legal, it's OK; work the gray areas; protect loopholes and don't give ground without a fight; economic performance dominates evaluations and rewards	The code of ethics, if it exists, is an internal document; "Don't do anything to harm the organization"; "Be a good corporate citizen"	Ford Pinto Firestone 500 Nestlé Infant Formula R. J. Reynolds Philip Morris
Stage III – the responsive organization	Management understands the value of not acting solely on a legal basis, even though they believe they could win; management still has a reactive mentality; a growing balance between profits and ethics, although a basic premise still may be a cynical "ethics pays"; management begins to test and learn from more responsive actions	There is a growing concern for other corporate stakeholders other than owners; culture begins to embrace a more "responsible citizen" attitude	Codes are more externally oriented and reflect a concern for other publics; other ethics vehicles are undeveloped	Procter & Gamble (Rely Tampons) Abbott Labs Borden
Stage IV – the emerging ethical organization	First stage to exhibit an active concern for ethical outcomes; "We want to do the 'right' thing"; top management values become organizational values; ethical perception has focus but lacks organization and long-term planning; ethics management is characterized by successes and failures	Ethical values become part of culture; these core values provide guidance in some situations but questions exist in others; a culture that is less reactive and more proactive to social problems when they occur	Codes of ethics become action documents; code items reflect the core values of the organization; handbooks, policy statements, committees, ombudsmen are sometimes used	Boeing General Mills Johnson & Johnson (Tylenol) General Dynamics Caterpillar Levi Strauss
Stage V – the ethical organization	A balanced concern for ethical and economic outcomes; ethical analysis is a fully integrated partner in developing both the mission and strategic plan; SWOT (Strengths, Weaknesses, Opportunities, Threats) analysis is used to *anticipate* problems and analyze alternative outcomes	A total ethical profile, with carefully selected core values which reflect that profile, directs the culture; corporate culture is planned and managed to be ethical; hiring, training, firing, and rewarding all reflect the ethical profile	Documents focus on the ethical profile and core values; all phases of organizational documents reflect them	????????

Figure 10.5   Stages of moral development. (*Source*: R.E. Reidenbach and D.P. Robin (1991) "A conceptual model of corporate model development", *Journal of Business Ethics*, 10, p. 282. Reprinted with kind permission from Kluwer Academic Publishers.)

responsive companies there is a growing concern for balance between profits and ethics, and for stakeholders. Nevertheless, their approach remains somewhat cynical: ethics pays. The fourth stage, the **emerging ethical** organization demonstrates an active approach to ethics, providing support and measures of ethical behavior, to encourage people to do the "right" thing, developing shared values of ethical behavior. Finally, the **ethical** organization thoroughly integrates questions of ethical behavior with developing strategy and mission, thereby addressing the fundamental issue of organizational integrity – what a company *is* rather than what it *does*.

Harvard Professor Lynne Paine provides the guidelines for developing strategies for integrity, as shown in Figure 10.6. Thus for managers and companies, the ethical decisions taken and the corresponding rationale, for legal (fear of getting caught) versus moral reasons, reflect different stages of moral development. In fact, by making something legal, it may no longer be considered as an ethical issue. This may be one way of creating a level "ethical" playing field, albeit to the lowest moral common denominator.

While it may help to clarify what is ethical and what is legal, this does not necessarily resolve the moral dilemma. Consider, for example, making corruption illegal (as did the United States). Although it may be legally permissible to give payments to officials to facilitate routine government action (so you can pay $25 to get your belongings through customs) or to use other legal kinds of currency, such as information, prestige, and contacts, does this not avoid the ethical issue? Is there a difference between a bribe and providing infrastructure or building a hospital? Or by having the country's president visit another country in order to get a government bid accepted? Or are we (as George Bernard Shaw argued in his indecent proposal) quibbling about the price, not the act? Why should best price be more valued than best relationship?

Thus there are many gray areas that need to be resolved. Creating a legal/ethical matrix can help to provide guidelines for conduct: what is neither ethical nor legal should be avoided; what is both legal and ethical can be embraced. But managers will still have to decide whether being legal or illegal makes it ethical or not: legal/unethical or illegal/

1. Guiding values and commitments make sense and are clearly communicated

2. Company leaders are personally committed, credible, and willing to take action on the values they espouse

3. Espoused values are integrated into the normal channels of management decision-making and are reflected in the organization's critical activities

4. Company systems and structures support and reinforce its values

5. Managers throughout the company have the decision-making skills, knowledge, and competencies needed to make ethically sound decisions on a day to day basis

Figure 10.6 Developing corporate integrity. (*Source*: L.S. Paine (1994) "Managing for organizational integrity", *Harvard Business Review*, March–April, p. 112.)

ethical (such as prostitution, child labor, birth control, abortion, designated mothers and fathers, assisted suicide, genetic engineering). Many such ethical dilemmas are outside the law, which cannot keep up with advances, say in technology and medicine.[77] Consider the ethical issues provoked by the Internet and subsequent calls for censorship.

Towards a global civilization

In order to address these issues of what is ethical and what guidelines need to be followed, companies need to provide opportunity for open discussion, without fear of punishment. It may be that ". . . levels of moral reasoning and judgment are likely to be higher when managers get together and discuss ethical issues than when these choices have to be made in solitude".[78]

Most ethics courses designed for managers or MBA students have been criticized as too theoretical (deontology/Kant), too general (questioning economic and political systems), or too impractical.[79] De Bettignies recommends that such courses need to be experiential, conceptual, practical, prospective, and imaginative, where ethical dilemmas can be brought into the open and debated publicly by multidisciplinary and multicultural teams.[80]

> The purpose of these discussions and debates is not to impose values or give solutions but to enhance awareness, to provide frames of reference, to give analytical tools to explore in-depth tradeoffs among short and long term alternative decisions, to involve individual managers in assessing their own values and paradigms in order to be more lucid and responsible in their own choices.[81]

Puffer and McCarthy recommend creating a framework of what is considered ethical/unethical in each country to clarify the issues and to provide the starting point in working together to develop mutually acceptable ethical standards. This helps managers to recognize where there are differences and to understand the reasons for these differences. For example, the ambiguity and ambivalence about business ethics in Russia are strongly related to the current political and economic uncertainties, as well as the previous methods found necessary for survival. Nevertheless, both US and Russian managers were found to share universal values of honesty, integrity, trust, and fairness.[82]

Thus certain ethical standards may be universal: honesty, integrity, and protection of society, customer, and employees. Others may remain culturally specific: reciprocity (gift-giving), whistle-blowing, profit maximization, social welfare, patent protection, and price-fixing. These reflect cultural differences in importance placed on what is good for the group, rather than what is good for the individual, on achievement rather than belonging, and on social harmony rather than adherence to abstract principles.

What is important is to recognize where there are similarities and where there are differences, what are the cultural or institutional reasons for these differences, and how to arrive at some shared way of resolving them. One recommendation made by Dunfee is "to identify and make explicit diverse ethical norms and evaluate them against certain universal, but minimalist, moral principles".[83]

154

Efforts have been made to create a common set of business ethics, at the supranational level such as the United Nations code of conduct for multinationals and at the industry level. According to a report in the *Financial Times*,[84] in 1994, business leaders from Europe, Japan, and the United States met in Switzerland to develop an international code of ethics; to set a world standard against which business behavior could be measured and a benchmark to help companies devise their own codes. The Caux Round Table sought to identify shared values and reconcile differing values in an attempt to reduce trade tensions with Japan. A seven-point set of principles for doing business was drawn from two ethical traditions: Japanese *kyosei* ("living and working together for the common good of mankind") and human dignity.

Ultimately, the way that these decisions are taken by companies and managers will most likely remain culturally determined. Those from **individualist** cultures, such as Americans, will look within themselves, asking if they can personally live with the decisions taken. Those from **collectivist** cultures will look to those around them and ask how the others will live with them. In **low-context** cultures, ethical standards are likely to be made explicit, to be found in writing, and in law. In **high-context** cultures, ethical standards are likely to be more implicit, assumed to be shared by members of the community. This may result in some countries adhering to the letter of the law, in other cultures to the spirit of the law. In cultures that are **universalist**, the laws will be expected to apply to everyone; in **particularist** cultures, more attention will be paid to the situation and people involved.

Perhaps globalization of the economy will necessitate the convergence of rules and regulations for doing business, and perhaps even ethics. Nevertheless, the assumptions underlying economic and political integration, however deeply rooted (or near to one's heart), need to be acknowledged and challenged. The very ideologies of free market, of democracy, and of equal opportunity carry with them ethical baggage. We too often accept them as given. The lack of questioning of their own world-view is what leads to the perception of Americans as "playing moral police" in their mission to "make the world safe for democracy".

Yet, there are perhaps some fundamentals which need not be questioned. It may be possible to arrive at a shared view of morality and ethical behavior, in line with such efforts as the Helsinki agreements (against torture and murder). To arrive at such criteria for global citizenship requires acknowledging and utilizing cultural differences, enabling us to choose from a broader menu of desirable values: life, liberty, and the pursuit of happiness; liberty, equality, fraternity; filial piety, frugality, and hard work; Do unto others . . . . For Aristotle, "moral" simply meant "practical". He thus advocated "virtue", which meant toughness, "willingness to do what is necessary" as humanely as possible. Virtue also includes courage, fairness, sensitivity, persistence, honesty, and gracefulness.[85]

Now, coming to the end of our journey, rather than finding a global village, we discover yet another road. This road (whether paved with yellow bricks or gold) will hopefully lead towards a "global civilization". This destination promises greater riches through a fruitful coexistence of differences, and sharing of fundamental values. In the words of Harold Perlmutter, Professor of International Business at Wharton,

155

By the first global civilization we mean a world order, with shared values, processes, and structures: 1) whereby nations and cultures become more open to influence by each other, 2) whereby there is recognition of identities and diversities of peoples in various groups, and ethnic and religious pluralism, 3) where peoples of different ideologies and values both cooperate and compete but no ideology prevails over all the others, 4) where the global civilization becomes unique in a holistic sense while still being pluralist, and heterogeneous in its character, and 5) where increasingly these values are perceived as shared despite varying interpretations, such as we currently see for the values of openness, human rights, freedom, and democracy.[86]

Thus rather than corporate soldiers sent out to the battlefield to wage economic warfare, managers become global citizens engaged in making the world a better place through economic development.

Notes

1. Ricoeur, P. (1990) *Soi-même comme un Autre*, Paris: Seuil.
2. Vogel, D. (1991) "Business ethics: New perspectives on old problems", *California Management Review*, Summer, pp. 101–17.
3. *Ibid.*, p. 103.
4. Furnham, A. and Koritsas, E. (1990) "The protestant work ethic and vocational preference", *Journal of Organizational Behavior*, 11, 43–55, p. 44.
5. Furnham, A. (1990) *The Protestant Work Ethic: The Psychology of Work-related Beliefs and Behaviors*, London: Routledge.
6. Weber, M. (1905) *The Protestant Ethic and the Spirit of Capitalism*, New York: Scribners.
7. Puffer, S.M. and McCarthy, D.J. (1995) "Finding the common ground in Russian and American business ethics", *California Management Review*, 37(2), pp. 29–47.
8. Hofstede, G. (1991) *Culture and Organization: Software of the Mind*, London: McGraw-Hill.
9. Hofstede, G. and Bond, M.H. (1988) "The Confucius connection: From cultural roots to economic growth", *Organizational Dynamics*, Spring, pp. 4–21.
10. Ghoshal, S. and Bartlett, C.A. (1987) "Matsushita Electric Industrial (MEI) in 1987", Harvard Business School case.
11. Trompenaars, F. (1993) *Riding the Waves of Culture*, London: The Economist Books.
12. Japan study, source unknown.
13. Santos, J.P., International executive and professor of management, Universidade Catolica Portuguesa, personal communication.
14. Cole, R.E. (1992) "Work and leisure in Japan", *California Management Review*, 34(3), pp. 52–63.
15. Grundling, E. (1991) "Ethics and working with the Japanese", *California Management Review*, Spring, 25–39, p. 33.
16. "Herman Miller: How green is my factory", *Business Week*, September 23, 1991, pp. 57–8.
17. Bartlett, C. (1993) "The Body Shop International", Harvard Business School case No. 9-392-032.
18. "Body Shop International: What selling will be like in the '90s", *Fortune*, January 13, 1992, pp. 47–8.
19. Bruce, R. (1992) "Can 'ethics' square money and nature?", *International Herald Tribune*, March 14–15, p. 14.

156

20. Baker, M. (1992) "Get rich, feel good: Is this moral?", *International Herald Tribune*, March 14–15, p. 15.
21. *Ibid.*
22. "Can ethics be taught? Harvard gives it the old college try", *Business Week*, April 6, 1992, p. 36.
23. Vogel, D. (1988) "Ethics and profits don't always go hand in hand", *Los Angeles Times*, December 28, p. 7.
24. "Managing by values: Is Levi Strauss' approach visionary – or flaky", *Business Week*, September 12, 1994, pp. 38–43.
25. Paine, L.S. (1994) "Managing for organizational integrity", *Harvard Business Review*, March–April, pp. 106–17.
26. Simon,W.E. (1976) "A challenge to free enterprise" in I. Hill (ed.) *The Ethical Basis of Economic Freedom*, Chapel Hill, NC: American Viewpoint, pp. 405–6.
27. Mallet, V. (1994) "Confucius or convenience? Asian leaders say their ideology must be taken seriously by the west, but critics say the philosophy is cynically self serving", *Financial Times*, March 5, p. 26.
28. "Something's rotten in France, Spain . . .", *Business Week*, June 20, 1994, pp. 16–18.
29. Glover, J. (1994) "A death in Tangentopoli", *Institutional Investor*, May, pp. 55–63.
30. Hager, B. (1991) "What's behind business' sudden fervor for ethics", *Business Week*, September 23, p. 39.
31. "Now it's Germany's turn for a scandal", *Business Week*, September 23, 1991, p. 17.
32. "Something's rotten in France, Spain . . .", *Business Week*, June 20, 1994, pp. 16–18.
33. Toy, S. (1994) "The real scandal in France is over", *Business Week*, July 25, p. 18.
34. Becker, H. and Fritzsche, D.J. (1987) "A comparison of the ethical behavior of American, French and German managers", *Columbia Journal of World Business*, Winter, 87–95, p. 87.
35. D'Iribarne, P. (1989) *La Logique de l'Honneur*, Paris: Seuil.
36. Muzaffar, C. (1980) "The scourge of corruption", Presented at the seminar of *Corruption and Society*.
37. Worthy, F.S. (1989) "When somebody wants a payoff", *Fortune*, Pacific Rim, pp. 91–3.
38. Becker and Fritzsche, *Op. cit.*
39. Dolecheck, M.M. and Dolecheck, C.C. (1987) "Business ethics: A comparison of attitudes of managers in Hong Kong and the United States", *The Hong Kong Manager*, April–May, pp. 28–43.
40. Berenbeim, R.E. (1986) *Corporate Ethics*, New York: The Conference Board.
41. Langlosis, C.C. and Schlegelmilch, B.B. (1990) "Do corporate codes of ethics reflect national character? Evidence from Europe and the United States", *Journal of International Business Studies*, Fourth quarter, pp. 519–39.
42. Vogel, D. (1992) "The globalization of business ethics: Why America remains distinctive", *California Management Review*, Fall, pp. 30–49.
43. *Ibid.*, p. 45.
44. *Ibid.*, pp. 44–5.
45. de Bettignies, H.-C. (1991) "Ethics and international business: A European perspective", presented at the Tokyo Conference on the Ethics of Business in a Global Economy, Kashiwa-shi, Japan.
46. Grundling, *Op. cit.*, p. 27.
47. Markus, H.R. and Kitayama, S. (1991) "Culture and the self: Implications for cognition, emotion, and motivation", *Psychological Review*, 98(2), pp. 224–53.
48. Vogel, *Op. cit.*
49. Paine, *Op. cit.*
50. Vogel, *Op. cit.*
51. *Ibid.*, p. 43.

52. Gellerman, S.W. (1986) "Why 'good' managers make bad ethical choices", *Harvard Business Review*, July–August, pp. 85–9.
53. De Bettignies, H.-C., Professor INSEAD, lecture notes.
54. Nash, N.C. (1995) "Germans look to their corporate ethics", *International Herald Tribune*, July 21, pp. 1, 10.
55. Vogel, *Op. cit.*
56. *Ibid.*
57. "Ethics: Part of the game at Citicorp", *Fortune*, October 26, 1987.
58. "The best laid ethics program", *Business Week*, March 9, 1992, pp. 59–60.
59. Weiser, B. (1996) "An ex-employee as hostile witness: Honda faces unusual critic", *International Herald Tribune*, March 6, pp. 13, 17.
60. "When in Rome . . .", *Business Week*, June 7, 1993, p. 20.
61. Schneider, S.C. and Wittenberg-Cox, A. and Hanson, L. (1990) Honeywell, Europe, INSEAD case.
62. Schmidt, E. (1980) *Decoding Corporate Camouflage: U.S. Business Support for Apartheid*, Institute for Policy Studies, Washington, DC, p. 78.
63. "Companies try a new tack: Civil disobedience", *Business Week*, October 13, 1985, p. 27.
64. Sherman, S.P. (1984) "Scoring corporate conduct in South Africa", *Fortune*, July 9, pp. 168–72.
65. "As Americans pull out of South Africa, Europeans and Asians move in", *Business Week*, March 17, 1986, pp. 22–3.
66. Rolfe, R. (1988) "South Africa: The next wave of pullouts", *International Management*, April, pp. 51–5.
67. Gladwin, T.N. and Walter, I. (1980) *Multinationals Under Fire*, New York: John Wiley.
68. Stark, A. (1993) "What's the matter with business ethics?", *Harvard Business Review*, May–June, pp. 38–48.
69. Worthy, *Op. cit.*.
70. Badaracco, J.L. and Webb, A.P. (1995) "Business ethics: A view from the trenches", *California Management Review*, 37(2), pp. 8–28.
71. Labisch, K. (1992) "The new crisis in business ethics", April 20, *Fortune*, pp. 99–102.
72. *Ibid.*
73. Magnet, M. (1986) "The decline and fall of business ethics", *Fortune*, December 8, pp. 65–72.
74. Kohlberg, L. (1981) *Essays on Moral Development*, San Francisco: Harper & Row.
75. Snell, R.S. (1996) "Complementing Kohlberg: Mapping the ethical reasoning used by managers for their own dilemma cases", *Human Relations*, 49(1), pp. 23–49.
76. Drummond, J. (1994) "Management: Saints and sinners – How to achieve an ethical balance in business operations", *Financial Times*, March 23, p. 12.
77. De Bettignies, lecture.
78. Posner, B.Z. and Schmidt, W.H. (1984) "Values and the American manager: An update", *California Management Review*, 26(3), pp. 210–12.
79. Stark, *Op. cit.*
80. de Bettignies, *Op. cit.*
81. *Ibid.*, p. 15.
82. Puffer and McCarthy, *Op. cit.*
83. Stark, *Op. cit.*
84. Dickson, T. (1994) "The search for universal ethics: The launch of a new set of business principles", *Financial Times*, July 22, p. 11.
85. Stark, *Op. cit.*
86. Perlmutter, H.V. (1991) "On the rocky road to the first global civilization", *Human Relations*, 44(9), 897–920, p. 898.

Chapter Eight

———— • ————

Ethical Issues
in International Business

PERHAPS THE MOST important development in business in the past decade has been the recognition that markets are now international. Every U.S. firm realizes that competitors for its market share could come from any corner of the globe. Even fairly small regional firms now attempt to market their products internationally. Any firm concerned with its survival must adopt an international perspective.

Of course there is much more to the awareness of international issues than the development of international markets. International travel is becoming more prevalent, and many more people from abroad are visiting the United States. In addition, many problems that affect one country have an impact on other nations. For example, the disaster at the Soviet nuclear power plant in Chernobyl illustrated that pollution respects no national boundaries.

The subject of ethical issues in international business has no shortage of topics. Bribery is a common problem, as is the marketing of pesticides and the obligations of wealthy economies to so-called lesser developed countries. Before we can address these specific issues with much authority, an overarching problem needs to be addressed. There is a wide variety of opinion on what is acceptable conduct in international business, and a general skepticism prevails that questions whether there are any universal norms for ethical business practice. Since opinions on whether U.S. companies should bribe when conducting business in certain foreign countries depend in part on whether one believes there is a universal norm that bribery is unethical, the issue of international business norms needs to be addressed at the outset.

ARE THERE INTERNATIONAL NORMS
OF BUSINESS PRACTICE?

A U.S. company involved in business abroad must face the question, "When in Rome, should it behave as the Romans do?" This question arises not only for U.S. firms doing business abroad but for non-U.S. firms doing business in the United

514   **160**

States. One is tempted to answer the question as follows: When operating abroad, a firm should always obey the law of the host country. But this answer is inadequate on a number of grounds. First, many differences in business practices between the home country (where the firm is headquartered) and host country are not matters governed by host country law. As noted in Chapter 5, employment at will is both legal and widely practiced in the United States. In Japan employment at will is not the customary business practice. When Japanese auto companies built auto assembly plants in the United States, the executives of these companies could not have looked to U.S. law to instruct them as to whether they should adopt the U.S. employment-at-will practice. Under U.S. law, employment at will is legally permitted, but it is not legally required. Second, it is immoral for a company to obey an unjust law. The most that can be said is that corporations should obey the law of the host country as long as the law does not require the corporation to violate a universal moral norm.

How should a corporation behave when business norms of the host country differ from those of the home country and when host country law is silent concerning how business must behave? The multinational firm has at least four options: (1) Follow the norms of its home country because that is the patriotic thing to do; (2) follow the norms of the host country to show proper respect for the host country's culture; (3) follow whichever norm is most profitable; (4) follow whichever norm is morally best. (Note that these four alternatives are not all mutually exclusive; for example, following the fourth option might require following the second one as well.)

There may be no one appropriate course of action for a multinational business to take. In highly developed industrialized countries, option 3 seems to be a permissible course of action. One might think that choosing option 3 would require following option 2 as well because the most profitable way to conduct business is to follow the practices of the host country. However, Japanese companies operating in the United States have consistently not followed U.S. norms (option 2). Rather, Japanese companies have imported traditional Japanese management practices into the United States.[1] The results have been mixed, but on balance Japanese businesses operating in the United States that obey Japanese management principles are equal or superior in profitability to competing U.S. firms. One U.S. Honda plant that is operated on Japanese management principles is even more productive than comparable Honda plants in Japan. The importing of Japanese management practices with respect to employees into the United States has not created any appreciable resentment from U.S. citizens.

In his article, Iwao Taka provides the religious and philosophical basis for business ethics in Japan. As a result, certain practices that would be morally questionable in our culture are seen as morally appropriate or even required in Japanese culture. Consider the keiretsu system which is so often criticized in the United States as being anticompetitive and hence unfair. In a keiretsu system the capital for each firm is supplied by the banks in that firm's keiretsu, and the firm uses a limited number of suppliers from that firm's keiretsu. The fact that a supplier outside the keiretsu could provide a product at a cheaper price is not normally a decisive criterion. Since foreign (non-Japanese) firms are not members of any Japanese keiretsu, they have an especially difficult time breaking into the Japanese market. However, as Taka points out, the special treatment given keiretsu members is consistent with what Taka calls the Concentric Circles view of ethical obligations. One's ethical obligations are greatest to those close to you, e.g., family, and are least to those most different from you, e.g., foreigners. As Taka says, this ethical point of view rests in turn on Confucianism which permits "people to treat others in proportion to the intimacy of their relations."

Understanding Japanese ethics also explains some of the criticisms that the Japanese level against American business practice. They believe that American firms are short-sighted, focusing only on the short term, that American executives are paid too highly, and that American companies lay off workers too quickly.

On the other hand, Taka realizes that Japan's ethical system is also subject to criticism. Japan should take its obligations to non-Japanese more seriously, even if foreigners are in the outermost circle. Japan also has been criticized for discriminating against women and for driving workers too hard so that some literally die from overwork (karoshi).

This discussion illustrates the importance of establishing the existence and content of international moral norms for business. In his article, Norman Bowie contends that any appeals to justify home country practices over host country practices or vice versa require an appeal to international moral norms. Bowie appeals to three considerations on behalf of international moral norms. First, widespread agreement already exists among nations, as illustrated by the large number of countries that are signatories to the United Nations Declaration of Universal Human Rights and by the existence of numerous international treaties establishing norms of business practice. Second, certain moral norms must be endorsed by each society if society is to exist at all. Corporations ought to accept the moral norms that make society, and hence business practice itself, possible. Third, certain moral norms are required if business practice is to function at all. Bowie uses Kantian arguments to show that business requires a moral norm that corporations keep their contracts. However, similar arguments could be based on utilitarian considerations. If certain moral rules or traits such as truth telling or honesty give a multinational corporation a competitive advantage, then eventually these moral norms or traits will be adopted by all multinationals because those that do not will not survive.

Thomas Donaldson argues that multinationals have a moral duty to honor fundamental rights. Donaldson proposes a threefold test that any rights claim must pass if it is to be considered a fundamental right. He proposes a list of ten such fundamental rights such as the right to own property, the right to physical security, and the rights to subsistence and a minimal education. A morally responsible multinational must honor the rights of the people in host countries. Does that mean that a company has an unlimited obligation to feed the poor and provide education? Donaldson argues that honoring fundamental rights imposes no such obligation, and he distinguishes three ways that rights can be infringed: (1) A person or corporation can take action to deprive people of their rights; (2) a person or corporation can fail to protect people from having their rights violated; and (3) a person or corporation can fail to aid people in achieving their rights. Donaldson argues that the duties of multinationals are limited. Multinationals do not have a duty to aid people in achieving their rights, nor do they have an unlimited duty to provide food and education. However, multinationals do have a duty to avoid depriving people of any of their fundamental rights. In the case of six fundamental rights, multinationals have an additional duty to help people from being deprived of their fundamental rights. The reader is invited to see how persuasive Donaldson's analysis is and how many conflicts between home and host country practices Donaldson's analysis can resolve. Sometimes it might be difficult to distinguish failing to aid (which is permitted) from failing to protect (which for six of the fundamental rights is not permitted). Conflicts also exist between home and host country business practices that the rights portion of Donaldson's theory may not resolve.

Moreover, the existence of universal moral norms or fundamental human rights does not mean that business practice need be the same in all countries even when there are significant differences in the economic development of countries. Neither does it mean that a multinational from a highly industrialized society has the same moral obligations when it does business in a poor country that the local businesses have. These points are convincingly argued by Richard De George, who considers what business ethics amounts to in Russia and Eastern Europe. Although De George believes that there are universal norms of business ethics, he also argues that in a country that lacks adequate property rights, that is plagued by corruption, and that has inadequate law enforcement, local business firms are permitted to deviate from some of the requirements of normal ethical business practice, for example, the paying of bribes for legitimate services. However, the fact that Russians are permitted to bribe does not mean that American or Japanese firms doing business in Russia are morally permitted to bribe. After all, a U.S. or Japanese multinational has alternative means to get the services it needs.

THE REGULATION OF INTERNATIONAL BUSINESS

At first one might think that international business cannot be regulated. After all, Ian Maitland's arguments against self-regulation in Chapter Three would apply with even greater force in the international arena. Secondly, there is no true international government. The authority of the United Nations is severely limited, especially its authority over business.

However, some regulation of international business is conducted by national governments. Do the laws of the United States protect U.S. citizens when they work for U.S. companies abroad? Rulings of the Supreme Court indicate that they do when Congress specifically indicates that they do. Whether Congress actually intended the protection of Title VII of the Civil Rights Act of 1964 to apply to U.S. citizens working abroad for a U.S. company was the subject in 1991 of U.S. Supreme Court case *Boureslan v. Aramco* (reprinted in part in the Legal Perspectives section of this chapter). When the Court ruled that Congress had not explicitly included citizens working for U.S. companies abroad, Congress was forced quickly to amend the law so that they could be included.

What about the rights of foreigners who are injured abroad by U.S. corporations? Do they have any rights to relief in American courts? Normally they do not under the doctrine of *forum non conveniens* (it is not the convenient forum). It makes more practical sense for foreigners to seek relief in the country where the injury took place. But, in *Dow Chemical Company and Shell Oil Company v. Domingo Castro Alfaro et. al.,* the Supreme Court of Texas disagrees. The reasoning of the Court is presented in the Legal Perspectives section of this chapter.

Perhaps the most controversial instance of the U.S. government's regulation of business practice abroad is the attempt to prevent American business people from paying bribes to government officials in order to secure business. In 1977 Congress passed the Foreign Corrupt Practices Act (FCPA), which made it illegal for U.S. companies to pay bribes in order to do business abroad. Several highly publicized incidents led to the passage of the act, but the most prominent was the resignation of Japanese Premier Tanaka in 1974 after being indicted for accepting $1.7 million in bribes from the Lockheed Corporation.

Before discussing the FCPA, a distinction should be made among facilitating payments, extortion, and bribery. These distinctions are important because the FCPA permitted facilitating payments by exempting customs agents and bureaucrats whose jobs were essentially ministerial and clerical and it permitted payments in cases of genuine extortion. The chief difference between bribery and extortion is who does the initiating of the act. A corporation pays a bribe when it offers to pay or provide favors to a person or persons of trust to influence the latters' judgment or conduct. A corporation pays extortion money when it yields to a demand for money in order to have accomplished what it has a legal right to have accomplished without the payment. The difference between extortion and a facilitating payment is often one of degree.

These distinctions are important because discussion and criticism of the FCPA often confuses these activities. For example, the major criticism of the act was that the FCPA made it difficult to do business abroad and put U.S. firms at a competitive disadvantage. Stories of government officials or employees of corporations who demand payment to unload perishables or get a telephone installed are used to attack the FCPA, but such payments are not bribes under the act and hence are permitted. These payments are considered to be facilitating payments.

Business leaders have argued that the FCPA has put U.S. firms at a competitive disadvantage and that U.S. export business has been hurt as a result. There is also a belief that U.S. companies are less likely to offer bribes. There is empirical evidence against these beliefs. For example, a study by Kate Gillespie showed that U.S. export business in the Middle East had not been lost.[2] Her analysis was based on data showing the share of U.S. exports of the total exports to the countries in the region from 1970–1982. The sole exception was Iran, and the explanation for the loss there had nothing to do with the FCPA. She also showed that from 1975 to 1979, U.S. corporations were nearly twice as often involved in financial scandals in the Middle East as were the multinationals of other countries, even though the U.S. share of the exports to these countries was never more than 20 percent. Gillespie did not distinguish cases of bribery from cases of extortion, so the data might show that U.S. companies were more likely to pay extortion money than other multinationals. In any case, a picture that paints the U.S. companies as moral heroes and their foreign competitors as bribers is not accurate. A recent analysis showed that most U.S. firms did not consider the FCPA a major impediment to obtaining markets abroad.[3]

Yet another criticism of the FCPA was that it was an example of moral imperialism in which the United States was forcing its moral views on the rest of the world. This argument is fallacious for at least three reasons. First, the FCPA did not force other countries or the multinationals of other countries to follow U.S. morality. It simply required U.S. companies to follow U.S. moral norms with respect to bribery when doing business abroad. Second, as seen in the discussion of pesticides, good reasons often dictate that U.S. companies should adopt U.S. standards rather than those of host countries. Third, the belief that bribery is an unethical business practice is not unique to the United States. Nearly all countries believe that bribery is wrong. The practice of bribery may vary among countries, but the belief that bribery is wrong is universal — or nearly so. Evidence for this claim can be found in the public reaction when it is exposed. Throughout the world there is moral outrage when bribery is discovered. The bribe taker is morally disgraced and is sometimes sent to prison. Recall that Japanese Premier Tanaka resigned in disgrace when it was discovered that he was a bribe taker. This reaction is hardly to be expected in a country where bribery is morally permitted.

Despite these empirical and moral arguments, FCPA critics were sufficiently influential to have the FCPA amended in 1988. Those favoring the amendments believe that the law still outlaws bribery but is less disadvantageous to U.S. multinationals. Critics of the amendments believe that the FCPA has been gutted. Bartley A. Brennan in his article provides a detailed analysis of the 1988 amendments and refers to them as the "death" of a law. Despite Brennan's arguments, some American firms believe the FCPA still has real teeth.[4]

Since there is no world government and since business practice differs throughout the world, in this age of internationalization of business some common standards for business practice are imperative. This need is particularly acute in light of the criticisms against multinationals launched by representatives of the lesser developed countries. Many informed commentators fear a growing split between the "haves" in the northern hemisphere and the "have nots" in the southern hemisphere. In addition, government officials in many countries are growing concerned about the ability of multinationals to subvert government economic activities. For example, multinationals can often use overseas operations to avoid taxes. Generally, government officials complain that multinationals use their economic power to gain favorable legislation or consideration at the expense of the public good. Although this complaint is most commonly made in lesser developed countries, it has been made in nearly every country. A few years ago, some U.S. officials contended that the Federal Reserve kept interest rates up so that the Japanese would not move their investment funds elsewhere and create a credit crunch. Some negotiated codes for the international conduct of business might lessen the number and intensity of the conflicts.

The advantages for domestic industry-wide codes discussed in Chapter 2 apply equally well for international industry-wide codes. Unfortunately the disadvantages of codes are even more acute in the international arena. Since a truly international code must apply to a number of different cultures, the drafters try to make code provisions general enough so that the codes win acceptance. As a result, however, international codes tend to be too general to implement in specific situations. Since most multinationals are from highly industrialized countries and since many of the criticisms of multinationals are from host countries that are underdeveloped countries, the latter advocate strict enforcement procedures with penalties for violation. The representatives of the developed countries resist such penalties, and disputes become political, contentious, and ultimately intractable. This inability to reach agreement has already occurred at meetings of the United Nations Conference on Trade and Development.

Despite great difficulties in negotiating international codes, the benefits justify the effort. International codes can take a number of forms. One of the more interesting codes emanating from the business community itself is the Caux Round Table Principles for Business. These principles, which are included in this chapter, originated as the Minnesota principles because they were developed by the Minnesota Center for Corporate Responsibility. These principles were based on the stakeholder philosophy discussed in detail in Chapter 2. Ryuzaburo Kaku, then Chairman of Canon, Inc., thought the Minnesota Principles had much in common with the Japanese concept of *kyosei* (roughly translated as "living together in harmony"). After the kyosei concept was incorporated into the principles, they were endorsed by a number of business leaders from Europe, Japan, and the United States who were meeting in Caux, Switzerland, in 1993. Efforts are now under way to increase the endorsements worldwide. In 1995 the principles were introduced to the Chinese, who are considering them. The attempt to have the principles endorsed worldwide is an extraordinary effort at international business self-regulation.

Other efforts at regulating international business are being undertaken by the U.N. and by regional governments. Several codes regulating international business are already working their way through the United Nations, but progress is often excruciatingly slow. For example, the United Nations Code of Conduct in Transnational Corporations has been under discussion since 1972. Other codes are more regional in nature and thus agreement is often quicker. Some of the agreements of the European Economic Community provide good models e.g. the "Guidelines for Multinational Enterprises" adopted by the Organization of Economic Cooperation and Development (OECD). Still another possibility for the development of international codes are self-regulatory codes developed by the industries in the different countries themselves. With respect to exporting hazardous products, guidelines have been adopted by the international pharmaceutical associations and the International Group of National Associations of Agrochemical Producers. As the United Nations or groups of sovereign states establish codes of conduct governing international business practice, one would predict a corresponding increase in the development of selfregulatory codes. The 1990s should be a fertile time of the development of international codes of business practice.

In his article, William Frederick examines six international codes of business practice to see if he can identify any common themes. He identifies a number of common themes such as the way multinationals should treat corporate stakeholders as well as guidelines on political payments and basic human rights. Having identified these common themes, Frederick wonders how this commonality arose. Some of it is based on shared experiences. As business becomes international, people become more knowledgeable about cultural differences in business practice and more aware of the difficulties these differences can create. Given the advantageous nature of international business, there is an incentive to resolve the difficulties those different business practices present. Common norms are then negotiated.

Interestingly, Frederick also appeals to Kantian norms, which seem to have a universal claim to validity. We are thus back at our starting point. Are there international norms of business conduct? Yes, but opinions might differ concerning how they arose. Some have argued that there are norms that are valid across cultures and that all or nearly all cultures recognize them. Others would argue that the utilitarian advantages of international business require that nations develop such norms in order to overcome the difficulties that different business practices create. On this view, the nations cannot afford not to have universal norms for business.

NOTES

1. For example, see "The Difference Japanese Management Makes," *Business Week*, July 14, 1986, pp. 47–50.
2. Kate Gillespie, "Middle East Response to the Foreign Corrupt Practices Act," *California Management Review* 29 (Summer 1987): 9–30.
3. "A World of Greased Palms," *Business Week*, November 6, 1995, 36–38.
4. "Greasing Wheels: How U.S. Concerns Compete in Countries Where Bribes Flourish," *Wall Street Journal*, September 29, 1995.

The Moral Obligations of Multinational Corporations

Norman Bowie

Now that business ethics is a fashionable topic, it is only natural that the behavior of multinational corporations should come under scrutiny. Indeed, in the past few decades multinationals have allegedly violated a number of fundamental moral obligations. Some of these violations have received great attention in the press.

Lockheed violated an obligation against bribery. Nestlé violated an obligation not to harm consumers when it aggressively and deceptively marketed infant formula to uneducated poor women in Third World countries. Union Carbide violated either an obligation to provide a safe environment or to properly supervise its Indian employees.

Other violations have received less attention. After the Environmental Protection Agency prohibited the use of the pesticide DBCP, the American Vanguard Corporation continued to manufacture and export the product in Third World countries. U.S. cigarette companies are now aggressively marketing their products abroad. Such actions have been criticized because they seem to treat the safety of foreigners as less important than the safety of U.S. citizens. Other charges involve the violation of the autonomy of sovereign governments. Companies such as Firestone and United Fruit have been accused of making countries dependent on one crop, while Union Miniere and ITT were accused of attempting to overthrow governments.[1]

The charges of immoral conduct constitute a startling array of cases where multina-
tionals are alleged to have failed to live up to their moral obligations. However, the charges are of several distinct types. Some have also been brought against purely domestic U.S. firms — for example, issues involving a safe working environment or safe products. Other charges are unique to multinationals — the charge that a multinational values the safety of a foreigner less than the safety of a home country resident. Still others are charges that companies try to justify behavior in other countries that is clearly wrong in the United States, for example, the bribing of government officials.

In this essay, I will focus on the question of whether U.S. multinationals should follow the moral rules of the United States or the moral rules of the host countries (the countries where the U.S. multinationals do business). A popular way of raising this issue is to ask whether U.S. multinationals should follow the advice "When in Rome, do as the Romans do." In discussing that issue I will argue that U.S. multinationals would be morally required to follow that advice if the theory of ethical relativism were true. On the other hand, if ethical universalism is true, there will be times when the advice would be morally inappropriate. In a later section, I will argue that ethical relativism is morally suspect. Finally, I will argue that the ethics of the market provide some universal moral norms for the conduct of multinationals. Before turning to these questions, however, I will show briefly that many of the traditional topics dis-

From Norman Bowie, "The Moral Obligations of Multinational Corporations," *Problems of International Justice* (edited by Steven Luper-Foy), 1988. Reprinted by permission of the author.

cussed under the rubric of the obligations of multinationals fall under standard issues of business ethics.

OBLIGATIONS OF MULTINATIONALS THAT APPLY TO ANY BUSINESS

As Milton Friedman and his followers constantly remind us, the purpose of a corporation is to make money for the stockholders — some say to maximize profits for the stockholders. According to this view, multinationals have the same fundamental purpose as national corporations. However, in recent years, Friedman's theory has been severely criticized. On what moral grounds can the interests of the stockholders be given priority over all the other stakeholders?[2] For a variety of reasons, business ethicists are nearly unanimous in saying that no such moral grounds can be given. Hence, business executives have moral obligations to all their stakeholders. Assuming that Friedman's critics are correct, what follows concerning the obligations of multinationals?

Can the multinationals pursue profit at the expense of the other corporate stakeholders? No; the multinational firm, just like the national firm, is obligated to consider all its stakeholders. In that respect there is nothing distinctive about the moral obligations of a multinational firm. However, fulfilling its obligations is much more complicated than for a national firm. A multinational usually has many more stakeholders. It has all the classes of stakeholders a U.S. company has but multiplied by the number of countries in which the company operates.[3]

It also may be more difficult for the multinational to take the morally correct action. For example, one of the appealing features of a multinational is that it can move resources from one country to another in order

to maximize profits. Resources are moved in order to take advantage of more favorable labor rates, tax laws, or currency rates. Of course, the pursuit of such tactics makes it more difficult to honor the obligation to consider the interests of all stakeholders. Nonetheless, the increased difficulty does not change the nature of the obligation; multinationals, like nationals, are required to consider the interests of all corporate stakeholders.

Should a multinational close a U.S. plant and open a plant in Mexico in order to take advantage of cheap labor? That question is no different in principle from this one: Should a national firm close a plant in Michigan and open a plant in South Carolina in order to take advantage of the more favorable labor climate in South Carolina? The same moral considerations that yield a decision in the latter case yield a similar decision in the former. (Only if the interests of Mexican workers were less morally significant than were the interests of U.S. workers could any differentiation be made.)

These examples can be generalized to apply to any attempt by a multinational to take advantage of discrepancies between the home country and the host country in order to pursue a profit. Any attempt to do so without considering the interests of all the stakeholders is immoral. National firms and multinational firms share the same basic obligations. If I am right here, there is nothing distinctive about the many problems faced by multinationals, and much of the discussion of the obligations of multinationals can be carried on within the framework of traditional business ethics.

DISTINCTIVE OBLIGATIONS

Certain obligations of multinationals do become distinctive where the morality of the host country (any country where the multinational has subsidiaries) differs from or contradicts the morality of the home country (the country where the multinational was legally created). The multinational faces a modern version of the "When in Rome, should you do as the Romans do?" question. That question is the focus of this essay.

On occasion, the "when in Rome" question has an easy answer. In many situations the answer to the question is yes. When in Rome a multinational is obligated to do as the Romans do. Because the circumstances Romans face are different from the circumstances Texans face, it is often appropriate to follow Roman moral judgments because it is entirely possible that Romans and Texans use the same moral principles, but apply those principles differently.

This analysis also works the other way. Just because a certain kind of behavior is right in the United States does not mean that it is right somewhere else. Selling infant formula in the United States is morally permissible in most circumstances, but, I would argue, it is not morally permissible in most circumstances to sell infant formula in Third World countries. U.S. water is safe to drink.

Many moral dilemmas disappear when the factual circumstances that differentiate two cultures are taken into account. It is important to note, however, that this judgment is made because we believe that the divergent practices conform to some general moral principle. The makers of infant formula can sell their product in an advanced country but not in a Third World country because the guiding principle is that we cannot impose avoidable harm on an innocent third party. Selling infant formula in underdeveloped countries would often violate that common fundamental principle; selling the formula in developed countries usually would not.

This situation should be contrasted with cases where the home and the host country have different *moral* principles. Consider dif-

ferent moral principles for the testing of new drugs. Both countries face the following dilemma. If there are fairly lax standards, the drug may have very bad side effects, and if it is introduced too quickly, then many persons who take the drug are likely to be harmed — perhaps fatally. On the other hand, if a country has very strict standards and a long testing period, the number of harmful side effect cases will be less, but a number of people who could have benefited from benign drugs will have perished because they did not survive the long testing period. Where is the trade-off between saving victims of a disease and protecting persons from possible harmful side effects? To bring this problem home, consider a proposed cure for cancer or for AIDS. Two different countries could set different safety standards such that plausible moral arguments could be made for each. In such cases, it is morally permissible to sell a drug abroad that could not yet be sold in the United States.

If all cases were like this one, it would always be morally permissible to do as the Romans do. But alas, all cases are not like this one. Suppose a country totally ignores the problem of side effects and has no safety standards at all. That country "solves" the trade-off problem by ignoring the interests of those who might develop side effects. Wouldn't that country be wrong, and wouldn't a multinational be obligated not to market a drug in that country even if the country permitted it?

If the example seems farfetched, consider countries that are so desperately poor or corrupt that they will permit companies to manufacture and market products that are known to be dangerous. This is precisely the charge that was made against American Vanguard when it exported the pesticide DBCP. Aren't multinationals obligated to stay out even if they are permitted?

That question leads directly to the question of whether multinationals always should

170

do in Rome as the Romans do. To sort through that issue, Figure 1 may be useful. Thus far, I have focused on I and IIA. The remainder of the essay considers the range of ethical problems found in IIB.

In IIB4, the multinational has an obligation to follow the moral principles of the host country because on the issue at hand those of the host country are justified while those of the home country are not. Although Americans may believe that there are few such obligations because their moral principles are far more likely to be justified, it is not hard to think of a contrary case. Suppose it is a moral obligation in a host country that no corporation fire someone without due cause. In other words, in the host country employ-

ment at will is morally forbidden. Although I shall not argue for it here, I think the employment-at-will doctrine cannot stand up to moral scrutiny. Hence, in this case, multinationals are obligated to follow the moral principle of the host country. Except for economic reasons (falling demand for one's product), a multinational is morally obligated not to fire an employee without just cause.

In IIB3, if the moral principles with respect to a given issue are not justified, then the multinational is under no moral obligation to follow them (except in the weak sense where the multinational is under a legal obligation and hence under a moral obligation to obey the law). Actually, IIB3 can be

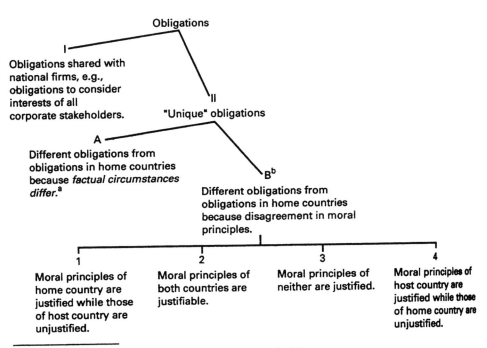

ᵃIn my view, different obligations still conform to universal principles.
ᵇIt is assumed that the different moral principles referred to here and below refer to the same moral issue. It is also stipulated that "unjustified" in IIB1 and IIB4 means that the unjustified principles are in conflict with the canons of justification in ethics.

FIGURE 1. Obligations of Multinationals

171

further subdivided into cases where the moral principles are not justified and where the moral principles cannot be justified. Theocratic states with moral principles based on revelation but not in contradiction with rationally justified moral principles are examples of the former. When the "moral" principles based on revelation are in contradiction with rationally justified moral principles, we have an example of the latter. In this latter case, a multinational is obligated not to follow the moral principles of the host country. In these cases, when in Rome, multinationals are not to do as the Romans do.

In Case IIB2, multinationals may do in Rome as the Romans do. In this case, the moral principles of the host country are justified.

Finally, in case IIB1, the multinational is obligated not to follow the moral principles of the host country. In these cases, the principles of the host country are contrary to the canons of ethics.

In summary, then, U.S. multinationals are obligated to do as the Romans do in IIB4, are permitted to do as the Romans do in IIB2 and in IIB3 where the moral principles of the Romans are consistent with what morality would justify. U.S. multinationals are obligated *not* to do as the Romans do in IIB1 and IIB3 where the moral principles of the Romans are inconsistent with what morality would justify.

Notice, however, that the entire analysis assumes there is some means of justifying ethical principles independent of the fact that a society believes they are justified. Otherwise, for example, I could not say that the moral principles of a home country are not justified while those of the host country are. But who is to say whether the moral principles of a country are justified or when they run counter to universal morality. Besides, perhaps there is no universal morality. What then?

RELATIVISM

Cultural relativism is the doctrine that what is right or wrong, good or bad, depends on one's culture. If the Irish consider abortion to be morally wrong, abortion *is* morally wrong in Ireland. If the Swedes do not consider abortion to be morally wrong, then abortion *is not* morally wrong in Sweden. There is no universal principle to which the Swedes and the Irish can appeal that determines whether abortion really is wrong or not.

If a person is a cultural relativist, then the implications for our discussion may seem quite clear. A corporation has an obligation to follow the moral principles of the host country. When one is in Rome, one is obligated to do as the Romans do. On our chart, IIB1, IIB3, and IIB4 have no referents. There are no members of those classes just as there are no members of the class of unicorns.

The officers and managers of many multinationals often speak and act as if cultural relativism were true. Who are we, they argue, to impose our moral standards on the rest of the world? For example, the U.S. Foreign Corrupt Practices Act, which prohibits the payment of unrecorded bribes to foreign governments or officials, has come under intense attack. After all, if the payment of bribes is morally acceptable in country X, why should we impose our moral views about bribery on that country. Besides, if U.S. multinationals do not bribe, German and Japanese multinationals will — or so the argument goes. Former president Jimmy Carter's attempt to include a country's record on violating or not violating fundamental human rights when making foreign policy decisions came under the same kind of criticism. Who is the United States to impose its moral values on others?

This relativistic way of thinking has always been prominent in the thinking of many so-

172

cial scientists. After all, discoveries by anthropologists, sociologists, and psychologists have documented the diversity of moral beliefs and punctured some of the pseudo-justifications that had been given for the superiority of white Western male ways of thinking. Philosophers, by and large, welcomed the corrections to prejudicial moral thinking, but, nonetheless, found the doctrine of cultural relativism seriously flawed.

Recently, however, the situation in philosophy has taken a surprising turn. A number of prominent philosophers have either seemed to embrace cultural relativism or have been forced by the "critics" to admit that their own philosophical positions may be consistent with it. Three examples should make the point.

In 1971, John Rawls published his monumental work *A Theory of Justice*. In that work, Rawls intended to develop a procedure (the original position) that would provide principles for a just society. Although these principles might be implemented in different ways by different societies, Rawls seemed to think that *any* just society would conform to these principles. In part, Rawls held this view because he believed the original position provided a universal justification for the principles of justice the original position produced. Early critics charged that the assumptions behind the original position were individualistic, liberal, Western, and democratic. The original position was biased in favor of individualistic Western democracies; it did not provide a universal method of justification. In a 1985 article in *Philosophy and Public Affairs*, Rawls admitted that his critics were right.

> In particular justice as fairness is framed to apply to what I call the basic structure of a modern constitutional democracy. . . . Whether justice as fairness can be extended to a general political conception for different kinds of societies existing under different historical and social conditions or whether it can be extended

to a general moral conception . . . are altogether separate questions. I avoid prejudging these larger questions one way or the other.[4]

Another highly influential book in ethics, Alasdair MacIntyre's *After Virtue*, argued that the recent emphasis by ethicists on utilitarianism and deontology was seriously skewed. MacIntyre argued that a full moral theory must give a central place to the virtues. His own account was rich in description of the place of virtue in various societies. . . . However, MacIntyre's critics pointed out that what was considered a virtue in one society was frequently not considered a virtue in another — indeed one culture's virtue might be another culture's vice. MacIntyre now concedes that his earlier attempts to avoid these relativistic implications have largely failed.[5]

In theory, a cultural relativist could have two responses to CEOs of multinationals who wanted to know whether their personnel should behave, when in Rome, as the Romans do. Given that the morality of one culture cannot be shown to be superior to the morality of another, the personnel should follow the moral principles of the host country. Such an attitude of tolerance is the traditional response of most relativists.

But another response is possible. Even though the morality of one culture cannot objectively be shown to be superior to the morality of another, rather than embrace tolerance, once could simply assert the superiority of one's own culture. This is the approach taken by Richard Rorty, who has written extensively on the pretensions to objectivity in philosophy. In his 1984 article "Solidarity or Objectivity," he points out that the objectivist tries to create a dilemma for any subjectivist position. The dilemma is that

> either we attach a special privilege to our own community, or we pretend an impossible tolerance for every other group. I have been argu-

ing that we pragmatists should grasp the ethno-centric horn of this dilemma. We should say that we must, in practice, privilege our own group, even though there can be no noncircular justification for doing so.... We Western liberal intellectuals should accept the fact that we have to start from where we are, and that this means that there are lots of views which we simply cannot take seriously.[6]

But how would Rorty's quotation strike the CEO of a U.S. multinational? In this case, the personnel of a multinational should *not* follow the moral principles of the host country unless they are consistent with U.S. principles. But what would this mean in terms of business practice? Given that in U.S. culture, the capitalist Friedmanite principle — maximize profits! — is the cultural norm, a U.S. multinational with a plant in South Africa would not refuse to follow the rules of apartheid or pull out. It would locate in South Africa and conform to local custom so long as it could make a profit.

Although I argued earlier that the classical view of profit maximization is seriously flawed, I did not do so from Rorty's ethnocentric position. I assumed an objective universal moral standpoint, as have those who have criticized the classical view. If Rorty's theory is correct, there is no transcultural objective perspective; because the classical view is a central principle in U.S. business and legal culture, I assume Rorty would have to accept it.

Hence, whether we are cultural relativists or ethnocentrists, some disconcerting implications seem to follow.

1. A corporation has no obligation to follow the Sullivan principles[7] in South Africa.
2. A corporation that wants to do business with the Arabs has no moral obligation to refuse participation in a boycott against Israel as a condition for doing business with the Arabs.
3. A corporation has no obligation to refrain from doing business with a state that is in systematic violation of human rights.

If these implications do follow, there seems to be something wrong with the position that entails them. Even Ronald Reagan has forbidden U.S. firms from doing business with Libya. Some set of criteria is needed for indicating when multinationals are permitted to follow the moral principles of the host country and when multinationals are forbidden to follow host-country principles. What is also needed are some principles that tell U.S. multinationals when they have an obligation to refrain from doing business either *with* a foreign (host) government or *in* a host country. However, unless cultural relativism is false, these principles will never be forthcoming.

THE ADEQUACY OF CULTURAL RELATIVISM

Although our primary concern is the obligations of multinationals, some considerations of the adequacy of cultural relativism must be made before we can speak meaningfully about the obligations of multinationals. As a starting point, I adopt a strategy used by Derek Parfit to undermine the doctrine of prudentialism.[8] Consider a continuum with three positions:

Individual Relativism	Cultural Relativism	Universalism

Individual relativism is the view that what is right or wrong, good or bad, depends on the feelings or attitudes of the individual. If an individual believes abortion is wrong, then abortion is wrong for that individual. If another individual believes abortion is not wrong, then abortion is not wrong for that individual. There is no valid cultural norm that will tell us which individual is objectively right.

The strategy is to show that any argument the cultural relativist uses against universalism can also be used by the individual relativist against cultural relativism. Similarly, any argument the cultural relativist uses against the individual relativist can be used by the universalist against the cultural relativist. As Parfit would say, the cultural relativist is constantly fighting a war on two fronts.

In this discussion, one example of this strategy will have to suffice. First, against an individual relativist, a cultural relativist would often argue that if individual relativism were the prevailing view, a stable society would be impossible. Arguments from Thomas Hobbes or decision theory would prove the point. If individual relativism were the prevailing norm, life would be "nasty, brutish, and short."

But in the present world, any arguments that appeal to social stability will have to be applied universally. In the atomic age and in an age where terrorism is an acceptable form of political activity, the stability problems that afflict individual relativism equally afflict cultural relativism. If the necessity for social stability is a good argument for a cultural relativist to use against an individual relativist, it is an equally good argument for a universalist to use against a cultural relativist.

This brief argument has not refuted relativism. It has only shown that if the stability argument works for the cultural relativist against the individual relativist, the argument also works for the universalist against the cultural relativist. Moreover, to accept the argument this far is only to show that some universal moral norms are required for stable relationships. The argument itself does not provide those universal moral norms. Multinational CEOs are likely to accept the argument thus far, however, because multinationals need a stable international environment if they are to make a profit in the long run. As any adviser for any multinational will verify,

one of the chief factors affecting an investment decision in a foreign country is the political stability both of that individual country and of the region surrounding it. An unstable country or region is highly inimical to the conduct of international business.

THE MORAL MINIMUM FOR SOCIETY

Thus far we have established that multinational business requires stability and that commonly accepted moral rules are necessary for stability. But what specifically are these moral rules? To answer that question I will appeal to conceptual arguments that will assist in providing answers.

One argument that is especially effective against the charge of moral imperialism develops the point that some universal standards of conduct already have been accepted by all parties. Despite appearances to the contrary, a great deal of morality has already been internationalized either explicitly through treaty, through membership in the U.N., or implicitly through language and conduct. . . .

Note the following: The word *democracy* or *democratic* has become an honorific term. Nearly all national states claim they are democracies — people's democracies, worker democracies, but democracies nonetheless. The August 4, 1986, *Newsweek* carried a story about repression and the denial of civil rights in Chile. The president of Chile responded to his critics by calling his dictatorship a "democratic government with authority." I have yet to come across a state that brags it is not a democracy and has no intention of being one. (Some nations do indicate they do not want to be a democracy like the United States.) Hence, there is no moral imperialism involved in saying that host countries should be democracies. The controversy involves the question, What must a government be like to be properly characterized as a democracy?

A notion of shared values can be of assistance here as well. There is a whole range of behavior, such as torture, murder of the innocent, and racism, that nearly all agree is wrong. A nation-state accused of torture does not respond by saying that a condemnation of torture is just a matter of subjective morality. The state's leaders do not respond by saying, "We think torture is right, but you do not." Rather, the standard response is to deny that any torture took place. If the evidence of torture is too strong, a finger will be pointed either at the victim or at the morally outraged country. "They do it, too." In this case the guilt is spread to all. Even the Nazis denied that genocide took place. What is important is that *no* state replies there is nothing wrong with genocide or torture. Hence, the head of a multinational need have no fear of cultural imperialism when she or he takes a stand in favor of democracy and against torture and genocide.

This conceptual argument is buttressed by another. Suppose an anthropologist discovers a large populated South Pacific island. How many tribes are on the island? Part of the answer to that question will be determined by observing if such acts as killing and murder are permitted and if they are permitted, against whom are they permitted? If they are not permitted, that counts as evidence that there is only one tribe. If people on the northern half of the island permit stealing directed against southerners but do not permit northerners to steal from one another, that provides evidence that there are at least two tribes. What often distinguishes one society from another is the fact that society A does not permit murder, lying, and stealing against members of A — society A could not permit that and still be a society — but society A does permit that kind of behavior against society B. What this strategy shows is that one of the criteria for having a society is that there be a shared morality among the individuals that make up the society.

What follows from this is that there are certain basic rules that must be followed in each society — for example, do not lie; do not commit murder. There is a moral minimum in the sense that if these specific moral rules are not generally followed, then there will not be a society at all. These moral rules are universal, but they are not practiced universally. That is, members of society A agree that they should not lie to each other, but they think it is okay to lie to the members of other societies. Such moral rules are not relative; they simply are not practiced universally.

However, multinational corporations are obligated to follow these moral rules. Because the multinational is practicing business in the society and because these moral norms are necessary for the existence of the society, the multinational has an obligation to support those norms. Otherwise, multinationals would be in the position of benefiting from doing business with the society while at the same time engaging in activity that undermines the society. Such conduct would be unjust.

THE MORALITY OF THE MARKETPLACE

Given that the norms constituting a moral minimum are likely to be few in number, it can be argued that the argument thus far has achieved something — that is, multinationals are obligated to follow the moral norms required for the existence of a society. But the argument has not achieved very much — that is, most issues surrounding multinationals do not involve alleged violations of these norms.

Perhaps a stronger argument can be found by making explicit the morality of the marketplace. That there is an implicit morality of the market is a point that is often ignored by most economists and many businesspersons.

Although economists and businesspersons assume that people are basically self-interested, they must also assume that persons involved in business transactions will honor their contracts. In most economic exchanges, the transfer of product for money is not simultaneous. You deliver and I pay or vice versa. As the economist Kenneth Boulding put it: "without an integrative framework, exchange itself cannot develop, because exchange, even in its most primitive forms, involves trust and credibility."[9]

Philosophers would recognize an implicit Kantianism in Boulding's remarks. Kant tried to show that a contemplated action would be immoral if a world in which the contemplated act was universally practiced was self-defeating. For example, lying and cheating would fail Kant's tests. Kant's point is implicitly recognized by the business community when corporate officials despair of the immoral practices of corporations and denounce executives engaging in shady practices as undermining the business enterprise itself.

Consider what John Rawls says about contracts:

> Such ventures are often hard to initiate and to maintain. This is especially evident in the case of covenants, that is, in those instances where one person is to perform before the other. For this person may believe that the second party will not do his part, and therefore the scheme never gets going. . . . Now in these situations there may be no way of assuring the party who is to perform first except by giving him a promise, that is, by putting oneself under an obligation to carry through later. Only in this way can the scheme be made secure so that both can gain from the benefits of their cooperation.[10]

Rawls's remarks apply to all contracts. Hence, if the moral norms of a host country permitted practices that undermined contracts, a multinational ought not to follow them. Business practice based on such norms could not pass Kant's test.

In fact, one can push Kant's analysis and contend that business practice generally requires the adoption of a minimum standard of justice. In the United States, a person who participates in business practice and engages in the practice of giving bribes or kickbacks is behaving unjustly. Why? Because the person is receiving the benefits of the rules against such activities without supporting the rules personally. This is an example of what John Rawls calls freeloading. A freeloader is one who accepts the benefits without paying any of the costs.

> In everyday life an individual, if he is so inclined, can sometimes win even greater benefits for himself by taking advantage of the cooperative efforts of others. Sufficiently many persons may be doing their share so that when special circumstances allow him not to contribute (perhaps his omission will not be found out), he gets the best of both worlds. . . . We cannot preserve a sense of justice and all that this implies while at the same time holding ourselves ready to act unjustly should doing so promise some personal advantage.[11]

This argument does not show that if bribery really is an accepted moral practice in country X, that moral practice is wrong. What it does show is that practices in country X that permit freeloading are wrong and if bribery can be construed as freeloading, then it is wrong. In most countries I think it can be shown that bribery is freeloading, but I shall not make that argument here.

177

The implications of this analysis for multinationals are broad and important. If activities that are permitted in other countries violate the morality of the marketplace — for example, undermine contracts or involve freeloading on the rules of the market — they nonetheless are morally prohibited to multinationals that operate there. Such multinationals are obligated to follow the moral norms of the market. Contrary behavior is inconsistent and ultimately self-defeating.

Our analysis here has rather startling implications. If the moral norms of a host country are in violation of the moral norms of the marketplace, then the multinational is obligated to follow the norms of the marketplace. Systematic violation of marketplace norms would be self-defeating. Moreover, whenever a multinational establishes businesses in a number of different countries, the multinational provides something approaching a universal morality — the morality of the marketplace itself. If Romans are to do business with the Japanese, then whether in Rome or Tokyo, there is a morality to which members of the business community in both Rome and Tokyo must subscribe — even if the Japanese and Romans differ on other issues of morality.

THE DEFENSE OF MARKETPLACE MORALITY

Up to this point I have argued that multinationals are obligated to follow the moral minimum and the morality of the marketplace. But what justifies the morality of the marketplace? Unless the marketplace morality can be justified, I am stuck in Rorty's ethnocentrism. I can start only where I am, and there are simply a lot of views I cannot take seriously. If a CEO of a U.S. multinational should adopt such an ethnocentric position, she or he would be accused of cultural imperialism. The claim of objectivity remains the central issue for determining the obligations of multinationals.

One possible argument is that capitalism supports democratic institutions. For example, Milton Friedman argues in *Capitalism and Freedom* that capitalism institutionally promotes political freedom.

> Economic arrangements play a dual role in the promotion of a free society. On the one hand freedom in economic arrangements . . . is an end in itself. In the second place economic freedom is also an indispensable means toward the achievement of political freedom. . . .
>
> No one who buys bread knows whether the wheat from which it is made was grown by a Communist or a Republican, by a constitutionalist or a Fascist, or for that matter by a Negro or a white. This illustrates how an impersonal market separates economic activities from political views and protects men from being discriminated against in their economic activities for reasons that are irrelevant to their productivity — whether these reasons are associated with their views or their color.[12]

Friedman also points out that freedom of speech is more meaningful so long as alternative opportunities for employment exist. However, these alternatives are impossible if the government owns and operates the means of production. In a private diversified economic community someone has a better chance to publish views that are contrary to the views of a given editor, the government, or even a majority of the public. Usually one can find some audience that is interested. Moreover, even publishers who disagree might still publish. Fear of competition often overcomes the distaste for certain ideas.

Indeed, one of the arguments for morally permitting multinationals to operate in nondemocratic countries is an extension of Friedman's point. Capitalism is allegedly a catalyst for democratic reform. If capitalism promotes democracy, then a moral argument can be made to justify capitalist investment in repressive regimes because investment will serve the moral end of making the government less repressive. This is precisely the argument that many have used to justify U.S. investment in South Africa. Indeed, the South African situation can serve as an interesting case study. The point of the Sullivan principles is to provide moral guidelines so that a company may be morally justified in having plants in South Africa without becoming part of the system of exploitation. The Sullivan principles also prevent profit-seeking corporations from morally justifying immoral behavior. No company can passively do as the South Africans do and then claim that its presence will bring about a more democratic, less racist regime. After all, if it is plausible to argue that capitalism can help create a democracy, it seems equally plausible to argue that a totalitarian regime may corrupt capitalism. The Sullivan principles help keep multinationals with South African facilities morally honest.

Moreover, the morality of the Sullivan principles depends on an empirical claim that profit-seeking corporations behaving in accordance with marketplace morality and acknowledging universally recognized human rights will in fact help transform totalitarian or repressive regimes into more democratic, more humane regimes. If that transformation does not take place within a reasonable amount of time, the moral justification for having facilities in that country disappears. Leon Sullivan recognized that point when he set May 31, 1987, as the deadline for reform of the South African government. When that reform was not forthcoming, he insisted that U.S. companies suspend operations in South Africa. . . .

What about the issue of human rights? Can multinationals ignore that question? No, they cannot. Part of what it means to be a

democracy is that respect be shown for fundamental human rights. The only justification for a multinational's doing business with a regime that violates human rights is the claim that in so doing, the country's human rights record will improve. Again, business activity under that justification will have to be judged on results.

Even if the "contribution to democracy argument" is not convincing, there is another argument on behalf of the morality of the marketplace. On the assumption that a multinational business agreement is a voluntary exchange, the morality of the marketplace is voluntarily accepted. Economic prosperity seems to be highly desired by all countries. Given that multinational business is a device for achieving prosperity, participating countries voluntarily accept the morality of the market.

CONCLUSION

I have argued that on occasion multinationals have obligations that would require them *not* to do in Rome as the Romans do — for example, in those cases where Roman practice is in violation of marketplace morality. I have also provided arguments on behalf of marketplace morality, although those arguments require that businesses have obligations to pull out of oppressive countries if there is little hope of reform.

But the appeal to the morality of the marketplace has an added benefit. What often is forgotten by business is that the market is not a morally neutral, well-oiled machine; rather, it is embedded in morality and depends upon the acceptance of morality for its success. Ultimately, the obligations of multinationals, whether in Rome, Tokyo, or Washington, are the obligations required by the market. If corporations live up to those obligations, and if capitalism really could advance the cause of democracy and human rights throughout the world, then the morally responsible multinational could be a force for social justice. However, I regret to say that I am discussing a goal and a hope rather than a reality.

NOTES

I wish to thank Steven Luper-Foy for his helpful comments on an earlier version of this essay.

1. See "There's No Love Lost Between Multinational Companies and the Third World," *Business and Society Review* (Autumn 1974).

2. For the purpose of this discussion, a stakeholder is a member of a group without whose support the organization would cease to exist. The traditional list of stakeholders includes stockholders, employees, customers, suppliers, lenders, and the local community where plants or facilities are located.

3. Of course, one large U.S. company with 10 plants in 10 different states has more classes of stakeholders than 1 U.S. company with 1 U.S. plant and 1 foreign subsidiary.

4. John Rawls, "Justice as Fairness: Political Not Metaphysical," *Philosophy and Public Affairs* 14, no. 3 (Summer 1985):224–226. Also see John Rawls, *A Theory of Justice* (Cambridge, Mass.: Harvard University Press, 1971).

5. The most explicit charge of relativism is made by Robert Wachbroit, "A Genealogy of Virtues," *Yale Law Journal* 92, no. 3 (January 1983):476–564. For Alasdair MacIntyre's discussion, see "Postscript to the Second Edition" in *After Virtue,* 2nd ed. (Notre Dame: University of Notre Dame, 1984) and his Eastern Division American Philosophical Association Presidential Address, "Relativism, Power and Philosophy" in *Proceedings and Addresses of the American Philosophical Association* 59, no. 1 (September 1985):5–22. Also see Michael Walzer, *Spheres of Justice* (New York: Basic Books, 1983).

6. Richard Rorty, "Solidarity or Objectivity," in *Post-Analytic Philosophy,* John Rajchman and Cornel West, eds. (New York: Columbia University Press, 1985), pp. 12–13.

7. The Sullivan code affirms the following principles: (1) that there be nonsegregation of the races in all eating, comfort, and work facilities; (2) that equal and fair employment practices be instituted for all employees; (3) that all employees doing equal or comparable work for the same period of time receive equal pay; (4) that training programs be developed and implemented that will prepare substantial numbers of blacks and other non-whites for supervisory, administrative, technical, and clerical jobs; (5) that the number of blacks and other nonwhites in management and supervisory positions be increased; and (6) that the quality of employees' lives outside the work environment be improved — this includes housing, transportation, schooling, recreation, and health facilities.

8. See Derek Parfit, *Reasons and Persons* (New York: Oxford University Press, 1986), pp. 126–127.

9. Kenneth E. Boulding, "The Basis of Value Judgments in Economics," in *Human Values and Economic Policy,* Sidney Hook, ed. (New York: New York University Press, 1967), p. 68.

10. John Rawls, *A Theory of Justice* (Cambridge, Mass.: Harvard University Press, 1971), p. 569.

11. Ibid., p. 497.

12. Milton Friedman, *Capitalism and Freedom* (Chicago: University of Chicago Press, 1962), pp. 8, 21.

Fundamental Rights
and Multinational Duties

Thomas Donaldson

RIGHTS

Rights establish minimum levels of morally acceptable behavior. One well-known definition of a "right" construes it as a "trump" over a collective good, which is to say that the assertion of one's right to something, such as free speech, takes precedence over all but the most compelling collective goals, and overrides, for example, the state's interest in civil harmony or moral consensus.[1]

Rights are at the rock bottom of modern moral deliberation: Maurice Cranston writes that the litmus test for whether something is a right or not is whether it protects something of "paramount importance."[2] If I have a right to physical security, then you should, at a minimum, refrain from depriving me of physical security (at least without a rights-regarding and overriding reason). It would be nice, of course, if you did more: if you treated me charitably and with love. But you must *at a minimum* respect my rights. Hence, it will help to conceive the problem of assigning minimal responsibilities to multinational corporations through the question, "What specific rights should multinationals respect?"

Notice that the flip side of a right typically is a duty.[3] This, in part, is what gives aptness to Joel Feinberg's well-known definition of a right as a "justified entitlement *to* something *from* someone."[4] It is the "from someone" part of the definition that reflects the assumption of a duty, for without a correlative obligation that attaches to some moral agent

or group of agents, a right is weakened — if not beyond the status of a right entirely, then significantly. If we cannot say that a multinational corporation has a duty to keep the levels of arsenic low in the workplace, then the worker's right not to be poisoned means little.

Often, duties fall upon more than one class of moral agent. Consider, for example, the furor over the dumping of toxic waste in West Africa by multinational corporations. During 1988, virtually every country from Morocco to the Congo on Africa's west coast received offers from companies seeking cheap sites for dumping waste.[5] In preceding years, the United States and Europe had become enormously expensive for dumping, in large part because of the costly safety measures mandated by U.S. and European governments. In February of 1988, officials in Guinea-Bissau, one of the world's poorest nations, agreed to bury 15 million tons of toxic wastes from European tanneries and pharmaceutical companies. The companies agreed to pay about 120 million dollars, which is only slightly less than the country's entire gross national product. And in Nigeria in 1987, five European ships unloaded toxic waste containing dangerous poisons such as polychlorinated biphenyls, or PCBs. Workers wearing thongs and shorts unloaded the barrels for $2.50 a day, and placed them in a dirt lot in a residential area in the town of Kiko. They were not told about the contents of the barrels.[6]

Who bears responsibility for protecting the workers' and inhabitants' rights to safety in such instances? It would be wrong to place it entirely upon a single group of agents such as the governments of West African nations. As it happens, the toxic waste dumped in Nigeria entered under an import permit for "nonexplosive, nonradioactive and non-self-combusting chemicals." But the permit turned out to be a loophole; Nigeria had not meant to accept the waste and demanded its removal once word about its presence filtered into official channels. The example reveals the difficulty many developing countries have in formulating the sophisticated language and regulatory procedures necessary to control high-technology hazards. It seems reasonable in such instances, then, to place the responsibility not upon a single class of agents, but upon a broad collection of them, including governments, corporate executives, host country companies and officials, and international organizations. The responsibility for not violating the rights of people living in West Africa to be free from the dangers of toxic waste, then, potentially falls upon every agent whose actions might harm, or contribute to harming, West African inhabitants. Nor is one agent's responsibility always mitigated when another "accepts" responsibility. To take a specific instance, corporate responsibility may not be eliminated if a West African government explicitly agrees to accept toxic waste. There is always the possibility — said to be a reality by some critics — that corrupt government officials will agree to accept and handle waste that threatens safety in order to fatten their own Swiss bank accounts.

In wrestling with the problem of which rights deserve international standing, James Nickel recommends that rights that possess international scope be viewed as occupying an intermediary zone between abstract moral principles such as liberty or fairness on the one hand, and national specifications of rights on the other.[7] International rights must be more specific than abstract principles if they are to facilitate practical application, but less specific than the entries on lists of rights whose duties fall on national governments if they are to preserve cosmopolitan relevance. . . .

As a first approximation, then, let us interpret a multinational's obligations by asking which *international rights* it should respect. We understand international rights to be the sort of moral precepts that lie in a zone between abstract moral principles and national rights specifications. Multinationals, we shall assume, should respect the international rights of those whom they affect, especially when those rights are of the most fundamental sort. . . .

[Donaldson then proposes three conditions that any purported rights claim must pass if it imposes a valid duty on a corporation. Ed.]

1. The right must protect something of very great importance.
2. The right must be subject to substantial and recurrent threats.
3. The obligations or burdens imposed by the right must satisfy a fairness-affordability test.

Let us further stipulate more precisely for our own purposes what shall be meant by the fairness — affordability test in condition number 3. The affordability part of the test implies that for a proposed right to qualify as a genuine right, all moral agents (including nation-states, individuals, and corporations) must be able under ordinary circumstances, and after receiving any share of charitable help due them, to assume the various burdens and duties that fairly fall upon them in honoring the right. "Affordable" here implies literally being *capable of paying for;* it does not imply that something is necessarily unaffordable because paying for it would constitute an inefficient use of funds, or would necessitate trading off other more valuable economic goods.

This use of the term "affordability" means that — at least under unusual circumstances — honoring a right may be a fundamental moral duty for a given multinational even when the result is financial loss to the particular firm. For example, it would be "affordable" in the present sense for multinational corporations to employ older workers and to refuse to hire eight-year-old children as full-time, permanent laborers, and hence doing so would be mandatory even in the unusual situation where a particular firm's paying the higher salaries necessary to hire older laborers would result in financial losses. By the same logic, it would probably not be "affordable" for either multinational corporations or nation-states around the world to guarantee kidney dialysis for all citizens who need it. This sense of the term also implies that any act of forbearance (of a kind involved in not violating a right directly) is "affordable" for any moral agent.[8] To put the last point another way, I can always "afford" to let you exercise your right to vote, no matter how much money it might cost me.

Turning to the "fairness" side of the test, the extent to which it is "fair" to distribute burdens associated with a given right in a certain manner will be controversial. We assume, however, that for any right to qualify as a genuine right, some "fair" arrangement for sharing the duties and costs among the various agents who must honor the right exists, and that such an arrangement makes it possible (although not necessarily probable) for the right to be enjoyed by most people in most instances.

Next, let us stipulate that satisfying all three of the revised conditions qualifies a prospective right as what we shall call a "fundamental international right," and, in turn,

as a right that must be respected by the three major types of international actors: individuals, nation-states, and corporations. This definition does not mean that individuals, nation-states, and corporations must "respect" the rights in precisely the same manner. That is, it does not entail that the correlative duties flowing from the rights are the same for each type of actor. It entails only that each such actor must "respect" fundamental international rights in some manner, and that they possess some duties, however minimal, in consequence. . . .

FUNDAMENTAL INTERNATIONAL RIGHTS

We are now prepared to identify some of the items that should appear on a list of fundamental international rights, as well as to lay the groundwork for interpreting their application to multinational corporations. . . .

Though probably not complete, the following list contains items that appear to satisfy the three conditions and hence to qualify as fundamental international rights:

1. The right to freedom of physical movement
2. The right to ownership of property
3. The right to freedom from torture
4. The right to a fair trial
5. The right to nondiscriminatory treatment (freedom from discrimination on the basis of such characteristics as race or sex.)
6. The right to physical security
7. The right to freedom of speech and association
8. The right to minimal education
9. The right to political participation
10. The right to subsistence

This is a minimal list. Some will wish to add entries such as the right to employment, to social security, or to a certain standard of living. . . . Disputes also may arise about the wording or overlapping features of some rights: for example, is not the right to freedom from torture included in the right to physical security, at least when the latter is properly interpreted? We shall not attempt to resolve such controversies here. Rather, the list as presented aims to suggest, albeit incompletely, a description of a *minimal* set of rights and to serve as a beginning consensus for evaluating international conduct. If I am correct, many would wish to add entries, but few would wish to subtract them. . . .

Because by definition the list contains items that all three major classes of international actors must respect, the next task is to spell out the correlative duties that fall upon our targeted group of international actors, namely, multinational corporations.

This task requires putting the "fairness-affordability" condition to a second, and different, use. This condition was first used as one of the three criteria generating the original list of fundamental rights. There it demanded satisfaction of a fairness-affordability threshold for each potential respecter of a right. For example, if the burdens imposed by a given right are not fair (in relation to other bona fide obligations and burdens) or affordable for nation-states, individuals, and corporations, then presumably the prospective right would not qualify as a fundamental international right.

In its second use, the "fairness-affordability" condition goes beyond the judgment *that* a certain fairness-affordability threshold has been crossed to the determination of *what* the proper duties are for multinational corporations in relation to a given right. In its second use, in other words, the condition's notions of fairness and affordability are invoked to help determine *which* obligations properly fall upon corporations, in contrast to individuals and nation-states. The condition can help determine the correlative du-

ties that attach to multinational corporations in their honoring of fundamental international rights.

As we look over the list of fundamental rights, it is noteworthy that except for a few isolated instances multinational corporations have probably succeeded in fulfilling their duty not to *actively deprive* persons of their enjoyment of the rights at issue. But correlative duties involve more than failing to actively deprive people of the enjoyment of their rights. Henry Shue, for example, notes that three types of correlative duties are possible for any right: (1) to avoid depriving; (2) to help protect from deprivation; and (3) to aid the deprived.[9]

While it is obvious that the honoring of rights clearly imposes duties of the first kind, to avoid depriving directly, it is less obvious, but frequently true, that honoring them involves acts or omissions that help prevent the deprivation of rights. If I receive a note from Murder, Incorporated, and it looks like it means business, my right to security is clearly threatened. If a third party has relevant information which if revealed to the police would help protect my right, it is not a valid excuse for the third party to say that it is Murder, Incorporated, and not the third party, who wishes to kill me. Hence, honoring rights sometimes involves not only duties to *avoid depriving*, but to *help protect from deprivation* as well. Many critics of multinationals, interestingly enough, have faulted them not for the failure to avoid depriving, but for the failure to take reasonable protective steps.

The duties associated with rights often include ones from the third category, that of *aiding the deprived*, as when a government is bound to honor the right of its citizens to adequate nutrition by distributing food in the wake of a famine or natural disaster, or when the same government in the defense of political liberty is required to demand that an employer reinstate or compensate an employee fired for voting for a particular candidate in a government election.

Nonetheless, the honoring of at least some of the ten fundamental rights by multinational corporations requires only the adoption of the first class of correlative duties, that is, only the duty to avoid depriving. The correlative duties for corporations associated with some rights do not extend to protecting from deprivation or to aiding the deprived, because of the "fairness-affordability" condition discussed earlier. . . .

It would be unfair, not to mention unreasonable, to hold corporations to the same standards of charity and love as human individuals. Nor can they be held to the same standards to which we hold civil governments for enhancing social welfare — since many governments are formally dedicated to enhancing the welfare of, and actively preserving the liberties of, their citizens. The profit-making corporation, in contrast, is designed to achieve an economic mission and as a moral actor possesses an exceedingly narrow personality. It is an undemocratic institution, furthermore, which is ill-suited to the broader task of distributing society's goods in accordance with a conception of general welfare. The corporation is an economic animal; . . . although its responsibilities extend beyond maximizing return on investment for shareholders, they are informed directly by its economic mission. . . .

[T]he application of the "fairness-affordability" criterion . . . impl[ies] that duties of the third class, to aid the deprived, do not fall upon for-profit corporations except, of course, in instances in which a corporation itself has done the depriving. Barring highly unusual circumstances, . . . whatever duties corporations may have to aid the deprived are "maximal," not "minimal," duties. They are duties whose performance is not required as a condition of honoring fundamental rights or of preserving the corporation's moral right to exist. . . .

The same, however, is not true of the second class of duties, to protect from deprivation. These duties, like those in the third class, are also usually the province of government, but it sometimes happens that the rights to which they correlate are ones whose protection is a direct outcome of ordinary corporate activities. For example, the duties associated with protecting a worker from the physical threats of other workers may fall not only upon the local police, but also to some extent upon the employer. These duties, in turn, are properly viewed as correlative duties of the right — in this instance, the workers' right — to personal security. This will become clearer in a moment when we discuss the correlative duties of specific rights.

The following table lists correlative duties that reflect the second-stage application of the "fairness-affordability" condition to the earlier list of fundamental international rights. It indicates which rights do, and which do not, impose correlative duties of the three various kinds upon multinational corporations.

A word of caution should be issued for interpreting the table: the first type of correlative obligation, not depriving directly, is broader than might be supposed at first. It includes *cooperative* as well as individual actions. Thus, if a company has personnel policies that inhibit freedom of movement, or if a multinational corporation operating in South Africa cooperates with the government's restrictions on pass laws, then those companies may be said to actively deprive persons of their right to freedom of movement, despite the fact that actions of other agents (in this example, the South African government) may be essential in effecting the deprivation.[10]

Still, the list asserts that at least six of the ten fundamental rights impose correlative duties upon corporations of the second kind, that is, to protect from deprivation. What fol-

185

Correlative Corporate Duties

	Minimal Correlative Duties of Multinational Corporations		
Fundamental Rights	*To Avoid Depriving*	*To Help Protect From Deprivation*	*To Aid the Deprived*
Freedom of physical movement	X		
Ownership of property	X		
Freedom from torture	X		
Fair trial	X		
Nondiscriminatory treatment	X	X	
Physical security	X	X	
Freedom of speech and association	X	X	
Minimal education	X	X	
Political participation	X	X	
Subsistence	X	X	

lows is a brief set of commentaries discussing sample applications of each of those six rights from the perspective of such correlative duties.

SAMPLE APPLICATIONS

Discrimination

The obligation to protect a person from deprivation of the right to freedom from discrimination properly falls upon corporations as well aᵉ governments insofar as everyday corporate activities directly affect compliance with that right. Because employees and prospective employees possess the moral right not to be discriminated against on the basis of race, sex, caste, class, or family affiliation, it follows that multinational corporations have an obligation not only to refrain from discrimination, but in some instances to protect the right to nondiscriminatory treatment by establishing appropriate procedures. This may require, for example, offering notice to prospective employees about the company's policy of nondiscriminatory hiring, or

educating lower-level managers about the need to reward or penalize on the basis of performance rather than irrelevant criteria.

Physical Security

The right to physical security similarly entails duties of protection. If a Japanese multinational corporation operating in Nigeria hires shop workers to run metal lathes in an assembly factory, but fails to provide them with protective goggles, then the corporation has failed to honor the workers' moral right to physical security (no matter what the local law might decree). Injuries from such a failure would be the moral responsibility of the Japanese multinational despite the fact that the company could not be said to have inflicted the injuries directly.

Free Speech and Association

In the same vein, the duty to protect from deprivation the right of free speech and association finds application in the ongoing corporate obligation not to bar the creation of

186

labor unions. Corporations are not obliged on the basis of human rights to encourage or welcome labor unions; indeed they may oppose them using all morally acceptable means at their disposal. But neither are they morally permitted to destroy them or prevent their emergence through coercive tactics; for to do so would violate their workers' international right to association. The corporation's duty to protect from deprivation the right to association, in turn, includes refraining from lobbying host governments for restrictions that would violate the right in question, and perhaps even to protesting host government measures that do violate it. The twin phenomena of commercial concentration and the globalization of business, both associated with the rise of the multinational, have tended to weaken the bargaining power of labor. Some doubt that labor is sharing as fully as it once did from the cyclical gains of industrial productivity. This gives special significance to the right of free speech and association.

Minimal Education

The correlative duty to protect the right of education may be illustrated through the very example used to open this essay: the prevalence of child labor in developing countries. A multinational in Central America is not entitled to hire an eight-year-old for fulltime, permanent work because, among other reasons, doing so blocks the child's ability to receive a minimally sufficient education. What counts as a "minimally sufficient" education may be debated, and it seems likely, moreover, that the specification of the right to a certain level of education depends at least in part upon the level of economic resources available in a given country; nevertheless, it is reasonable to assume that any action by a cor-

poration which has the effect of obstructing the development of a child's ability to read or write would be proscribed on the basis of rights.

Political Participation

Clearly in some instances corporations have failed to honor the correlative duty of protecting from deprivation the right to political participation. Fortunately, the most blatant examples of direct deprivation are becoming so rare as to be nonexistent. I am referring to cases in which companies directly aid in overthrowing democratic regimes, as when United Fruit Company allegedly contributed to overthrowing a democratically elected regime in Guatemala during the 1950s.

A few corporations continue indirectly to threaten this right by failing to protect it from deprivation, however. Some persist, for example, in supporting military dictatorships in countries in which democratic sentiment is growing, and others have blatantly bribed publicly elected officials with large sums of money. Perhaps the most famous example of the latter occurred in 1972 when the prime minister of Japan was bribed with 7 million dollars by the Lockheed Corporation to secure a lucrative Tri-Star Jet contract. Here, the complaint from the perspective of this right is not against bribes or "sensitive payments" in general, but to bribes in contexts where they serve to undermine a democratic system in which publicly elected officials hold a position of public trust.

Even the buying and owning of major segments of a foreign country's land and industry has been criticized in this regard. As Brian Barry has remarked, "The paranoia created in Britain and the United States by land purchases by foreigners (especially Arabs, it seems) should serve to make it understandable that the citizenry of a country might be unhappy with a state of affairs in which the most important natural resources are in foreign ownership." At what point would Americans regard their democratic control threatened by foreign ownership of U.S. industry and resources? At 20 percent ownership? At 40 percent? At 60 percent? At 80 percent? The answer is debatable, yet there seems to be some point beyond which the right to national self-determination, and national democratic control, is violated by foreign ownership of property.[11]

Subsistence

Corporations also have duties to protect from deprivation the right to subsistence. Consider the following scenario: a number of square miles of land in an underdeveloped country has been used for many years to grow beans. Further, the bulk of the land is owned, as it has been for centuries, by two wealthy landowners. Poorer members of the community work the land and receive a portion of the crop, a portion barely sufficient to satisfy nutritional needs. Next, imagine that a multinational corporation offers the two wealthy owners a handsome sum for the land, because it plans to grow coffee for export. Now *if* — and this, admittedly, is a critical "if" — the corporation has reason to *know* that a significant number of people in the community will suffer malnutrition as a result, that is, if it has convincing reasons to believe that either those people will not be hired by the company or will not be paid sufficiently if they are hired, or that if forced to migrate to the city they will receive less than subsistence wages (wages inadequate to provide food and shelter), then the multinational may be said to have failed in its correlative duty to protect individuals from the deprivation of the right to subsistence. This is true despite the fact

that the corporation would never have stooped to take food from workers' mouths, and despite the fact that the malnourished will, in Samuel Coleridge's words, "die so slowly that none call it murder."

Disagreements: The Relevance of . . . Culture

The foregoing commentaries obviously are not intended to complete the project of specifying the correlative duties associated with fundamental international rights; they only begin it. Furthermore, . . . it may be that some of the fundamental rights on our list would not be embraced, at least as formulated here, by cultures different from ours. Would, for example, the Fulanis, a nomadic cattle culture in Nigeria, subscribe to this list with the same eagerness as the citizens of Brooklyn, New York? What list would they draw up if given the chance? And could we, or should we, try to convince them that our list is preferable? Would such a dialogue even make sense?[12]

I want to acknowledge that rights may vary in priority and style of expression from one cultural group to another. Yet . . . I maintain that the list itself is applicable to peoples even when those peoples would fail to compose an identical list. Clearly the Fulanis do not have to *accept* the ten rights in question for it to constitute a valid means of judging their culture. If the Fulanis treat women unfairly and unequally, then at least one fundamental international right remains unfulfilled in their culture, and their culture is so much the worse as a result. . . .

The Drug Lord Problem

One of the most difficult aspects of the proposed rights list concerns the fairness-affordability condition, a problem we can see more

188

clearly by reflecting on what might be called the "drug lord" problem.[13] Imagine that an unfortunate country has a weak government and is run by various drug lords (not, it appears, a hypothetical case). These drug lords threaten the physical security of various citizens and torture others. The government — the country — cannot afford to mount the required police or military actions that would bring these drug lords into moral line. Or, perhaps, this could be done but only by imposing terrible burdens on certain segments of the society which would be unfair to others. Does it follow that members of that society do not have the fundamental international right not to be tortured and to physical security? Surely they do, even if the country cannot afford to guarantee them. But if that is the case, what about the fairness-affordability criterion?

Let us begin by noting the "affordability" part of the fairness-affordability condition does imply some upper limit for the use of resources in the securing of a fundamental international right (for example, at the present moment in history, kidney dialysis cannot be a fundamental international right). With this established, the crucial question becomes *how* to draw the upper limit. The argument advanced in this essay commits us to draw that limit as determined by a number of criteria, two of which have special relevance for the present issue: first, compatibility with other, already recognized, international rights; and second, the level of importance of the interest, moral or otherwise, being protected by the right, that is, the first of the three conditions. In terms of the compatibility criterion, we remember that the duties imposed by any right must be compatible with other moral duties. Hence, a *prima facie* limit may be drawn on the certification of a prospective right corresponding to the point at which other bona fide international rights are violated. As for the importance of the

right, trade-offs among members of a class of prospective rights will be made by reference to the relative importance of the interest being protected by the right. The right not to be tortured protects a more fundamental interest than, say, the right to an aesthetically pleasing environment.

This provides a two-tiered solution for the drug lord problem. At the first tier, we note that the right of people not to be tortured by the drug lords (despite the unaffordability of properly policing the drug lords) implies that people, and especially the drug lords, have a duty not to torture. Here the solution is simple. The argument of this essay establishes a fundamental international right not to be tortured, and it is a right that binds all parties to the duty of forbearance in torturing others. For on the first application of the fairness-affordability condition, that is, when we are considering simply the issue of which fundamental international rights exist, we are only concerned about affordability in relation to *any* of the three classes of correlative duties. Here we look to determine only whether duties of *any* of the three classes of duties are fair and affordable, where "affordable" means literally capable of paying for. And with respect to the issue of affordability, clearly the drug lords, just as every other moral agent, can "afford" to refrain from actively depriving persons of their right not to be tortured. They can afford to refrain from torturing. (Earlier in this essay, the fairness-affordability condition was interpreted to imply that any act of forbearance, of a kind involved in not violating a right directly, is "affordable" for any moral agent.) It follows that people clearly have the fundamental international right not to be tortured, which imposes at least one class of duties upon all international actors, namely the duty of forbearance.

At the second tier, on the other hand, we are concerned with whether the right not to be tortured includes a duty of the government to mount an effective prevention system against torture. Here the fairness-affordability criterion is used in a second application, which helps establish the specific kinds of correlative duties associated with the already-acknowledged-to-exist right not to be tortured. Surely all nation-states can "afford" under ordinary circumstances to shoulder duties of the second and third categories of helping prevent deprivation and of aiding the deprived, although the specific extent of those duties may be further affected by considerations of fairness and affordability. For example, in the instance described in the drug lord problem, it seems questionable that all countries could "afford" to *succeed* completely in preventing torture, and hence the duty to help prevent torture presupposed by a fundamental international right to freedom from torture probably cannot be construed to demand complete success. Nonetheless, a fairly high level of success in preventing torture is probably demanded by virtue of international rights since, as noted earlier, the ordinary protection of civil and political rights, such as the right not to be tortured, carries a negative rather than positive economic cost. We know that the economic cost of allowing the erosion of rights to physical security and fair trial — as an empirical matter of fact — exceeds the cost of maintaining them.

What the list of rights and correlative corporate duties establishes is that multinational corporations frequently do have obligations derived from rights when such obligations extend beyond simply abstaining from depriving directly to actively protecting from deprivation. It implies, in other words, that the relevant factors for analyzing a difficult issue, such as hunger or high-technology agriculture, include not only the degree of factual correlation existing between multinational policy and hunger, but also the recognition of the existence of a right to subsistence along with a specification of the corporate correlative duties entailed.

I have argued that the ten rights identified in this essay constitute minimal and bedrock moral considerations for multinational corporations operating abroad. Though the list may be incomplete, the human claims that it honors, and the interests those claims represent, are globally relevant. The existence of fundamental international rights implies that no corporation can wholly neglect considerations of racism, hunger, political oppression, or freedom through appeal to its "commercial" mission. These rights are, rather, moral considerations for every international moral agent, although, as we have seen, different moral agents possess different correlative obligations. The specification of the precise correlative duties associated with such rights for corporations is an ongoing task that this chapter has left incomplete. Yet the existence of the rights themselves, including the imposition of duties upon corporations to protect — as well as to refrain from directly violating — such rights, seems beyond reasonable doubt.

NOTES

1. Ronald Dworkin, *Taking Rights Seriously* (Cambridge, Mass.: Harvard University Press, 1977). For other standard definitions of rights see James W. Nickel, *Making Sense of Human Rights: Philosophical Reflections on the Universal Declaration of Human Rights* (Berkeley: University of California Press, 1987), especially chapter 2; Joel Feinberg, "Duties, Rights and Claims," *American Philosophical Quarterly* 3 (1966): 137–44. See also Joel Feinberg, "The Nature and Value of Rights," *Journal of Value Inquiry* 4 (1970): 243–57; Wesley N. Hohfeld, *Fundamental Legal Conceptions* (New Haven, Conn.: Yale University Press, 1964); and H. J. McCloskey, "Rights — Some Conceptual Is-

sues," *Australasian Journal of Philosophy* 54 (1976): 99–115.

2. Maurice Cranston, *What Are Human Rights?* (New York: Tamlinger, 1973), p. 67.

3. H. J. McCloskey, for example, understands a right as a positive entitlement that need not specify who bears the responsibility for satisfying that entitlement. McCloskey, "Rights — Some Conceptual Issues," p. 99.

4. Feinberg, "Duties, Rights and Claims"; see also Feinberg, "The Nature and Value of Rights," pp. 243–57.

5. James Brooke, "Waste Dumpers Turning to West Africa," *New York Times*, July 17, 1988, p. 1, 7.

6. Ibid. Nigeria and other countries have struck back, often by imposing strict rules against the acceptance of toxic waste. For example, in Nigeria officials now warn that anyone caught importing toxic waste will face the firing squad. p. 7.

7. James W. Nickel, *Making Sense of Human Rights*, pp. 107–8.

8. I am indebted to Lynn Sharp Paine who, in critiquing an earlier draft of this essay, made me see the need for a clearer definition of the "fairness — affordability" criterion.

9. Henry Shue, *Basic Rights: Subsistence, Affluence and U.S. Foreign Policy* (Princeton, N.J.: Princeton University Press, 1980) p. 57.

10. I am indebted to Edwin Hartman for establishing this point. Hartman has suggested that this warrants establishing a fourth significant kind of duty, i.e., "avoiding helping to deprive." For a more detailed account of this interesting suggestion, see Edwin Hartman, "Comment on Donaldson's 'Rights in the Global Market,'" in Edward Freeman, ed., *Business Ethics: The State of the Art* (New York: Oxford University Press, 1991, pp. 163–72).

11. Brian Barry, "Humanity and Justice in Global Perspective," in J. Roland Pennock and John W. Chapman, eds., *Ethics, Economics, and the Law: Nomos Vol. XXIV* (New York: New York University Press, 1982), pp. 219–52. Companies are also charged with undermining local governments, and hence infringing on basic rights, through sophisticated tax evasion schemes. Especially when companies buy from their own subsidiaries, they can establish prices that have little connection to existing market values. This, in turn, means that profits can be shifted from high-tax to low-tax countries with the result that poor nations can be deprived of their rightful share.

12. Both for raising these questions, and in helping me formulate answers, I am indebted to William Frederick.

13. I am indebted to George Brenkert for suggesting and formulating the "drug lord" problem.

International Business Ethics: Russia and Eastern Europe

Richard T. De George

An American firm hires Russian scientists for $40 a month, which is above the average wage of the Russian worker but well below what their work is worth to the company. Although the American firm is willing to pay more, the Russian scientists do not want to earn too much more than their colleagues and are content to be able to continue their research. Both the American firm and the Russian scientists benefit. The American firm is accused by Americans of exploitation.

A truck full of toxic waste crosses the border from Germany into Poland and in a Polish border town dumps its hot load into a

From Richard DeGeorge, "International Business Ethics: Russia and Eastern Europe," *Social Responsibility: Business, Journalism, Law, and Medicine*, 19 (1993), pp. 5–23. Used by permission.

large, unprotected landfill. The German company has solved its problem of disposing of toxic waste. A group of Polish entrepreneurs has found a way of getting hard currency. What each side does is not against the law. The town's inhabitants, and probably others downstream, will eventually bear the cost.

A small Russian entrepreneur tries to set up a small plumbing business. He finds that all pipe and other supplies are allocated to big industries and that the only way he can get any at all is through bribes. He defends his paying these as being necessary and de facto the way business is done.

A former East German professor, who has lived in his apartment for forty years, is evicted when the building is privatized by the manager and sold to a West-German buyer who raises the rent beyond the professor's means.

These are just a few samples of the ethical issues that form part of daily life in Russia and Eastern Europe as they go through the torturous and unprecedented journey from socialist ownership and a centralized command economy to private ownership and a market economy. Marx claimed that the initial accumulation of capital was a result of plunder and theft of a variety of kinds and that capitalism was based on exploitation of the workers. Many in the former socialist countries seem to believe that this is in fact the situation they now face and that the system they are attempting to adopt is the system of capitalism as described by Marx.

In discussing business ethics in Russia and Eastern Europe I shall do three things. First, I shall present an overview of both the business and the ethical climate in these countries. Second, I shall investigate issues of business ethics for and from the point of view of the citizens of these countries. Third, I shall ask, given these two foundations, what are the

obligations of foreign firms — especially American firms — that wish to operate in these countries.

I. THE BUSINESS AND ETHICAL CLIMATE OF PRIVATIZATION

Following the October Revolution in 1917, Lenin and his followers started a new society governed by Marxist principles. The newly established Soviet Union entered unchartered waters as it moved from an early capitalist country to socialism. No country had done what this fledgling country did: seize the private instruments of production — all land, all buildings, all firms and business enterprises, large and small — and convert them to state property. There was no compensation given, no ethical qualms entertained. The exploiters and expropriators held their wealth and position unjustly and had no ethical or legal claim to them under the new rules. In theory, the move from capitalism to socialism was easy. The state simply had to nationalize what previously had been private without thought of weighing owner's rights, competing claims, or other similar considerations. Nonetheless, the years of War Communism following the revolution were an economic disaster. This led Lenin to introduce the New Economic Policy, which permitted some small free enterprise and which allowed the peasants to sell some of their produce on the open market. Stalin put an end to that policy and forcibly collectivized the farms, killing millions of kulaks in the process. The period from 1917 to 1933 can be considered the fifteen years it took to change over from a capitalist economy to a socialist one, and the change involved enormous hardships for the people and cost many lives.

The change from a socialist to a free market economy in the former Soviet Union and

192

in Eastern Europe is unprecedented as well. It is even more difficult and complicated than the change in the other direction. And it cannot be understood or appreciated without our being aware of the socialist background out of which these countries are moving.

I shall touch on only three aspects: the ethical and social background, the development of free enterprises, and the privatization of industry.

A) Government control in the USSR and in the socialist countries of Eastern Europe was ubiquitous. The state or government was the owner of all the means of production, including all the land. Housing was state owned, just as was industry. The government was the sole employer, and it in turn provided highly subsidized housing, free education, free medical care, old age pensions. The standard of living was not very high and productivity was correlatively low. There were laws, but there was no real rule of law. Nonetheless, the state provided security. Government control was total, and hence other sources of control were minimal. In 1961 the Communist Party issued a Moral Code of the Builders of Communism, which listed the norms that were to guide Soviet citizens. The norms were collective. Conscience was not something private to be respected but something social to be molded. Any notion of internal norms was undermined by a view of ethics that was external and in the service of the state.

One result was that the vast majority of the population ignored the official morality. They learned how to get around official rules whenever possible. There was little in the way of a work ethic. The standard joke was, "We pretend to work, and the State pretends to pay us." And there was also little in the way of a shared public ethic. People still valued their families and friends, but the values of the state were never successfully inculcated into the people. Except for those who privately nurtured religious values, the moral fabric of the country was seriously weakened. The old morality had been undermined and the new morality was ineffective. Falsehood was expected from the government and from the Communist Party, and people became immune to Party propaganda. For over seventy years the Soviet Union had preached Marxism-Leninism, and most of those alive today in the former Soviet republics have never known any other approach to history, society, or economics. They think in Marxist terms, and they learned about the West and capitalism from their Marxist texts, which tended to vilify both.

The overthrow of the Communist regime was a protest against the domination by the Party and its control. It was not a fight for capitalism or free enterprise. And how much of socialism the people want to give up is still an open question. The problems are many. Having overthrown communism and repudiated the former system, they are left with little in the way of a system under which to operate. Socialist laws have not yet been effectively replaced by other laws, and the question of which laws to adopt is a continuing topic of debate. With the legal system under revision, the police and the courts are less and less effective — and not free of corruption. As the traditional background institutions that lend stability to a society disintegrate, there is more and more need for morality to function as a source of social order; but there is little public morality left to play that essential role.

The ordinary worker — who has little, who earns an average of 5,000 rubles a month (less than $10 at the May 1993 rate of exchange), and whose savings have disappeared with rampant inflation — considers anyone able to succeed under these circumstances as

193

being crooked: they must be a former communist official or a bureaucrat who is taking advantage of his or her past position; or a member of the "mafia," criminally amassing wealth; or an entrepreneur exploiting others.

This is the social background for the development of free enterprise and for privatization.

B) The development of small entrepreneurs has been officially both encouraged and hampered. It has been encouraged because it is clear that one of the failures of the old system, which relied exclusively on centralized control, was simply not effective. Hence, some of those presently in charge realize, at least in theory, the need for entrepreneurs to develop small businesses and for decentralization to replace the former command economy.

The difficulty is that the former state structures of distribution are for the most part still in place. Large factories and enterprises are still the dominant economic reality, and sources of supplies are still geared toward those enterprises. The result is that small businesses have a very difficult time receiving the wherewithal to conduct their business. If goods are earmarked for the large factories and are not available to the small entrepreneur, the latter effectively cannot operate. The only way they can operate, given the skewed — and, they claim, unfair — allocation system, is by getting what they can where, when, and how they can. In practice, this most often means paying bribes to those who have access to the needed materials — whether they are managers in factories willing to sell what has been allocated to them, or shippers and middle men who divert shipments to the small business for a fee, or black market and other people who steal what they can sell.

The climate for the entrepreneur is very volatile. The laws are constantly changing. The tax rates and rules are similarly in a state of flux. The status of ownership of whatever property they have is uncertain. In addition, there is a growing crime rate, with extortion not uncommon, and there are reports of a Russian mafia becoming more and more powerful.[1] Dmitri Rozanov, a Russian entrepreneur, says, "Without paying off the local powers-that-be, it's almost impossible to stay in business,"[2] — a view that is echoed by most Russian business persons.

C) The status of privatization is equally unsettled. Privatization has been described as the state's selling enterprises worth nothing to people who have nothing. A major difficulty in the present situation is the amassing of industrial capital. The people have savings that amount to only about 4% of the estimated value of state enterprises. Clearly they cannot buy them. But under socialism they were said to be the owners of the means of production: hence they should not have to buy them because they already own them. One problem is that simply owning the factories, shops, stores does no good if they are not productive, and most of them need an influx of money to retool and modernize. A second problem is great confusion about who owns former state property and who has the right to privatize it.

What is the ethically right, the just, the fair way to privatize state property? When Britain privatized its state-owned industries it did so according to established rules. It was clear who owned the industries, who had a right to sell them, and who would get the proceeds. In the former Soviet Union and Eastern Europe none of this is the case. It is not clear who owns what (since in theory everyone owned everything), who has the right to sell anything, and who should get the proceeds. Issues of fairness and justice arise as competing, conflicting, incompatible claims, with no mechanism for dispute resolution in place and a sense of urgency to make the transition quickly, before reactionary forces can turn the clock back to state ownership. Yelena Kotova, former director of Moscow's privatization, says, "Moral notions are essentially inappropriate, because it's a cruel process."[3]

Privatization is proceeding in a number of different ways — none of which is wholly fair to all. In Czechoslovakia and Russia the government has issued vouchers that may be used to purchase shares in firms of the individual's choosing. In October 1992, the Russian government issued vouchers of 10,000 rubles each and expected to make available all small and medium enterprises and about 5,000 large enterprises in 1993.[4] The vouchers may be sold or the stock one buys may be traded, although capital markets are just now being organized and are still rudimentary. The vouchers were originally worth $40 at the current rate of exchange; by February 1993 they were worth $17 and were selling for half that on the commodities exchange.[5] . . . The voucher system sounds like a good solution, since everyone in theory owned everything. But one can hardly expect the ordinary Russian citizen to believe that his or her share of the nation's wealth was, at best, $40.

A second form of privatization, followed to a large extent in Poland, consists of turning a factory or enterprise over to the workers. But some of the enterprises were favored under the state system and are productive while others were not. Is it fair to treat them all the same? Is it fair for a worker who has been at a plant for two years to get the same share as one who has been there for twenty years? And is it fair to turn over a non-productive factory to workers who have no prospects of making it productive? What of those who were in the service sector, like teachers? In some cases, managers have taken the initiative and sold the enterprise, sometimes to themselves at ridiculously low prices, sometimes to foreign investors and others who had available cash — again often at ridiculously low prices.

Some firms are being privatized by government auction. Poland has used this method, among others. This provides immediate revenue, but it works only for productive enterprises and has been criticized for turning factories over to foreigners. In an attempt to overcome the former problem, Poland is restructuring and intends to sell whole industries rather than just the strongest companies.[6]

A fourth form of privatization is the selling off of the assets of a company piecemeal to whomever will buy the pieces. This has even been done by military units, which are selling off their arms and even in some instances their tanks to whoever is willing to buy them.[7]
. . .

Other forms of privatization include: the state's organizing holding companies (which in fact tend to resemble state-owned enterprises) to help the transition; or, as in Hungary, the selling of individual firms through the State Property Agency to investors who ask to buy them; or allowing companies to go private on their own. Each method has advantages and disadvantages, and from an ethical point of view each raises problems. In Russia, if enterprises were simply turned over to the workers, 70% of the population would be left out.[8]

The situation in East Germany and Poland is further complicated because the new regimes are recognizing the legal claims of former owners on property that the state confiscated from them or their families immediately after World War II.

The result is a condition of great confusion and uncertainty. The state is ineffective in its new role. Market forces are not yet in place. The transition period has led to high unemployment and the closing of many factories that simply cannot compete. They were able to sell shoddy goods in the former command economy but not in an economy where goods are available from the West. The social services formerly provided by the state are no longer readily available. The status of apartments and housing is often in dispute, and ownership is not clear. Do the apartments belong to the occupants, to the city, to the state? Who is responsible for their upkeep and repair?

It is within this system that I now turn to the question of business ethics, to consider it first from the point of view of the local entrepreneur and then from the point of view of the foreigner.

II. BUSINESS ETHICS AND RUSSIAN ENTREPRENEURS

What can we say of business ethics from the Russian point of view? The first answer is that it is a perceived problem, at least by some. In June 1993 the Academy of National Economy of the Russian Federation Graduate School of International Business sponsored an international conference on "Business Ethics in New Russia." What a conference can do is certainly minimal, and bears on the insignificant. But it is an indication of the realization on the part of at least some that a move to free enterprise is possible only if it is accompanied by a set of background institutions — laws, enforceable contracts, social understandings, accepted business practices, and acceptability by the general population, which is where ethics enters. Ethics provides the legitimation for the system of business, and it provides both the glue that keeps it together and the oil that allows it to function. Without basic trust, no contracts will be signed, no goods delivered. Markets rely on information, and hence truth becomes a value. Property is central, and hence respect for property is essential. . . .

The issue of ethics in a corrupt system is a difficult one. The claim that in order to operate as a small entrepreneur one must pay bribes and buy supplies where and when one finds them, without questioning their source, is probably correct. Let us suppose that it is. Is one ethically allowed to operate one's business this way? The obvious answer is No, if there is any alternative. But if the allocation system is itself unfair and corrupt, if government bureaucrats get their share of payments and ignore or condone the diverting of goods based on bribes, can the small entrepreneur be held to a standard of ethical behavior proper in a less corrupt environment? To hold one to that standard is, in effect, to preclude one's being a private entrepreneur and to leave all enterprise to the criminal element.

The tax laws keep changing, and no standard method of bookkeeping is in place. In some cases no bookkeeping is required.

Under the circumstances, basic fundamental ethical norms still apply. Extortion, physical harm and threats, robbery, lying, producing defective goods, dumping toxic wastes, all remain unethical — whether or not they are effectively policed. The outright stealing of goods by some of the managers, who receive materials and immediately ship and sell them abroad for below their market value, is unethical by any standard.

But in the given circumstances I believe that some practices that would be clearly wrong, for instance, in the United States, may be ethically justified for people in those circumstances. When, for example, might the paving of bribes to receive legitimate supplies necessary for one's business be allowed? One justifiable answer is that they are justifiable when they are not bribes but part of the cost of doing business. Bribes are payments made to receive special advantage at the expense of others under some orderly system of entitlements. Absent an orderly system of entitlements, and absent the special advantage and the harm done to others, we are no longer describing what is generally thought of as bribery. We have a disorderly system in which goods are not rationally allocated, either by the market or by the government, and in which there is no fair market price. The price of goods is determined by supply and demand in a rough sense. But if all private entrepreneurs are in the same system, and if goods are available to all only through the payment of fees beyond those listed on an invoice (if there is one), then that is the way, and the cost, of doing business. The payments do not undermine a free market but in this case are part of a developing one.

A kind of utilitarian argument might also be mounted according to which both society as a whole and consumers benefit from private entrepreneurs taking the risks of private business and providing goods and services under the present inefficient and chaotic system. Both the entrepreneurs and society will benefit more than if such businesses were not carried on, leaving people without goods and services, and all enterprise to criminal initiatives.

This justification is clearly conditional and temporary. As the system becomes organized and regularized, the status of such payments changes and becomes disruptive rather than productive, unethical rather than justifiable. Moreover, at best this line of reasoning justifies those who are forced to pay what we shall continue to call bribes. It does not justify the actions of government officials who demand bribes, or of police who require bribes to not enforce what law there is. These actions are part of the problem and can in no way be considered a waystation toward the solution.

Similarly, it is difficult for the small entrepreneur to know what his taxes are when the government, for all intents and purposes, does not know and is unable to provide adequate information or to police any rules it does establish. In such a situation, is failure to pay one's taxes unethical? While it is unethical to avoid paying one's fair taxes in an ordinary system, one can hardly call the present Russian situation a system in any functional sense. Hence the small entrepreneur can plausibly follow whatever rules there are that are most favorable to him — possibly even delaying paying where it is not clearly illegal to delay.

The appropriate generalization in these conditions is that more cannot be asked of those in business than the situation warrants. General ethical demands must be placed in context, and in the Russian context the conclusions one comes to, from an ethical point of view, diverge from the conclusions one would come to in a normal situation. That is true primarily because of the lack of any stable or just background institutions.

At the present time it is difficult to know what "just" or "fair" mean in a great many instances having to do with property — because property is a bundle of rights relative to a system of rights. What constitutes property in the United States is a function of our laws that grant property rights and provide a system under which property can be legitimately transferred. Under the Soviet system, private property was not allowed and the system of rights that developed was significantly different from the system of property in the United States. What was fair or just, as well as what was possible under the two systems, differed. But under which system are Russia and the countries of Eastern Europe now, and which notions of property and justice apply? The problem is that no clear system has yet emerged in any of these countries.

This fact makes the problems of privatization and of developing private enterprises very difficult to judge from the point of view of fairness or justice. If what constitutes property, and what is fair with respect to its transfer or control, are a function of a system, then absent a clear system there is no clear answer to the question. The practical difficulty is that privatization is taking place be-

197

fore any coherent system has been put in place. In some ways, then, business ethics requires a background system within which to operate.

This does not mean that there are no norms common to all systems. As we have already seen, both the ordinary citizen and outside observers appropriately condemn violence, outright robbery, the misuse of political or police power for private gain, and the like.

This leads to my third consideration: how should foreign — for instance, American — firms, act in this environment?

III. MULTINATIONALS IN RUSSIA AND EASTERN EUROPE

I have already claimed that the basic norms of respecting life, honoring agreements and contracts, and telling the truth are basic to any society and economic system. The norms are not universally adhered to; but that is consistent with the necessity for basic norms to exist. If basic norms are breached in any significant numbers, the very possibility of social life and hence of doing business is undermined.

Nor does the fact that some moral issues are dependent on the background institutions of a society mean that when in Rome one should do as the Romans do. In the first place, what the Romans do may be unethical and unjustifiable in itself. If some society practices slavery and protects it by law, that does not mean that American companies are ethically allowed to similarly practice slavery in that country. In South Africa under the apartheid laws, American companies could not morally abide by those laws and enforce apartheid within their operations. This led to the Sullivan principles, which precluded firms from following the apartheid laws and yet allowed them to operate in the country in

the hope that they could weaken apartheid from within. After ten years, Leon Sullivan, who had proposed the principles in the first place, declared the experiment a failure and maintained that following his principles no longer could provide justification for continued operation in South Africa.

Although American companies are not required to do business in Eastern Europe and Russia exactly as they do in the United States, they are also not allowed to ignore moral norms, even if these are neither enacted into law nor effectively enforced in the host country. The situation of the multinational that can choose whether to operate in these countries, and the conditions under which it will operate, is different from the situation of native entrepreneurs. The latter's choices are much more restricted if they choose to set up a business.

The example of MacDonald's is a case in point. When MacDonald's first started operating in Moscow, it made provision to receive almost all of its supplies from foreign sources because of the unreliability of Soviet sources. Slowly, as it found reliable local suppliers, it switched from foreign to local sources. This option would not be open to local entrepreneurs. But even though the policy was possible for MacDonalds, it is clear that American firms cannot justify bribery and illegality by arguing that because this is the way business is done in Russia, it is the only way our firm can do business there.

Does this not imply a double standard, since I gave a limited defense of local entrepreneurs working within the system? The answer is No. The reason is that the situation of the local entrepreneur and of the American multinational is very different. One can plausibly argue that the local entrepreneur has no choice but to operate within a corrupt system or not to operate at all. The American multinational, on the other hand, has a very real option of not operating there at all, while continuing to operate everywhere else that it already does. Second, the multinational does not need to engage in bribery. It has available hard currency, which is in such great demand that, if anything, it needs to give some attention to the fact that it can skew the allocation of resources to the serious disadvantage of local firms. If bribes are demanded, an American company can and should point to the American Foreign Corrupt Practices Act as an added reason precluding its paying bribes to public officials. If bribes are actually necessary to conduct business, the American company can protest through official governmental and intergovernmental channels; it can use the media to expose the demands; and it can band together with other American companies similarly situated to jointly refuse to pay such demands. In short, an American company has a wide variety of options available that are not available to the local entrepreneur. Therefore, the multinationals have no justification for engaging in such practices.

The multinational in the given context, because of the strength of its position, has a positive obligation to set an example of ethics in business and to encourage the development of background institutions conducive to stability and to business practices that benefit the society as a whole. As an outside interest entering the country for the company's benefit, it should not be exploitive or seek its own good to the disadvantage of the local population. To do otherwise is the carpetbagger syndrome, exploitive and unethical, even if legal.

Of the stories with which we began, clearly the Western firm that transported its toxic waste to Poland and knew it would be dumped in unprotected landfills acted unethically, even though not yet illegally. It took advantage of the need of the people for hard currency and collaborated with a group of private entrepreneurs willing, for their own

profit, to endanger a considerable number of people. Even if the town as a whole had consented to the deal and shared in the proceeds, the Western company would have been taking advantage of them. There are some deals, such as selling oneself into slavery, that are not allowable, even if done with the apparent consent of the disadvantaged party. Using one's backyard for toxic wastes indicates either desperation or lack of appreciation of the consequences of one's act; in any case, it shows flagrant disregard for those who will be adversely affected without their consent.

What of the American firm that hired Russian scientists for $40 a month — as both AT&T and Corning have done? AT&T Bell Laboratories signed a one year agreement with the General Physics Institute of the Russian Academy of Sciences in Moscow, hiring about 100 of the Institute's 1200 scientists and researchers. Corning hired 115 scientists and technicians at Vavilov State Optical Institute in St. Petersburg, which has several thousand scientists.[9] Are the American firms guilty of exploiting the scientists by paying them $480 a year, while a comparable top scientist in the U.S. working, say, in fiber optics could command an annual salary of about $70,000? Despite appearances, the answer is No. In these cases the wages were set by the Russian scientists, who know they could get more but who did not want to be paid too much more than their Russian counterparts. Since $40 a month is well above the average Russian worker's wage, it is sufficient to live at a standard common to large numbers of people in that society. The labor is not forced, and the wage is set by the workers, who have the Russian right to patents on whatever they develop. Hence there is no exploitation in this case. There is rather a mutually satisfactory and ethically justifiable arrangement.

The issues of wages is a difficult one for American companies in many countries abroad. If they pay the going wage — which by American standards seems pitifully low — they are accused by Americans of exploiting the local workers. If they pay well above the going wage, they are accused by local companies of stealing away their best workers and of attempting to drive wages up so as to put them out of business. No matter what the going wage, an American multinational can and should pay at least wages that are sufficient for the worker to live at a standard of living considered acceptable in that country, providing that it is at least sufficient for the worker to live in accordance with general norms of human dignity. These guidelines are admittedly vague, and they are necessarily so because there is no one just wage. Above a certain minimum necessary for decent living conditions, the amount of which varies from country to country, the market can ethically be allowed to operate. What is ethically demanded everywhere is respect for the human rights of workers, which means not only adequate wages but fair treatment and relatively safe and sanitary working conditions.

What of the West German who buys the Berlin apartment building? I have already indicated that in Russia and in some other East European countries it is not clear to whom such property belongs. Nor is it clear how to decide what is a fair way to privatize. No one can legitimately sell what does not belong to him. The difficulty facing an outside buyer is to determine that what he is buying legitimately belongs to the seller, that the title the buyer receives will be legally recognized, and that the attached rights will be upheld and enforced.

In the German case, the buyer knows that German law applies. The fact that long-time residents of the apartment building could not pay the new rent and were forced to leave is an unfortunate consequence of privatization. The buyer, the seller, or the government might try to alleviate the residents'

plight by helping them relocate. But that is an ethical ideal and not an ethical requirement. In itself the transaction is not unethical. It differs from the toxic dumping case because of the difference in the harm done and foreseen in the two cases. Had the building existed prior to World War II, and had it been nationalized by the East Germans, the former owner might have some claim on it. What the claim amounts to and how such claims are to be adjudicated is presently being decided by German courts. Had the apartments been given to the tenants, as the state has done in many cases in Russia, the situation would obviously be different. The fact that persons who had important positions under the Communist regime and had correspondingly favorable housing are now being forced to relocate to more modest housing does not seem unjust, on the face of it. The German laws are adequate to handle difficult cases of homelessness and eviction rights. This case — as opposed to somewhat similar cases in other East European countries that were not able to adopt wholesale a preexisting system of laws — shows the pain many in Eastern Europe are suffering in the period of transition. . . .

What general conclusions can we draw?

The first is that international business ethics is not and cannot be the imposition of American business ethics — whatever one means by that — on all nations. Ethics is one of the restraints on business, and in each country it operates in conjunction with a host of other restraints, demands, and expectations. As we have noted in passing, the system of law, the view of property, the standard of living, and the customs and traditions of the people are all important considerations. This does not imply ethical relativism, or the view that whatever any society says is ethical is in fact ethical — as the cases of slavery and apartheid show. But it does imply that norms appropriately vary in their application, and that one should be cautious of overgeneralization based exclusively on American experience.

A second conclusion has to do with American multinationals. A company that wishes to act with integrity must have its own values to which it adheres. If a company changes its values from country to country, and if the norms it follows are determined exclusively by the enforced local laws, it is questionably a company of integrity. I have suggested that, given the conditions of Eastern Europe and Russia, American companies, and companies from other industrially developed countries, have a special obligation not to abuse the special advantages they have vis-à-vis these countries. They are ethically precluded from exploitation, from cooperating with criminal elements (whether as suppliers or as go-betweens), from paying bribes, and from violating the human rights of workers or consumers — whether or not any of this is precluded by enforced laws.

A third conclusion has to do with international business ethics in general. Business ethics is itself a fairly recent subject of study. It developed in the United States in the 1970s and has grown since then. It has spread to various countries in Europe and more recently to centers in Japan, Brazil, Australia, and elsewhere. But although business is clearly global, there is still a great deal of confusion among both academicians and business people about international or global business ethics: what it means and how it can be implemented. The most significant difference between business ethics in the United States and on a global level is the absence on the global level of what can be called background institutions: laws, agreements, understandings, traditions, and the like. The need worldwide is to adopt agreements, understandings, and rules that make mutually advantageous trade possible and that keep the playing field of competition level.

I suggest that these background institutions should not be established by the imposition of American standards on the world, but that they should be the result of negotiation between all affected parties. Only if all those seriously affected agree to the justice of those institutions will they be stable and perform the function that comparable background institutions play in most developed countries.

Russia and some East European countries are now in a state of economic and social chaos. In such a situation ethics is needed, but even more important are ethically justifiable structures — laws and procedures. The development of such structures is a precondition for any full-fledged consideration of business ethics in Russia and Eastern Europe in the foreseeable future.

NOTES

1. See Stephen Handelman, "Inside Russia's Gangster Economy." *The New York Times Magazine*, January 24, 1993, 12 ff.
2. Cynthia Scharf, "The Wild, Wild East: Everyone's a Capitalist in Russia Today and Nobody Knows the Rules," *Business Ethics*, vol. 6, No. 6, (Nov./Dec. 1992), 21.
3. "Russians Privatize by Looting State Goods," *The Washington Post*, May 17, 1992, A1.
4. "Citizens of Russia To Be Given Share of State's Wealth," *The New York Times*, October 1, 1992, A1, A10.
5. *Christian Science Monitor*, February 10, 1993, 3.
6. "In East Europe, There's More Than One Capitalist Road," *Chicago Tribune*, October 25, 1992, Sec. 7, 1.
7. "Selling Off Big Red," *Newsweek*, March 1, 1993, 50–51; "Russians Privatize by Looting State Goods," *The Washington Post*, May 17, 1992, A1.
8. "Russia's Big Enterprises Privatize, With Communists at the Ready," *Christian Science Monitor*, February 10, 1993, 3.
9. "Russian Scientists for A.T.&T. and Corning," *The New York Times*, May 27, 1992, D1.

Business Ethics: A Japanese View

Iwao Taka

I. TWO NORMATIVE ENVIRONMENTS — RELIGIOUS DIMENSION

In order to evaluate the traditional ethical standards of the Japanese business community, it is necessary to describe the Japanese cultural context or background. When it comes to cultural or ethical background, we can classify Japanese conscious and unconscious beliefs into a "religious dimension" and a "social dimension," in that Japanese culture cannot be understood well in terms of only one of the two dimensions. While the former is closely combined with a metaphysical concept or an idea of human salvation, the latter is based on how Japanese observe or conceive their social environment. Stated otherwise, while the former is "ideal-oriented," the latter is "real-oriented."

First, the religious dimension. This dimension supplies a variety of concrete norms of behavior to the Japanese in relation to the ultimate reality. As a consequence, I shall call this dimension the "normative environment."

By this I mean the environment in which most events and things acquire their own meanings pertaining to something beyond the tangible or secular world. Following this definition, there are mainly two influential normative environments in Japan: the "transcendental normative environment" and the "group normative environment."

1. Transcendental Normative Environment

One of the famous Japanese didactic poems says, "Although there are many paths at the foot of a mountain, they all lead us in the direction of the same moon seen at the top of the mountain." This poem gives us an ontological equivalent of "variety equals one." To put it in another way, though there are innumerable phenomena in this tangible world, each individual phenomenon has its own "numen" (soul, spirit, reason-d'être, or spiritual energy), and its numen is ultimately connected with the unique numen of the universe. In Japanese, this ultimate reality is often called "natural life force," "great life force of the universe," *"michi"* (path of righteousness), *"ri"* (justice), *"ho"* (dharma, laws), and the like.

"Transcendentalism" is the philosophy that every phenomenon is an expression of the great life force and is ultimately connected with the numen of the universe. It follows that the environment where various concrete norms come to exist may be called the "transcendental normative environment." What is more, the set of these norms is simply called "transcendental logic."

In this transcendental environment, everyone has an equal personal numen. This idea has been philosophically supported or strengthened by Confucianism and Buddhism. That is to say, in the case of neo-Confucianism, people are assumed to have a

---

From Iwao Taka, "Business Ethics: A Japanese View" from *Business Ethics Quarterly* 4:1, (1994). Used with permission.

microcosm within themselves, and are considered condensed expressions of the universe (macrocosm). Their inner universe is expected to be able to connect with the outer universe.

In the case of Buddhism, every living creature is said to have an equal Buddhahood, a Buddhahood which is very similar with the idea of numen and microcosm. Buddhism has long taught, "Although there are differences among living creatures, there is no difference among human beings. What makes human beings different is only their name."

In addition, however, under the transcendental normative environment, not only individuals but also jobs, positions, organizations, rituals, and other events and things incorporate their own "numina." Needless to say, these numina are also expected to be associated with the numen of the universe.

Deities of Shintoism, Buddhism, and the Japanese new religions, which have long been considered objects of worship, are often called the "great life force of the universe," or regarded as expressions of that force. In this respect, the life force can be sacred and religious. On the other hand, however, many Japanese people have unconsciously accepted this way of thinking without belonging to any specific religious sect. In this case, it is rather secular, non-religous, and atheistic. Whether it is holy or secular, the significant feature of Japan is that this transcendental normative environment has been influential and has been shared by Japanese people.

2. Meaning of Work
in the Transcendental Environment

Inasmuch as Japanese people live in such a normative environment, the meaning of work for them becomes unique. That is to say, work is understood to be a self-expression of the great life force. Work is believed to have its own numen so that work is one of the ways to reach something beyond the secular world or the ultimate reality. Accordingly, Japanese people unconsciously and sometimes consciously try to unify themselves with the great life force by concentrating on their own work.

This propensity can be found vividly in the Japanese tendency to view seemingly trivial activities — such as arranging flowers, making tea, practicing martial arts, or studying calligraphy — as ideal ways to complete their personality (or the ideal ways to go beyond the tangible world). Becoming an expert in a field is likely to be thought of as reaching the stage of *kami* (a godlike state). Whatever job people take, if they reach the *kami* stage or even if they make a strong effort to reach it, they will be respected by others.

M. Imai has concluded that whereas Western managers place priority on innovation, Japanese managers and workers put emphasis on *Kaizen* (continuous improvement of products, of ways to work, and of decision-making processes). While innovation can be done intermittently only by a mere handful of elites in a society, *Kaizen* can be carried on continuously by almost every person.

Technological breakthroughs in the West are generally thought to take a Ph.D., but there are only three Ph.D.s on the engineering staff at one of Japan's most successfully innovative companies — Honda Motor. One is founder Soichiro Honda, whose Ph.D. is an honorary degree, and the other two are no longer active within the company. At Honda, technological improvement does not seem to require a Ph.D.[1]

The transcendental normative environment has contributed to the formation of this Japanese propensity to place emphasis on *Kaizen*. Work has been an important path for Japanese people to reach the numen of the universe. Thus, they dislike skimping on their work, and instead love to improve their products, ways of working, or the decision-making processes. These Japanese attitudes are closely linked with the work ethics in the transcendental normative environment. Kyogoku describes this as follows:

> In marked contrast with an occidental behavioral principle of "Pray to God, and work!" at the cloister, in Japan, "Work, that is a prayer!" became a principle. In this context, devotion of one's time and energy to work, concentration on work to such a degree that one is absorbed in the improvement of work without sparing oneself, and perfectionism of "a demon for work," became institutional traditions of Japan.[2]

In this way, the transcendental environment has supplied many hard workers to the Japanese labor market, providing an ethical basis for "diligence." Nonetheless, it has not created extremely individualistic people who pursue only their own short-term interests. Because they have hoped for job security and life security in the secular world, they have subjectively tried to coordinate their behavior so as to keep harmonious relations with others in the group. Within this subjective coordination, and having the long-term perspective in mind, they pursue their own purposes.

3. Group Normative Environment

The second or group normative environment necessarily derives from this transcendental normative environment, insofar as the latter gives special raisons d'être not only to individuals and their work, but also to their groups. As a result of the transcendental environment, every group holds its own numen. The group acquires this *raison d'être*, as long as it guarantees the life of its members and helps them fulfill their potentials.

But once a group acquires its *raison d'être*, it insists upon its survival. An environment in which norms regarding the existence and prosperity of the group appear and affect its members is called the "group normative environment," and the set of the norms in this environment is called "group logic."

In Japan, the typical groups have been: *ie* (family), *mura* (local community), and *kuni* (nation). After World War II, although the influence of *ie* and *kuni* on their members has been radically weakened, one cannot completely ignore their influence. *Mura* has also lost much power over its members, but *kaisha* (business organization) has taken over many functions of *mura*, in addition to some functions of *ie*. These groups are assumed to have their own numen: *ie* holds the souls of one's ancestors, *mura* relates to a *genius loci* (tutelary deity), *kaisha* keeps its corporate tradition (or culture), and *kuni* has Imperial Ancestors' soul. . . .

Groupism and a group-oriented propensity, which have often been pointed out as Japanese characteristics, stem from this group normative environment.

II. THE ETHICAL DILEMMA OF LIVING BETWEEN TWO ENVIRONMENTS

Japanese often face an ethical dilemma arising from the fact that they live simultaneously in the two different influential normative environments. In the transcendental environment, groups and individuals are regarded as equal numina and equal expressions of the great life force. In the group environment, however, a group (and its representatives) is considered to be superior to its ordinary members, mainly because while the group is expected to be able to connect with the numen of the universe in a direct way, the members are not related to the force in

204

the same way. The only way for the members to connect with the life force is through the activities of their group.

Depending on which normative environment is more relevant in a given context, the group stands either above or on an equal footing with its members. Generally speaking, as long as harmonious human relations within a group can be maintained, discretion is allowed to individuals. In this situation, the transcendental logic is dominant.

But once an individual begins asking for much more discretion than the group can allow, or the group starts requiring of individuals much more selfless devotion than they are willing to give, ethical tension arises between the two environments. In most cases, the members are expected to follow the requirements of the group, justified by the group logic. . . .

The assertion or gesture by a group leader to persuade subordinate members to follow, is called *tatemae* (formal rule). *Tatemae* chiefly arises from the need of the group to adapt itself to its external environment. In order to adjust itself, the group asks its members to accept changes necessary for the group's survival. In this moment, the group insists upon *tatemae.* On the other hand, the assertion or gesture by the members to refuse *tatemae,* is called *honne* (real motive). *Honne* mainly comes from a desire to let the subordinates' numen express itself in a free way.

Usually, a serious confrontation between *tatemae* and *honne* is avoided, because both the leader and subordinates dislike face-to-face discussions or antagonistic relations. Stated otherwise, the members (the leader and the subordinates) tend to give great weight to harmonious relations within the group. Because of this, the leader might change his or her expectation toward the subordinates, or the subordinates might refrain from pursuing their direct self-interest. In either case, the final decision-maker is un-

likely to identify whose assertion was adopted, or who was right in the decision-making, since an emphasis on who was correct or right in the group often disturbs its harmony.

Simply described, this ambiguous decision-making is done in the following way. The group lets the subordinates confirm a priority of group-centeredness, and requires their selfless devotion. This requirement is generally accepted without reserve in the group normative environment. But if the subordinate individuals do not really want to follow the group orders, they "make a wry face," "look displeased," "become sulky," or the like, instead of revealing their opinions clearly. These attitudes are fundamentally different from formal decision-making procedures. In this case, taking efficiency and the harmonious relation of the group into consideration, the group "gives up compelling," "relaxes discipline," or "allows *amae*" of the subordinates.

If the failure to follow the norms endangers the survival of the group, the leader repeatedly asks the members to follow the order. In this case, at first, the leader says, "I really understand your feeling," in order to show that he or she truly sympathizes with the members. And then he or she adds, "This is not for the sake of me, but for the sake of our group." Such persuasion tends to be accepted, because almost everybody implicitly believes that the group has its own numen and the group survival will bring benefits to all of them in the long run. . . .

III. ETHICS OF CONCENTRIC CIRCLES — SOCIAL DIMENSION

Due to human bounded cognitive rationality or cultural heritage, Japanese moral agents, whether individuals or corporations, tend to conceptualize the social environment in a centrifugal order similar to a water ring. Although there are many individuals, groups, and organizations which taken together constitute the overall social environment, the Japanese are likely to categorize them into four concentric circles: family, fellows, Japan, and the world. On the basis of this way of thinking, Japanese people and organizations are likely to attribute different ethics or moral practices to each circle. Let us look at the concentric circles of individuals and of corporations respectively.

* * *

1. The Concentric Circles of Corporations

Just as individuals understand their social environment as concentric circles, so groups such as corporations have a similar tendency to characterize their environment. For the sake of simplicity, I shall classify the corporate environment into four circles: quasi-family, fellows, Japan, and the world.

First, corporations have a quasi-family circle. Of course, though corporations do not have any blood relationships, they might still have closely related business partners. For example, parent, sister, or affiliated companies can be those partners. "Vertical *keiretsu*" (Vertically integrated industrial groups like Toyota, Hitachi, or Matsushita groups) might be a typical example of the quasi-family circle. In this circle we find something similar to the parent-child relationship.

The main corporate members (about 20 to 30 companies in each group) of "horizontal *keiretsu*" (industrial groups such as Mitsubishi, Mitsui, Sumitomo, Dai Ichi Kangyo, Fuyo, and Sanwa groups) might be viewed as quasi-family members. Nonetheless, most of the cross-shareholding corporations in the horizontal *keiretsu* should be placed in the second circle, because their relations are less intimate than commonly understood.

In the second circle, each corporation has its own main bank, fellow traders, distant affiliated firms, employees, steady customers, and the like. If the corporation or its executives belong to some outside associations like *Nihon Jidousha Kogyo Kai* (Japanese Auto Manufactures Association), *Doyukai* (Japan Association of Corporate Executives), *Keidanren* (Japan Federation of Economic Organizations), etc., the other members of such outside associations might constitute part of the second circle of the corporation. And if the corporation is influential enough to affect Japanese politics or administration, the Japanese governmental agencies or ministries, and political parties might constitute part of this circle.

Recognition within the fellow circle requires that there must be a balance between benefits and debts in the long run. On account of this, if a corporation does not offer enough benefits to counterbalance its debts to others in this circle, the corporation will be expelled from the circle, being criticized for neither understanding nor appreciating the benefits given it by others. On the other hand, if the corporation can successfully balance benefits and debts or keep the balance in the black, it will preferentially receive many favorable opportunities from other companies or interest groups. For these reasons, every corporation worries about the balance sheet of benefits and debts in the fellow circle.

This way of recognizing the business context is closely related to original Confucianism, in that Confucianism allows people to treat others in proportion to the intimacy of their relations. Unlike Christianity, Confucianism does not encourage people to love one another equally. It rather inspires people to love or treat others differentially on the grounds that, if people try to treat everybody equally in a social context, they will often face various conflicts among interests. This does

206

not mean that Confucianism asserts that people should deny love to unacquainted people. The main point of this idea is that, although people have to treat all others as human beings, they should love intensely those with whom they are most intimate; those who cannot love this way cannot love strangers either. I can call this "the differential principle" in Confucianism. Influenced or justified by this differential principle, Japanese corporations also classify their business environment in this way.

In the Japan circle, the fellow circle ethics is substantially replaced by "the principle of free competition." Competitors, unrelated-corporations, ordinary stockholders, consumers, (for ordinary corporations, the Japanese government constitutes part of this circle) and so forth, all fall within this circle. Yet almost all corporations in this circle know well that the long-term reciprocal ethics is extremely important in constructing and maintaining their business relations, because of their similar cultural background. This point makes the third circle different from the world circle.

In the fourth or world circle, corporations positively follow "the principle of free competition," subject to the judicial system, with less worrying about their traditional reputations. Roughly speaking, the behavioral imperatives for corporations turn out to be producing or supplying high quality and low price products, dominating much more market share, and using the law to resolve serious contractual problems.

As in the case of the individuals, the world circle is conceived as a relatively chaotic sphere causing corporate attitudes to become contradictory. On the one hand, Japanese corporations tend to exclude foreign counterparts that do not understand the extant Japanese business practices, hoping to maintain the normative order of its own business community. Notwithstanding these closing attitudes, on the other hand, they yearn after

foreign technologies, know-how, products, and services which are expected to help corporations to be successful and competitive in the Japanese and world market. In particular, western technologies have long been objects of admiration for Japanese companies. This tendency vividly shows their global attitudes.

2. Dynamics of the Concentric Circles

Now that I have roughly described the static relations among the concentric circles (of individuals and of corporations), I need to show the dynamic relations among these circles, that is to say, how these circles are interrelated.... In order to describe these complicated relations in a parsimonious light, I shall limit my discussion to the relations between the members of an "ideal big Japanese corporation" and its business environment. By a "big Japanese corporation," I mean the "idealized very influential organization" in an industry that places priority on the interests of employees, and holds a long-term strategic perspective. By "operation base" in this context, I mean the place where the members can relax, charge their energy, and develop action programs to be applied to the business environment. Whether the corporation can be such a base or not heavily depends on its members' abilities with respect to human relations: their ability to sympathize or understand other members' feelings, their ability to put themselves in the others' position, their ability to internalize other members' expectations toward them, and the like.

It has been said that in Japanese corporations, many people have such abilities. For instance, E. Hamaguchi has called people with these abilities "the contextuals" in contrast with "the individuals."

An "individual" is not a simple unit or element of a society, but a positive and subjective member. This so-called "individual-centered model of man" is the typical human model of the western society.

This model, however, is clearly different from the Japanese model. The Japanese human model is a "being between people" or an internalized being in its relations. This can be called "the contextual" in contrast with the individual.[3]

To be sure, these abilities have also positively contributed to the performance of Japanese corporations. The corporations have not rigidly divided work into pieces and distributed them to each employee so as to clarify the responsibilities each has to take. The corporations have rather let employees work together so that the contextual members make up for the deficiencies of one another allowing the quality of products and efficiency of performance to be surprisingly improved.

On the contrary, the business environment as a "battlefield" is reckoned to be a strenuous sphere, where "the law of the jungle" is the dominant ethical principle. In the market, the principle of free competition replaces the ethics expected in an operation base (quasi-family and fellow circles). What is more, this principle of free competition is justified by the transcendental logic, because, as I have described earlier, in the transcendental environment, work is one of the most important "ways" or "paths" to reach something sacred or the ultimate reality. In this way, "the principle of free competition" in the battlefield and "the transcendental logic" are coincidentally combined to encourage people to work hard, an encouragement which results in survival and the development of the corporation.

Wealth, power, market share, competitive advantage, or other results acquired in this business context become important scales to measure the degree of the members' efforts to proceed on the "path" to the ultimate

stage. And based on these scales, contributors are praised within the operation base, namely in a corporation, in an industrial group, or in Japan.

For example, the Japanese government, administrative agencies, or ministries have so far endorsed the efforts of corporations under the present *Tenno* system (the Emperor System of Japan). The decoration and the Order of Precedence at the Imperial Court have been given to corporate executives who have contributed to the development of the Japanese economy.

Theoretically speaking, it is very hard to compare the performance of various corporations in different industries of a nation, simply because each industry has its own scale or own philosophy to measure performance. In the case of Japan, however, the annual decoration and attendance at the Imperial Court plays the role of a unitary ranking scale, applied to every industry as well as non-business-related fields. Since the Japanese mass-media makes the annual decoration and attendance public, the Japanese people know well who or which corporations are praiseworthy winners.

3. The Group Environment and the Concentric Circles

Now that I have explained both the group normative environment and the concentric circles of corporations, I should make clear the relationship between the group normative environment and the concentric circles. According to the group logic, each group has its own numen and has different social status. For example, even if the R&D unit of corporation A has its own numen, the status of the unit is lower than that of A itself. The status of A is also lower than that of the leading company B in the same industry. The status of B is lower than that of the Japanese government. But if I observe their relations from the viewpoint of concentric circles, these groups can be members of the same fellow circle of corporation C. Namely, the R&D unit of corporation A, company B, and the government can constitute part of the fellow circle of C. Therefore, even if they are in the same fellow circle, it does not mean that all members have equal status in the group normative environment.

For these reasons, reciprocal relations within the fellow circle are varied according to the members' status in the group normative environment. For instance, because, in most cases, the Japanese government is regarded as a powerful agent in the fellow circle of large corporation C, C makes efforts to maintain its good relations with the government and is likely to depend on the government.

The main reason why *gyosei-shido* (administrative guidance) has so far worked well in Japan comes from this dependent trait of the corporation and from the fact that the administrative agencies or ministries have a very important status in the second circle of the large Japanese corporations.

Each Japanese corporation also maintains relations with the business associations such as *Keidanren* and *Doyukai*. Once an authoritative business association declares *tatemae*, the member corporations make efforts to follow the formal rules, even though they might have some doubts about *tatemae*, simply because those associations hold socially or politically higher status in the group normative environment.

IV. JAPANESE RECOGNITION OF THE AMERICAN BUSINESS COMMUNITY

Because Japanese follow the transcendental logic, group logic, and concentric circles' ethics, their way of observing other business societies might appear to be idiosyncratic. And this idiosyncrasy might bring serious misunderstanding to trading partners such as the United States, European industrialized countries, Asian NIEs, and the other developing countries.

Because of this, I would like to clarify how Japanese conceive the American business community: how the American business community is seen in the eyes of the Japanese business people who adopt the two normative logics and the concentric circles' ethics.

1. Job Discrimination and the Transcendental Logic

First, as noted earlier, in the transcendental normative environment, whatever job people take, they are believed to reach the same goal or the same level of human development. Because of this logic, Japanese are unlikely to evaluate others in terms of their "job" (specialty). They would rather evaluate one another in terms of their "attitudes" toward work.

To be concrete, it is not important for Japanese to maintain the principle of the division of labor. Of importance is the process and the result of work. If people cannot attain goals in the existing framework of the division of labor, they are likely to try other alternatives which have not been clearly defined in the existing framework. This kind of positive attitude toward work is highly appreciated in Japan.

On the contrary, a society such as the United States, where jobs are strictly divided, is perceived as not only inefficient but also discriminatory in Japanese eyes. To be sure, this society might hold a belief that the division of labor makes itself efficient or makes it possible for diverse people to utilize their own abilities. The Japanese business community, however, is likely to assume that people's reluctance to help others' work in the same group is based on job discrimination.

In America, in a large retail shop, for instance, often those who sell a heavy consumer product are reluctant to carry it for the customer. They have a specific person, whose job is just to carry goods, do so. If the person is busy with other goods, the salespeople will ask the customer to wait until the person is finished carrying the other goods.

Similarly, those who manage a large shop typically do not clean up the street in front of their shop. They let a janitor do so. Even if they find garbage there, when the janitor has not come yet, they are likely to wait for the janitor. This kind of attitude of salespeople or managers is regarded as inefficient and discriminatory by Japanese.

2. Employees' Interest and the Group Logic

Second, in the group normative environment, the group is believed to hold its own numen and expected to guarantee the members' life. That is to say, a corporation is thought to exist for its employees rather than for its shareholders.

Because of this logic, the Japanese business community ethically questions American general attitudes toward the company where many accept the ideas that 1) a company is owned by its shareholders, 2) executives should lay off the employees whenever the layoff brings benefits to the shareholders, 3) executives should buy other companies and sell part of their own company whenever such a strategy brings benefits to the shareholders, etc.

Of course, even in Japan, shareholders are legal owners of a company so that the shareholders might use their legal power to change the company in a favorable way for themselves. Therefore, many Japanese corpo-

rations have invented a legitimate way to exclude the legal rights of shareholders, i.e. "cross-shareholding." This is the practice in which a corporation allows trusted companies to hold its own shares, and in return the corporation holds their shares. By holding shares of one another and refraining from appealing to the shareholders' rights, they make it possible to manage the companies for the sake of the employees.[4] Because this cross-shareholding is based on mutual acceptance, any attempts to break this corporate consortium from the outside, whether Japanese or foreigners, are often stymied by the consortium of the member corporations.

For example, in April 1989, Boone Company, controlled by T. Boone Pickens, bought a 20 percent stake in Koito Manufacturing, Japanese auto parts maker. In 1990, Pickens increased it to 25 percent, becoming Koito's largest single shareholder.[5] But because Pickens asked for seats on Koito's board for himself as well as three Boone Company associates, and requested an increase in Koito's annual dividend, he was labeled as a "greenmailer" in the Japanese business community. As a result, the other consortium members cooperatively protected Koito from the Pickens' attack.[6] . . .

In addition, the layoff of employees and the high salaries of American executives are also regarded as unethical by the Japanese business community. . . . In Japan, when executives face serious difficulties, they first reduce their own benefits, then dividends and other costs, and, after that, employees' salary or wage. If the situation is extremely hard to overcome with these measures, they sell assets and only as a last resort do they lay off workers. Even in this case, the executives often find and offer new job opportunities for those who are laid off, taking care of their family's life.

Because of this, Japanese executives criticize the American business climate in which only salaries of executives keep rising, even while they lay off employees (especially in the 1980s). This criticism is also based on the Japanese group normative logic.

3. Claims Against the Japanese Market and the Concentric Circles' Ethics

As I have noted above, because of the framework of concentric circles, especially of the ethics of the fellow circle, foreign corporations often face difficulties entering the Japanese market. Although Japanese admit that the market is very hard to enter, a majority of them believe that it is still possible to accomplish entry.

Even if the Japanese market has many business-related practices such as semi-annual gifts, entertainment, cross-shareholding, "triangular relationship" among business, bureaucracy, and the Liberal Democratic Party, the long-term relationship is formed mainly through a series of business transactions.

That is to say, the most important factor in doing business is whether suppliers can respond to the assemblers' requests for quality, cost, the date of delivery, and the like, or on how producers can respond to the retailers' or wholesalers' expectations. . . .

Foreign corporations might claim that because they are located outside Japan, they cannot enter even the Japan circle. On this claim, the Japanese business community is likely to insist that if they understand the "long-term reciprocal ethics," they can enter the Japan circle; and what is more, might be fellows of Japanese influential corporations. As I have described, what makes the Japan circle different from the world circle is that people in the Japan circle know well the importance of this ethics. In fact, successfully enjoying the Japanese market are foreign corporations such as IBM, Johnson & Johnson,

McDonald, Apple, and General Mills which have understood well this ethics.

In this respect, realistically, the Japanese business community interprets the criticism by the American counterpart of the Japanese market as unfair and unethical. To put it differently, Japanese believe that if foreign corporations understand the long-term ethics, they will easily be real members of the Japanese business community.

V. ETHICAL ISSUES OF THE JAPANESE BUSINESS COMMUNITY

I have shown how Japanese people conceive the American business society and its business-related practices from the viewpoint of the two normative environments and the concentric circles. Yet this does not mean that the Japanese business community has no ethical problems. On the contrary, there are many issues it has to solve. What are the ethical issues of the Japanese business community? . . .

1. Discrimination and the Transcendental Logic

I will shed light on the organizational issues (opening the Japanese organizations) from the prime value of transcendental logic. The prime value here is "everybody has an equal microcosm." Whether men or women, Japanese or foreigners, hard workers or non-hard workers, everybody has to be treated equally as a person. When I observe the organizational phenomena from the viewpoint of this value, there are at least the following two discriminatory issues.

First, the transcendental logic has worked favorably only for male society. That is, in this normative environment, Japanese women have been expected to actualize their potentials through their household tasks. Those tasks have been regarded as their path toward the goal. Of course, insofar as women voluntarily agree with this thinking, there seems to be no ethical problem. And in fact, a majority of women have accepted this way of living to date. Nonetheless, now that an increasing number of women work at companies and hope to get beyond such chores as making tea to more challenging jobs, the Japanese corporations have no longer been allowed to treat women unequally.

Second, the transcendental normative logic itself has often been used to accuse certain workers of laziness. As far as a worker voluntarily strives to fulfill his or her own potential according to the transcendental logic, this presents no ethical problems. Nevertheless, once a person begins to apply the logic to others and evaluate them in terms of their performance, the transcendental logic easily becomes the basis for severe accusations against certain workers.

For example, even if a man really wants to change his job or company, his relatives, colleagues, or acquaintances are unlikely to let him do so, because they unconsciously believe that any job or any company can lead him to the same high stage of human development, if he makes efforts to reach it. Put in a different way, it is believed that despite the differences between the jobs or companies, he can attain the same purpose in either. On account of this, many Japanese say, "once you have decided and started something by yourself, you should not give up until reaching your goal." This is likely to end up justifying a teaching that "enough is as good as a feast."

If the person does not follow this teaching, thereby refusing overtime or transfers, he will jeopardize his promotion and be alienated from his colleagues and bosses, since he is not regarded as a praiseworthy diligent worker. Even if he is making efforts to fulfill his potential in work-unrelated fields, he is not highly appreciated, simply because what he is doing is not related to the company's work.

Analyzing those practices from the viewpoint of the prime value (everybody has equal microcosm), I cannot help concluding that the Japanese business community should alter its organizational climate.

2. Employees' Dependency and the Group Logic

In the group normative environment, groups are regarded as having a higher status than their individual members. Because the members are inclined to take this hierarchical order for granted, they come to be dependent on the groups. And their groups also come to be dependent on the next higher groups. This dependency of the agents, whether of individuals or groups, brings the following two problems into the Japanese business community. Because of the dependent trait, 1) the individual members of the group refrain from expressing their opinions about ethical issues, and 2) they tend to obey the organizational orders, even if they disagree with them. The first tendency is related to decision-making, while the second affects policy-implementation. . . .

One of the typical examples which show this tendency of members to waive their basic rights is *karoshi* (death caused by overwork). In 1991, the Japanese Labor Ministry awarded 33 claims for *karoshi*. Since it is very hard to prove a direct and quantifiable link between overwork and death, this number is not large enough to clarify the actual working condition, but is certainly large enough to show that there is a possibility of turning the group logic into unconditional obedience.

This corporate climate not only jeopardizes the employees' right to life, but also

212

hampers the healthy human development of the individual members. Because of this, the Japanese business community has to alter this group-centered climate into a democratic ground on which the individuals can express their opinions more frankly than before.

3. Exclusiveness of the Concentric Circles

The Japanese conceptualization of the social environment in a centrifugal framework is closely connected with Confucianism (the differential principle): it allows people to treat others in proportion to the intimacy of their relationships. As I touched upon before, however, the main point of this principle is not that people should deny love to strangers, but rather that those who cannot love their most intimate relatives intensely are surely incapable of loving strangers. Stated otherwise, even if the way to achieve a goal is to love differentially, the goal itself is to love everybody. Therefore, "to love everybody" should be regarded as the prime value of the concentric circles' ethics.

If I look at the Japanese market (opening the Japanese market) from the viewpoint of this prime value, there appear to be at least the following two issues. 1) The Japanese business community has to make an effort to help foreigners understand the concept of long-term reciprocal ethics. This effort will bring moral agents of the world circle into the Japan circle. 2) The Japanese community has to give business opportunities to as many newcomers as possible. This effort will bring the newcomers into the fellow circles.

The first issue is how to transfer foreign corporations from the world circle to the Japan circle. . . . This "fairness" implies that they treat foreign companies the same as they treat other Japanese firms. To put it differently, the concept of "fairness" encourages

the Japanese corporations to apply the same ethical standard to all companies.

Although this is a very important point of "fairness," there is a more crucial problem involved in opening the market. That is how to let newcomers know what the rules are and how the Japanese business community applies the rules. As mentioned before, for the purpose of constructing and maintaining business relationships with a Japanese company (a core company), a foreign firm has to be a fellow of the company. In this fellow circle, every fellow makes efforts to balance benefits and debts with the core company in material and spiritual terms in the long run, since making a long-term balance is the most important ethics. Yet balancing them is too complicated to be attained for the foreign corporation, as long as benefits and debts are rather subjective concepts.

For example, in Japan, if company A trusts the executive of company B and helps B, when B is in the midst of serious financial difficulties, then B will give the most preferential trade status to A after overcoming its difficulties. B will rarely change this policy, even if B finishes repaying its monetary debts to A. Moreover, even if A's products are relatively expensive, as long as the price is not extraordinarily unreasonable, B will continue to purchase A's output. If A's products are not sophisticated enough to meet B's standard, B will often help A to improve A's products in various ways.

If A's help is understood only as financial aid, this close relationship between A and B will not appear reasonable. In Japan, in most cases, B is deeply impressed by the fact that A has trusted B (even if B is in serious difficulties) so that B continues to repay its spiritual debts to A as long as possible. Yet if B were to change this policy soon after repaying the borrowed capital to A, and if it began buying the same but cheaper products from company C, not only A but also other corporations which have been aware of this process from the beginning will regard B as an untrustworthy company in their business community.

"Fairness" in a Japanese sense might involve asking foreign companies to follow the former way of doing business. Nonetheless, foreign companies, especially Americans, do not understand "fairness" this way. Their understanding is rather similar to the latter behavior of B: switching from A to C. This difference of understanding "fairness" between Americans and Japanese undoubtedly causes a series of accusations against each other.

The Japanese business community should not let this happen over and over again. If the community takes the prime value seriously, as the first duty, it has to explain the long-term reciprocal ethics to foreign counterparts in an understandable way. This effort will help the foreigners enter the Japan circle.

But even if they can enter the Japan circle successfully, there still remains another problem. That is how those foreigners, which have been already in the Japan circle, enter the fellow circles of influential Japanese corporations. This is related to the second issue of opening the Japanese market.

Even when foreign companies understand and adopt long-term reciprocal ethics, they might not be able to enter those fellow circles, if they rarely have the chance to show their competitive products or services to the influential corporations. On account of this, as an ethical responsibility, the Japanese corporations should have "access channels" through which every newcomer can equally approach.

To be sure, the "mutual trust" found in the fellow circle should not be blamed for everything. But if the trust-based business relation is tightly combined among a few influential corporations, it tends to exclude newcomers. As long as such a relation is not against the Japanese Antimonopoly Law, it is safe to say that efforts to maintain the relationship are not problematic, because most of the corporations do so according to their free will. Despite that, if I look at the exclusive tendency of a fellow circle like that of the Japanese distribution system, I cannot help saying that the trust-based relation is a critical obstacle for newcomers.

If the Japanese business community follows the prime value (to love everybody) of the concentric circles' ethics, it has to make an effort to remove the obstacles to entry. One of the ideal ways to do so is to give newcomers more competitive bids than before. Of course, it is not obligatory for Japanese corporations to accept every bidder as a fellow after the tender. If a bidder is not qualified as an ideal business partner in terms of its products or services, Japanese corporations do not need to start transactions with the bidder. But as a minimum ethical requirement, Japanese corporations should have access channels through which every newcomer can equally approach them. . . .

NOTES

1. M. Imai, *Kaizen* (New York: McGraw-Hill Publishing Company, 1986), p. 34.

2. Kyogoku, *Nihon no Seiji* (Politics of Japan) (Tokyo: Tokyo University Press, 1983) pp. 182–83.

3. E. Hamaguchi, *"Nihon Rashisa" no Saihakken (Rediscovery of Japaneseness)* (Tokyo; Kodansha, 1988), pp. 66–67.

4. This practice was basically formed for a purpose of defending Japanese industries from foreign threats. But at the same time, Japanese people thought this threat might destroy the employee-centered management. T. Tsuruta, *Sengo Nihon no Sangyo Seisaku (Industrial Policies of Post-War Japan)* (Nihon Keizai Shinbunsha, 1982), pp. 121–30.

5. W. C. Kester, *Japanese Takeovers: The Global Contest for Corporate Control* (Cambridge: Harvard Business School Press, 1991), pp. 258–59.

6. *Mainichi Daily News* (May 15, 1990).

Introduction to
Managerial Economics

- The Nature and Scope of Managerial
  Economics

THE NATURE
AND SCOPE
OF MANAGERIAL
ECONOMICS

CHAPTER OUTLINE

KEY TERMS
(in order of their appearance)

Managerial economics
Economic theory
Microeconomics
Macroeconomics
Model
Mathematical economics
Econometrics

Functional areas of business
   administration studies
Firm
Circular flow of economic activity
Theory of the firm
Value of the firm
Constrained optimization

Satisficing behavior
Business profit
Explicit costs
Economic profit
Implicit costs
Internationalization of economic
   activity

3

I n this chapter we examine the nature and scope of managerial economics. We begin with a definition of managerial economics and a discussion of its relationship to other fields of study. We then go on to examine the theory of the firm. Here, we discuss the reason for the existence of firms and their functions, and we define the value of the firm, examine the constraints faced by firms, and examine the limitations of the theory of the firm. Subsequently, we examine the nature of profits by distinguishing between economic and business profits, by presenting several theories of profits, and by analyzing their function in a free-enterprise system. Finally, we examine the importance of introducing an international dimension into managerial economics to reflect the globalization of production and distribution in today's world.

Each section of the chapter includes a case study which clearly illustrates with a real-world example or application the major concept introduced in the particular section. This is an important chapter because it defines the subject matter of managerial economics, it clearly shows its relationship to other fields of study, and it examines the great importance and relevance of managerial economics in all business and economics decision-making situations and programs in today's global economy.

1-1 THE SCOPE OF MANAGERIAL ECONOMICS

In this section we define the function of managerial economics and examine its relationship to economic theory, management decision sciences, and functional areas of business administration studies.

1-1a Definition of Managerial Economics

Managerial economics* refers to the application of economic theory and the tools of analysis of decision science to examine how an organization can achieve its aims or objectives most efficiently. The meaning of this definition can best be examined with the aid of Figure 1-1.

Management decision problems (see the top of Figure 1-1) arise in any organization—be it a firm, a not-for-profit organization (such as a hospital or a university), or a government agency, when it seeks to achieve some goal or objective subject to some constraints. For example, a firm may seek to maximize profits subject to limitations on the availability of essential inputs and in the face of legal constraints. A hospital may seek to treat as

---

*The definition of all bolded terms, arranged alphabetically, is provided in the Glossary at the end of the book.

4

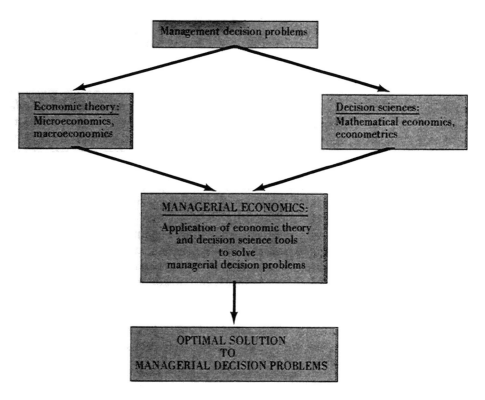

FIGURE 1-1 THE NATURE OF MANAGERIAL ECONOMICS
Managerial economics refers to the application of economic theory and decision science tools to find the optimal solution to managerial decision problems.

many patients as possible at an "adequate" medical standard with its limited physical resources (physicians, technicians, nurses, equipment, beds) and budget. The goal of a state university may be to provide an adequate education to as many students as possible, subject to the physical and financial constraints it faces. Similarly, a government agency may seek to provide a particular service (which cannot be provided as efficiently by business firms) to as many people as possible at the lowest possible cost. In all these cases, the organization faces management decision problems as it seeks to achieve its goal or objective, subject to the constraints it faces. The goals and constraints may differ from case to case, but the basic decision-making process is the same.

1-1b Relationship to Economic Theory
The organization can solve its management decision problems by the application of economic theory and the tools of decision science. **Economic**

theory refers to microeconomics and macroeconomics. **Microeconomics** is the study of the economic behavior of *individual* decision-making units, such as individual consumers, resource owners, and business firms, in a free-enterprise system. **Macroeconomics,** on the other hand, is the study of the total or aggregate level of output, income, employment, consumption, investment, and prices for the economy *viewed as a whole.* While the (microeconomic) theory of the firm is the single most important element in managerial economics, the general macroeconomic conditions of the economy (such as the level of aggregate demand, rate of inflation, and interest rates) within which the firm operates are also very important.

Economic theories seek to predict and explain economic behavior. Economic theories usually begin with a **model.** This abstracts from the many details surrounding an event and seeks to identify a few of the most important determinants of the event. For example, the theory of the firm assumes that the firm seeks to maximize profits, and on the basis of that it predicts how much of a particular commodity the firm should produce under different forms of market structure or organization. While the firm may have other (multiple) aims, the profit-maximization model accurately predicts the behavior of firms, and, therefore, we accept it. Thus, the methodology of economics (and science in general) is to accept a theory or model if it predicts accurately and if the predictions follow logically from the assumptions.[1]

1-1c Relationship to the Decision Sciences

Managerial economics is also closely related to the decision sciences. These utilize the tools of mathematical economics and econometrics (see Figure 1-1) to construct and estimate decision models aimed at determining the optimal behavior of the firm (i.e., how the firm can achieve its goals most efficiently). Specifically, **mathematical economics** is used to formalize (i.e., to express in equational form) the economic models postulated by economic theory. **Econometrics** then applies statistical tools (particularly regression analysis) to real-world data to estimate the models postulated by economic theory and for forecasting.

For example, economic theory postulates that the quantity demanded (Q) of a commodity is a function of or depends on the price of the commodity (P), the income of consumers (Y), and the price of related (i.e., complementary and substitute) commodities (P_C and P_S, respectively). Assuming

---

[1]See M. Friedman, "The Methodology of Positive Economics," in *Essays in Positive Economics* (Chicago: University of Chicago Press, 1953) and M. Blaug, *The Methodology of Economics and How Economists Explain* (Cambridge, England: Cambridge University Press, 1980).

constant tastes, we may postulate the following formal (mathematical) model:

$$Q = f(P, Y, P_C, P_S) \qquad (1\text{-}1)$$

By collecting data on Q, P, Y, P_C, and P_S for a particular commodity, we can then estimate the empirical (econometric) relationship. This will permit the firm to determine how much Q would change by a change in P, Y, P_C, and P_S, and to forecast the future demand for the commodity. These data are essential in order for management to achieve the goal or objective of the firm (profit maximization) most efficiently.

To conclude, "managerial economics" refers to the application of economic theory and decision science tools to find the optimal solution to managerial decision problems.

1-1d Relationship to the Functional Areas of Business Administration Studies

Having defined the subject matter of managerial economics and its function, we can now examine the relationship between managerial economics and the **functional areas of business administration studies.** The latter include accounting, finance, marketing, personnel or human resource management, and production. These disciplines study the business environment in which the firm operates and, as such, they provide the background for managerial decision making. Thus, managerial economics can be regarded as an overview course that *integrates* economic theory, decision sciences, and the functional areas of business administration studies, and it examines how they interact with one another as the firm attempts to achieve its goal most efficiently.

Most students taking managerial economics are likely to have some knowledge (from other courses) of some of the topics presented and tools of analysis utilized in managerial economics. While reviewing these topics and studying the others, the student should pay particular attention to the overall decision-making process by which the firm can achieve its objective, since this is the ultimate goal of managerial economics.

In short, managerial economics is not the study of a number of topics but the utilization of economic theory and management science tools to examine how a firm can achieve its objective most efficiently within the business environment in which it operates. If all students in a managerial economics course had already taken courses in microeconomic and macroeconomic theory, in mathematical economics and econometrics, and in the functional areas of business, then managerial economics could concentrate exclusively on its integrating and synthesizing role in analyzing the decision-making process. As it is, most students have had some of those courses but not all. Thus, a managerial economics course, while stressing the process of reaching optimal managerial decisions, must also present the theories and tools required to make such optimal managerial decisions.

CASE STUDY

DECISION MAKING IN BUSINESS AND MILITARY STRATEGY

According to William E. Peackock, president of two St. Louis companies and former Assistant Secretary of the Army under Jimmy Carter, decision making in business has much in common with military strategy. While business managers' actions are restricted by laws and regulations to prevent unfair practices and the objective of managers, of course, is not to literally destroy the competition, there is much that they can learn from military strategists. Peackock points out that, down through history, military conflicts have produced a set of Darwinian basic principles that are an excellent guideline to business managers in meeting the competition in the marketplace. Neglecting these principles can make the difference between business success and failure.

In business as in war, it is crucial to have a clear objective as to what the organization wants to accomplish and to explain this objective to all employees. The benefits of a simple marketing strategy that all employees can understand are clearly evidenced by the success of McDonald's. Both business and warfare also require the development of a strategy for attacking. Being aggressive is important because few competitions are ever won by being passive. Furthermore, both business and warfare require unity of command to pinpoint responsibility. Even in decentralized companies with informal lines of command, there are always key individuals who must make important decisions. Finally, in business as in war, the element of surprise and security (keeping your strategy secret) is crucial. For example, Lee Iacocca stunned the competition in 1964 by introducing the immensely successful Mustang.

More than ever before, today's business leaders must learn how to tap employees' ideas and energy, manage large-scale rapid change, anticipate business conditions five or ten years down the road, and muster the courage to steer the firm in radical new directions when necessary. Above all, firms must think and act strategically in a world of increasing global competition.

Source: W. E. Peackock, *Corporate Combat* (New York: Facts on File Publication, 1984); W. B. Wriston, "The State of American Management," *Harvard Business Review*, vol. 90, January-February 1990; and "Making Global Alliances Work," *Fortune*, December 17, 1990, pp. 121–126.

1-2   THE THEORY OF THE FIRM

In this section, we examine first the reason for the existence of firms and their principal functions. Then we define the value of the firm and the constraints under which it operates. Finally, we discuss the limitations of the theory of the firm. This is a most important section since the theory of firm behavior is the centerpiece and central theme of managerial economics.

1-2a   Reason for the Existence of Firms and Their Functions

A **firm** is an organization that combines and organizes resources for the purpose of producing goods and/or services for sale. There are millions of firms in the United States. These include proprietorships (firms owned by one individual), partnerships (firms owned by two or more individuals), and corporations (owned by stockholders). Firms produce more than 80 percent of all goods and services consumed in the United States. The remainder is produced by the government and not-for-profit organizations, such as private colleges, hospitals, museums, and foundations.

Firms exist because it would be very inefficient and costly for entrepreneurs to enter into and enforce contracts with workers and owners of capital, land, and other resources for each separate step of the production and distribution process. Instead, entrepreneurs usually enter into longer-term, broader contracts with labor to perform a number of tasks for a specific wage and fringe benefits. Such a general contract is much less costly than numerous specific contracts and is highly advantageous both to the entrepreneurs and to the workers and other resource owners. By internalizing many transactions (i.e., by performing within the firm many functions), the firm also saves on sales taxes and avoids price controls and other government regulations, which apply only to transactions among firms.

On the other hand, firms do not continue to grow larger and larger indefinitely because of limitations on management ability to effectively control and direct the operation of the firm as it becomes larger and larger. It is true that up to a point, a firm can overcome these internal disadvantages of large size or diseconomies of scale by establishing a number of semi-autonomous divisions (i.e., by decentralizing). Eventually, however, the increased communication traffic that is generated coupled with the further and further distancing of top management from the operation of each division imposes sufficient diseconomies of scale to limit the growth of the firm. Furthermore, the firm will reach a point where the cost of supplying additional services within the firm exceeds the cost of purchasing these services from other firms. An example is provided by some highly technical (legal, medical, or engineering) service that the firm may need only occasionally.

The function of firms, therefore, is to purchase resources or inputs of labor services, capital, and raw materials in order to transform them into goods and services for sale. Resource owners (workers and owners of capital, land, and raw materials) then use the income generated from the sale of their services or other resources to firms to purchase the goods and services produced by firms. The **circular flow of economic activity** is thus complete.[2] In the process of supplying the goods and services that society demands, firms provide employment to workers and pay taxes that government utilizes to provide services (such as national defense, education, and fire protection) that firms could not provide at all or as efficiently.

1-2b The Objective and Value of the Firm

Managerial economics begins by postulating a theory of the firm, which it then uses to analyze managerial decision making. Originally, the theory of the firm was based on the assumption that the goal or objective of the firm was to maximize current or short-term profits. Firms, however, are often observed to sacrifice short-term profits for the sake of increasing future or long-term profits. Some examples of this are expenditures on research and development, new capital equipment, and an enhanced promotional campaign.[3] Since both short-term as well as long-term profits are clearly important, the **theory of the firm** now postulates that the primary goal or objective of the firm is to maximize the wealth or **value of the firm.** This is given by the present value of all expected future profits of the firm. Future profits must be discounted to the present because a dollar of profit in the future is worth less than a dollar of profit today.[4]

Formally stated, the wealth or value of the firm is given by

$$PV = \frac{\pi_1}{(1 + r)^1} + \frac{\pi_2}{(1 + r)^2} + \cdots + \frac{\pi_n}{(1 + r)^n} \qquad (1\text{-}2)$$

$$= \sum_{t=1}^{n} \frac{\pi_t}{(1 + r)^t} \qquad (1\text{-}2\text{a})$$

where PV is the present value of all expected future profits of the firm, π_1, $\pi_2, \ldots, \pi_n$ represent the expected profits in each of the n years considered,

---

[2]For a more extensive discussion, see D. Salvatore, *Microeconomics: Theory and Applications* (New York: HarperCollins, 1991), pp. 8–9.

[3]Many managers, however, complain that the pressure to report profits every year or every quarter forces them to take actions which are very detrimental to the long-term profitability of the firm.

[4]A $1 investment today at 10 percent interest will grow to $1.10 in one year. Therefore, $1 is defined as the present value of $1.10 due in one year. For the purpose of this chapter, this is all that needs to be known. A detailed presentation of the concepts of present value and compound interest, which are required for understanding Chapter 13 on risk analysis and Chapter 14 on long-term investment decisions, is given in Appendix A at the end of the book.

and r is the appropriate discount rate used to find the present value of future profits. In Equation 1-2a, Σ refers to "the sum of" and t assumes the values from 1 up to the n years considered. Thus, $\Sigma_{t=1}^{n}$ means "sum or add" all the $\pi_t/(1 + r)^t$ terms resulting from substituting the values of 1 to n for t. Hence, Equation 1-2a is an abbreviated but equivalent form of Equation 1-2. The introduction of the time dimension in Equations 1-2 and 1-2a also allows for the consideration of uncertainty. For example, the more uncertain is the stream of expected future profits, the higher is the discount rate that the firm will use, and, therefore, the smaller is the present value of the firm.

Since profits are equal to total revenue (TR) minus total costs (TC), Equation 1-2a can be rewritten as

$$\text{Value of firm} = \sum_{t=1}^{n} \frac{TR_t - TC_t}{(1 + r)^t} \tag{1-3}$$

Equation 1-3 provides a unifying theme for the analysis of managerial decision making and, indeed, for this entire text. Specifically, TR depends on sales or the demand for the firm's output and the firm's pricing decisions. These are the major responsibility of the marketing department and are discussed in detail in Part Two (Chapters 3 through 5) and Part Four (Chapters 9 through 11), respectively. The TC depends on the technology of production and resource prices. These are the major responsibility of the production and personnel departments and are discussed in detail in Part Three (Chapters 6 through 8). The discount rate (r) depends on the perceived risks of the firm and on the cost of borrowing funds. These are the major responsibility of the finance department and are discussed in detail in Chapters 13 and 14 (in Part Five).

Equation 1-3 can also be used to organize the discussion of how the various departments within the firm interact with one another. For example, the marketing department can reduce the cost associated with a given level of output by promoting off-season sales. The production and personnel departments can stimulate sales by quality improvements and the development of new products. The accounting department can provide more timely information on sales and costs. All these activities increase the efficiency of the firm and reduce its risk, thereby allowing the firm to use a lower discount rate to determine the present value of its expected future profits (which increases the value of the firm).

1-2c Constraints on the Operation of the Firm
We have seen above that the goal or objective of the firm is to maximize wealth or the value of the firm. In trying to do this, however, the firm faces many constraints. Some of these constraints arise from limitations on the

availability of essential inputs. Specifically, a firm may not be able to hire as many skilled workers as it wants, especially in the short run. Similarly, the firm may not be able to acquire all the specific raw materials it demands. It may also face limitations on factory and warehouse space and in the quantity of capital funds available for a given project or purpose. Government agencies and not-for-profit organizations also face similar resource constraints. Besides resource constraints, the firm also faces many legal constraints. These take the form of minimum wage laws, health and safety standards, pollution emission standards, as well as laws and regulations that prevent firms from employing unfair business practices. In general, society imposes these constraints on firms in order to modify their behavior and make it more nearly consistent with broad social welfare goals.

So important and pervasive are the constraints facing firms that we speak of **constrained optimization.**[5] That is, the primary goal or objective of the firm is to maximize wealth or the value of the firm subject to the constraints it faces. The existence of these constraints restricts the range of possibilities or freedom of action of the firm and limits the value of the firm to a level that is lower than in the absence of such constraints (unconstrained optimization). Within these constraints, however, the firm seeks to maximize wealth or its value. While government agencies and not-for-profit organizations may have goals other than wealth or value maximization, they also face constraints in achieving their goals or objectives, whatever these goals or objectives might be. Most of the discussion in the rest of the text will be in terms of constrained optimization, and we will develop and use powerful techniques such as linear programming to examine how the firm achieves constrained optimization.

1-2d Limitations of the Theory of the Firm

The theory of the firm which postulates that the goal or objective of the firm is to maximize wealth or the value of the firm has been criticized as being much too narrow and unrealistic. In its place, broader theories of the firm have been proposed. The most prominent among these are models that postulate that the primary objective of the firm is the maximization of sales, the maximization of management utility, and satisficing behavior.

According to the sales maximization model introduced by William Baumol and others, managers of modern corporations seek to maximize sales, after an adequate rate of profit has been earned to satisfy stockholders.[6] Indeed, some early empirical studies found a strong correlation be-

---

[5]We refer to *optimization* rather than maximization in order to allow for cases where the firm wants to *minimize* costs and other objectives, subject to the constraints it faces.

[6]See W. J. Baumol, *Business Behavior, Value and Growth* (New York: Macmillan, 1959).

tween executives' salaries and sales, but not between salaries and profits. More recent studies, however, found the opposite. Oliver Williamson and others have introduced a model of management utility maximization, which postulates that with the advent of the modern corporation and the resulting separation of management from ownership, managers are more interested in maximizing their utility, measured in terms of their compensation (salaries, fringe benefits, stock options, etc.), the size of their staff, extent of control over the corporation, lavish offices, etc., than in maximizing corporate profits.[7] However, managers who maximize their own interests rather than the corporation's profits are likely to be replaced either by the stockholders of the corporation or as a result of the corporation's being taken over (merged) with another firm that sees the unexploited profit potential of the first.

Finally, Richard Cyert and James March, building on the work of Herbert Simon, pointed out that because of the great complexity of running the large modern corporation, a task complicated by uncertainty and a lack of data, managers are not able to maximize profits but can only strive for some satisfactory goal in terms of sales, profits, growth, market share, and so on. Simon called this **satisficing behavior.** That is, the large corporation is a satisficing, rather than a maximizing, organization.[8] This, however, is not necessarily inconsistent with profit or value maximization and, presumably, with more and better data and search procedures, the modern corporation could conceivably approach profit or value maximization.

While these alternative and broader theories of the firm stress some relevant aspect of the operation of the modern corporation, they do not provide a satisfactory alternative to the theory of the firm postulated in Section 1-2b. Indeed, the stiff competition prevailing in most product and resource markets as well as in managerial and entrepreneurial talent today forces managers to pay close attention to profits—lest the firm go out of business or they be replaced. As a result, we retain our theory of the firm (in terms of profit or value maximization) in the rest of the text as the basis for analyzing managerial decisions, because it is from this vantage point that the behavior of the firm can be studied most fruitfully. The assumptions of the theory may be somewhat unrealistic, but the theory predicts the behavior of the firm more accurately than any of its alternatives.

---

[7]See O. E. Williamson, "A Model of Rational Managerial Behavior," in R. M. Cyert and J. G. March, eds., *A Behavioral Theory of the Firm* (Englewood Cliffs, N.J.: Prentice-Hall, 1963).

[8]See R. M. Cyert and J. G. March, eds., *A Behavioral Theory of the Firm,* and H. A. Simon, "Theories of Decision-Making in Economics," *American Economic Review,* vol. 49, June 1949.

CASE STUDY

THE OBJECTIVE AND STRATEGY OF FIRMS IN THE CIGARETTE INDUSTRY

The objective of firms in the cigarette industry seems to be to maximize profits over the long run or the value of the firm, as postulated by the theory of the firm. Different firms, however, pursue these goals differently. The doubling of the federal excise tax on each pack of cigarettes, which came into effect on January 1, 1983, as well as the rise in other state taxes since then, resulted in a sharp increase in cigarette prices and a reduction in consumption. In order to lure customers from rivals and maintain profit levels, the weaker three of the nation's six major producers introduced generic cigarettes. These contain cheaper tobacco, come in plain black-and-white packages, are advertised very little, and sell for a price about 20 percent lower than name brands.

The other three major producers, instead, followed the more traditional marketing strategy of brand proliferation. That is, they introduced a large number of brands to appeal to every conceivable taste or consumer group and spent hundreds of millions of dollars on advertising. They resisted the introduction of generic cigarettes because these cigarettes have very low profit margins. But, as sales of generic cigarettes rose, these other major producers responded with the introduction of discounts—brand-name cigarettes that cost more than generics but less than the traditional brands. Thus, while the goal of both groups of cigarette producers is the same (i.e., long-term profit maximization or maximizing the value of the firm), their strategy is different. Those companies that suffered very large declines in sales and profits as a result of increased cigarette prices and declining consumption introduced generic cigarettes. The others adopted a more traditional strategy and introduced discount brands. Both groups of cigarette producers, however, greatly expanded sales abroad, where antismoking campaigns are either in their infancy or still nonexistent, cigarettes can still be heavily advertised on television, and sales of American cigarettes are growing rapidly (as compared with a declining market in the United States).

Source: "Big Tobacco Toughest Road," *U.S. News & World Report*, April 17, 1989, p. 26, and "Tobacco Suit Exposes Ways Cigarette Firms Keep the Profits Fat," *The Wall Street Journal*, March 5, 1990, p. 1.

1-3 THE NATURE AND FUNCTION OF PROFITS

In this section we examine the nature and function of profits. We distinguish between business and economic profits, present various theories of profits, and examine the function of profits in a free-enterprise economy.

1-3a Business versus Economic Profit

To the general public and the business community, profit or **business profit** refers to the revenue of the firm minus the explicit or accounting costs of the firm. **Explicit costs** are the actual out-of-pocket expenditures of the firm to purchase or hire the inputs it requires in production. These expenditures include the wages to hire labor, interest on borrowed capital, rent on land and buildings, and the expenditures on raw materials. To the economist, however, **economic profit** equals the revenue of the firm minus its explicit costs and implicit costs. **Implicit costs** refer to the value of the inputs owned and used by the firm in its own production processes.

Specifically, implicit costs include the salary that the entrepreneur could earn from working for someone else in a similar capacity (say, as the manager of another firm) and the return that the firm could earn from investing its capital and renting its land and other inputs to other firms. The inputs owned and used by the firm in its own production processes are not free to the firm, even though the firm can use them without any actual or explicit expenditures. Their implicit costs are what these same inputs could earn in their best alternative use outside the firm. Accordingly, economists include both explicit and implicit costs in their definition of costs. That is, they include a normal return on owned resources as part of costs, so that economic profit is revenue minus explicit and implicit costs. While the concept of business profit may be useful for accounting and tax purposes, it is the concept of economic profit that must be used in order to reach correct investment decisions.

For example, suppose that a firm reports a business profit of $30,000 during a year, but the entrepreneur could have earned $35,000 by managing another firm and $10,000 by lending out his capital to another firm facing similar risks. To the economist this entrepreneur is actually incurring an economic loss of $15,000 because, from the *business* profit of $30,000, he would have to subtract the implicit or opportunity cost of $35,000 for his wages and $10,000 for his capital. A business profit of $30,000, thus, corresponds to an economic loss of $15,000 per year. Even if the entrepreneur owned no capital, he would still incur an economic loss of $5,000 per year by continuing to operate his own firm and earning a business profit of $30,000 rather than working for someone else in a similar capacity for $35,000.

Similarly, if one firm is fully capitalized (i.e., does not borrow any capital) while another pays $50,000 per year on borrowed capital, the first will show a *business* profit per year $50,000 larger than the second if both firms are otherwise identical. The *economic* profit of both firms, however, is the same. It should also be pointed out that while the man in the street may use the business concept of profit in his conversations, he intuitively applies the economic concept of profit and will close his coffee shop if he earns a "profit" of $25,000 but knows he can earn more than that by managing a coffee shop for someone else.[9] Thus, it is the economic, rather than the business, concept of profit that is important in directing resources to different sectors of the economy. In the rest of the text we will use the term *profit* to mean economic profit and *cost* to mean the sum of explicit and implicit costs.

1-3b Theories of Profit

Profit rates usually differ among firms in a given industry and even more widely among firms in different industries. Firms in such industries as steel, textiles, and railroads generally earn very low profits both absolutely and in relation to the profits of firms in pharmaceutical, office equipment, and other high-technology industries. Several theories attempt to explain these differences.

Risk-Bearing Theories of Profit   According to this theory, above-normal returns (i.e., economic profits) are required by firms to enter and remain in such fields as petroleum exploration with above-average risks. Similarly, the expected return on stocks has to be higher than on bonds because of the greater risk of the former. This will be discussed in greater detail in Chapter 3.

Frictional Theory of Profit   This theory stresses that profits arise as a result of friction or disturbances from long-run equilibrium. That is, in long-run, perfectly competitive equilibrium, firms tend to earn only a normal return (adjusted for risk) or zero (economic) profit on their investment. At any time, however, firms are not likely to be in long-run equilibrium and may earn a profit or incur a loss. For example, at the time of the energy crisis in the early 1970s, firms producing insulating materials enjoyed a sharp increase in demand, which led to large profits. With the sharp decline in petroleum prices in the mid 1980s, many of these firms began to incur losses. When profits are made in an industry in the short run, more firms are attracted to the industry in the long run, and this tends to drive profits down to zero (i.e., to firms earning only a normal return on investment). On the other hand, when losses are incurred, some firms leave the industry. This leads to higher prices and the elimination of the losses.

Monopoly Theory of Profits   Some firms with monopoly power can restrict output and charge higher prices than under perfect competition, thereby earning a profit. Because of restricted entry into the industry, these firms can continue to earn profits even in the long run. Monopoly power may arise from the firm's owning and controlling the entire supply of a raw material required for the production of the commodity, from

---

[9]Unless, of course, he values even more the freedom of being "his own boss."

economies of large-scale production, from ownership of patents, or from government restrictions that prohibit competition. The causes, effects, and control of monopoly are examined in detail in Chapters 9, 11, and 12.

Innovation Theory of Profit   The innovation theory of profit postulates that (economic) profit is the reward for the introduction of a successful innovation. For example, Steven Jobs, the founder of the Apple Computer Company, became a millionaire in the course of a few years by introducing the Apple Computer in 1977 (see Case Study 1-3). Indeed, the U.S. patent system is designed to protect the profits of a successful innovator in order to encourage the flow of innovations. Inevitably, as other firms imitate the innovation, the profit of the innovator is reduced and, eventually, eliminated. This is, in fact, what happened to the Apple Computer Company in the early 1980s.

Managerial Efficiency Theory of Profit   This theory rests on the observation that if the average firm tends to earn only a normal return on its investment in the long run, firms that are more efficient than the average would earn above-normal returns and (economic) profits.

All of the above theories of profit have some element of truth, and each may be more applicable to some industries. Indeed, profits often arise from a combination of factors, including differential risk, market disequilibrium, monopoly power, innovation, and above-average managerial efficiency. This was, for example, the case of the Apple Computer Company when it was established.

1-3c Function of Profit

Profit serves a very crucial function in a free-enterprise economy, such as our own. High profits are the signal that consumers want more of the output of the industry. High profits provide the incentive for firms to expand output and for more firms to enter the industry in the long run. For a firm of above-average efficiency, profits represent the reward for greater efficiency. On the other hand, lower profits or losses are the signal that consumers want less of the commodity and/or that production methods are not efficient. Thus, profits provide the incentive for firms to increase their efficiency and/or produce less of the commodity and for some firms to leave the industry for more profitable ones. Profits, therefore, provide the crucial signals for the reallocation of society's resources to reflect changes in consumers' tastes and demand over time.

To be sure, the profit system is not perfect, and governments in free-enterprise economies often step in to modify the operation of the profit system to make it more nearly consistent with broad societal goals. For example, governments invariably regulate the prices charged for electricity by public utility companies to provide shareholders with only a normal return on their investment. Governments also pass minimum wage legislation and pollution emission controls to internalize to polluting firms the social cost of the pollution they create. While not perfect, the profit system is the most efficient form of resource allocation available. In societies such as the Soviet Union and the People's Republic of China, where profits were not allowed, a committee of the party performed this function in a much less efficient manner.

CASE STUDY

PROFITS IN THE PERSONAL COMPUTER INDUSTRY

In 1976, Steven Jobs, then 20 years old, dropped out of college and together with a friend developed a prototype desktop computer. With financing from an independent investor, the Apple Computer Company was born, which revolutionized the computer industry. Sales of Apple Computers jumped from $3 million in 1977 to over $1.9 billion in 1986, with profits of over $150 million. The immense success of Apple was not lost on potential competitors, and by 1984 more than 75 companies had jumped into the market. Even IBM, which had originally chosen not to enter the market, soon put all its weight and muscle behind the development of its own version of the personal computer—the IBM PC. Because of increased competition, however, many of the early entrants had dropped out by 1986 and profits fell sharply. For example, profit margins for the 11 largest U.S. computer companies averaged 11.5 percent from 1980 to 1985 but only 6.5 percent from 1986 to 1990.

This is a classic example of the source, function, and importance of profits in our economy. While Jobs is not doing as well today as he did a few years ago (he actually was ousted from the company in 1985 after a power struggle with the company's president, John Scully, and is trying a comeback with his NeXT computer), he is still a multimillionaire. His huge rewards resulted from correctly anticipating, promoting, and satisfying an important type of market demand. Competitors, attracted by the huge early profits, were quick to follow, thereby causing profits in the industry to fall sharply. In the process, however, more and more of society's resources were attracted to the computer industry, which supplied consumers with rapidly improving personal computers at sharply declining prices.

Source: "Apple Era Behind Him, Steve Jobs Tries Again, Using a New System," *The Wall Street Journal*, October 13, 1990, p. A1, and "Computers Become a Kind of Commodity, to Dismay of Makers," *The Wall Street Journal*, September 5, 1991, p. A1.

1-4   THE INTERNATIONAL FRAMEWORK OF MANAGERIAL ECONOMICS

Many of the commodities we consume today are imported, and American firms purchase many inputs abroad and sell an increasing share of their products overseas. Even more important, domestic firms face increasing competition from foreign firms in the U.S. market and around the world. The international flow of capital, technology, and skilled labor has also reached unprecedented dimensions. In short, there is a rapid movement in the world today toward the internationalization of production and consumption. Thus, it is essential to introduce an international dimension in the study of managerial economics to reflect these present-world realities.

Specifically, as consumers, we purchase Japanese Toyotas and German Mercedes, Italian handbags and French perfumes, Hong Kong clothes and Taiwanese hand calculators, English Scotch and Swiss chocolates, Canadian fish and Mexican tomatoes, Costa Rican bananas and Brazilian coffee. Often, we are not even aware that the products we consume, or parts of them, are in fact made abroad. For example, imported cloth is used in American-made suits, many American brand-name shoes are entirely manufactured abroad, and a great deal of the orange juice we drink is imported. American multinational corporations produce and import many parts and components from abroad and export an increasing share of their output. For example, most of the parts and components of the IBM PC are in fact manufactured abroad and more than one-third of IBM revenues and profits are generated abroad. The strongest competition and challenge faced by IBM today is not from the American Digital Equipment Corporation (DEC) but from Japanese Mitsubishi and Hitachi. General Motors, Ford, and Chrysler face increasing competition from Toyota, Nissan, and Honda. U.S. steel companies almost collapsed during the 1980s as a result of rising steel imports and today survive only after merging with foreign steel producers, mostly Japanese and French.

In view of such an **internationalization of economic activity** it would be entirely unrealistic to study managerial economics in an international vacuum, as if U.S. firms did not in fact face serious and increasing competition from foreign firms. This text will explicitly introduce and integrate this essential international dimension into the study of managerial decision making. All of the topics examined in traditional managerial economics are covered but the focus is broadened to reflect the globalization of most economic activities in the world today.

CASE STUDY

THE RISE OF THE GLOBAL CORPORATION

One of the most significant business and economic trends of the late twentieth century is the rise of global or "stateless" corporations. These are companies that have research and production facilities in many countries, are run by an international team of managers, and sell their products, finance their operation and are owned by stockholders throughout the world. The trend toward global corporations is unmistakable and is accelerating. Going global has become a competitive strategy. Global corporations maintain a balance between functioning as a global organism while customizing products to local tastes. Both geographic and product managers report to top managers at the companies' headquarters, who reconcile differences. Companies that were entirely domestic and merely exported some of their output as late as a decade ago are now finding that in order to remain competitive they have to become global players. The necessity to be insiders in most major world markets rather than mere exporters is rapidly growing. Even smaller companies are often finding it necessary to form joint ventures with foreign companies in order to expand abroad and remain competitive at home. Today a large number of corporations with headquarters in the United States, Europe, and Japan sell more of their products and earn more profits abroad than in the country where the corporation headquarters are located. Table 1-1 shows a small sample of such corporations.

TABLE 1-1 GLOBAL CORPORATIONS

Company	Home Country	Total 1989 Sales (billions)	Sales Outside Home Country	Assets Outside Home Country	Shares Held Outside Home Country
Nestle	Switzerland	$39.9	98.0%	95.0%	Few
Phillips	Netherlands	30.0	94.0	85.0	46.0%
Electrolux	Sweden	13.8	83.0	80.0	20.0
Volvo	Sweden	14.8	80.0	30.0	10.0
ICI	Britain	22.1	78.0	50.0	16.0
Michelin	France	9.4	78.0	NA	0.0
Canon	Japan	9.4	69.0	32.0	14.0
Sony	Japan	16.3	66.0	NA	13.6
Bayer	Germany	25.8	65.4	NA	48.0
Gillette	United States	3.8	65.0	63.0	10.0
Colgate	United States	5.0	64.0	47.0	10.0
Honda	Japan	26.4	63.0	35.7	6.9
Daimler Benz	Germany	45.5	61.0	NA	25.0
IBM	United States	62.7	59.0	NA	NA
Coca-Cola	United States	9.0	54.0	45.0	0.0
Digital	United States	12.7	54.0	44.0	NA
Dow Chemical	United States	17.6	54.0	45.0	5.0
Saint-Gobain	France	11.6	54.0	50.0	13.0
Xerox	United States	12.4	54.0	51.8	0.0
Caterpillar	United States	11.1	53.0	NA	NA
Hewlett-Packard	United States	11.9	53.0	38.6	8.0

Source: "The Stateless Corporation," *Business Week*, May 14, 1990, pp. 98–105.

SUMMARY

1. "Managerial economics" refers to the application of economic theory (microeconomics and macroeconomics) and the tools of analysis of decision science (mathematical economics and econometrics) to examine how an organization can achieve its aims or objectives most efficiently. The functional areas of business administration studies (accounting, finance, marketing, personnel, and production) provide the environmental background for managerial decision making.

2. Firms exist because the economies that they generate in production and distribution confer great benefits to entrepreneurs, workers, and other resource owners. The theory of the firm postulates that the primary goal or objective of the firm is to maximize wealth or the value of the firm. This is given by the present value of the expected future profits of the firm. Since the firm usually faces many resource, legal, and other constraints, we speak of "constrained optimization." Alternative theories of the firm postulate other objectives for the firm, but profit or value maximization predicts the behavior of the firm more accurately than does any of its alternatives.

3. "Business profit" refers to the revenue of the firm minus its explicit costs. The latter are the actual out-of-pocket expenditures of the firm. Economic profit equals the revenue of the firm minus its explicit and implicit costs. The latter refer to the value of the inputs owned and used by the firm in its own production processes. Economic profit can result from one or a combination of the following: risk bearing, frictional disturbances, monopoly power, the introduction of innovations, or managerial efficiency. Profits provide the signal for the efficient allocation of society's resources.

4. Many of the commodities we consume today are imported, and American firms purchase many inputs abroad, sell an increasing share of their output to other nations, and face increasing competition from foreign firms operating in the United States. Furthermore, the international flow of capital, technology, and skilled labor has also reached unprecedented dimensions. In view of such internationalization of economic activity in the world today, it is essential to introduce an international dimension into the study of managerial economics.

DISCUSSION QUESTIONS

1. What is the relationship between the field of managerial economics and (a) microeconomics and macroeconomics? (b) Mathematical economics and econometrics? (c) The fields of accounting, finance, marketing, personnel, and production?

2. Managerial economics is often said to help the business student integrate the knowledge gained in other courses. How is this integration accomplished?

3. What is the methodology of science in general and of managerial economics in particular?
4. What might be the objective of a museum?
5. Why do firms exist? Who benefits from their existence?
6. How does the theory of the firm differ from short-term profit maximization? Why is the former superior to the latter?
7. How does the theory of the firm provide an integrated framework for the analysis of managerial decision making across the functional areas of business?
8. What effect would each of the following have on the value of the firm? (a) A new advertising campaign increases the sales of the firm substantially. (b) A new competitor enters the market. (c) The production department achieves a technological breakthrough which reduces production costs. (d) The firm is required to install pollution-control equipment. (e) The work force votes to unionize. (f) The rate of interest rises. (g) The rate of inflation changes.
9. How is the concept of a normal return on investment related to the distinction between business and economic profit?
10. What factors should be considered in determining whether profit levels are excessive in a particular industry?
11. Why does the government regulate telephone and electric power companies if the profit motive serves such an important function in the operation of a free-enterprise system?
12. Why is it crucial to introduce an international dimension into managerial economics?

PROBLEMS

The ▨ *symbol indicates problems that can be solved using the Analytical Software Diskette, provided free to adopters of the text.*

1. Find the present value of $100 due in one year if the discount rate is 5 percent, 8 percent, 10 percent, 15 percent, 20 percent, and 25 percent.
2. Find the present value of $100 due in *two* years if the discount rate is 5 percent, 8 percent, 10 percent, 15 percent, 20 percent, and 25 percent.
*3. The owner of a firm expects to make a profit of $100 for each of the next two years and to be able to sell the firm at the end of the second year for $800. The owner of the firm believes that the appropriate discount rate for the firm is 15 percent. Calculate the value of the firm.
4. A firm is contemplating an advertising campaign that promises to yield $120 one year from now for $100 spent now. Explain why the firm should or should not undertake the advertising campaign.
*5. Determine which of two investment projects a manager should choose if the discount rate of the firm is 10 percent. The first project promises a profit of $100,000 in each of the next four years, while the second project promises a profit of $75,000 in each of the next six years.

6. Determine which of the two investment projects of Problem 5 the manager should choose if the discount rate of the firm is 20 percent.

7. Explain the effect that the timing in the receipt of the profits from project 1 and project 2 in Problems 5 and 6 has on the present value of the two investment projects.

*8. The cost of attending a private college for one year is $6,000 for tuition, $2,000 for the room, $1,500 for meals, and $500 for books and supplies. The student could also have earned $15,000 by getting a job instead of going to college and 10 percent interest on expenses he or she incurs at the beginning of the year. Calculate the explicit, implicit, and the total economic costs of attending college.

9. A woman managing a duplicating (photocopying) establishment for $25,000 per year decides to open her own duplicating place. Her revenue during the first year of operation is $120,000, and her expenses are as follows:

Salaries to hired help	$45,000
Supplies	15,000
Rent	10,000
Utilities	1,000
Interest on bank loan	10,000

Calculate (a) the explicit costs, (b) the implicit costs, (c) the business profit, (d) the economic profit, and (e) the normal return on investment in this business.

10. According to Milton Friedman, "Business has only one social responsibility—to make profits (so long as it stays within the legal and moral rules of the game established by society). Few trends could so thoroughly undermine the very foundations of our society as the acceptance by corporate officials of a social responsibility other than to make as much money for their stockholders as possible." Explain why you agree or disagree with such a statement.

11. Apply the decision-making model developed in this chapter to your decision to attend college.

12. **Integrating Problem**

Semantha Jones has a job as a pharmacist earning $30,000 per year, and she is deciding whether to take another job as the manager of another pharmacy for $40,000 per year or to purchase a pharmacy that generates a revenue of $200,000 per year. To purchase the pharmacy, Semantha would have to use her $20,000 savings and borrow another $80,000 at an interest rate of 10 percent per year. The pharmacy that Semantha is contemplating purchasing has additional expenses of

$80,000 for supplies, $40,000 for hired help, $10,000 for rent, and $5,000 for utilities. Assume that income and business taxes are zero and that the repayment of the principal of the loan does not start before three years. (a) What would be the business and economic profit if Semantha purchased the pharmacy? Should Semantha purchase the pharmacy? (b) Suppose that Semantha expects that another pharmacy will open nearby at the end of three years and that this will drive the economic profit of the pharmacy to zero. What would the revenue of the pharmacy be in three years? (c) What theory of profit would account for profits being earned by the pharmacy during the first three years of the operation? (d) Suppose that Semantha expects to sell the pharmacy for $50,000 at the end of three years and that she requires a 15 percent return on her investment. Should she still purchase the pharmacy?

SUPPLE-MENTARY READINGS

A paperback in the Schaum's Outline Series in economics that presents a problem-solving approach to managerial economics and that can be used with this and other texts is:

Salvatore, Dominick: *Theory and Problems of Managerial Economics* (New York: McGraw-Hill, 1989).

For a general description of the scope of managerial economics and its relationship to other fields of study, see:

Beasley, Howard W.: "Can Managerial Economics Aid the Chief Executive Officer?" *Managerial and Decision Economics*, vol. 2, September 1981.

Baumol, William J.: "What Can Economic Theory Contribute to Managerial Economics?" *American Economic Review*, vol. 51, May 1961.

A more extensive discussion of the theories of the firm is found in:

Baumol, William J.: *Business Behavior, Value and Growth* (New York: Macmillan, 1959).

Williamson, Oliver F.: "A Model of Rational Managerial Behavior," in R. M. Cyert and J. G. March, eds., *A Behavior Theory of the Firm* (Englewood Cliffs, N.J.: Prentice-Hall, 1963).

Cyert, Richard M. and James G. March, eds.: *A Behavior Theory of the Firm* (Englewood Cliffs, N.J.: Prentice-Hall, 1963).

Simon, Herbert A.: "Theories of Decision-Making in Economics," *American Economic Review*, vol. 49, June 1959.

On the theories of profit, see:

Solomon, David: "Economic and Accounting Concepts of Income," *The Accounting Review*, vol. 36, July 1961.

Wong, Robert E.: "Profit Maximization and Alternative Theories: A Dynamic Reconciliation," *American Economic Review*, vol. 65, September 1975.

Goodpaster, Kenneth E. and **John B. Mathews, Jr.:** "Can a Corporation Have a Conscience?" *Harvard Business Review,* vol. 60, January–February 1982.

For the globalization of managerial decision making, see:

Salvatore, Dominick: *International Economics,* 4th ed. (New York: Macmillan, 1993), Chap. 1.

Davidson, William H. and **Jose' de la Torre:** *Managing the Global Corporation: Case Studies in Strategy and Management* (New York: McGraw-Hill, 1989).

Systems Thinking

- What is a System?

1

what is a system?

A million candles can be lit from one flame.

This book is an introduction to systems thinking – what systems are, the key ideas they embody, how to think about them and why they are important. What do we mean by a 'system'? We are going to use the word in its everyday, intuitive sense:

A system is an entity that maintains its existence and functions as a whole through the interaction of its parts.

Systems thinking looks at the whole, and the parts, and the connections between the parts, studying the whole in order to understand the parts. It is the opposite to reductionism, the idea that something is simply the sum of its parts. A collection of parts that do not connect is not a system. It is a heap.

A System	A Heap
Interconnecting parts functioning as a whole.	A collection of parts.
Changed if you take away pieces or add more pieces. If you cut a system in half, you do not get two smaller systems, but a damaged system that will probably not function.	Essential properties are unchanged whether you add or take away pieces. When you halve a heap, you get two smaller heaps.
The arrangement of the pieces is crucial.	The arrangement of the pieces is irrelevant.
The parts are connected and work together.	The parts are not connected and can function separately.
Its behaviour depends on the total structure. Change the structure and the behaviour changes.	Its behaviour (if any) depends on its size or on the number of pieces in the heap.

When you look at the patterns that connect the parts rather than simply the parts themselves, a remarkable fact emerges. Systems made from very different parts having completely different functions follow the same general rules of organization. Their behaviour depends on how the parts are connected, rather than what the parts are. Therefore you can make predictions about their behaviour without knowing the parts in detail. You can understand and influence very different systems – your body, your business, your finances and your relationships – using the same principles. Instead of seeing separate fields of knowledge all needing years of study to understand, systems thinking lets you see the connection between different disciplines. It enables you to predict the behaviour of systems, whether the system is a road traffic network, a belief system, a digestive system, a management team or a marketing campaign.

Why is systems thinking so important? Because, as already mentioned, you are a system living in a world of systems. We live in the hugely complex system of the natural environment, and build towns and cities that also work as systems. We have mechanical systems like computers, cars and automated factories. We talk of political systems, economic systems and belief systems. Each one works as a complete functioning whole that combines many separate parts (although how *well* it functions is another matter entirely). Systems can be simple, like a central heating thermostat, or very complex, like the weather. At present we face unprecedented problems due to the impact of pollution and technology on the system we call 'nature'. Wherever we look there are systems. We study molecules, cells, plants and animals as systems. You are made of cells, which in turn build into organ systems, under the control of the nervous system. You are part of your family system, which is turn is part of a local community, which joins other communities to form cities, regions and nations. They are all systems in their own right and subsystems of a larger system. The planet Earth itself can be looked on as a system, part of the solar system, the galaxy and even the universe. We may use the word 'system' lightly, but systems are interwoven into everything we do and in order to gain more influence over them, to gain a better quality of life, we need to understand how they work.

A system, then, is a number of parts acting as a single entity. It may itself be composed of many smaller systems or form part of a larger system. Within the body, for instance, there is the digestive system, the immune system, the nervous system and the blood system. You can study any of these in isolation and also how they work together in the larger system of the human body. A car is a mechanical system made up of different sub-systems: the cooling system, the exhaust system and the fuel system. All these systems work together to produce the smoothly working car that takes you where you want to go. You do not bother to think about the smaller systems until the car breaks down and then you discover why reductionism is so frustrating. You have all the bits of the car, but if they are not working together it is basically a heap of scrap metal.

There is a limit to how big a man-made system can grow. Everything else being equal, at a certain point it will become unwieldy, hard to manage and more prone to breakdown. So, as systems grow bigger, it makes sense to divide them into smaller systems and establish different levels of control. In a business, say, a team of six may work well together, but a team of 600 would not be able to do anything unless it divided itself into smaller groups. There is also a limit to how large anything in the natural world can grow and still live. In the world of systems, bigger does not mean better, it usually means worse. Every system has an optimum size and if it is made much larger or smaller than this without other changes, it will not function.

Emergence – Whirlpools and Rainbows

There are some startling implications to our simple definition of a system. First, systems function as a whole, so they have properties above and beyond the properties of the parts that comprise them. These are known as *emergent properties* – they 'emerge' from the system when it is working. Imagine 100 pictures of Mickey Mouse all slightly different. Not very interesting. Now run them very quickly one after another and Mickey seems to move. You've got a cartoon. When the different pictures are a smooth progression, the movement is also smooth. It is an emergent property.

Because we live with emergent properties, we take them for granted. Yet they are often unpredictable and surprising. (We suppose 'emergency' really ought to be the word here rather than the rather clumsy 'emergent properties', but language has hijacked 'emergency' for unpredictable, sudden and usually unpleasant surprises – a pity.)

Emergent properties arise from systems like those three-dimensional pictures that suddenly pop out from the random swathes of coloured patterns in the infuriating and attractive 'magic eye' books. There is no way you can predict the picture from the pattern you immerse yourself in. Likewise, watch the turbulent flow of water in a river. No amount of knowledge of the molecular structure of water would prepare you for a whirlpool. (Nor would it let you predict the wetness of water!) You could study acoustics and the physics of sound for years without suspecting the beauty and emotional power of music. Put two eyes together and you do not simply get a bigger picture but three-dimensional vision. Two ears do not simply give you the ability to hear twice as well, they give you the ability to hear in stereo. When you put together the colours of the spectrum, you do not get a muddy brown, but white light. We take these daily

246

miracles for granted, but would you have predicted them if you did not know them already? Properties can emerge like the beauty of a rainbow when the rain, atmosphere and angle of sunlight fit together absolutely right.

Our brains seem to delight in creating these emergent properties. And remember that we are part of the system, for without our senses these properties would not exist.

Consciousness itself is an emergent property. Who could have predicted that the billions of interconnections in the brain would allow the feeling of being aware of ourselves? And all your senses are part of your whole self. You see, not your eyes. Put an eye by itself on the table and it would see nothing. You cannot find sight, hearing, touch, taste or smell in any of the parts of a body. Your life is dependent on your parts working together. When the parts are isolated from the body, they die. Post mortems do not discover the secret of life, but death.

To take another example, the movement of a car is also an emergent property. A car needs a carburettor and the fuel tank in order to move, but put the carburettor or the fuel tank on the road and see how far they go on their own.

The balance of nature, too, is an emergent property. Plants, animals and weather conditions work together to create a flourishing environment, even though within that environment animals may prey on each other. When the environment is disturbed, that particular balance may be lost, some species may die out, others may dominate, but overall, another balance will emerge.

In short:

Systems have emergent properties that are not found in their parts. You cannot predict the properties of a complete system by taking it to pieces and analysing its parts.

When you take a system apart, you do not find its essential properties anywhere. These properties arise only when the whole system is working. The only way to find out what they are is to run the system.

Emergent Properties

Here are some emergent properties. Can you think of more?

- life
- whirlpools
- tornadoes
- temperature
- pressure
- computer software bugs
- computer graphics
- emotions
- music
- magic eye graphics
- rainbows
- culture
- flames
- consciousness
- team morale
- clouds
- health and well-being
- hunger
- laughter
- memories
- dreams
- pain

The nice thing about emergent properties is that you do not have to understand the system to benefit – you do not have to have a degree in electronics to switch on the light, nor understand how a car works to drive. You don't have to understand the millions of lines of software code before playing a computer game. Do you know how computer graphics appear on the screen? Joseph never really thought about it, until one day, as he switched off his computer, his eight-year-old daughter asked him, 'Daddy, where do the pictures go when you switch off?'

'They don't really go anywhere. The computer just doesn't make them any more.'

'But how does the computer remember to make the same picture when you switch on again?'

'They're stored in the computer's memory.'

'What! All those pictures?'

'No, more like how to make them when we tell it to.'

'Where is its memory?'

Joseph started to flounder.

'The computer stores the picture as a pattern of bits that mark the exact position of every small part, so it can remake the whole picture when we ask it to.'

'Where does it store the bits?'

'In the bits of plastic and metal inside the computer we call chips.'

'If we look inside the chips can we see the pictures?'

We had reached the veil between the worlds of silicon and sight.

'No, they're too small.'

'Could we see them with a magnifying glass?'

'No, they are more like patterns of bits like a jigsaw puzzle that the computer knows how to put together. When you tip out the pieces of your jigsaw puzzle, you have to put the pieces together.'

She wasn't very impressed with the explanation, but trying to explain the electrical flows inside a computer with graphics as an emergent property would have been even worse. We cannot break open the computer casing to look for the picture, just as we would not take apart a piano to look for the sound.

'Emergent properties' is also a charitable name for computer bugs. Have you ever had the experience of a computer suddenly behaving very oddly for no apparent reason, while you are doing something you have done hundreds of times before without any problems? We certainly have. Sometimes the computer seems to be actively mischievous or even malevolent. (Shortly after typing this, the computer decided to give us a 'live' demonstration – the program crashed. It wouldn't type, delete or save anything. Cursing the inert heap of silicon, and simultaneously grateful we had saved a few moments before, we rebooted the computer.)

The second critical feature of systems is a mirror image of the first. Just as the properties of the system are shown by the whole system and not by its parts, so if you take the system apart it loses those properties. When you take a piano apart, for example, not only will you not find the sound, but it is also impossible to produce the sound until you reassemble it. You cannot find a rainbow in the rain or a picture inside a television. When you cut a system in half, you do not get two smaller systems, but a broken or dead system.

Analysis is the name for taking something to pieces to find out how it works. This is very useful for certain types of

250

problems or for seeing how a large system is made up of smaller subsystems. *You gain knowledge through analysis.* However, you cannot understand the whole system properties by breaking the system into its constituent parts.

The complement of analysis is synthesis – building the parts into a whole. *You gain understanding through synthesis.* The only way to find out how a system functions and what its emergent properties are is to see it in action as a whole.

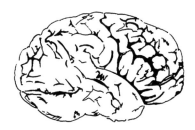

The Most Complex System We Think We Know

The world is a very complex system. We need a complex system to make sense of it.

The human brain is the most complex structure within the known universe. Weighing 3–4 lb (around 1.5 kg), it consists of over 100 billion neurons or nerve cells – as many stars as there are in the Milky Way. The front part of the brain, or cerebral cortex, has over 10 billion neurons. The connections *between* the nerve cells are more important than the cells themselves, just as systems thinking would suggest. A single neuron can have up to 100,000 inputs and continually integrate 1,000 inputs. The brain is not like a computer, but every nerve cell works like a small computer. The cortex has over one million billion connections. If you were to count one every second, it would take you 32 million years.

No two brains are alike. We are born with all the neurons we need, but up to 70 per cent of them will die in our first year of life. The surviving neurons form an ever more complex web of connections. Certain connections are reinforced by use and others wither as we learn about the world. The brain is not independent of the world, it is shaped by it – the outside system of the world moulds the inside system of our brain.

The brain has the task of extracting pattern and sense from the huge flood of sensory information it receives. The very act of perception also makes meaning of that perception and so the brain in turn shapes the world as it appears to us. Interpretation is part of sensation.

The brain has been described by neuroscientists as an interconnected, decentralized, parallel processed, distributed network of simultaneous waves of interactive resonance patterns. In other words, a very complex system.

The brain is every bit as complex as our vanity hoped and our intellect feared.

Simple and Complex Systems

A system maintains itself through the interaction of its parts, and so it is the relationships and the mutual influence between the parts that is important, rather than the number or size of the parts. These relationships, and therefore the systems, can be simple or complex.

There are two very different ways that anything can be complicated. When we think something is complex, we usually think of it having many different parts. That is complexity of detail. When you look at a 1,000-piece jigsaw puzzle, you are looking at complexity of detail. We can usually find a way of simplifying, grouping and organizing this sort of detail, and there is only one place for every piece to fit. Computers are good at dealing with this sort of complexity, especially if it can be sequenced.

The other type of complexity is dynamic complexity. This is when the elements can relate to each other in many different ways, because each part has many different possible states, so a few parts can be combined in a myriad of different ways. It is misleading to judge complexity on the number of separate bits, rather than the possible ways of putting them together. It is not necessarily true that the smaller the number of parts, the simpler to understand and deal with. It all depends on the degree of dynamic complexity.

Consider a business project team. Each person's mood can change from moment to moment. There are many, many different ways they can relate to each other. So a system may have a few parts but a great deal of dynamic complexity. Problems that look simple on the surface may reveal a great deal of dynamic complexity when we probe them.

New connections between parts of a system add complexity and adding another piece can create many new connections. When you add one new piece, the number of *possible connections* does not increase by one. It may increase *exponentially* – in other words, for every one you add you get a bigger increase than you got from adding the one before it. For example, suppose you start with just two pieces, A and B. There are two possible links and pathways of influence: A on B and B on A. Now let's add another part. Now there are three parts: A, B and C. The number of possible connections, however, has increased to six; 12 if we allow two parts to form alliances and influence the third (e.g. A plus B influences C). You can see that it does not take many parts to create a dynamically complex system, even when the parts have only one state. We know this from experience – two people are more than twice as hard to manage as one, there is more chance of difficulty miscommunication, and a second child brings far more than twice the work and twice the joy to the parents.

The simplest systems will have a few parts that have only a few states and a few simple relationships between those parts. A plumbing system or a thermostat are good examples. They have limited detail complexity and limited dynamic complexity.

A very complex system may have many parts or subsystems, all of which can have different states which may change in response to other parts. Mapping this kind of complex system would be like finding your way through a maze that changed itself completely depending on what direction you took at any time. A game involving strategy, like chess, is a game of dynamic complexity because whenever you make a move you alter the whole board because your move changes the relationships between the pieces. (An even more dynamically complex chess game would have a piece changing into a different piece every time it made a move!)

254

The first lesson of systems thinking is to know whether you are dealing with detail or dynamic complexity – a jigsaw or a chess game.

The relationship between the different parts of the system determines how it works, so each part, however small, can affect the behaviour of the whole. For example, your hypothalamus, a small gland the size of a pea which is located in the middle of your brain, regulates your temperature, breathing rate, water balance and blood pressure. Likewise your heart rate affects your whole body. When it speeds up you may feel anxious, excited or exhilarated. When it slows down you feel more relaxed.

All parts of a system are interdependent, they all interact. How they relate to each other gives them the power to affect the whole system. This suggests an interesting rule for influencing systems, particularly groups: the more connections you have, the more possible influence. Networking brings influence. Indeed, research suggests that successful managers spend four times as much time networking as their less successful colleagues.[1]

Different parts can also combine to affect the whole. Groups form alliances that make a difference in government, organizations and teams.

The System as a Web

Complex systems are bound together by many links, so they are usually very stable. The French phrase *plus ça change, plus c'est la même chose* sums it up perfectly: whatever changes also stays the same in important ways. It is easy to see why this is so. Imagine a system as a kind of web with each part influencing and connected to many others. The more parts there are, the more complex the system is in detail. The more the parts can change state and form shifting alliances, the more possible connections there are between the parts, and the more dynamically complex the system.

Imagine a complex system like a web. Say, some of the possible elements of the government of a fictional state called Dystopia (see figure). You could also make this hypothetical system represent a business, where the factors are such things as established procedures, job responsibilities, reward and appraisal systems and management styles. It could also be made to represent people in an organization, factors in an advertising campaign, different ideas in a belief system, a team, an extended family or parts of your body.

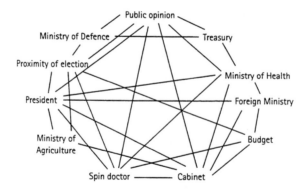

The government of Dystopia

This system has 11 elements. Let's suppose the government is stable, all the pieces fit together and the system works. The links between the parts keep it steady. Now, imagine you want to change how the budget is calculated, but you cannot do this without taking all the other pieces it is linked to into account.

Changing it will affect all the other parts of the system that it is linked to. They will resist the change because it means they will have to change as well.

This is the problem with political reforms. The political system is very complex and many a political career has ended in disappointment because the system resists change. New governments inherit a vast bureaucracy that is notoriously cautious. The BBC television comedy *Yes, Minister* showed the hapless government minister Jim Hacker (later promoted beyond his level of competence to Prime Minister) struggling in vain against the Machiavellian wiles of his civil servants. Whatever initiative he wanted to take, whatever shift he wanted to make, somehow he always seemed to end up reinforcing the very system he wanted to change. The Civil Service was the personification of the resistance of a complex system to the quick change (or indeed any change).

A system will act like a strong elastic net – when you pull one piece out of position it will stay there only for as long as you actually exert force on it. When you let go, you may be surprised and annoyed that it springs back to where it was before. Yet when you see this obstinacy as part of a system rather than isolated maliciousness, its resistance is not only understandable but inevitable.

New Year's resolutions are a good example. Suppose you have a habit you want to change. A habit, especially if you do not approve of it, seems to be 'outside' you, something you could just drop and be the better for it. But these habits are part of your total system of behaviour. You may not like them, but they connect with many other parts of your life. On New Year's Day you resolve to change, but somehow the habit persists unless you make a constant effort. You feel the strain – literally. Trying harder may not help. It is not the habit or behaviour that is so strong in itself – the strength of resistance comes from all the other parts that it is bound into. You are not just pulling on it alone, but on all the habits and experiences it links to. From a systems thinking point of view, you would expect such resolutions to be very difficult to keep.

Stability and Leverage

How stable a system is depends on many factors, including the size, number and variety of the subsystems within it and the type and degree of connectivity between them. A complex system is not necessarily an unstable one: Many complex systems are remarkably stable and therefore resistant to change. For example, different political parties can gain power without the whole democratic system of government being overthrown. Families tolerate arguments and disagreements without falling apart, and businesses can still function even when there are policy disagreements between different departments. Also, part of your body may not work very well, yet overall you can still function. This stability is really important, for without it your health would fluctuate wildly, businesses would fail or boom erratically and every disagreement would threaten your friendships. This overall stability is a positive aspect, but it comes (of course) with a price. The price is resistance to change.

So political parties struggle with their civil servants and reforms meet a constant series of checks. Families may be unhappy, but they live with it. New business practices are usually resisted, as people feel comfortable with the old ways of doing things. It is not that people are being difficult, it is the system that they are in. Whenever you make a change in any complex system – a business, a family or your own way of doing things – expect resistance. You cannot have stability without resistance, they are two sides of the same coin.

Reformers often make the mistake, particularly in business, of pushing and pushing, and finally exhausting the system's resilience, at which point it breaks down completely, to everybody's cost.

When systems do change, they tend to do so relatively rapidly and often quite drastically. The Berlin Wall is a good example. It had divided East and West Berlin since August 1961, a symbol of the East German government's long-standing hostility towards the West, yet in November 1989 the government collapsed and the wall was demolished by enthusiastic people using their bare hands in an incredible scene of elation and release. There were many political and economic reasons behind this, it was not a simple process, but the actual event was quick and dramatic. At the same time, Communist governments that had been stable for decades were falling one after another.

When pressure for change builds up in a system, it can suddenly burst like a balloon. There is a threshold beyond which a system will suddenly change or break down. If the system is under a lot of pressure it only takes a small trigger, just as a small crack in a dam can lead to its collapse because of the pressure of water behind it. The more stressed you feel, the less provocation it takes for you to lose your temper. It is the straw that breaks the camel's back.

So, if you put a system under enough pressure for long enough, it can suddenly collapse. Systems can also suddenly change if you find just the right combination of actions. This comes from understanding the system and is known as *the principle of leverage*. This principle is simple. Again, imagine a system as a web with many parts connected. Suppose you want to change the position of one part. When you pull on it directly, it seems to resist, but really the whole system resists. However, cutting a small link in another place may free this piece, like undoing a crucial knot in a tangle of string. You need to know how the system is made up to know which knot to undo. Ian was working in a business some years ago where it was well known that if you wanted something done in a certain department you had to speak to the secretary of the departmental head. Speaking directly to the senior managers had no effect.

Leverage and sudden change also relate to how smoothly the system functions over time and how it responds in special circumstances. Complex systems are not always smoothly continuous in their behaviour. System behaviour is described as continuous when it behaves predictably through its range of states. For example, you can test a car through its range of speeds and you can be fairly sure that if it works at 70 miles an hour and 10 miles an hour, it will also work at all the speeds in between. It is not suddenly going to come apart at $35\frac{1}{2}$ mile per hour. Its behaviour is continuous throughout the range of speeds.

Living systems and some mechanical systems like computer software may behave very differently. Discontinuous system behaviour is when something weird happens given the right special set of circumstances. The computer crashes, the person loses their temper or the body becomes ill. The possibility was always there, it's just that the exact circumstances never cropped up in the tests, that the system is too complex to control all the variables. Two pieces of software that work perfectly well on their own may not work together and cause the computer to crash. Two people who do excellent work independently may be at each other's throats when they work together.

Medical drugs are another example. They have to undergo stringent tests over a long period. But even so, many drugs react badly with other drugs or have side-effects that do not manifest until years afterwards. The presence of another drug, or a long time period (or both), is a special set of circumstances. The more complex the system, the less you can rely on sampling to predict the effects.

The same process is at work when you lose your temper. For example, perhaps you have had a day when everything goes wrong and your mood inexorably worsens. You feel under pressure. Then something trivial happens – another motorist makes a mistake or someone makes a chance remark that irks you. It is the last straw and you explode with anger.

However, there is good news too (of course). If system failure can happen under what seems like trivial circumstances, then other, more desirable changes can also happen with little effort. Change can be surprisingly easy if you identify the right connections. This doesn't mean piling on the pressure, but knowing *where* to intervene so that a small effort can get a huge result. This is *leverage*.

How do you apply the idea of leverage? Instead of wasting effort in directly pulling or pushing, which could exhaust both you and the system, ask the key systems question: *What stops the change?*

Look at the connections that are holding the part you want to change in place. Cut or weaken these and the change may be easy. This is a key principle of systems thinking.

Some parts of a system are more critical than others, that is, they exercise a higher degree of control. A head injury is far more dangerous than a leg injury, because the brain has a higher level of control over the body than the leg. In business, when you make a change at head office, the effects ramify down through all the local branches. Changing a manager at a local branch is less likely to affect the policy of the whole business – although it is possible, as complex systems are full of surprises. As a general rule, however, the greater the control of the system of the part you change, the more pervasive and wide-ranging the effects.

Side-Effects

This leads on to another consequence of the connectedness of the pieces in a system. When you change one part, the influence radiates out like ripples from a stone thrown into a pool. What you do may affect other parts of the system which may then affect still others that are far from the original change.

When you are dealing with a system you can never just do one thing.

Medical drugs are again a good example. All drugs have side-effects. The only question is whether they are noticeable, and if so, how uncomfortable or dangerous the side-effects are and whether they are worth putting up with for the positive effects of the drug. Antibiotics, for instance, are very effective against bacterial infections. The stomach upsets they cause (because they kill the naturally occurring and beneficial bacteria in the gut as well as the dangerous bacteria that have made you ill) are usually a small price to pay.

262

The side-effects of drugs may appear years after treatment and it is hard to make the connection between the two. For example, steroid drugs are used to treat a whole variety of conditions: inflammation, asthma, eczema and arthritis. Yet they can also cause muscle wasting, high blood sugar, diabetes, water retention, insomnia, mood changes, menstrual problems and osteoporosis, All these are listed in the official *Physician's Desk Reference*. The more powerful the drug, the more likely there are to be side-effects.

Sometimes, however, the side-effects can be utilized in another context. For example, aspirin, as well as being a potent pain reliever, also has the side-effect of thinning the blood when taken in larger quantities. It is a cheap, readily available and familiar drug and is now widely used as a way of preventing strokes in patients who have suffered heart attacks or those with constricted blood vessels. Aspirin still has unpleasant side-effects – stomach upsets, nausea and sometimes allergic responses and anaemia – because it can deplete the body of essential vitamins and minerals, particularly iron.

We are very careful with medical drugs, but not so careful with the equivalents of drugs in our environment – the pesticides and chemicals we use. The most infamous example of this is the insecticide DDT. Invented in 1939 (it helped earn the discoverer a Nobel Prize), it was used by farmers as an insecticide and was particularly effective in controlling mosquitoes and thus preventing the spread of malaria. However, by 1950, there was mounting evidence that DDT was toxic to many animals. By 1970, when its use was finally controlled, it had worked its way up the food chain and was found in human tissue.

Nor was it effective as an insecticide in the long term. At the beginning, the insects ate the DDT but the insectivores (animals who feed on insects) ate the poisoned insects. When the insectivores started to die, the insect population (which had started to become immune to DDT anyway) increased, so paradoxically, the insect population got larger, not smaller.

Consider, there are over 65,000 industrial chemicals now in regular commercial use and up to five more come on the market every day. Eighty per cent of these chemicals are not tested for toxicity.[2] We are discovering their side-effects to our cost as time passes.

Another principle of systems thinking, then, is:

Expect side-effects.

They may be surprising. They may be unpleasant. But when you do understand the system you can begin to predict them, so that you can design your change to have the desired effects with few detrimental side-effects. Or even you can have the desired change as a side-effect of another change by applying the principle of leverage.

For example, we know a family where one of the children, a boy of 10 named Tom, had got into trouble at his school. He would pick fights with other children in the playground and get into kicking matches with them. He was also extremely demanding in class, continually asking for the teacher's attention. The school spoke with the parents and they all agreed that the family should receive some counselling. After a number of sessions, it turned out that the leverage point was in the parents' attitude to discipline. They set broad limits, because they wanted to encourage the boy to be self-reliant and to discover ideas for himself. They believed that limits are much stronger and better when they are internalized rather than imposed. This approach

264

had worked very well with Tom's older brother. What Tom needed, however, was much clearer boundaries. He needed to be told exactly what to do. Without a clear sense of acceptable boundaries he felt insecure, so he kept pushing to the limit to find out where they were.

As an experiment, and with the counsellor's support, the parents became very directive with Tom. After a few difficult weeks, he started to respond – he became much calmer, stopped fighting at school and started to work in a more self-directed way in class. Paradoxically (again that word!), the parents got the result they wanted by doing the opposite. The effects spread beyond Tom to the parents, to the elder brother and to the school. The class teacher was less stressed and so the whole class was happier.

In this example, no one was to blame and no one wanted the initial situation. Everyone agreed it had to change, but how? The action taken was indirectly on Tom and directly on the parent's beliefs. They acted differently, which led to Tom acting differently.

We shall see that very often the most critical point for leverage in any system is the beliefs of the people in it, because it is the beliefs that sustain the system as it is.

---

1 Luthans, Paul, *Real Managers*, Ballinger Publishing Company, 1988

2 World Commission on Environment and Development, *Our Common Future*, Oxford University Press, 1987

Post Industrial Society

- Daniel Bell
- The New Society of Organizations

CHAPTER 7

DANIEL BELL

Daniel Bell is one of the foremost American sociologists and social theorists. His work for the last twenty years, framed around the concept of the emerging post-industrial society, has become the conceptual and intellectual centerpiece of thinking in the U.S. and among the other advanced industrialized nations in the interpretation of the broad sweep of economic, technological, social, cultural and political change in which we are enmeshed. While Bell is universally seen as a premier futurist, he prefers to see himself as a student of long term and fundamental social and institutional change.

KEY VIEWS ABOUT THE FUTURE

1. The post-industrial society will be increasingly dependent on information, especially on scientifically-grounded theoretical knowledge. Information and service jobs will predominate.
2. The success of capitalism grounded in a Protestant ethic contains the seed of its own decline. Prosperity and education move successive generations to self-centered gratification, and away from deferred gratification and a sense of *civitas*, i.e., a collective or community-oriented set of values.
3. The nation-state is too small for the big problems of life, and too big for the small problems.
4. Accompanying the central role of theoretical knowledge are new technologies which reflect: broad application of electronics, miniaturization, digitalization, and an expanding competence to design to specifications.
5. Intellectual technologies will be increasingly crucial to the management of complexity.
6. Human capital is appreciating.
7. The three realms of society, the technoeconomic, the polity, and the culture, are only loosely coupled, so that changes in one do not necessarily have direct anticipatible effects on the other. Each realm is also a boundary constraint and an influence on change in the other realms.

BIOGRAPHICAL NOTE

Daniel Bell, Henry Ford Professor of Social Sciences at Harvard University, graduated from the College of the City of New York in 1938 and earned his doctorate at Columbia. He was a staff writer and later managing editor of the *New Leader* (1939-44). He then became managing editor of *Common Sense* (1945) and took his first academic assignment as assistant professor of social sciences at the University of Chicago (1945-48). He was labor editor for *Fortune* magazine for a decade. He started lecturing in sociology at Columbia in 1942, and was made professor in 1958. In 1969 he migrated to Harvard. Bell has served on numerous commissions. He was the U.S. representative to the Organization for Economic Cooperation and Development (OECD) Interfutures Project (1976-79) and a member of the President's Commission on Technology, Automation, and Economic Progress.

Bell was chairman of the American Academy of Arts and Sciences Commission on the Year 2000, which in 1968 resulted in *Toward the Year 2000: Work in Progress* and stimulated a distinguished cadre of thinkers, including Herman Kahn, to turn their attention to what was then the last third of a century.

He is a prolific author. The present chapter draws from *The Coming of the Post Industrial Society: A Venture in Social Forecasting* (1973), and its complement, *The Cultural Contradictions of Capitalism* (1976).

We have also drawn on a 1977 paper, "The Future World Disorder: A Structural Context for Crises," prepared for the OECD and reprinted in *The Winding Passage*.

Bell pointed out the significance of his chapter, "The Social Framework of the Information Society," which appears in *The Computer Age: A Twenty Year View*, edited by Michael Dertouzos and Joel Moses. We have also found Bell's introductory essay, "The Year 2000—The Trajectory of an Idea" in *Toward the Year 2000*, valuable in highlighting the origins of his interest in the future. Bell has generously supplied us with unpublished notes and charts, and we had the advantage of hearing his engaging and informal lecture at the Congressional Office of Technology Assessment, September 15, 1986.

As a student of both Marxist and non-Marxist socialism of the 19th century, he has characterized himself as a post-Marxist thinker, presumably by way of satisfying the demands of those who would push us each into labeled boxes. He is indebted to scores of other 19th century thinkers and draws on a panorama of contemporary analysts and social thinkers, extracting, interpreting, re-interpreting, and integrating concepts and ideas into his own comprehensive framework. Karl

Daniel Bell

Mannheim and Max Weber rank with Marx in influence. His own teacher at Columbia, Robert McIver, was also an influence. Bell acknowledges the contributions of the Australian economist, Colin Clark, for his pathbreaking conceptualization of economic activity in three sectors, the primary sector of extractive industry, the secondary sector, manufacturing and transportation, and the tertiary or services sector.

WORLDVIEW

The Realms of Modern Society

Bell rejects the notion that society is an integrated whole, a complex system. Rather, for him, it is an amalgam of three realms; the social structure, including the techno-economic structure, the polity, and the culture. His concept of the post-industrial society refers primarily to the first realm, the techno-economic. In Bell's view, changes in that realm do not determine either the polity or the culture. He is inclined to the contrary view that the cultural and political orders dominate—or at least constrain—technological choices. Exhibit 7-1 outlines this general social schema. One can find and interpret many conflicts within our society in terms of this three-part division of society into distinctive realms. For example, under the first column of axial principles, the economic criteria of functional rationality, efficiency, and effectiveness, characteristic of business decisions, is at odds with the political pressure for equality. Each of these in turn is at cross purposes with a cultural characteristic, the drive toward self-realization with its intense focus on the individual. The concerns of the individual work against a requirement for political stability, shared beliefs, and a willingness to compromise.

Next, consider the column on the relation of the individual to society. The traditional industrial society has segmented people's roles. One is professionally a lawyer or a physician or an assembly line operator. On the other hand the polity emphasizes participation in decisions affecting one's interests while the cultural realm celebrates the whole person.

The Post-Industrial Society

Exhibit 7-2 summarizes Bell's concept of the post-industrial society. A key feature is the shift in the labor force from predominantly fabrication, material production, and manufacturing to post-industrial society's emphasis on service sector employment. More subtle, less visible, and in the long pull, more important, is the shift to dependence on codified theoretical knowledge as a directing force for change. Every

Exhibit 7-1

The Disjunctive Realms of Modern Society

1. Realms	Techno-Economic	Polity	Culture
2. Axial Principles	Functional Rationality	Equality	Self-Realization
3. Axial Structures	Bureaucracy	Representation	"The Democratization of Genius"
4. Central Value Orientation	Material Growth	Government by Consent of Governed	The Value of the "New"
5. Relations of Individual to Society	Segmentation into Roles	Participation in Decision	The Emphasis on the Whole Person
6. Basic Processes	Specialization	Negotiation-Conflict	Break-up of Genres and Distinctions
7. Structural Problematics	Reification of Institutions and Persons	Entitlements	The Question Judgements of What is Value

General Schema of Society

1. Realms	Techno-Economic	Polity	Culture
2. Axial Principles	Tools for Increase of Resources	Stipulation of Power	Existential Meanings
3. Axial Structures	Organization of Production	Legal or Customary Institutions	Sacral and Esthetic Authorities

4. Central Value Orientation	Control over Nature	Justice	Transcendence
5. Relations Individual to Society	Instrumental — Labor as Means	Jural Standing	Self to an Ultimate
6. Basic Processes	Differentiation	Definitions of Actors and Arenas	Syncretism
7. Structural Problematics	Disruption of Custom Scarcities	Legitimacy	Dialectic of Release and Restraint
8. Patterns of Social Change	Linear	Alternation	Ricorsi

society has operated on the basis of knowledge. The critical difference between the industrial and the post-industrial society is the switch from experimental, empirical knowledge and know-how, to theoretical knowledge. The great society-shaping technologies of the 19th century were created by amateurs, by tinkerers, by empirical geniuses. Theoretical knowledge either followed or was ignored by the developers of the 19th century technologies. Today, theoretical knowledge dominates in electronics and in material science. Coming out of the post-industrial transformation is the new class, the knowledge and information workers.

A stream of new conflicts accompanies the transformation from the industrial to the post-industrial society. For example, the ownership of intellectual property will become more important because theoretical knowledge does not fit the traditional property categories of the industrial society. Theoretical knowledge must be protected and rewarded if we are to have incentives for its effective development. The concept of "technology" itself must expand, since technology has historically meant the physical, and more recently, the physical and biological. One must embrace institutional and intellectual technology inventions, since these will become more important factors in shaping, organizing, and managing our world.

Exhibit 7-2

The Postindustrial Society: A Comparative Schema [1]

Mode of Production	Preindustrial Extractive	Industrial Fabrication	Postindustrial Processing; Recycling Services
Economic sector	**Primary** Agriculture Mining Fishing Timber Oil and gas	**Secondary** Goods-producing Manufacturing Durables Nondurables Heavy construction	**Tertiary** Transportation Utilities **Quaternary** Trade Finance Insurance Real estate **Quinary** Health Education Research Government Recreation
Transforming resource	**Natural power** Wind, water, draft animal, human muscle	**Created energy** Electricity—oil gas, coal, nuclear power	**Information** Computer and data-transmission systems
Strategic resource	Raw materials	Financial capital	Knowledge
Technology	Craft	Machine technology	Intellectual technology
Skill base	Artisan, manual worker, farmer	Engineer, semi-skilled worker	Scientist, technical and professional occupations

Daniel Bell

Methodology	Commonsense, trial and error experience	Empiricism, experimentation	Abstract theory, Models, Simulations, Decision theory Systems analysis
Time perspective	Orientation to the past	Ad hoc adaptiveness, Experimentation	Future orientation: Forecasting and planning
Design	Game against nature	Game against fabricated future	Game between persons
Axial principle	Traditionalism	Economic growth	Codification of theoretical knowledge

Another emerging conflict will frame itself around those workers whose incomes rise rapidly because they are backed by new theoretical knowledge and those other workers in our society such as nurses, policemen, and teachers whose work is more or less inelastic to technology driven productivity gains. The labor conflicts will be over closing the wage gaps.

Education for the new world will create its own problems as will the rise of the adversarial culture and the resistances of bureaucracy to change.

Bell has a metaphor for his trichotomy of societies:

. . .pre-industrial society is a 'game against nature'. . . .industrial society is a 'game against fabricated nature'. . . . a post-industrial society is a 'game between persons'. . . .[2]

Cultural Contradictions

"Irony" is a term not extensively used by Bell but is implicit to his analysis of many problems. In Bell's cultural realm, one of the

275

consequences of the success of the industrial era has been an extraordinary degree of personal freedom and opportunity as well as the development of strong attention to the self, self-realization, self-fulfillment, or "self-actualization." This concentration on the self is reflected in the way we in the U.S. ransack the world to acquire its benefits in a helter-skelter, self-engorging way. A further mark of modernity is that there is a shift from the old, including our roots, to a concentration on the new and the future. The epitome of this is the bourgeois entrepreneur and his relentless search for the new, the sensational, the stimulating. This ubiquitous self-centeredness undercuts the very values of hard work and deferred gratification which made it all possible. For Bell, "modernism has thus been the seducer."[3]

The Changing Market System

From the point of view of the polity, Bell sees five forces or elements together structurally transforming the old market system:

- The institutionalization of expectations in the form of entitlements has led Bell to coin a phrase, "a revolution of rising entitlements," to describe the situation. We have moved away from the concept of earning, saving, husbanding, and preparing for the future with this new sense of entitlements. At the low end of the economic scale the expectation is welfare. In the middle class it is free or heavily subsidized public education.
- The incompatibility of our numerous wants and diverse values is breeding inescapable problems of choice.
- The rise of spillover or secondary effects of economic growth are important factors in our collective concerns.
- Worldwide inflation reflects expanding demand and lagging capacity.
- The shift in many crucial decisionmaking processes is from the marketplace to the political domain.

Put in a different way, the West has lost a sense of *civitas*, the willingness to make sacrifices for the collective good. In the absence of of *civitas* we are adrift in setting our priorities.

Bell argues strongly the need for a "public household" but tells us nearly nothing about who, how, when, or by what means we might achieve that objective. He celebrates the value of religion and hopes that its restoration will help provide that public value. On the other hand, it

Daniel Bell

would be hard to believe that he sees the current prominence of religious fundamentalism as a positive step in the direction of a renewed *civitas*.

SPECIFIC ISSUES

Values

A key value for Bell is lost in the decline of a strong Protestant ethic, presumably including the Protestant work ethic. He encapsulates his harsh judgment in terms of installment buying and the credit card, which pushes us to excessive consumption, eroding a traditional Protestant commitment to saving for the future.

Women

Bell's structural analysis sheds light on the status of women and their emergence as a major segment of the workforce. Two conditions were necessary for this emerging role of women. First was the now decades old shift in cultural attitudes and second was the more recent institutionalization of a market. The cultural attitudes changed decades ago but only recently has there been the rise of the human services sector which has led to the institutionalization of a market for women's employment.

Emerging Technologies

Bell is working on a book, tentatively entitled, *The Next Technological Revolution*, developing his notion that we are moving to a knowledge based society, dependent increasingly on theoretical knowledge. The characteristic example of his concept is seen in the shift in the way materials are handled. Until quite recently, there were a small number of relatively standardized materials, a variety of iron and steels, copper, brass, aluminum, polyethylene, polyvinyl-chloride, etc. If we chose to build or make something, we had to work within the boundaries of the capabilities of those materials, thereby limiting our ability to meet our goals. A radical, if not revolutionary, change has transformed our approach to selection and use of materials. We now can literally specify the performance characteristics of the material we want and most likely create that material in the laboratory and introduce it successfully into commerce. For Bell the new capability is both revolutionary in the materials domain itself and in the paradigm of our emerging technological capabilities across the board.

Information and Telecommunications

In the post-industrial society,

A new social framework based on telecommunications may be decisive in the way in which economic and social exchanges are conducted, the way knowledge is created and retrieved, and the character of occupations and work in which men engage. [4]

Closely tied to this central role of telecommunications or more properly, "compunications" (a somewhat awkward term conceived by Anthony Oettinger of Harvard and more euphoniously captured by "telematics"), is the shift from goods-producing to a service society. The second is the strong role of theoretical knowledge and third is the emergence of intellectual technologies as key tools for social management, where the intellectual technologies include such things as systems analysis and decision theory. The key to the intellectual technology is the substitution of knowledge, wisdom, experience and intuitive judgment by some formal algorithm. A big problem in the information society is the virtual absence of any economic theory of information. Information obviously is not a commodity or an article of commerce in the traditional sense. For example, when sold or given away it still remains. It has characteristics which will take time to understand and codify. In terms of information technology, Bell sees five emerging problem areas:

- The meshing of telephone and computer systems.
- The substitution of electronic media for paper processing.
- The expansion of television through cable.
- The reorganization of storage and retrieval to allow for interaction.
- The expansion of the education system through computer aided instruction.

Coming out of these transformational technological changes are numerous emerging issues. Consider, for example, the infrastructure.

Transportation, Energy, and Communication

Society has three basic clusters of infrastructure. The first is transportation, the second is energy, and third is communication. Bell sees little likelihood of radical developments in transportation. On the other hand, should a ballistic airplane be developed which would link New York to Tokyo in 3 to 5 hours or London to Sydney, etc., the increased banding together of the world surely would be a change.

Daniel Bell

There may be some significant new developments in the energy infrastructure but the really big actions will be in the communications infrastructure. The communications infrastructure will raise the crucial question of the best techno-economic organization to achieve the most efficient and effective use of the technology. Do we go competitive or integrated? Do we create monopolies or promote competition? Bell sees unregulated competition rather than government regulated spheres as being far more productive.[5]

How the third infrastructure develops depends on some issues of the polity such as:

- The location of cities.
- The possibility of more centralized or national planning.
- The roles of centralization and privacy.
- The possible divisions of society between the elite and the masses.
- The international organization of telematics.

World Disorders

Bell is pessimistic about the global situation. He has epitomized it in the observation that "the national state is too small for the big problems of life and too big for the small problems."[6] The scope and urgency of problems arising from this mismatch must drive us to seek new political arrangements to preserve freedom and peace in our shrinking world.

His international analysis done in 1977 is as cogent and applicable today as it was then, primarily because Bell chooses to address issues at the structural level and structure changes slowly. That structural situation is as follows:

There have been two major sociological and geopolitical transformations in the Western world:

- The rise of the welfare state, especially "the revolution of rising entitlements" and the greater freedom in culture and morals.
- The end of the old international order and the emergence of a large number of heterogeneous, diverse states.
- Separate and distinct but interacting with the above are the technological revolutions in transportation and communication, tying the world together in real time and the rise of the science based industries of the post-industrial era, the associated global integration of manufacturing, and displacement of jobs in manufacturing from the advanced to the less developed nations.

Coming out of these structural changes is a new class struggle not between labor and management or owner and worker as in the 19th century, but between larger interest groups. Associated with this is the rise of more political intervention in the economic sector.

Four structural problems will affect the advanced nations:

- Growing interconnectedness and interdependence creates a double bind in the advanced economies; the need for someone to think about the system as a whole, since everything is systemic, conflicting with the rise of special, legitimate, powerful, individual interests.
- Data and protectionism.
- The demographic tidal wave.
- The rich and poor nations. While that difference will always exist, we have run into new problems with international industrialization. For example, international manufacturing will lead to an international labor base.

Bell sees situations among the advanced nations similar to the crisis in the 1920s and 1930s arising, in which there will be many insoluble problems, a parliamentary impasse with little or no likelihood of any group commanding a majority, growth of an unemployed, an educated intelligentsia, and the spread of private violence, which regimes are unable to check.

The Multinational Corporation

For Bell, the multinational corporation is a primary instrument for the transfer of technology to the developing nations. As part of the long-term integration and shift to a global economy, the U.S. is likely to move more toward a "headquarters economy" as more regularized, standardized processes migrate overseas.[7] That division of labor between rich and poor nations is one of the factors pushing the U.S. toward a more service based economy and a high technology service based economy at that.

Intellectual Technologies

Technology is a broad concept for Bell, going well beyond traditional, physical, and biological technologies, to embrace almost the full range of notions associated with Jacques Ellul, for whom technology is virtually equivalent to technique. An emerging critical part of the new family of technologies will be intellectual technologies, framed primarily around the management of complexity. Among the new intellectual technologies are the techniques for rationalizing our decisionmaking such as operations research, the techniques for the formalization of judgment, and the application of empirical and mathematical rules. Along with the rise of intellectual technologies is the observation that the period of great scientific achievement based on specialization is now being overtaken by growing cross relationships among theories. We are beginning to reintegrate our knowledge of the world.

Among the intellectual technologies are Markov chain applications, the Monte Carlo technique, information theory, cybernetics, and game theory.

Modeling Society

Bell is pessimistic about the ability to model society. We do not have the knowledge or the theory, although from the technological point of view we do have some insights into how society changes. Adding futher difficulty to the modeling of society is its increasing openness. The strength of models is in closed systems.

Bell also makes a sharp distinction between prediction and forecasting and has relatively little interest in prediction, that is, in statements about the probabilities of particular events. Forecasting requires a basic understanding of structural forces at play as a route to anticipating some of their potential consequences. Bell does, however, see that an approach through multiple "social frameworks" can be the basis of insight into social forecasting. His seven frameworks are:

1. The geopolitical relationships and the strategic variables assumed to be associated with each of them. So, for example, in the dimensions of conflict between East versus West, West versus West, North versus South, East versus East, each one has these strategic variables to consider: demographic transitions, energy dependency, minerals and metal resources, agricultural status, industrial status, science and technology capabilities, and military capabilities.
2. The post-industrial framework.
3. The infrastructure. As already noted, the basic infrastructure variables are transportation, energy, and communications.
4. The matching of scale. Many issues arise from the fact that the nation states are too small for the big problems and too big for the small problems.
5. Centripetal and centrifugal tendencies including possible political and economic integration in Europe, the Mediterranean basin, and the Mideast. At the same time we have sub-national fragmentation working vigorously in the U.K., France, Spain, Yugoslavia, and the Soviet Union. There are emergent world structures in finance,

science, and health. There are trans-national organizations, and there is the growing recognition of vulnerabilities and societal susceptibilities to shock and economic maladjustments and adjustments, terrorism, and so on.

6. New technological changes.
7. The new belief systems, including the revival of traditional religions, especially fundamentalism in Islam and in Christianity, the rise of cults, new "primordial attachments" such as ethnicity, the rise of irrationalism, and the decay of Communist ideologies.

Limits to Forecasting

Several central concepts in Bell's views set a severe limit on the expectations which he or others may have about social forecasting. First with regard to his concept of realms discussed earlier, he sees that they change in different ways; the techno-economic sectors do not change in the ways that culture changes. There is no single general principle which acts in determinant fashion and which one can use as a guide to isolate the leading and lagging elements of change. A second limiting factor is clear in his book on post-industrial society. That whole activity is conducted in the spirit of "as if" in the sense that he draws out social science fictions as logical constructs trying to identify dimensions and then see how the future would come out with and without interventions. Put differently, the idea of an industrial society is a principle. Whether societies can or cannot move in that direction is an empirical, not a logical issue for Bell.

Bell also rejects the concept of the pace of change as not useful. He is more comfortable with using scale as the metric with regard to what is changing. An example of the mismatch of scale is the international economy which has greatly expanded, multiplied in the number of actors, and increased in volatility and velocity of actions, yet its political management is on a totally inadequate scale.

Finally, it should be noted that in his current research and work not yet published, Bell is developing methodologies for tracking technology and for using the social frameworks discussed above to see how technologies may change our ways of acting.

UNDERLYING CAUSES

From the point of view of day-to-day life, life in the year 2000 is more likely to be similar than it is to be different from that in the previous decades. However, the changes that will occur will be driven by four major forces:

Daniel Bell

- Technological change. Bell notes in the area of technological change that among the critical developments are a move toward

  — miniaturization,
  — the intrusion of electronics into all kinds of devices and services,
  — the application of theoretical knowledge, and,
  — digitalization of all information.

- Diffusion of goods and social claims throughout the economy.
- Structural developments in society, such as the centralization of the political economy, the shift to the service sector, the rise of the university as gatekeeper, and the increasing importance of human capital.
- The relationship of the U.S. and the rest of the world, which could in some sense be the most important of these basic factors.

EXHIBIT 7-3

FORCES INFLUENCING THE FUTURIST THINKING OF

DANIEL BELL

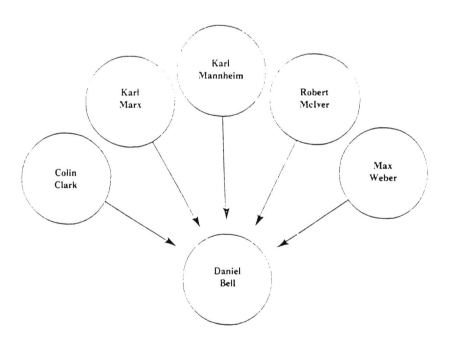

REFERENCES

1. Daniel Bell, "The Social Framework of the Information Society," in Michael L. Dertouzos and Joel Moses, eds., *The Computer Age: A Twenty Year View*, The MIT Press, Cambridge, MA 1979, pp. 166-167.
2. Daniel Bell, *The Coming of Post-Industrial Society*, Basic Books, Inc., New York, 1976, p. 116.
3. *The Cultural Contradictions of Capitalism*, Basic Books, Inc., New York, 1976, p. 19.
4. "The Social Framework," p. 163.
5. "The Social Framework," p. 196.
6. "The World Future Disorders: The Structural Context of Crisis" (1977), reprinted in Daniel Bell's *The Winding Passage*, Basic Books, Inc., New York, 1980, p. 227.
7. *The Coming of Post-Industrial Society*, p. 485.

Additional Readings:

Daniel Bell, "The World and the United States in 2013," *Daedalus*, Journal of the American Academy of Arts and Sciences, 116:3, Summer 1987.

In the knowledge society, managers must prepare to abandon everything they know.

The New Society of Organizations

by Peter F. Drucker

Peter F. Drucker is the Clarke Professor of Social Science and Management at the Claremont Graduate School in Claremont, California. This article is adapted from his new book, Post-Capitalist Society, to be published in early 1993 by Harper/Collins. This is Mr. Drucker's thirtieth article for HBR.

E very few hundred years throughout Western history, a sharp transformation has occurred. In a matter of decades, society altogether rearranges itself – its world view, its basic values, its social and political structures, its arts, its key institutions. Fifty years later a new world exists. And the people born into that world cannot even imagine the world in which their grandparents lived and into which their own parents were born.

Our age is such a period of transformation. Only this time the transformation is not confined to Western society and Western history. Indeed, one of the fundamental changes is that there is no longer a "Western" history or a "Western" civilization. There is only world history and world civilization.

Whether this transformation began with the emergence of the first non-Western country, Japan, as a great economic power or with the first computer – that is, with information – is moot. My own candidate would be the GI Bill of Rights, which gave every American soldier returning from World War II the money to attend a university, something that would have made absolutely no sense only 30 years earlier at the end of World War I. The GI Bill of Rights and the enthusiastic response to it on the part of America's veterans signaled the shift to a knowledge society.

In this society, knowledge is *the* primary resource for individuals and for the economy overall. Land, labor, and capital – the economist's traditional factors of production – do not disappear, but they become secondary. They can be obtained, and obtained easily, provided there is specialized knowledge. At the same time, however, specialized knowledge by itself produces nothing. It can become productive only when it is integrated into a task. And that is why the knowledge society is also a society of organizations: the purpose and function of every organization, business and non-business alike, is the integration of specialized knowledges into a common task.

If history is any guide, this transformation will not be completed until 2010 or 2020. Therefore, it is risky to try to foresee in every detail the world that is emerging. But what new questions will arise and where the big issues will lie we can, I believe, already discover with a high degree of probability.

In particular, we already know the central tensions and issues that confront the society of organizations: the tension created by the community's need for stability and the organization's need to destabilize; the relationship between individual and organization and the responsibilities of one to another; the tension that arises from the organization's need for autonomy and society's stake in the Common Good; the rising demand for socially responsible organizations; the tension between specialists with specialized knowledges and performance as a team. All of these will be central concerns, especially in the developed world, for years to come. They will not be resolved by pronunciamento or philosophy or legislation. They will be resolved where they originate: in the individual organization and in the manager's office.

Society, community, and family are all conserving institutions. They try to maintain stability and to prevent, or at least to slow, change. But the modern organization is a destabilizer. It must be organized for innovation and innovation, as the great Austro-American economist Joseph Schumpeter said, is "creative destruction." And it must be organized for the systematic abandonment of whatever is established, customary, familiar, and comfortable, whether that is a product, service, or process; a set of skills; human and social relationships; or the organization itself. In short, it must be organized for constant change. The organization's function is to put knowledge to work – on tools, products, and processes; on the design of work; on knowledge itself. It is the nature of knowledge that it changes fast and that today's certainties always become tomorrow's absurdities.

Skills change slowly and infrequently. If an ancient Greek stonecutter came back to life today and went to work in a stone mason's yard, the only change of significance would be the design he was asked to carve on the tombstones. The tools he would use are the same, only now they have electric batteries in the handles. Throughout history, the craftsman who had learned a trade after five or seven years of apprenticeship had learned, by age eighteen or nineteen, everything he would ever need to use during his lifetime. In the society of organizations, however, it is safe to assume that anyone with any knowledge will have to acquire new knowledge every four or five years or become obsolete.

This is doubly important because the changes that affect a body of knowledge most profoundly do not, as a rule, come out of its own domain. After Gutenberg first used movable type, there was practically no change in the craft of printing for 400 years – until the steam engine came in. The greatest challenge to the railroad came not from changes in railroading but from the automobile, the truck, and the airplane. The pharmaceutical industry is being profoundly changed today by knowledge coming from genetics and microbiology, disciplines that few biologists had heard of 40 years ago.

And it is by no means only science or technology that creates new knowledge and makes old knowledge obsolete. Social innovation is equally important and often more important than scientific innovation. Indeed, what triggered the present worldwide crisis in that proudest of nineteenth-century institutions, the commercial bank, was not the computer or any other technological change. It was the discovery by nonbankers that an old but hitherto rather obscure financial instrument, commercial paper, could be used to finance companies and would thus deprive the banks of the business on which they had held a monopoly for 200 years and which gave them most of their income: the commercial loan. The greatest change of all is probably that in the last 40 years purposeful innovation – both technical and social – has itself become an organized discipline that is both teachable and learnable.

Nor is rapid knowledge-based change confined to business, as many still believe. No organization in the 50 years since World War II has changed more than the U.S. military. Uniforms have remained the same. Titles of rank have remained the same. But weapons have changed completely, as the Gulf War of 1991 dramatically demonstrated; military doctrines and concepts have changed even more drastically, as have the armed services' organizational structures, command structures, relationships, and responsibilities.

Similarly, it is a safe prediction that in the next 50 years, schools and universities will change more and more drastically than they have since they assumed their present form more than 300 years ago when they reorganized themselves around the printed book. What will force these changes is, in part, new technology, such as computers, videos, and telecasts via satellite; in part the demands of a knowledge-based society in which organized learning must become a lifelong process for knowledge workers; and in part new theory about how human beings learn.

For managers, the dynamics of knowledge impose one clear imperative: every organization has to build the management of change into its very structure.

On the one hand, this means every organization has to prepare for the abandonment of everything it

does. Managers have to learn to ask every few years of every process, every product, every procedure, every policy: "If we did not do this already, would we go into it now knowing what we now know?" If the answer is no, the organization has to ask, "So what do we do now?" And it has to *do* something, and not say, "Let's make another study." Indeed, organizations increasingly will have to *plan* abandonment rather than try to prolong the life of a successful product, policy, or practice – something that so far only a few large Japanese companies have faced up to.

On the other hand, every organization must devote itself to creating the new. Specifically, every

Managers must learn to ask every few years, "If we did not do this already, would we go into it now?"

management has to draw on three systematic practices. The first is continuing improvement of everything the organization does, the process the Japanese call *kaizen*. Every artist throughout history has practiced kaizen, or organized, continuous self-improvement. But so far only the Japanese – perhaps because of their Zen tradition – have embodied it in the daily life and work of their business organizations (although not in their singularly change-resistant universities). The aim of kaizen is to improve a product or service so that it becomes a truly different product or service in two or three years' time.

Second, every organization will have to learn to exploit its knowledge, that is, to develop the next generation of applications from its own successes. Again, Japanese businesses have done the best with this endeavor so far, as demonstrated by the success of the consumer electronics manufacturers in developing one new product after another from the same American invention, the tape recorder. But successful exploitation of their successes is also one of the strengths of the fast-growing American pastoral churches.

Finally, every organization will have to learn to innovate – and innovation can now be organized and must be organized – as a systematic process. And then, of course, one comes back to abandonment, and the process starts all over. Unless this is done, the knowledge-based organization will very soon find itself obsolescent, losing performance capacity and with it the ability to attract and hold the skilled and knowledgeable people on whom its performance depends.

The need to organize for change also requires a high degree of decentralization. That is because the organization must be structured to make decisions quickly. And those decisions must be based on closeness – to performance, to the market, to technology, and to all the many changes in society, the environment, demographics, and knowledge that provide opportunities for innovation if they are seen and utilized.

All this implies, however, that the organizations of the post-capitalist society must constantly upset, disorganize, and destabilize the community. They must change the demand for skills and knowledges: just when every technical university is geared up to teach physics, organizations need geneticists. Just when bank employees are most proficient in credit analysis, they will need to be investment counselors. But also, businesses must be free to close factories on which local communities depend for employment or to replace grizzled model makers who have spent years learning their craft with 25-year-old whiz kids who know computer simulation.

Similarly, hospitals must be able to move the delivery of babies into a free-standing birthing center when the knowledge base and technology of obstetrics change. And we must be able to close a hospital altogether when changes in medical knowledge, technology, and practice make a hospital with fewer than 200 beds both uneconomical and incapable of giving first-rate care. For a hospital – or a school or any other community organization – to discharge its social function we must be able to close it down, no matter how deeply rooted in the local community it is and how much beloved, if changes in demographics, technology, or knowledge set new prerequisites for performance.

But every one of such changes upsets the community, disrupts it, deprives it of continuity. Every one is "unfair." Every one destabilizes.

Equally disruptive is another fact of organizational life: the modern organization must be *in* a community but cannot be *of* it. An organization's members live in a particular place, speak its language, send their children to its schools, vote, pay taxes, and need to feel at home there. Yet the organization cannot submerge itself in the community nor subordinate itself to the community's ends. Its "culture" has to transcend community.

It is the nature of the task, not the community in which the task is being performed, that determines the culture of an organization. The American civil servant, though totally opposed to communism, will understand immediately what a Chinese colleague tells him about bureaucratic intrigues in Beijing. But he would be totally baffled in his own Washington, D.C. if he were to sit in on a discussion of the next week's advertising promotions by the managers of the local grocery chain.

To perform its task the organization has to be organized and managed the same way as others of its

Businesses must be free to close factories that communities depend on or replace grizzled employees with 25-year-old whiz kids.

type. For example, we hear a great deal about the differences in management between Japanese and American companies. But a large Japanese company functions very much like a large American company; and both function very much like a large German or British company. Likewise, no one will ever doubt that he or she is in a hospital, no matter where the hospital is located. The same holds true for schools and universities, for labor unions and research labs, for museums and opera houses, for astronomical observatories and large farms.

In addition, each organization has a value system that is determined by its task. In every hospital in the world, health care is considered the ultimate good. In every school in the world, learning is considered the ultimate good. In every business in the world, production and distribution of goods or services is considered the ultimate good. For the organization to perform to a high standard, its members must believe that what it is doing is, in the last analysis, the one contribution to community and society on which all others depend.

In its culture, therefore, the organization will always transcend the community. If an organization's culture and the values of its community clash, the organization must prevail – or else it will not make its social contribution. "Knowledge knows no boundaries," says an old proverb. There has been a "town and gown" conflict ever since the first university was established more than 750 years ago. But such a conflict – between the autonomy the organization needs in order to perform and the claims of the community, between the values of the organization and those of the community, between the decisions facing the organization and the interests of the community – is inherent in the society of organizations.

The issue of social responsibility is also inherent in the society of organizations. The modern organization has and must have social power – and a good deal of it. It needs power to make decisions about people: whom to hire, whom to fire, whom to promote. It needs power to establish the rules and disciplines required to produce results: for example, the assignment of jobs and tasks and the establishment of working hours. It needs power to decide which factories to build where and which factories to close. It needs power to set prices, and so on.

And nonbusinesses have the greatest social power – far more, in fact, than business enterprises. Few organizations in history were ever granted the power the university has today. Refusing to admit a student or to grant a student the diploma is tantamount to debarring that person from careers and opportunities. Similarly, the power of the American hospital to deny a physician admitting privileges is the power to exclude that physician from the practice of medicine. The labor union's power over admission to apprenticeship or its control of access to employment in a "closed shop," where only union members can be hired, gives the union tremendous social power.

The power of the organization can be restrained by political power. It can be made subject to due process and to review by the courts. But it must be exercised by individual organizations rather than by political authorities. This is why postcapitalist society talks so much about social responsibilities of the organization.

It is futile to argue, as Milton Friedman, the American economist and Noble-laureate does, that a business has only one responsibility: economic performance. Economic performance is the *first* re-
sponsibility of a business. Indeed, a business that does not show a profit at least equal to its cost of capital is irresponsible; it wastes society's resources. Economic performance is the base without which a business cannot discharge any other responsibilities, cannot be a good employee, a good citizen, a good neighbor. But economic performance is not the *only* responsibility of a business any more than educational performance is the only responsibility of a school or health care the only responsibility of a hospital.

Unless power is balanced by responsibility, it becomes tyranny. Furthermore, without responsibility power always degenerates into nonperformance, and organizations must perform. So the demand for socially responsible organizations will not go away but rather widen.

Fortunately, we also know, if only in rough outline, how to answer the problem of social responsibility. Every organization must assume full responsibility for its impact on employees, the environment, customers, and whomever and whatever it touches. That is its social responsibility. But we also know that society will increasingly look to major organizations, for-profit and nonprofit alike, to tackle major social ills. And there we had better be watchful because good intentions are not always socially responsible. It is irresponsible for an organization to accept – let alone to pursue – responsibilities that would impede its capacity to perform its main task and mission or to act where it has no competence.

Organization has become an everyday term. Everybody nods when somebody says, "In our organization, everything should revolve around the customer" or "In this organization, they never forget a mistake." And most, if not all, social tasks in every developed country are performed in and by an organization of one kind or another. Yet no one in the United States – or anyplace else – talked of "organizations" until after World War II. *The Concise Oxford Dictionary* did not even list the term in its current meaning in the 1950 edition. It is only the emergence of management since World War II, what I call the "Management Revolution," that has allowed us to see that the organization is discrete and distinct from society's other institutions.

Unlike "community," "society," or "family," organizations are purposefully designed and always specialized. Community and society are defined by the bonds that hold their members together, whether they be language, culture, history, or locality. An organization is defined by its task. The symphony orchestra does not attempt to cure the sick; it plays music. The hospital takes care of the sick but does not attempt to play Beethoven.

Indeed, an organization is effective only if it concentrates on one task. Diversification destroys the performance capacity of an organization, whether it is a business, a labor union, a school, a hospital, a community service, or a house of worship. Society and community must be multidimensional; they are environments. An organization is a tool. And as

Every organization is in competition for its most essential resource: qualified, knowledgeable people.

with any other tool, the more specialized it is, the greater its capacity to perform its given task.

Because the modern organization is composed of specialists, each with his or her own narrow area of expertise, its mission must be crystal clear. The organization must be single-minded, or its members will become confused. They will follow their own specialty rather than apply it to the common task.

They will each define "results" in terms of their own specialty and impose its values on the organization. Only a focused and common mission will hold the organization together and enable it to produce. Without such a mission, the organization will soon lose credibility and, with it, its ability to attract the very people it needs to perform.

It can be all too easy for managers to forget that joining an organization is always voluntary. De facto there may be little choice. But even where membership is all but compulsory – as membership in the Catholic church was in all the countries of Europe for many centuries for all but a handful of Jews and Gypsies – the fiction of voluntary choice is always carefully maintained: the godfather at the infant's baptism pledges the child's voluntary acceptance of membership in the church.

Likewise, it may be difficult to leave an organization – the Mafia, for instance, a big Japanese company, the Jesuit order. But it is always possible. And the more an organization becomes an organization of knowledge workers, the easier it is to leave it and move elsewhere. Therefore, an organization is always in competition for its most essential resource: qualified, knowledgeable people.

All organizations now say routinely, "People are our greatest asset." Yet few practice what they preach, let alone truly believe it. Most still believe, though perhaps not consciously, what nineteenth-century employers believed: people need us more than we need them. But, in fact, organizations have to market membership as much as they market products and services – and perhaps more. They have to attract people, hold people, recognize and reward people, motivate people, and serve and satisfy people.

The relationship between knowledge workers and their organizations is a distinctly new phenomenon, one for which we have no good term. For example, an employee, by definition, is someone who gets paid for working. Yet the largest single group of "employees" in the United States is comprised of the millions of men and women who work several hours a week without pay for one or another nonprofit organization. They are clearly "staff" and consider themselves as such, but they are unpaid volunteers. Similarly, many people who work as employees are not employed in any legal sense because they do not work for someone else. Fifty or sixty years ago, we would have spoken of these people (many, if not most, of whom are educated professionals) as "independent"; today we speak of the "self-employed."

These discrepancies – and they exist in just about every language – remind us why new realities often demand new words. But until such a word emerges, this is probably the best definition of employees in the post-capitalist society: people whose ability to make a contribution depends on having access to an organization.

As far as the employees who work in subordinate and menial occupations are concerned – the sales-clerk in the supermarket, the cleaning woman in the hospital, the delivery-truck driver – the consequences of this new definition are small. For all practical purposes, their position may not be too different from that of the wage earner, the "worker" of yesterday, whose direct descendants they are. In fact, this is precisely one of the central social problems modern society faces.

But the relationship between the organization and knowledge workers, who already number at least one-third and more likely two-fifths of all employees, is radically different, as is that between the organization and volunteers. They can work only because there is an organization, thus they too are dependent. But at the same time, they own the "means of production" – their knowledge. In this respect, they are independent and highly mobile.

Knowledge workers still need the tools of production. In fact, capital investment in the tools of the knowledge employee may already be higher than the capital investment in the tools of the manufacturing worker ever was. (And the social investment, for example, the investment in a knowledge worker's education, is many times the investment in the manual worker's education.) But this capital investment is unproductive unless the knowledge worker brings to bear on it the knowledge that he or she owns and that cannot be taken away. Machine operators in the factory did as they were told. The machine decided not only what to do but how to do it. The knowledge employee may well need a machine, whether it be a computer, an ultrasound analyzer, or a telescope. But the machine will not tell the knowledge worker what to do, let alone how to do it. And without this knowledge, which belongs to the employee, the machine is unproductive.

Further, machine operators, like all workers throughout history, could be told what to do, how to do it, and how fast to do it. Knowledge workers cannot be supervised effectively. Unless they know more about their specialty than anybody else in the organization, they are basically useless. The marketing manager may tell the market researcher what the company needs to know about the design of a new product and the market segment in which it should be positioned. But it is the market researcher's job to tell the president of the company what market research is needed, how to set it up, and what the results mean.

During the traumatic restructuring of American business in the 1980s, thousands, if not hundreds of thousands, of knowledge employees lost their jobs. Their companies were acquired, merged, spun off, or liquidated. Yet within a few months, most of them found new jobs in which to put their knowledge to work. The transition period was painful, and in about half the cases, the new job did not pay quite as much as the old one did and may not have been as enjoyable. But the laid-off technicians, professionals, and managers found they had the "capital," the knowledge: they owned the means of production. Somebody else, the organization, had the tools of production. The two needed each other.

One consequence of this new relationship – and it is another new tension in modern society – is that loyalty can no longer be obtained by the paycheck. The organization must earn loyalty by proving to its knowledge employees that it offers them exceptional opportunities for putting their knowledge to work. Not so long ago we talked about "labor." Increasingly we are talking about "human resources." This change reminds us that it is the individual, and especially the skilled and knowledgeable employee, who decides in large measure what he or she will contribute to the organization and how great the yield from his or her knowledge will be.

Because the modern organization consists of knowledge specialists, it has to be an organization of equals, of colleagues and associates. No knowledge ranks higher than another; each is judged by its contribution to the common task rather than by any inherent superiority or inferiority. Therefore, the modern organization cannot be an organization of boss and subordinate. It must be organized as a team.

There are only three kinds of teams. One is the sort of team that plays together in tennis doubles. In that team – and it has to be small – each member adapts himself or herself to the personality, the skills, the strengths, and the weaknesses of the other member or members. Then there is the team that plays European football or soccer. Each player has a fixed position; but the whole team moves together (except for the goalie) while individual members retain their relative positions. Finally, there is the American baseball team – or the orchestra – in which all the members have fixed positions.

At any given time, an organization can play only one kind of game. And it can use only one kind of team for any given task. Which team to use or game to play is one of the riskiest decisions in the life of an organization. Few things are as difficult in an organization as transforming from one kind of team to another.

Traditionally, American industry used a baseball-style team to produce a new product or model. Research did its work and passed it on to engineering. Engineering did its work and passed it on to manufacturing. Manufacturing did its work and passed it on to marketing. Accounting usually came in at the manufacturing phase. Personnel usually came in only when there was a true crisis – and often not even then.

Then the Japanese reorganized their new product development into a soccer team. In such a team, each function does its own work, but from the beginning they work together. They move with the task, so to speak, the way a soccer team moves with the ball. It took the Japanese at least 15 years to learn how to do this. But once they had mastered the new concept, they cut development time by two-thirds. Where traditionally it has taken 5 years to bring out a new automobile model, Toyota, Nissan, and Honda now do it in 18 months. This, as much as their quality control, has given the Japanese the upper hand in both the American and European automobile markets.

Some American manufacturers have been working hard to reorganize their development work ac-cording to the Japanese model. Ford Motor Company, for instance, began to do so in the early 1980s. Ten years later, in the early 1990s, it has made considerable progress – but not nearly enough to catch up with the Japanese. Changing a team demands the most difficult learning imaginable: unlearning. It demands giving up hard-earned skills, habits of a lifetime, deeply cherished values of craftsmanship and professionalism, and – perhaps the most difficult of all – it demands giving up old and treasured human relationships. It means abandoning what people have always considered "our community" or "our family."

But if the organization is to perform, it must be organized as a team. When modern organizations first arose in the closing years of the nineteenth century, the only model was the military. The Prussian Army was as much a marvel of organization for the world of 1870 as Henry Ford's assembly line was for the world of 1920. In the army of 1870, each member did much the same thing, and the number of people with any knowledge was infinitesimally small. The army was organized by command-and-control, and business enterprise as well as most other institutions copied that model. This is now rapidly changing. As more and more organizations become information-based, they are transforming themselves into soccer or tennis teams, that is, into responsibility-based organizations in which every member must act as a responsible decision maker. All members, in other words, have to see themselves as "executives."

Even so, an organization must be managed. The management may be intermittent and perfunctory, as it is, for instance, in the Parent-Teacher Association at a U.S. suburban school. Or management may be a full-time and demanding job for a fairly large group of people, as it is in the military, the business enterprise, the labor union, and the university. But there have to be people who make decisions or nothing will ever get done. There have to be people who are accountable for the organization's mission, its spirit, its performance, its results. Society, community, and family may have "leaders," but only organizations know a "management." And while this management must have considerable authority, its job in the modern organization is not to command. It is to inspire.

The society of organizations is unprecedented in human history. It is unprecedented in its performance capacity both because each of its constituent organizations is a highly specialized tool designed for one specific task and because each bases itself on the organization and deployment of knowledge. It is unprecedented in its structure. But it is also unprecedented in its tensions and problems. Not all of these are serious. In fact, some of them we already know how to resolve – issues of social responsibility, for example. But there are other areas where we do not know the right answer and where we may not even be asking the right questions yet.

There is, for instance, the tension between the community's need for continuity and stability and the organization's need to be an innovator and destabilizer. There is the split between "literati" and "managers." Both are needed: the former to produce knowledge, the latter to apply knowledge and make it productive. But the former focus on words and ideas, the latter on people, work, and performance. There is the threat to the very basis of the society of organizations – the knowledge base – that arises from ever greater specialization, from the shift from knowledge to *knowledges*. But the greatest and most difficult challenge is that presented by society's new pluralism.

For more than 600 years, no society has had as many centers of power as the society in which we now live. The Middle Ages indeed knew pluralism. Society was composed of hundreds of competing and autonomous power centers: feudal lords and knights, exempt bishoprics, autonomous monasteries, "free" cities. In some places, the Austrian

Tyrol, for example, there were even "free peasants," beholden to no one but the Emperor. There were also autonomous craft guilds and transnational trading leagues like the Hanseatic Merchants and the merchant bankers of Florence, toll and tax collectors, local "parliaments" with legislative and tax-raising powers, private armies available for hire, and myriads more.

Modern history in Europe – and equally in Japan – has been the history of the subjugation of all competing centers of power by one central authority, first called the "prince," then the "state." By the middle of the nineteenth century, the unitary state had triumphed in every developed country except the United States, which remained profoundly pluralistic in its religious and educational organizations. Indeed, the abolition of pluralism was the "progressive" cause for nearly 600 years.

But just when the triumph of the state seemed assured, the first new organization arose – the large business enterprise. (This, of course, always happens when the "End of History" is announced.) Since then, one new organization after another has sprung up. And old organizations like the university, which in Europe seemed to have been brought safely under the control of central governments, have become autonomous again. Ironically, twentieth-century totalitarianism, especially communism, represented the last desperate attempt to save the old progressive creed in which there is only one center of power and one organization rather than a pluralism of competing and autonomous organizations.

That attempt failed, as we know. But the failure of central authority, in and of itself, does nothing to

Since the Middle Ages, no society has had as many centers of power as the one in which we now live.

address the issues that follow from a pluralistic society. To illustrate, consider a story that many people have heard or, more accurately, misheard.

During his lifetime, Charles E. Wilson was a prominent personality in the United States, first as president and chief executive officer of General Motors, at that time the world's largest and most successful manufacturer, then as secretary of defense in the Eisenhower administration. But if Wilson is remembered at all today it is for something he did *not* say: "What is good for General Motors is good for the United States." What Wilson actually said in his 1953 confirmation hearings for the De-

Who will take care of the Common Good? Who will define it?

fense Department job was: "What is good for the United States is good for General Motors."

Wilson tried for the remainder of his life to correct the misquote. But no one listened to him. Everyone argued, "If he didn't say it, he surely believes it – in fact he *should* believe it." For as has been said, executives in an organization – whether business or university or hospital or the Boy Scouts – must believe that its mission and task are society's most important mission and task as well as the foundation for everything else. If they do not believe this, their organization will soon lose faith in itself, self-confidence, pride, and the ability to perform.

The diversity that is characteristic of a developed society and that provides its great strength is only possible because of the specialized, single-task organizations that we have developed since the Industrial Revolution and, especially, during the last 50 years. But the feature that gives them the capacity to perform is precisely that each is autonomous and specialized, informed only by its own narrow mission and vision, its own narrow values, and not by any consideration of society and community.

Therefore, we come back to the old – and never resolved – problem of the pluralistic society: Who takes care of the Common Good? Who defines it? Who balances the separate and often competing goals and values of society's institutions? Who makes the trade-off decisions and on what basis should they be made?

Medieval feudalism was replaced by the unitary sovereign state precisely because it could not answer these questions. But the unitary sovereign state has now itself been replaced by a new pluralism – a pluralism of function rather than one of political power – because it could neither satisfy the needs of society nor perform the necessary tasks of community. That, in the final analysis, is the most fundamental lesson to be learned from the failure of socialism, the failure of the belief in the all-embracing and all-powerful state. The challenge that faces us now, and especially in the developed, free-market democracies such as the United States, is to make the pluralism of autonomous, knowledge-based organizations redound both to economic performance and to political and social cohesion. ▽

Reprint 92503